RACE, CLASS, AND AFFIRMATIVE ACTION

RACE, CLASS, AND AFFIRMATIVE ACTION

Sigal Alon

Russell Sage Foundation • New York

The Russell Sage Foundation

The Russell Sage Foundation, one of the oldest of America's general purpose foundations, was established in 1907 by Mrs. Margaret Olivia Sage for "the improvement of social and living conditions in the United States." The foundation seeks to fulfill this mandate by fostering the development and dissemination of knowledge about the country's political, social, and economic problems. While the foundation endeavors to assure the accuracy and objectivity of each book it publishes, the conclusions and interpretations in Russell Sage Foundation publications are those of the authors and not of the foundation, its trustees, or its staff. Publication by Russell Sage, therefore, does not imply foundation endorsement.

BOARD OF TRUSTEES
Sara S. McLanahan, Chair

Larry M. Bartels
Kenneth D. Brody
Karen S. Cook
W. Bowman Cutter III
Sheldon Danziger

Kathryn Edin
Lawrence F. Katz
Nicholas Lemann
Peter R. Orszag
Claude M. Steele

Shelley E. Taylor
Richard H. Thaler
Hirokazu Yoshikawa

Library of Congress Cataloging-in-Publication Data

Alon, Sigal.
  Race, class, and affirmative action / Sigal Alon.
    pages cm
  Includes bibliographical references and index.
  ISBN 978-0-87154-001-0 (pbk. : alk. paper) — ISBN 978-1-61044-854-3 (ebook) 1. Affirmative action programs in education—United States. 2. Affirmative action programs in education—Israel. 3. Minority college students—United States. 4. Low income college students—Israel. 5. Education, Higher—Social aspects—United States. 6. Education, Higher—Social aspects—Israel. I. Title.
  LC213.52.A55 2015
  306.430973—dc23
                          2015018417

Copyright © 2015 by Russell Sage Foundation. All rights reserved. Printed in the United States of America. No part of this publication may be reproduced, stored in a retrieval system, or transmitted in any form or by any means, electronic, mechanical, photocopying, recording, or otherwise, without the prior written permission of the publisher.

Reproduction by the United States Government in whole or in part is permitted for any purpose.

The paper used in this publication meets the minimum requirements of American National Standard for Information Sciences—Permanence of Paper for Printed Library Materials. ANSI Z39.48-1992.

Text design by Genna Patacsil.

RUSSELL SAGE FOUNDATION
112 East 64th Street, New York, New York 10065
10 9 8 7 6 5 4 3 2 1

To Joel, Omri, Assaf, and Neta, with all my love.

CONTENTS

	List of Illustrations	ix
	About the Author	xv
	Preface	xvii
	Acknowledgments	xix
PART I	**Introduction**	**1**
Chapter 1	The Search for an Alternative Affirmative Action Policy in American Higher Education	3
PART II	**The Problem**	**25**
Chapter 2	Affirmative Action in American Higher Education: A Story About Race	27
Chapter 3	Social, Economic, and Academic Trends and Their Impact on Inequality in Higher Education	41
Chapter 4	Broad Diversity at Elite Colleges	64
PART III	**Class-Based Affirmative Action**	**77**
Chapter 5	What Is Class-Based Affirmative Action?	79
Chapter 6	Israel: Contours of Inequality, Higher Education, and Class-Based Affirmative Action at the Elite Universities	98

PART IV	**Implications for Feasibility and Diversity**	**127**
Chapter 7	The Feasibility and Diversity Dividends of Affirmative Action Policy in Israel	129
Chapter 8	The Feasibility and Diversity Dividends of Affirmative Action Policy in the United States	159
PART V	**Implications for Academic Outcomes and Mobility**	**189**
Chapter 9	The Academic Outcomes and Mobility Dividends of Affirmative Action Policy in Israel	191
Chapter 10	The Academic Outcomes and Mobility Dividends of Affirmative Action Policy in the United States	213
PART VI	**Insights from a Comparative Outlook**	**231**
Chapter 11	Race, Class, and Affirmative Action	233
	Appendix	259
	Notes	275
	References	297
	Index	313

LIST OF ILLUSTRATIONS

Figure 2.1	The Race-Ethnicity of Students Attending Competitive Four-Year Institutions, 1972–2004	33
Figure 3.1	Top 10 Percent Income Share in the United States, 1917–2013	43
Figure 3.2	Median Earnings of Full-Time, Year-Round Male Workers Ages Twenty-Five and Older, 1991–2010	46
Figure 3.3	Percentage of Recent High School Completers Enrolled in College, 1960–2011	49
Figure 3.4	Postsecondary Institutions Listed in *Barron's Profiles of American Colleges,* by Admissions Competitiveness Categories, 1972–2008	51
Figure 3.5	Admission Rates at Harvard, Yale, Cornell, and Penn, 1959–2012	53
Figure 3.6	Average Tuition and Fees and Room and Board Charges in 2012 Dollars, 1972–2012, Selected Years	60
Figure 4.1	The Socioeconomic Status of Students Attending "Very Competitive," "Highly Competitive," and "Most Competitive" Four-Year Institutions, 1972–2004	68
Figure 4.2	Students Attending "Most Competitive" and "Noncompetitive" Four-Year Institutions, by Socioeconomic Status, 2004	69
Figure 4.3	Receipt of Federal Grants by Full-Time, First-Time-Degree-Seeking Undergraduate Students, 1998–2010	72
Figure 6.1	The Earnings Gap Among Workers Ages Twenty-Seven to Twenty-Nine Who Had Attended an Institution of Higher Education, 2005–2008	104

Figure 6.2	Selected Characteristics of Local Authorities in Israel, by SES Cluster, 2010	106
Figure 6.3	Number of Undergraduate Students in Institutions of Higher Education in Israel, by Type of Institution, 1980–2013	110
Figure 6.4	Competition in Admission to TAU, HUJI, BGU, and TECH, 1999–2008	114
Figure 6.5	Disadvantage-Based Eligibility for the Israeli Affirmative Action Program	120
Figure 6.6	The Stages of Implementation of Israel's Affirmative Action Policy	123
Figure 6.7	Affirmative Action (AA) Status of Applicants to the Four Top Israeli Universities, from the Start of Each University's AA Regime to 2008	125
Figure 7.1	Mean Test Scores of Actual and Simulated Admits to Israeli Universities, AA Regime	138
Figure 7.2	The Share of Arabs and Mizrachi Jews Among Actual and Simulated Admits to Israeli Universities, AA Regime	139
Figure 7.3	The Share of Immigrants Among Actual and Simulated Admits to Israeli Universities, AA Regime	142
Figure 7.4	The Share of Actual and Simulated Admits to Israeli Universities from the Bottom Cluster (1–4) on the Localities Socioeconomic Index, AA Regime	145
Figure 7.5	The Districts of Residence of Actual and Simulated Admits to Israeli Universities Relative to the General Population, All Majors, AA Regime	147
Figure 7.6	The Districts of Residence of Actual and Simulated Admits to Israeli Universities Relative to the General Population, Most-Selective Majors, AA Regime	148
Figure 7.7	The Share of Residents of Development Towns Among Actual and Simulated Admits to Israeli Universities, AA Regime	149
Figure 7.8	The Share Among Actual and Simulated Admits to Israeli Universities with a Father out of the Labor Force or Unemployed, AA Regime	152
Figure 7.9	The Mean SEI Score of Father's Occupation for Actual and Simulated Admits to Israeli Universities, AA Regime	153

Figure 8.1	The Process of Simulating Class-Based Affirmative Action	169
Figure 8.2	Pre- and Post-Simulation Test Scores (Mean) at Elite U.S. Universities, 1995–1996	172
Figure 8.3	The Pre- and Post-Simulation Share of Underrepresented Minorities at Elite U.S. Universities, 1995–1996	175
Figure 8.4	Pre- and Post-Simulation Expected Family Contribution, Elite U.S. Universities, 1995–1996	179
Figure 8.5	The Pre- and Post-Simulation Share of Students at Elite U.S. Universities Who Have Parents Without a College Degree, 1995–1996	181
Figure 8.6	The Geographic Region of Actual and Simulated AA Admits to Elite U.S. Universities, 1995–1996	184
Figure 9.1	Admission Rates Before and During the AA Regime, by Locality SES Cluster, 1999–2008	195
Figure 9.2	Admission and Enrollment Outcomes of Individuals Who Fell Just Above and Just Below the Affirmative Action Threshold of Eligibility, AA Regime	204
Figure 9.3	Tracking Fields of Study from Application to Graduation for Individuals Who Fell Just Above and Just Below the Affirmative Action Threshold of Eligibility, AA Regime	210
Figure 10.1	The College Destinations of Individuals Eligible for the Simulated Class-Based Affirmative Action, 1995–1996	218
Figure 10.2	The Academic Integration of Students at the First Institution They Attended During the 1995–1996 Academic Year, by AA Status	220
Figure 10.3	Persistence Toward a Degree of Students Who Enrolled During the 1995–1996 Academic Year, by AA Status	222
Figure 10.4	Field of Study of Students Who Started College in 1995–1996 upon Graduation (When Last Enrolled) from First Institution, by Institution Type and AA Status	224
Figure 11.1	Pre- and Post-Simulation Student Body Characteristics Under Three Regimes for Class-Based Affirmative Action at Elite U.S. Universities: Class, Race-Within-Class, and Reform, 1995–1996	255
Figure A6.1	The Distribution of Disciplines and Admits to Israeli Universities, 1999–2008	259

Figure A6.2	The Components of the Disadvantage-Based Eligibility Scores of Applicants Admitted Under the Class-Based Affirmative Action Plan in Israel	260
Table 3.1	*Barron's* Institutional Classification, by Freshman Characteristics, 1992	50
Table 5.1	A Typology of Affirmative Action Policies	87
Table 6.1	Postsecondary Systems in Israel and the United States	109
Table 6.2	The Average Monthly Salary of Male University Graduates During Their First Two Years in the Labor Market, by Field of Study and University, 1999–2002	112
Table 7.1	The Characteristics of Arabs and Mizrachi Jews in the Class-Based and Race-Based Admit Pools of Israeli Universities, AA Regime	155
Table 8.1	Types of Simulation of Class-Based Affirmative Action Policy, by Prototype, 1996–2001	164
Table 9.1	Admits' Fields of Study Before and During the AA Regime, by Locality SES Cluster, 1999–2008	197
Table 9.2	Fields of Study of Individuals Who Were Eligible for the Simulated Ethnic-Based Affirmative Action, AA Regime	202
Table 9.3	Fields of Study of Admits Who Fell Just Above and Just Below the Affirmative Action Threshold of Eligibility, AA Regime	205
Table 9.4	Various Academic Outcomes of Students Who Fell Just Above and Just Below the Affirmative Action Threshold of Eligibility, AA Regime	208
Table A7.1	Characteristics of Actual and Simulated Admits to Israeli Universities: General Admit Pool, Class-Based Admits and Race-Based Admits, All Majors, AA Regime	262
Table A7.2	Characteristics of Actual and Simulated Admits to Israeli Universities: General Admit Pool, Class-Based Admits and Race-Based Admits, Most Selective Majors, AA Regime	263
Table A7.3	Characteristics of Actual and Simulated Admits to Israeli Universities (Including TECH): Class-Based Admits and Race-Based Admits (Arabs Only), All Majors, AA Regime	264

Table A7.4	Characteristics of Actual and Simulated Admits to Israeli Universities (Including TECH): Class-Based Admits and Race-Based Admits (Arabs Only), Most-Selective Majors, AA Regime	265
Table A8.1	Simulations Results: Characteristics of AA Admits to Elite U.S. Universities, by Prototype, 1995–1996	266
Table A8.2	Pre- and Post-Simulations Results: Characteristics of the Student Bodies of Elite U.S. Institutions, by Prototype, 1995–1996	268
Table A8.3	Pre- and Post-Sensitivity Analysis with Different Thresholds: Characteristics of the Student Bodies of Elite U.S. Institutions, by Prototype, 1995–1996	270
Table A8.4	The Likelihood of Attending College, by Institution Selectivity Level, Four-Year Institutions, Odds Ratios, 1995–1996	272
Table A8.5	The Characteristics of Students at Elite U.S. Institutions, Below and Above Category Thresholds, by URM Status, 1995–1996	273
Table A9.1	OLS and Logit Regression Models Predicting Various Academic Outcomes for Students at the Israeli Universities Who Fell Just Above and Just Below the Affirmative Action Threshold of Eligibility, AA Regime	274

ABOUT THE AUTHOR

SIGAL ALON is associate professor in the Department of Sociology and Anthropology at Tel-Aviv University, Israel.

PREFACE

In 2005, I took a sabbatical leave from Tel Aviv University, where I have been a faculty member since 2002, and headed to Princeton University's Office of Population Research to delve into a year of full-time research. At the time I was studying the link between financial aid and the education attainment gap between the haves and have-nots. In the spring of 2006, I met William Bowen, the president of the Mellon Foundation and a former president of Princeton University. With Derek Bok, former president of Harvard University, Bowen had coauthored the book *The Shape of the River*, a seminal text about affirmative action policy at elite U.S. colleges. Toward the end of the meeting, our conversation happened upon the topic of affirmative action. Bowen asked me, in passing, if there was an affirmative action program in place at Israeli universities. I told him that I knew something about a new program that had just been adopted by several Israeli universities, but that I wasn't familiar with the details. Ironically, as one who had been investigating the effects of public policy on class and racial-ethnic inequalities in U.S. higher education for over a decade, I knew much more about affirmative action in the United States than in Israel—despite the fact that I have studied inequality in both countries, have lived in both countries, and am a citizen of both countries. Nonetheless, this question piqued my curiosity.

Back in my office, I started to gather information about the affirmative action program in Israel and was soon astounded by what I learned. The program, adopted in the mid-2000s by four of the country's most selective universities, targets disadvantaged applicants and is completely race-neutral and need-blind. That is, in evaluating the eligibility of applicants, neither their financial status nor their ethnic origins are considered. The emphasis, rather, is on structural determinants of disadvantage, in particular on locality or neighborhood and on high school socioeconomic status (although certain individual hardships are also weighed). I realized that the Israeli affirmative action program was the first and only program of its kind in the world to ever be implemented in university admissions on a large scale. Thus, examining this policy is strategic for advancing our thinking about the promise and perils of race-neutral admissions.

The unique design of this program—class-based, structure-based, race-neutral, and need-blind—inspired me to think more exhaustively about the possibilities of preferential treatment—specifically, about the wide but mostly unexplored range of potential class-based policies beyond the socioeconomically based, need-sensitive model that is typically suggested—and remains popular—in the public debate about this issue. In light of the vehement controversy over race-based policy in the United States, I decided to investigate whether these class-based possibilities could be relevant in American higher education. And so, with the generous support of the Spencer Foundation, I began this journey.

This book is the culmination of my research on affirmative action in both countries—specifically, race-based admissions in the United States and class-based admissions in Israel. The overarching goal of this book is to develop new, and more global, insights about the potential of race-neutral public policy to promote equality in higher education. Specifically, how do class-based and race-based models of affirmative action compare in promoting social and economic mobility for underprivileged groups and in increasing broad-scale diversity at selective postsecondary institutions? In this book, the evidence regarding how alternative affirmative action models perform in both the United States and Israel guides the discourse about their costs, benefits, and optimal design. This inquiry does not, however, simply aim to feed the debate about the consequences of these choices; it is also my hope that it will shed light on how social policy can equalize educational opportunity.

ACKNOWLEDGMENTS

Writing a book is a long and excruciating endeavor. It would not have been possible without the cooperation and generosity of many friends, colleagues, and organizations.

I am in debt to the Spencer Foundation, and especially to Mike McPherson, who saw the potential in this study and made it possible. With their generous support, I was able to build the Israeli dataset of university administrative records. I also owe many thanks to the top officials at those Israeli universities, who granted me unprecedented access to their administrative records. The unbelievingly dedicated staff at the admission offices of these institutions helped me and my research team understand the structure of these complex databases.

Assembling the data for the Israeli-side analysis was not an easy feat. The database is considerably more complex in scope, volume, and range than the U.S. counterparts on which my previous research has relied. I was fortunate to have many young talents on my research team, who worked diligently on transforming the raw data we received from the universities into a state of the art dataset. My biggest debt is to Erez Garnai, who worked with me for more than five years on the analyses for this book. I benefited immensely from Erez's dedication, motivation, wisdom, tenacity, meticulousness, patience, and excellent quantitative skills. I'm grateful to Dafna Caspi-Dror, who was the first to join this project and helped me collect and assemble the database; to Dafna Gelbgiser, who helped in the early stages of data cleaning and the later stages of the analyses; to Anat Shalev, who helped me assemble and organize the material in the final stage of the project; and to Yael Gazit, Ori

Katz, Yannay Shanan, and Mor Zarenkin for providing general research assistance.

The Russell Sage Foundation (RSF) was instrumental in moving me from the data analysis stage to the manuscript writing stage. My residency at the foundation during the 2012–2013 academic year granted me the physical and mental space needed to transform this ambitious comparative study into a book. I would not have been able to devote myself to this task without the supportive environment of the foundation, and am grateful for the daily support and friendship of its staff. Special thanks go to Suzanne Nichols, director of publications, for her serenity, wit, and priceless advice, and to David Haproff, director of communications, for his friendship and open-mindedness. Both were instrumental in the production and marketing of this book, and guided me patiently through the maze of the publishing world. I also thank Patricia Woodford, Claire Gabriel, John Lee, Galo Falchettore, Chris Brogna, James Wilson, and Jackie Cholmondeley for making my stay at the RSF comfortable and enjoyable. I enjoyed the time I spent with all the visiting scholars enormously, and cherish our intellectual exchanges and casual dialogues. I am particularly thankful to Annette Lareau, James Gibson, and Edward Mulvey for inspiration, encouragement, and friendship.

There are many colleagues who provided guidance, advice, critique, and encouragement throughout the process of conducting this investigation and writing the manuscript. I'm especially indebted to Rachel Sur, whose indispensable advice on the content, prose, and structure of the manuscript helped me regain a much-needed focus, while also encouraging me to strive for breadth and depth in the manuscript; to Michele Warman for providing sage legal insight into my interpretation of Supreme Court rulings and civil rights legislation; and to Cynthia Buck for editing the manuscript for general readability and style. I am grateful for the two reviewers for their insightful comments and productive suggestions, which have greatly improved the manuscript. Thanks also go to Ernie Eichenbaum for providing useful advice on one chapter.

My research would never have culminated in such a book without the many colleagues who supported me throughout my academic career. While I cannot name them all, I am especially grateful to Marta Tienda, who taught me the secrets of the trade and introduced me to higher education research; to Bill Bowen, whose work has been a huge inspiration and who was the first to suggest studying the affirmative action practices of Israeli universities; to Eugene Tobin for his relentless faith in me and in this project, and his commitment to assist in any way possible; and to Ann Marcus, who I can always count on for generosity, support, and friendship.

The active support, kindness, serenity, wisdom, and unconditional love of my husband, Joel, made this project possible. I adore my smart, mature, compassionate, easygoing kids, Omri, Assaf, and Neta, for tolerating my infinite work hours and for enduring life on the Israel-U.S. route. I couldn't have written the book without the love, optimism, and encouragement of my family.

Sigal Alon
Tel Aviv

PART I

Introduction

CHAPTER 1

The Search for an Alternative Affirmative Action Policy in American Higher Education

In 1973 and 1974, a white U.S. military veteran named Allan Bakke applied to medical school at the University of California–Davis (UC Davis) and was twice rejected. At the time the student bodies of most American colleges and universities were overwhelmingly white, especially the professional schools, such as law and medical schools. In an attempt to remedy the underrepresentation of minorities, UC Davis had established an affirmative action program in the early 1970s, with the multiple goals of "reducing the historic deficit of traditionally disfavored minorities in medical schools and in the medical profession," "countering the effects of societal discrimination, increasing the number of physicians practicing in underserved communities," and "obtaining the educational benefits that flow from an ethnically diverse student body."[1] In furtherance of these aims, the medical school at UC Davis created two separate admission pools: one for standard applicants and another for minority applicants. Sixteen of the one hundred seats in the entering class were reserved for the latter group.[2]

Bakke was born in Minneapolis in 1940 to a middle-class family of Scandinavian descent and was raised in Florida. His father was a postal carrier and his mother was a schoolteacher. He received a bachelor's degree in engineering from the University of Minnesota in 1962 and joined the U.S. Marine Corps after graduation. He served as an engineer in the Marines for four years, including a seven-month stint in Vietnam, earning the rank of captain.

After his discharge, he worked as an engineer at NASA and completed a master's degree in engineering at Stanford University in 1970.[3]

Bakke first applied to medical school in 1973 at the age of thirty-three, a relatively late age at a time when medical schools throughout the United States were known to discriminate against older applicants.[4] After twice being rejected, Bakke sued the university, claiming racial discrimination, because his grades were higher than those of some of the school's minority admits. His lawyers argued that the minority quota at the medical school violated the Equal Protection Clause of the Fourteenth Amendment to the United States Constitution, as well as the 1964 Civil Rights Act. After several appeals, this case eventually reached the U.S. Supreme Court in 1977. Representing UC Davis, Archibald Cox argued that considering race as a positive factor in admissions, with the goal of overcoming the vestiges of slavery and discrimination, was legal and constitutional. The case, Regents of the University of California v. Bakke (1978), represented the first Supreme Court challenge to affirmative action policy in the history of American higher education.

ELITE COLLEGES AND UNIVERSITIES IN THE UNITED STATES

UC Davis was not alone in adopting affirmative action practices. In the late 1960s, toward the end of the civil rights era, several colleges and universities in the United States started to give black students special consideration in admissions. These schools, for the most part, were among the most selective in the nation. In fact, most U.S. postsecondary institutions do not need to give special treatment in admissions because they admit all applicants who seek admission; only 20 to 30 percent of four-year colleges in America have enough applicants to be able to pick and choose among them.[5] A very small percentage are so selective that they reject the majority of applicants, including the historic Ivy League universities, most of which were founded centuries ago. These eight bastions of the elite in the Northeast—Brown University, Columbia University, Cornell University, Dartmouth College, Harvard University, Princeton University, the University of Pennsylvania (UPenn), and Yale University—are the traditional symbols of academic excellence and selectivity. In 2014 the undergraduate divisions of Harvard and Yale admitted only 6 percent of applicants, while the University of Pennsylvania admitted 10 percent.

Today there are several other four-year institutions around the country, most of them private, that are on par with the Ivy League in terms of prestige and selectivity, such as Stanford University (5 percent acceptance rate) and Rice University in Texas (14 percent). Several public state universities have also managed to enter the circle of elite schools—among them the University of California–Berkeley (UC Berkeley), the University of California–Los Angeles (UCLA), the University of Michigan (UMich), and the University of Texas–Austin (UT Austin). These public institutions were established to provide students with a top-notch education—tantamount to what the most distinguished private universities offer—but at a much lower price. Nonetheless, as more and more applicants were attracted to these world-class public research universities, they became more expensive and even more selective.[6] The undergraduate acceptance rate at UC Berkeley was 17 percent in 2014, similar to that at Cornell University. Today UCLA admits 18 percent of its college applicants, and UMich admits about one-third.

Social elitism has always been associated with selective colleges and universities in the United States—most glaringly at the Ivy League schools, which until a few decades ago catered largely to the traditional American upper class: white Anglo-Saxon Protestants, especially the "old money" families of the Northeast. But today even selective public universities, which were founded on the principles of mass higher education and social mobility, are becoming more elitist as they become more competitive. The percentage of affluent students whose fathers and mothers have college degrees is rising in these schools, while the number of Pell Grant recipients (a form of federal financial aid given to students with financial need) is declining.[7] These public universities have also become bastions of privilege.

Once a magnet for prospective teachers and ministers, the Ivy League today, like other selective schools, draws its elite status from being the training ground for the nation's leaders and high-rung professionals. The alumni of elite colleges are more likely than other bachelor's degree holders to enter graduate and professional programs. Over half of those who entered a bachelor's program at one of thirty elite colleges in 1976 went on to complete an advanced degree, compared with fewer than one-quarter of their counterparts at other four-year colleges.[8] An education at an elite school is also closely associated with some of the most prestigious positions in the country. Fourteen of the forty-three U.S. presidents graduated from an Ivy League university: eight had degrees from Harvard, five from Yale, three from Columbia, and two from Princeton. The last four presidents all attended Ivy League schools for at least part of their education: George H. W. Bush was a Yale undergrad; Bill Clinton attended Yale Law School; George W. Bush attended Yale College and Harvard Business School; and Barack Obama was a Columbia undergrad and completed Harvard Law School. All nine sitting Supreme Court justices have a law degree from either Harvard or Yale. Three were undergrads at Princeton, two were at Stanford, and the rest studied at Harvard, Cornell, Georgetown, and College of the Holy Cross.

The common denominator at elite institutions in the 1950s and early 1960s was the notable absence of African American students.[9] Blacks constituted only 0.8 percent of the entering freshman classes of nineteen of the most selective colleges in 1951.[10] Jerome Karabel, a sociologist at Berkeley who studied the "Big Three" universities—Harvard, Yale, and Princeton, all Ivies—noted that the homogenous student body at these schools largely comprised the sons of alumni and members of the social and economic upper crust. In 1960 only fifteen blacks were in the entering class at the Big Three, among more than three thousand students. At Princeton only one black student could be found in the freshman class of over eight hundred students.[11] Even as late as 1965 blacks made up only 1 percent of enrolled students at selective colleges in New England.[12]

RACE-BASED AFFIRMATIVE ACTION

In the United States in the late 1960s, toward the end of the civil rights era, most leading colleges and professional schools—where the paths to leadership roles in America tend to be found—began to acknowledge their crucial role in facilitating the social and economic mobility of minorities and leveling the playing field between blacks and whites. They also began seeking diversity on campus as they discussed the importance to the education process of having an array of talents, backgrounds, and opinions in the classroom. For these reasons, elite institutions started to give black students special consideration in admissions. In the five decades since these policies were first implemented, the term "affirmative action" has become synonymous with admissions policies that consider race or ethnicity—that is, that adopt as a main criterion applicants' membership in specific racial and ethnic groups. During this period, race-based affirmative action has dominated policymaking, research, courts of law, and the public's attention in the United States.

(For the sake of parsimony, I refer here to any policy based on race or ethnic origin as a "race" or "race-based" policy—that is, "race" in this context can also denote ethnicity.)

Yet this model of preferential treatment—based on an ascribed trait (a characteristic that an individual is born with, such as gender, race, ethnicity, or caste)—is not a uniquely American phenomenon. In fact, several countries have implemented or permitted similar affirmative action programs in higher education that draw attention to an ascribed trait. India, for example, initiated a quota program after gaining independence from Britain in 1947. Under this program, a percentage of positions in government and higher education are reserved for members of the Scheduled Castes and Scheduled Tribes, the two most disadvantaged groups in India.[13] More recently, South Africa also joined the affirmative action "club" in higher education. In the post-apartheid years, the University of Cape Town, one of the most selective institutions in South Africa, introduced affirmative action for black and mixed-race students, who had rarely been represented in the student body during the apartheid years.[14] Several selective universities in Brazil began using race-conscious admissions policies around the turn of the millennium. For example, in 2004 the University of Brasilia began reserving 20 percent of its enrollment for black and mixed-race students.[15]

What is unique, however, about race-based affirmative action in the United States is that it is voluntary—that is, it is not mandated by the government, but permitted when narrowly tailored. Remarkably, decisions about whether to implement such a policy at all and, if so, which applicants should get an edge in admission are made at the discretion of each institution (unless legislatively banned). Quotas are illegal. This approach to affirmative action represents a notable divergence from race- and ethnicity-based policies in other countries, which are state-sanctioned programs or legally permissible, such as India's reservation policy and Brazil's new Law of Social Quotas (which went into effect in 2012), under which admission decisions are formula-driven and based on state-proffered quotas.

Interestingly, despite significant between-country differences, affirmative action programs in all of these countries have been subject to criticism, and all have come under pressure to account for other aspects of disadvantage. Suggestions have arisen in India that preferential treatment eligibility be based on multiple disadvantages (gender, economic, and geographic factors, as well as type of prior schooling), not on caste.[16] The South African debate on race-based affirmative action centers on whether the children of the emerging black middle and upper classes should continue to get the same break on admissions as impoverished black students.[17] It is reported that the University of Cape Town is developing race-neutral measures of disadvantage—such as the quality of an applicant's high school and the educational attainment of his or her parents—in order to broaden access to underprivileged students. Brazil has already shifted to a class-based model of affirmative action in college admissions, with its new Law of Social Quotas, but the race of an applicant is still a factor in determining eligibility.

The fiercest and longest ongoing controversy over affirmative action, however, has taken place in the United States. Despite its noble goals, simply no other policy in higher education has been as divisive and litigious as affirmative action. Attempts have been made to abolish these policies from the moment they began. In fact, the Bakke case, which received tremendous media attention, reached the Supreme Court only about a decade after race-based affirmative action policies were first implemented in certain American colleges and universities.

THE BAKKE CASE: LAYING DOWN THE LEGAL GROUNDWORK FOR CLASS-BASED AFFIRMATIVE ACTION

> The University, through its special admissions policy, excluded Bakke from participation in its program of medical education because of his race.[18]
>
> —Supreme Court justice John Paul Stevens

> UC Davis' goal of admitting minority students disadvantaged by the effects of past discrimination is sufficiently important to justify use of race-conscious admissions criteria.[19]
> —Supreme Court justices William J. Brennan, Byron White, Thurgood Marshall, and Harry Blackmun

On October 11, 1977, the day before the presentation of oral arguments, newspaper reporters and camera crews camped out across from the Supreme

Court plaza. The next day hundreds of spectators lined up to get seats in the courtroom, while protesters on both sides filled the stairs outside of the Court.[20] The question raised by the Bakke case hit a nerve in a society grappling with the aftermath of the civil rights era: what happens when promoting opportunity for minorities comes at the expense of the majority? This question expresses the inherent tension between the notions of equal opportunity and race neutrality: the policies promoting the former can clash with the latter. On the one hand, the law forbids institutions from discriminating on the basis of race or color and from privileging one racial group. On the other hand, it allows minorities to be given special consideration for the purpose of promoting diversity and opportunity in employment and higher education.

The Supreme Court justices were divided in the Bakke case, and they issued six different opinions as the controversy was decided. Four justices—William Brennan, Byron White, Thurgood Marshall, and Harry Blackmun—argued that UC Davis's special admissions program was permissible both constitutionally and under Title VI of the 1964 Civil Rights Act and that its use of a race-conscious program to correct social, legal, and historic wrongs was proper. On the opposing side, four justices—John Paul Stevens, Warren Burger, William Rehnquist, and Potter Stewart—voted to annul UC Davis's affirmative action program, deeming it unconstitutional and in violation of Title VI of the 1964 Civil Rights Act.

The one remaining justice, Justice Lewis Powell, wrote the pivotal opinion in the case, which consisted of two parts. The first part (joined by four of the justices) struck down the affirmative action program at UC Davis's medical school because it used a quota for minority admissions. Such quotas, he argued, are unconstitutional because they prevent people of other races from competing for the reserved seats and thus discriminate against them. The second part (joined by four other justices), however, upheld the constitutionality of considering race as one of a number of factors in college admissions to promote a diverse student body. In reversing the California court's judgment enjoining UC Davis from any consideration of race, Justice Powell ruled that "the State has a substantial interest that legitimately may be served by a properly devised admissions program involving the competitive consideration of race and ethnic origin."[21]

Despite the split among the justices, the Bakke case is often praised as the legal cornerstone for affirmative action in higher education. Justice Powell, by way of his plurality opinion, set the stage for what came to be known as the "diversity rationale" for race-conscious admissions policies—the argument that having a diverse student body in postsecondary institutions serves a compelling government interest because "the 'nation's future depends upon leaders trained through wide exposure' to the ideas and mores of students as diverse as this Nation of many peoples."[22] Race-conscious admissions, then, are permissible because, when narrowly tailored, they serve this substantial educational interest. All subsequent Supreme Court rulings on affirmative action in higher education have reaffirmed the diversity rationale established in Bakke. Following this ruling striking down UC Davis's quota system, Allan Bakke was admitted to the medical school in 1978 at the age of thirty-eight. After graduation, Bakke began his residency in anesthesiology at the Mayo Clinic in Minnesota.[23]

The ruling has not ended challenges, however, to race-based affirmative action in college admissions. Far from resolving the controversy, the case encapsulates the differences of opinion concerning affirmative action. For one, the strict scrutiny that the Court imposed in Bakke stipulates that the consideration of race in admissions must be "necessary" for achieving diversity objectives, and this requirement has been used as ammunition against affirmative action in later lawsuits.[24]

Moreover, the issues at the heart of the jurists' disagreements were not fully resolved in the melded-together Bakke ruling, and they inevitably reemerged in the various ensuing cases. As the late Ronald Dworkin, a constitutional law scholar, wrote shortly after the verdict: "The arithmetic of the opinions of various justices, and the narrow ground of the pivotal opinion of Justice Powell, mean that Bakke decided rather less than had been hoped and left more, by way of general principle as well as detailed application, to later Supreme Court cases that are now inevitable."[25] Indeed, the public outcry against race-sensitive admissions in American colleges and universities has gained fervor over time, prompting more and more lawsuits in recent years and even bans concerning the use of affirmative action in several states, including Texas, California, Washington, Florida, Michigan, Nebraska, Arizona, New Hampshire, and Oklahoma (through voter-approved initiatives, referenda, executive decisions, or legislative votes).

Today, owing to this growing controversy as well as recent Supreme Court rulings, affirmative action policy in U.S. higher education may be embarking on a new path. In Fisher v. University of Texas (2013), the Supreme Court affirmed the importance of diversity on college campuses, but instructed that universities may take race and ethnicity into account during admissions only if race-neutral solutions have been proven to be unworkable. The imposition of these guidelines is likely to increase the pressure on selective schools in the coming years to find new and creative ways of achieving campus diversity.

An obvious alternative to affirmative action based on race is affirmative action based on class—that is, giving special consideration in admission to the socioeconomically disadvantaged. Ironically, while the 1978 Bakke decision is often looked upon as the landmark ruling for legitimizing race-conscious admissions policies in higher education, it arguably did a better job of laying a legal groundwork for class-based affirmative action in three ways: (1) by shifting the rationale for affirmative action from reparation for past discrimination to promotion of diversity; (2) by pushing for broad diversity—that is, insisting that race be regarded as only one element in the overall diversity that enhances the learning environment; and (3) by imposing strict scrutiny, thereby permitting race to be considered as a factor in admissions only if no alternative policy can achieve similar goals. Justice Powell, in a sense, was the architect of class-based affirmative action.

In an era of widening inequality in both higher education and society at large, few would argue that selective colleges today no longer need policies that promote diversity. But the question is not whether affirmative action is needed, but whether it should be based only on race or on broader aspects of disadvantage as well.

WHAT DO WE KNOW ABOUT CLASS-BASED AFFIRMATIVE ACTION?

> Disadvantaged applicants of all races must be eligible for sympathetic consideration.[26]
> —Justice Lewis Powell

One problem with the term "class-based affirmative action" is that it's not so simple to define, and trying to do so raises several conceptual and practical concerns. First and foremost, how exactly do we define "class"? Clearly, the designers of any class-based policy have to decide which factors determine eligibility. The most popular, almost instinctive, answer is to target people based on demonstrated individual disadvantages, such as being poor or being the first in the family to attend college. Alternatively, class-based policy can be based on structural factors, such as attending a low-performing high school or living in a poor neighborhood. And of course, class-based affirmative action can consider multiple factors, including both individual and structural disadvantages. This is not a trivial decision. For one, the decision is linked to our notions of morality and justice. But there are also important practical considerations that influence how we weigh the multiple factors.

It is reasonable to assume that adopting a more variegated set of criteria increases the likelihood of identifying the truly disadvantaged, but implementing and administering such an inclusive policy entails determining the relevant indicators of eligibility and then collecting, verifying, and weighting a wide array of sensitive information. It is when pondering potential alternatives to the current policy that this insight sinks in: while the focus on a single group characteristic (race or ethnicity) is the primary objection to race-based policy, it is also what streamlines its logistics. In class-based affirmative action, the question of who is eligible is far more complex. As two prominent economists note, there are "some important procedural questions about how a university might implement such a class-based affirmative action policy, because measuring family background is much less straightforward than measuring an individual's race or gender."[27]

It is also unclear whether a class-based policy would enhance racial diversity at elite institutions, relative to the race-based plans currently in place. Can race-neutral affirmative action achieve *broad* diversity—that is, socioeconomic, geographic, *and* demographic diversity? Or is the consideration of race in admissions essential for generating demographic diversity? Some researchers have tried to answer these questions by simulating a model of class-based affirmative action using U.S. data sets.[28] These statistical models suggest that policies based only on income will not promote racial and ethnic diversity nearly as well as race-sensitive policies do. But these simulations focus on a very narrow definition of class (family income) that may not be an adequate predictor of disadvantage, especially when it is the only criterion used. These studies do not take into account many of the factors likely to be significant in fostering broad diversity, such as household net worth, the quality of secondary education, neighborhood influences, and family structure. The question, then, is whether a race-neutral model that considers an extended array of disadvantages in admissions will suffice to create both socioeconomic and racial-ethnic diversity in the student bodies of elite schools. In other words, can class-based affirmative action replace race-conscious admissions? Or, alternatively, should class-based policies supplement race-based policies so that applicants' race and socioeconomic background are both taken into account in making the admission decision?

An eligibility scheme that considers multiple factors in determining class disadvantage may create broad diversity but end up with a very small pool of applicants from socioeconomically disadvantaged backgrounds who also have stellar academic achievements that put them near the threshold of the nation's most selective colleges. The question thus arises: how many applicants out there who fit this description have somehow managed to beat the odds? This is a critical issue because the size of the pool determines the potential of this model to boost diversity.

There is also the issue of money. Admitting poor students to expensive schools is costly and requires boosting financial aid budgets. So even if selective colleges are able to find enough socioeconomically disadvantaged students with good enough grades and test scores to cope with the colleges' academic rigor, all of these students will need generous financial aid packages in order to enroll and persist until graduation. In contrast, the current race-conscious admissions policies include the pool of socioeconomically strong minorities who can pay, at least partly, for their education. In other words, the size of the financial aid budget will largely determine the potential of class-based policies to infuse elite institutions with poor students and to augment socioeconomic diversity on campus.

These are just some of the many issues involved in shifting from race to class in affirmative action, a move that is neither simple nor straightforward. The problem is compounded by how very little we know about how well class-based affirmative action works, mostly because, with the exception of sporadic experiments, it has never been implemented in the United States. And so, with few real examples of class-based programs to observe, we are left wondering about the impact of class-based policy on disadvantaged youth and campus diversity.

If we look beyond the United States—as this book aims to do—we find that while the class-based road is certainly less traveled, several countries are experimenting with various models of class-based affirmative action in higher education. These policies, I argue, open up an invaluable opportunity to see class-based admissions policy in action—specifically, to evaluate how others have dealt with the challenges of determining and implementing eligibility criteria, and to measure and compare diversity outcomes. Looking outside our borders may help us decide whether it is finally time for the United States to embark on the class-based path in affirmative action.

This book is rooted in this perspective—the idea that close observation of other nations' battles with inequality can teach us something about our own, and specifically about whether the class-based model is feasible and fitting for U.S. colleges and universities. This idea led me to look for a natural experiment somewhere in the world that would allow me to empirically examine class-based affirmative action that had been implemented in higher education on a large scale. I wanted to compare such a program to the race-based approach favored by advocates of affirmative action in the United States—to reveal the respective gains and pitfalls and highlight the contextual and institutional factors conducive to each set of practices. Such an analysis, I reasoned, might help steer the debate on affirmative action in the United States away from political talking points and toward understanding whether this alternative could replace or supplement the race-based policy currently in effect.

Brazil, at first glance, looked like a tempting case study for such a comparative analysis. As mentioned earlier, in 2012 Brazil enacted a new class-based affirmative action program, the Law of Social Quotas.[29] According to this law, the public universities in Brazil, which are the selective universities, are required to reserve at least half of their slots for students from public high schools, which serve a poorer population and perform worse overall than the country's private high schools. Furthermore, half of these reserved slots are set aside for low-income students.[30] However, while this policy's hybrid design is noteworthy, its relevance to the current debate on affirmative action in the United States is limited. First, the policy—which focuses on high school type, income, and race simultaneously—is not race-neutral, in that the allocation of reserved slots must match the racial makeup of each state. Thus, this model does not comply with the U.S. Supreme Court's instructions to give serious, good-faith consideration to race-neutral methods of boosting diversity. Second, a U.S. "law of social quotas" would be problematic because first, quotas have been held to be unconstitutional in U.S. higher education ever since the Bakke decision, and second, affirmative action practices are voluntary. Finally, because the Brazilian policy is so new, it will be many years before it can be properly evaluated.

Nonetheless, there is a country with a voluntary class-based affirmative action policy in place that is large-scale enough to study, feasible for replication in the United States, and available for scrutiny. That country is Israel, whose higher education system I have been investigating for years, alongside my work on the American postsecondary education system.

A NATURAL EXPERIMENT IN CLASS-BASED AFFIRMATIVE ACTION IN HIGHER EDUCATION

The Israeli affirmative action policy, the first of its kind to be implemented in university admissions anywhere in the world, was adopted in the mid-2000s by four of the country's most selective universities. The program targets disadvantaged applicants, but it is completely race-neutral and need-blind: in evaluating the eligibility of applicants, these universities consider neither financial status nor ethnic origins. The emphasis, rather, is on structural determinants of disadvantage, specifically on neighborhood and high school socioeconomic status. (Some individual hardships are also weighed.) This design, while unique, nevertheless has deep roots in the long tradition of sociological research on the heavy impact of social structures, such as neighborhoods and schools, on educational outcomes.

Just as the reliance on race-based affirmative action in American colleges is no indicator that class is not a problem in the United States, it would be a mistake to deduce from the race-neutral design of the Israeli program that ethnicity[31] is not a factor in inequality in Israel. Israeli society is in fact divided along ethnic lines, with two main demographic cleavages. The first cleavage is between Israeli Arabs (the majority of whom are Muslims), who account for approximately 20 percent of the population, and Israeli Jews, who make up the rest. The second cleavage exists within the Jewish population between Jews of European and American origin (hereinafter "Ashkenazi") and Jews of Asian and African origin (hereinafter "Mizrachi"). These differences in ethnic origin shape Israel's stratification system. The hierarchies of educational attainment, occupational status, and earnings are clear and have persisted for over fifty years: Ashkenazi Jews are at the top, followed by Mizrachi Jews, while the Arab citizens of Israel occupy the bottom rung of the socioeconomic ladder.[32] In light of this stratification, there are occasionally calls in Israel for affirmative action policies in higher education that would consider applicants' ethnicity in admissions, giving an edge to the country's ethnic minorities, Arabs and Mizrachi Jews. But to properly evaluate whether such a change is warranted, we must go beyond the arguments and opinions and look at the numbers.

In this book I study the class-based, race-neutral, and structure-based program of affirmative action at Israeli flagship universities and compare these results (in terms of feasibility, academic standing, diversification, mobility, and students' success) with what ethnic-based affirmative action could generate. Simultaneously, I examine U.S. race-based plans and assess how their outcomes measure up against those that could have been advanced by class-based affirmative action.

THE COMPARATIVE INVESTIGATION

The anchor of this book is a comparative study of actual and simulated race-based versus class-based affirmative action—which I refer to hereafter as simply "the comparative investigation." I use the United States as a case study of race-based affirmative action and Israel as a case study of class-based affirmative action. For each country I compare the model that has actually been implemented to a simulated scenario of the road not taken—the alternative policy type. For the Israeli case, I compare the actual class-based affirmative action in place to a simulated model of ethnic affirmative action. For the American case, I put the current race-based policies up against three simulated models of class-based affirmative action: one focusing on individual socioeconomic status as determined by family income, family wealth, and parents' education levels (this is the most popular model in public discussion); one targeting applicants in poor schools that focuses on group affiliation (with schools), not on individual disadvantages (this model most closely replicates the Israeli program); and one that combines aspects of the first two models by focusing on both individual- and school-level disadvantages. The simulations also examine a race-sensitive, class-based model—that is, a hybrid design that integrates race and ethnicity as another element in class-based affirmative action. These simulations let us observe how the diversity dividends of American race-conscious admissions programs measure up against those that could be advanced by different types of class-based affirmative action. They also tell us what model is practical and feasible and show us the likely impact on participating universities' academic selectivity (in terms of the test scores and grades of incoming classes) of shifting from race to class in affirmative action.

Diversity is not a class-based policy's only outcome of concern: students' mobility is also an important issue. As with race-based policies, the objective of Israel's class-based program is not only to diversify the student bodies of elite schools but also to pave the way for the social and economic mobility of disadvantaged populations. Thus, I evaluate the Israeli model by examining whether this policy helps its beneficiaries rise from the lower rungs of the ladder. Also pertinent is the ability of the beneficiaries of affirmative action to thrive and attain a degree. One of the claims against race-conscious admissions policies is that admitting minority students to elite schools harms these students and that they would be better off attending less rigorous schools.[33] Given this argument, the empirical investigation tracks the academic progress of students admitted under the Israeli policy during the college years and evaluates whether a policy that gives an edge to Arabs and Mizrachi Jews (ethnic minorities) produces a student body that is academically stronger or weaker in comparison. Similarly, I track the academic progress, pathways to degree attainment, and type of degrees obtained by the beneficiaries of the race-based affirmative action practiced by American colleges and universities. Documenting the mobility dividends and the repercussions for academic success of race- and class-based affirmative action—a topic that has not been fully addressed in the scholarly literature—is critical for evaluating preferential treatment policies and informing the ongoing debate about the shift from race- to class-based policy.

The comparative investigation allows me to examine how both types of affirmative action policy fare in terms of feasibility, diversification, mobility, and academic outcomes. Implementing such a simulation framework requires a wealth of reliable information about students' socioeconomic status. The empirical analyses of the U.S. side of the comparative investigation are based on a cohort that started college in the fall of 1995 (the 1995–1996 academic year) and whose data are found in the Beginning Postsecondary Students Longitudinal Study (BPS), a study linked to the National Postsecondary Student Aid Study (NPSAS) and conducted by the U.S. Department of Education. These data include detailed information about students' social, economic, and academic backgrounds, their parents' educational attainment, and the type of high school they attended, and are thus ideal for determining applicants' eligibility for various class-based affirmative action prototypes. The data set also contains details about the postsecondary institution students attended and their academic outcomes and attainment in college. The Israeli-side analyses are based on institutional administrative data (a data set constructed with the support of the Spencer Foundation) from the four elite universities that practice this preferential treatment: Tel Aviv University (TAU), The Hebrew University (HUJI), The Technion (TECH), and Ben-Gurion University (BGU).[34] This rich data set contains application information, admission decisions, and student transcripts. Attractive aspects of the Israeli data set include the availability of applicant transcripts (including applicants' field-of-study selections and institution decisions)[35] and the ability to single out all affirmative action applicants, admits, and students.

AN OUTLINE OF THE BOOK

As the search in the United States for effective models of class-based affirmative action in college admissions intensifies—especially in light of recent court rulings—it is imperative that we obtain empirical evidence about the feasibility and effectiveness of class-based policy compared with race-based policy. This is what I do in this book.

Part II provides context for the debate about the consequential and turbulent development of affirmative action policy in American higher education. Chapter 2 describes the birth of race-conscious admissions policies in the wake of the Civil Rights Act of 1964, as well as the current state of these policies in U.S. higher education. I review the success of this practice in enhancing racial and ethnic diversity at elite colleges and widening the path of mobility for minorities. The chapter presents statistics demonstrating the decline of blacks and Hispanics in postsecondary education that occurred when colleges were banned from using race in admission decisions and shows the public and individual dividends of affirmative action. This success has been accompanied, however, by mounting controversy and legal threats, which I document. I explain the controversy surrounding race-based admissions—specifically, the issues of justice and preference, the creaming of already advantaged individuals, and academic mismatch. I review the relevant Supreme Court cases and focus on the guidelines of the recent Fisher decision. This chapter not only covers the history of race-conscious admission but also helps to sharpen the race and class controversy by highlighting some of the evidence for why race may still need to be considered in the admission process.

The wave of dissent against race-conscious admissions policies in higher education is more complex, I argue, than media headlines suggest. In chapter 3, I delve into what has been feeding the growing frustration with race-based affirmative action by analyzing the changing American economic and social landscape and postsecondary system over the past several decades. Several forces have made it very difficult for a talented high school senior from an underprivileged background to obtain an education from one of the best colleges in the country. These economic, social, and academic forces include rising income inequality, declining mobility, and escalating tuition costs. These forces have converged to sharply increase the competition for admission to selective colleges, leading to a widening class divide and growing segmentation in American higher education. The evidence in this chapter clarifies the rising appeal of class-based affirmative action in the public eye.

How have elite institutions in the United States reacted to these dramatic social, economic, and academic shifts? I focus in chapter 4 on the answers to this question, which represent an important piece of the puzzle. I show that elite institutions, while claiming to have opened the gates to students from all walks of life, have focused mainly on enhancing racial and ethnic diversity. Consequently, underprivileged applicants are falling behind, since they are competing not just with other meritorious students but also with alumni children, students from high-performing private high schools, children of foreign-born dignitaries, and those with special, unusual, athletic, or artistic talents. In the absence of consideration of other types of disadvantage, socioeconomic diversity at the country's top colleges has declined. This chapter concludes that selective colleges have largely ignored the increasing class stratification in America. In hindsight, this appears to be a historic mistake on their part, one that may bring about the total prohibition of race and ethnicity as criteria in admissions. But the schools are not the only culprits. Despite its mandate to focus on "broad diversity," the Supreme Court has never been specific about what broad diversity is and how to achieve it. At a time of rising class and income inequality, which has been accentuated by the Great Recession, the misalignment between the broad diversity rationale and the narrowly defined practice of affirmative action has fed the frustration with race-conscious admissions and accelerated the search for race-neutral methods of promoting diversity, mobility, and equal opportunity in higher education.

Moving from race to class in affirmative action is not a simple proposition, however, as is explored in part III. Chapter 5 describes the conceptual and practical frameworks of class-based affirmative action, the different class-based policy options, and the dilemmas involved in shifting from racial to class considerations. Here I also explain the implications of focusing only on socioeconomic differences while ignoring structural ones—such as living in a poor community or attending a low-quality high school. However, even taking personal and structural economic disadvantages into account may pose problems that undermine the feasibility of class-based affirmative action and the representation of underrepresented minorities at elite campuses.

Chapter 6 discusses Israel's current voluntary class-based regime, thereby bringing the theoretical discussion into the practical sphere. The chapter begins by describing the main contours of inequality in Israeli society. Over the past several decades, Israel, like the United States, has been plagued by rising economic inequality, declining social and economic mobility, and persistent ethnic inequality. As in this country, the rising competition in Israel for entry into the most selective universities prompted the need for affirmative action policy that could widen the path to these schools, especially to their most prestigious and lucrative departments. In this chapter, I describe in detail the unique affirmative action program that the most selective Israeli universities implemented in the mid-2000s.

Both chapters in part IV deal with feasibility and diversity dividends. Chapter 7 focuses on the diversity dividends of Israel's class-based regime, juxtaposing the results with the potential dividends of a hypothetical program of ethnic-based affirmative action. Through simulation, I replace the actual beneficiaries of class-based affirmative action with the students who would have been eligible for ethnicity-based admissions and estimate the impact on admission to higher education institutions of an affirmative action policy that gives preference to ethnic minorities. I gauge which model of affirmative action—race-based or class-based—produces higher levels of broad diversity within elite Israeli universities along geographic, economic, and demographic lines.

The answers are not entirely straightforward. A race-based affirmative action program, as expected, would generate a much higher level of ethnic diversity in the top Israeli universities than the current race-neutral program does. Moreover, owing to the high level of residential segregation in Israel, the race-based model would enhance certain types of geographic diversity. Race-based affirmative action would also strengthen the academic standards of the elite universities (although the opposite would be the case if the policy targeted only Arabs). The effect of race-based affirmative action on socioeconomic diversity, however, would be rather limited. Interestingly, and in contrast to the race-based model, the class-based program does not excel at promoting one particular type of diversity. Rather, its hybrid and multidimensional design targets several aspects of disadvantage simultaneously, with the result that its diversity effects are more widespread. In addition to its effect on spatial diversity, the class-based program enhances the representation in elite universities of ethnic minorities, new immigrants, poor individuals, and individuals from poor localities.

In a similar vein, chapter 8 reports the results of simulations that I conducted using data on American students. The approach is similar in logic to the Israeli simulations, but the direction is reversed: I replace the beneficiaries of racial and ethnic affirmative action at elite schools in the United States with students who would have been eligible for various prototypes of class-based affirmative action, including one similar to the Israeli program. (In reality, the latter are rejected and attend less-selective four-year schools.) These simulations show that, with one exception, the academic selectivity of elite institutions would not be jeopardized if affirmative action shifted from race to class; that exception would be a class-based policy that targets multiple disadvantages. Targeting students with as many disadvantages as possible is fair and politically correct, but given that elite institutions are likely to admit only the highest-achieving among this group, the diversifying potential of such a policy would be limited by the short supply from which to draw extremely disadvantaged high-achieving students.

I then compare the diversity dividends of the class-based models with those generated by the actual race-based programs in place. As in the Israeli case, the results of the simulations are not straightforward. On the one hand, the student bodies of elite colleges would be substantially less diverse racially and ethnically under all types of class-based affirmative action relative to current race-based policy. On the other hand, admissions that target the socioeconomically underprivileged could boost the socioeconomic diversity at these bastions of privilege. Perhaps the best route for generating broad diversity would be a race-within-class model. The level of racial and ethnic diversity generated by nesting race preferences within class-based affirmative action policy approaches the current level, while also benefiting underprivileged nonminority applicants. The price of this outcome is the abandonment of race-neutrality.

Together, the findings of chapters 7 and 8 lead to a firm conclusion: there is no magic bullet solution to the issue of diversity at elite institutions. Neither race-based nor class-based models by themselves can generate broad diversity. Doing so would require a hybrid program that embedded, for example, the consideration of race within class-based affirmative action.

The two chapters of part V examine the mobility dividends of affirmative action policies in college admissions. Chapter 9 brings us back to Israel: using other statistical models, I show the implications for students' prospects of an edge in admission to an elite institution. The results show that such an edge allows Israeli applicants from disadvantaged backgrounds, including Arabs and Mizrachi Jews and those from poor localities and failing schools, to improve their chances at the admission stage of getting access not only to elite institutions but also to more competitive, profitable, and career-oriented majors within them. They maintain this edge until degree attainment and graduate from fields of study that are more rigorous, prestigious, and lucrative, on average, compared to their counterparts who did not make the cutoff for the program's eligibility.

Chapter 10 examines the effect of the affirmative action edge in admission on its beneficiaries in the United States and its contribution to their social and economic mobility. I show that blacks and Hispanic freshmen who benefit from race-based affirmative action at elite schools are better integrated on campus, both academically and socially, than their counterparts at less-selective schools. Having more contact with faculty and peers contributes to their ability to navigate the hurdles in the first year of college. They are more likely than their counterparts to move on to the second year and, eventually, to graduate. Like the beneficiaries of class-based affirmative action in Israel, they translate the edge in admission to academic credentials. The findings in both cases indicate that affirmative action at elite colleges and universities is a vehicle for mobility for disenfranchised students, whether they are racial and ethnic minorities or socioeconomically disadvantaged. None would be better off without an edge in admissions.

Together, the findings of chapters 9 and 10 lead to a firm conclusion: in both Israel and the United States, students who benefit from either race- or class-based affirmative action are not better off attending less prestigious schools.

In the concluding part VI, "Insights from a Comparative Outlook," chapter 11 summarizes the main findings of the comparative investigation regarding the mobility and diversity dividends of different types of affirmative action policy. I use these insights to revisit the key issues plaguing the debate about whether to switch from race-based to class-based considerations in American college admissions. One such issue is the politics surrounding the goal of broad diversity, whose ambiguity continues to stymy efforts to effectively reform affirmative action policy. Another issue is whether college admissions should be race-neutral or race-conscious. This chapter also weighs the broad-diversity implications of a reform that would eliminate legacies and other preferences. I reflect on more practical questions as well, such as whether affirmative action policy should aim to avoid creaming, whether a hybrid design is preferable to a rigid prototype, and, finally, whether to base eligibility on group affiliation or individual traits.

The public debate about affirmative action in U.S. higher education tends to involve many vehement claims about what is right and just and about what should and what can work. Glaringly missing from the discussion are evidence-based assessments of the effectiveness, feasibility, and implications of reforming affirmative action policy in college admissions—namely, of shifting the focus from race to class. These assessments are desperately needed at this stage, and this book is devoted to making them.

By focusing on two countries, the United States and Israel, and on two types of affirmative action policy, race-based and class-based, this investigation tries to answer some of the most pressing questions regarding the shift from race to class in affirmative action. While the United States and Israel have embarked on different affirmative action pathways, the dilemmas on both sides of the Atlantic are similar. Both types of policy, whether race- or class-based, raise questions about diversity outcomes, mobility dividends, academic selectivity, implementation, and feasibility.

This study shows that both the class-based and the race-based roads promote equal opportunity, social mobility, and diversity, but that they do so in different ways, achieving different outcomes. Class-based affirmative action is a solid alternative to race-conscious admissions policies, but lamentably, it is not a problem-free, superior alternative. Whether American colleges and universities decide to keep race-based affirmative action in place or switch to class-based affirmative action, they must be realistic about what each policy can and cannot accomplish.

PART II

The Problem

CHAPTER 2

Affirmative Action in American Higher Education: A Story About Race

The dream of America as the melting pot has not been realized by Negroes—either the Negro did not get into the pot, or he did not get melted down.[1]

—Justice Thurgood Marshall

The problem of the Twentieth Century is the problem of the color line.[2]

—W.E.B. Du Bois

On June 4, 1965, President Lyndon B. Johnson delivered the commencement address, entitled "To Fulfill These Rights," to the graduating class of Howard University in Washington, D.C. A private and federally chartered institution, Howard University opened its doors in 1867, just after the Civil War, determined to educate freed blacks, who were shut out of most postsecondary institutions on account of their skin color.[3] As the president spoke in 1965 the country was at the peak of the civil rights era. He had signed a landmark Civil Rights Act a year earlier, ending racial segregation in schools, workplaces, and public accommodations. Two months after the Howard speech, Johnson signed the Voting Rights Act, which provided for the mass enfranchisement of black voters in the South. To this mostly black university audience, the president said:

Ability is stretched or stunted by the family that you live with, and the neighborhood you live in—by the school you go to and the poverty or the richness of your surroundings. It is the product of a hundred unseen forces playing upon the little infant, the child, and finally the man. . . . You do not take a person who, for years, has been hobbled by chains and liberate him, bring him up to the starting line of a race and then say, "You are free to compete with all the others," and still justly believe that you have been completely fair. Thus it is not enough just to open the gates of opportunity. All our citizens must have the ability to walk through those gates.[4]

By invoking the plight of blacks in America and the dire need to remedy the wrongs of slavery and discrimination, Johnson was drawing on a sordid history of slavery, indentured servitude, and political disenfranchisement. The legacy of slavery, segregation, and discrimination had left its mark on the educational attainment of blacks. In 1959, 67 percent of twenty-five- to twenty-nine-year-old whites had high school diplomas, while only 40 percent of their black counterparts did.[5] Twelve percent of whites in this age bracket had graduated from college, but fewer than 5 percent of blacks had done so. In spite of the postwar economic growth of the late 1950s and 1960s, the economic prospects remained gloomy for blacks, who faced increasing discrimination not only in the workplace but also in the housing market.[6] The unemployment rate ratio of blacks to whites has held consistently at two-to-one since 1954, the first year the U.S. Bureau of Labor Statistics (BLS) published unemployment data by race.[7] Many of the blacks who did get jobs were stuck in dead-end minimum-wage positions. In 1959, for example, the average weekly earnings of employed black men were 57 percent of employed white men's weekly earnings.

Although the 1964 Civil Rights Act prohibited institutions that receive federal funding from discriminating in employment decisions on the basis of race, color, religion, sex, or national origin, this legislation, along with several executive orders, went further: it also required such institutions to take "affirmative action," including in their recruitment, mentoring, and training programs, to ensure equal opportunity for all qualified persons.[8] In his speech at Howard University, President Johnson suggested that "it is not enough just to open the gates of opportunity," providing the justification for moving beyond nondiscrimination to affirmative action.

THE BIRTH OF AFFIRMATIVE ACTION IN U.S. COLLEGE ADMISSIONS

In the wake of the civil rights movement, and especially after the enactment of the Civil Rights Act in 1964, most leading colleges and professional schools in the country came to believe that they had a role to play in changing this reality—that is, in educating black students and increasing the share of minorities on campus.[9] The universities were influenced not only by the new legislation and changes in public opinion in the country overall but also by student protests that pushed university leaders to participate in rectifying past racial injustices.

Given this changing tide of sentiment, selective colleges began to recruit black students in the early to mid-1960s, but because they neither lowered admission standards nor increased financial aid, these attempts were largely fruitless. Elite colleges soon realized that a more "affirmative" approach would be necessary if they were serious about increasing their share of black students. Thus, toward the late 1960s elite colleges and universities began giving qualified black applicants a slight edge in college admissions—that is, they started admitting some black applicants whose grades and test scores were a bit lower than those of the average white admit.[10] They also augmented their financial aid budgets in order to offer needy students larger aid packages.[11] These practices mark what was basically the beginning of affirmative action by American colleges and universities as we know it today in the United States. In the 1980s, Hispanic applicants also became beneficiaries of affirmative action policies at elite colleges and universities. The edge that affirmative action bestows lowered the academic barriers for underrepresented minorities (URM) compared to other applicants, making their admission to selective schools easier. For example, according to several studies, the administrative records of selective institutions indicate that the test score gap between blacks and whites admitted to elite institutions is in the ballpark of 170 to 200 points.[12]

Clearly, the main criterion for special consideration in admissions is group membership, specifically, the applicant's affiliation with a particular racial or ethnic group. This practice is rooted in the notion of "macrojustice," which posits that inequality and discrimination are generated at the societal level; thus, the correction, or redistribution, must also occur at the macro level.[13] That is, because discrimination causes collective damage in terms of self-confidence, self-esteem, and sense of entitlement, every individual who is part of a historically disenfranchised group is entitled to some compensation, regardless of his or her individual experience. Policies, then, must address injustice at the group level—not at the individual level—in order to redress historic discrimination and target the unfair distribution of outcomes within society. This outlook justifies reverse discrimination and possible harm to some individuals for the sake of justice at a societal level.

Over the years, several rationales have been given for why race-conscious admissions is a legitimate and desirable practice at selective colleges.[14] For some of the institutions with affirmative action programs, the rationale behind the practice was "reparation" for past societal discrimination and the legacy of slavery. The idea of reparation for blacks in various forms was once part of the political discourse, but the topic has almost vanished from public consciousness in recent decades. The journalist Ta-Nehisi Coates made a compelling attempt in a 2014 *Atlantic* article to put the topic of economic reparations for blacks back on the agenda by pointing to precedents such as the agreement between West Germany and Israel in 1951 to compensate Holocaust victims and U.S. government compensation to Americans of Japanese origin who were incarcerated in internment camps during World War II.[15] Yet applying the reparation rationale to affirmative action as it is practiced by elite colleges today is not straightforward. For one, all black applicants, regardless of their origin, are eligible for preferential treatment, including recent black immigrants.[16] The inclusion of Hispanics as affirmative action beneficiaries since the 1980s further weakens the reparation rationale in this context. Thus, the reparations argument today has little political support and has never been endorsed by the Supreme Court for higher education.

Most institutions were motivated by two other reasons. First, they wanted to increase the representation of racial and ethnic minorities in their student bodies. The belief that diversity is important took hold and became deeply rooted in American society after the civil rights movement, especially in academia and the workplace, and the "diversity" rationale made its Supreme Court debut in the Bakke case (1978). Justice Powell, the pivotal opinion in that case, ruled that race-based affirmative action serves a compelling educational interest by enhancing student body diversity on the grounds that the interaction between students with diverse backgrounds and perspectives enriches the educational process. Diversity, argued Justice Powell, creates an academic environment that is "conducive to speculation, experiment and creation—so essential to the quality of higher education."[17] Ever since, the diversity rationale has remained the main justification for affirmative action policy according to the Supreme Court. This rationale has become more popular over time as American society has become increasingly diverse: between 1960 and 2011, the share of whites in the school-age population (ages five to twenty-four) declined from 85 to 58 percent (largely as a result of Hispanic immigration).[18]

The second rationale for giving minority applicants an edge in admissions to elite institutions was to promote "equal opportunity" and "social mobility." President Johnson believed that preferential treatment for disadvantaged groups would boost their representation in business, government, and the professional sphere and that this unequal treatment was warranted because people's life chances had been unequal. He believed that affirmative action in the labor market and, perhaps more importantly, in higher education—at the institutions that serve as the gateways to these positions—would infuse prestigious occupations with diversity and create leaders in all walks of life. Accordingly, one goal of race-conscious admissions was to promote a black middle and upper class that would reach leadership positions in professional and political life and serve as role models for other blacks.

By implementing race-conscious admissions, elite institutions appeared to concur with the imperative to level the playing field: to compensate high-achieving but disenfranchised youth for the effects of discrimination, segregation, primary and secondary school disadvantage, and home disadvantage—all disadvantages that accumulate over generations—and partly offset the competitive advantages that accrue to those with privileged upbringings. Leveling the playing field, in turn, was supposed to expand opportunities for a quality education, just slightly out of reach for some, and to widen the avenue for social and economic mobility for groups at the bottom of the hierarchy. This line of reasoning has been advocated and invoked by the Supreme Court on several occasions, as in the 2003 Grutter v. Bollinger decision: "Moreover, because universities, and in particular, law schools, represent the training ground for a large number of the Nation's leaders . . . the path to leadership must be visibly open to talented and qualified individuals of every race and ethnicity. Thus, the Law School has a compelling interest in attaining a diverse student body."[19]

SUCCESSES ACHIEVED BY RACE-BASED AFFIRMATIVE ACTION

Many educators, business leaders, scholars, politicians, and members of the public believe in the important role of affirmative action in diversifying academia and the workplace and widening the path of mobility for minorities. In this section, I review the successes of race-based affirmative action in the United States in achieving these goals.

Diversity Dividends

The voluntary adoption of race-conscious admissions reflects the open and growing desire of elite schools to diversify the demographics of their student bodies. These policies have been relatively successful at achieving this aim: the share of minority students at elite institutions has grown significantly as a result of race-based affirmative action.[20] For example, the share of URM (blacks and Hispanics) at competitive four-year colleges (those classified in the top three categories according to *Barron's*) increased from 7 percent in 1972 to 13 percent in 2004 (see figure 2.1).

Perhaps the best indicator of this success is the sharp drop in the share of black and Hispanic students at selective institutions after certain states banned the use of race as a factor in admission decisions.[21] For example, after Proposition 209 passed in California in 1997, banning public colleges and universities in the state from considering race in admissions, the share of black students at UC Berkeley declined by 52 percent (from 7 to 3.2 percent) and that of Hispanics by 43 percent (from 14 to 7.8 percent).[22] Similar downswings took place at universities in Texas and Michigan after those states adopted similar bans. Colleges and universities in states that have banned the consideration of race in admissions have experienced a decline in racial diversity across a number of educational fields, including the natural sciences, business, medicine, and law. In Florida, California, Texas, and Washington—four states that implemented these bans in the late 1990s—there has been a 26 percent drop in minority enrollment in engineering programs (from 6.2 to 4.6 percent) and a 19 percent drop in the share of minorities studying natural sciences (from 7.8 to 7.3 percent).[23] Between 2000 and 2011, black

Figure 2.1 The Race-Ethnicity of Students Attending Competitive Four-Year Institutions, 1972–2004

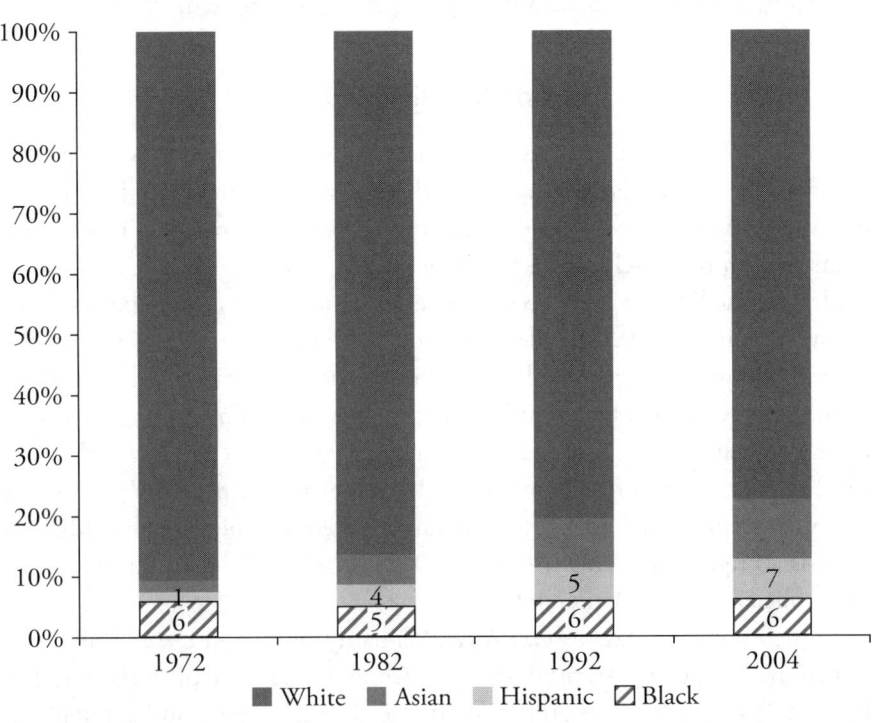

Source: Author's calculations using National Center for Education Statistics data sets: National Longitudinal Study of the High School Class of 1972 (NLS:72), High School and Beyond (HS&B), National Education Longitudinal Study of 1988 (NELS:88), and Education Longitudinal Study of 2004 (ELS:04).

Notes: The data are for high school graduates from four cohorts (1972, 1982, 1992, and 2004). The estimates are weighted. Competitive four-year institutions are those classified as very, highly, and most competitive (the top three categories) according to *Barron's* classification scheme. *Barron's* gives each college an academic rating (among other ratings) that indicates its competitiveness and selectivity as determined by the academic profile of the freshman class. The academic rating is based on median SAT or ACT scores, high school class rank, mean high school GPA, and the freshman admission rate (Barron's Educational Series 1982, 1992, 2003). These ratings are discussed in more detail in chapter 3.

students made up only 1.5 percent, on average, of the entering classes at the six business schools in the University of California system, down from 3.6 percent in 1996, the year before Proposition 209 was passed.[24]

Mobility Dividends

While blacks and Hispanics are still largely underrepresented at selective universities, the accumulated empirical evidence suggests that race-based affirmative action has broadened the educational opportunities of minority students and, in turn, helped push high-achieving URM up the socioeconomic ladder. By facilitating their access to better educational opportunities, affirmative action has increased the likelihood that minority students will graduate and obtain a job with good economic returns and contributed, as a result, to the emergence of a black middle class.[25] The share of blacks among physicians, for example, rose from 2.8 percent in 1960 to 6.4 in 2013, while the share among lawyers rose from about 1 percent to 4.2 percent.[26] URM are still underrepresented in prestigious and lucrative professional fields, but there is a huge improvement from the 1960s, before the first affirmative action policies were implemented.

In their book *The Shape of the River,* William Bowen and Derek Bok determined that 56 percent of black students who attended one of thirty elite colleges in 1976 went on to attain an advanced (graduate or professional) degree. This rate was much higher than the national average and matched that of whites at these schools. Among these black college graduates, 14 percent obtained a law degree and 11 percent became physicians—both higher rates of degree completion in these professions than among their white classmates. An additional 13 percent completed a business degree and 4 percent a doctoral degree. By 1995 the mean earned income of these black graduates was much higher than the average income of college graduates (although it was still lower than that of their white counterparts). The dividends of affirmative action extended into other spheres as well. For example, Bowen and Bok report that the black graduates of elite institutions, especially the men, were more likely than whites to be involved in civic activities, including community, social service, youth, and primary and secondary educational organizations. Many held leadership positions in these areas, serving as role models for minority youth.

Bowen and Bok conclude that not only is the premium associated with attending a selective college substantive, but this premium is higher for black students than for whites. This claim has been substantiated by several other studies. Although it is true that any student would benefit from graduating from an elite institution (more on this topic in the next chapter), the evidence suggests that the benefits of attending an elite institution, in terms of future educational attainment and occupational status, are larger for those who are least likely to attend these schools.[27] Put simply, blacks and Hispanics gain more than whites do from attending a more selective institution instead of a less selective one.[28] It appears that if you give a student with less access to elite institutions the opportunity to attend one, on average he or she will gain more from this experience—academically, socially, and professionally—than the typical elite student will. Given the disadvantaged student's starting point, he or she is likely to make the most of this opportunity.

Affirmative action in higher education probably begins to affect social mobility even before admissions decisions are made—by cultivating high school students' dreams, aspirations, and academic ambitions. Several studies demonstrate that the elimination of affirmative action in Texas, California, and Washington lowered minority students' propensity to apply to the most selective institutions.[29]

THE CONTROVERSY OVER RACE-BASED AFFIRMATIVE ACTION

All the evidence indicates that race-conscious admissions have been successful at widening the path to social and economic mobility and nurturing leadership for URM, all while enriching the learning environments of elite colleges and universities by increasing diversity. Most people would agree that affirmative action has left its mark on American society. Yet affirmative action has been as controversial as it has been successful. The discontent with race-sensitive admissions in higher education has recently prompted public referenda, statewide bans, and lawsuits against these programs.

Of the many charges that opponents hurl at race-conscious admissions, perhaps the most prevalent is that this practice runs counter to the core American values of individualism and egalitarianism, because the main criterion for eligibility is affiliation with a particular group—in this case, a racial or ethnic group.³⁰ By overlooking individual hardship, they argue, group-based affirmative action benefits the "wrong people." That is, while not all members of minority groups are disadvantaged, all members of these groups, even the most privileged among them, benefit from these policies. Thus, some observers claim, race-conscious admissions policies target the most advantaged of underrepresented minorities and not the truly disadvantaged—a practice referred to as "creaming."³¹ Indeed, the bulk of minority students at elite institutions are relatively affluent.³² Other critics contend that affirmative action sets up minority students for failure because its beneficiaries are ostensibly less prepared to succeed in elite academic settings.³³ Indeed, in the latest legal challenge to affirmative action, the lawsuits filed in 2014 against Harvard University and the University of North Carolina–Chapel Hill, plaintiffs made this argument about the "mismatch effect" of affirmative action.³⁴ The suits were filed by Asian American plaintiffs who had been denied admission.

Just in the past decade, the Supreme Court has heard *four* cases about race-conscious admissions. As mentioned, the first challenge to affirmative action in college admissions to reach the Supreme Court was Regents of the University of California v. Bakke in 1977. Two decades passed before the next cases against affirmative action in college admissions made it to the highest court. In 2003 the Supreme Court ruled on two such cases, in both of which white applicants were rejected from the University of Michigan (UMich): Gratz v. Bollinger (2003, brought by Jennifer Gratz, who applied to UMich's undergraduate program in 1995) and Grutter v. Bollinger (2003, brought by Barbara Grutter, who applied to UMich's law school in 1997). Both decisions relied on the Bakke ruling and were just as divided. In Gratz, the Court determined that UMich's undergraduate affirmative action program was in violation of both the Fourteenth Amendment of the Constitution and Title VI of the Civil Rights Act—and was thus unconstitutional because it used race and ethnicity as a decisive factor in admissions, not as one factor among many in admissions.³⁵

In the Grutter case, on the other hand, in a 5–4 ruling, the Court found that the law school's aim of diversifying its student body was a compelling interest and that its meticulous evaluation of each candidate was narrowly tailored to withstand strict scrutiny, as race was only one out of *many* factors considered in admissions and did not presumptively determine admissions outcomes. In some ways, Grutter, while endorsing and broadening Justice Powell's diversity rationale, also served to narrow the Bakke ruling.[36] Justice Sandra Day O'Connor's opinion required "serious, good faith consideration of workable race-neutral alternatives that will achieve the diversity the university seeks"[37] and also required that race-conscious programs be time-limited and subject to periodic reviews of the need for them.[38] Following Grutter, the state of Michigan banned affirmative action in schools and employment.[39]

The twenty-five-year hiatus in Supreme Court rulings on affirmative action in college admissions—from 1978 to 2003—may give the impression that affirmative action had become more widely accepted over time. However, the intense interest in Grutter, the continuing divisions on the Court, and mounting legislative bans suggest otherwise. Perhaps the most delicate case in recent times has been Fisher v. University of Texas (2013), brought by Abigail Noel Fisher, who was denied admission to the University of Texas–Austin (UT Austin) when she applied as a high school senior in 2008. Fisher, who is white, sued UT Austin for considering race and ethnicity in its admission decisions for a portion of its applicants. The Fisher case is quite distinctive because of its context—an affirmative action plan overlaid on Texas's Top Ten Percent Plan.

To understand Fisher's claim we first need to understand the admission policy at public universities in Texas designed after the 1996 Hopwood ruling, which prohibited the consideration of race in college and university admissions throughout the state.[40] In response to this ruling, Texas adopted a uniform admission policy that grants automatic admission to a fixed percentage of students at the top of the class of each public high school in the state. Under the state's HB 588 law, applicants who graduate in the top grade point average (GPA) decile of their senior high school class are guaranteed admission to the public postsecondary school of their choice anywhere in the state, regardless of their standardized test scores. This plan, known as the Top Ten Percent Plan, was intended to restore racial and ethnic diversity to Texas's public flagships—UT Austin and Texas A&M University (TAMU)—which had declined following the Hopwood ban. The expectation was that the high level of geographic segregation along ethnic lines in Texas—that is, the fact that whites and Hispanics do not reside in the same neighborhoods and do not attend the same high schools—would guarantee that the top students in high schools across the state represented various ethnic groups. Admitting students from this diverse pool would ensure diversity at Texas state universities.

However, despite the diversifying potential of this automatic admissions regime based exclusively on class rank, the policy was unable to fully support the University of Texas's diversity goal of attracting a broadly diverse student body of the highest caliber and in sufficient numbers to create a critical mass within the university and its classrooms. Although levels of racial and ethnic diversity at the state's flagship institutions did increase after the Top Ten Percent Plan was enacted, the University of Texas immediately recognized the educational need to supplement the plan with individual personal assessments to provide meaningful diversity in students' skills, experiences, and aptitudes, which were not captured simply by class rank. These individual assessments—which included race (following the Grutter decision) as one factor among many—were used in admissions for the 20 percent or fewer class seats not automatically populated by the Top Ten Percent Plan but available to all qualified applicants. This consideration of race and ethnicity as one of many factors lay at the heart of Fisher's complaint against the University of Texas.

When Abigail Fisher applied to UT Austin in 2008, she did not qualify under the Top Ten Percent Plan and thus had to compete with many others for the remaining 20 percent of freshman seats. After being denied admission, she sued the university, contending that her academic credentials exceeded those of certain minority students who were admitted that year. UT Austin claimed, in response, that it needed to consider race and ethnicity as one of many academic and non-academic factors in its holistic assessment of individual candidates in order to construct a richly diverse class of talents and perspectives that the simplistic Top Ten Percent Plan and the university's recruitment efforts alone did not achieve. The U.S. Court of Appeals for the Fifth Circuit affirmed the lower court's ruling that the University of Texas's consideration of race as one of many factors in its admissions process (for the 20 percent of seats not filled by the Top Ten Percent Plan) was constitutional. But Fisher appealed the decision, and the case was heard by the Supreme Court.

In Fisher v. University of Texas (2013), the justices reaffirmed that student body diversity is a compelling state interest that can justify the use of race in university admissions. However, in a 7–1 ruling, the Court held that universities can factor in race and ethnicity in admissions only *after* race-neutral solutions have been determined to be unworkable.

At first glance, the Fisher decision doesn't look like a big departure from previous Supreme Court rulings on this issue. In essence, all decisions since Bakke have maintained that the use of race as a factor in admission decisions should be "narrowly tailored" to achieving student body diversity, meaning that the policy must represent the least restrictive way of achieving this interest. Theoretically, a race-neutral policy would be less restrictive than a program that uses racial classifications. According to this logic, if there exists a race-neutral alternative that could achieve diversity, then race-conscious admissions are not necessary and would not pass strict scrutiny. But who is in charge of safeguarding that the search for alternative pathways has been adequately tried, if not exhausted? The answer to this question is shrouded in confusion. For example, in the Grutter case, the majority opinion ruled that the search for an alternative relies on the "good faith" of the institution.

The Fisher ruling imposed an exacting scrutiny of race-conscious measures: for the first time the Supreme Court made it clear that deferring to the good faith of universities was not enough. In the Court's words: "The reviewing court must ultimately be satisfied that no workable race-neutral alternatives would produce the educational benefits of diversity. [If] a nonracial approach . . . could promote the substantial interest about as well and at tolerable administrative expense, then the university may not consider race." Strict scrutiny requires "a careful judicial inquiry into whether a university could achieve sufficient diversity without using racial classifications."[41] In other words, strict scrutiny requires that the university demonstrate, before turning to racial classifications, that available and workable race-neutral alternatives do not suffice. In effect, the Court clamped down on the application of strict scrutiny, tightening the rein on race-conscious admissions policies by insisting that universities demonstrate that they cannot diversify their student bodies without using race and ethnicity as criteria. The Court was not deferring to their say-so. And so the Fifth Circuit scrutinized the University of Texas's plan on remand. In July 2014, in a 2–1 ruling, the Appellate Court again upheld UT Austin's consideration of race in admissions.[42] But neither this saga nor the affirmative action debate is over: after the en banc court in the Fifth Circuit affirmed the three-judge panel decision, the lawyers for Abigail Fisher filed another petition for certiorari in the Supreme Court. In June 2015, the Court announced it will hear the Fisher case for a second time. The case would be heard in the 2015–2016 term.[43]

In sum, the recent Fisher ruling made it clear that the race-conscious admissions policies of elite universities will be subject to strict scrutiny by the courts. As a result, selective schools are likely in the coming years to consider class-based affirmative action.

CONCLUSION

This review of the status of race-based affirmative action in the United States makes it clear that the public controversy surrounding affirmative action policy in higher education, alongside the mounting legal threats to its implementation, has intensified in recent years—despite the finding in a 2014 Pew Research Center survey that 63 percent of respondents thought that "affirmative action programs designed to increase the number of black and minority students on college campuses" were a good thing.[44] Opponents of affirmative action may not represent the majority of the U.S. population, but they are loud and organized, and they have steadily gained support. This wave of dissent runs deeper, however, than the media headlines suggest.

CHAPTER 3

Social, Economic, and Academic Trends and Their Impact on Inequality in Higher Education

> Analysts of inequality occupy something like the position of seismographers. In the explanation of earthquakes . . . the shifting of great tectonic plates beneath the earth's surface causes much of the heaving and cleaving in that surface.[1]
>
> —Charles Tilly

How did we get here? How did we get to the point where states are banning race-conscious admissions policies and the Supreme Court is pushing universities to abandon them? What has fueled the frustration with affirmative action policy in American higher education? In this chapter, I uncover several social, economic, and academic trends that have shaped the lives of all Americans during the past three decades. This changing landscape is intimately linked to the opposition to race-based affirmative action that has erupted over the last two decades, as well as to the shift in public opinion and the Supreme Court's continued unease. Exposing the relevant "tectonic plates," if we are to use Tilly's analogy, will help us situate the surface outcomes, such as policy and laws, in their broader context. This is not a historic exercise, since understanding the roots of the rising discontent with race-conscious admissions will give us insight into the fundamental questions of the current debate on affirmative action: Do we still need affirmative action policy in colleges and universities? Do we need to alter current policy, and if so, what types of policies are likely to draw consensus?

THE SOCIAL AND ECONOMIC CONTEXT

Rising Economic Inequality and Industrial Restructuring

Income inequality is one of the best indicators of changing social and economic realities in the United States over recent decades. Economic inequality in this country started to rise in the mid-1980s and has continued to grow ever since. In their recent and much-acclaimed study, the economists Emmanuel Saez and Thomas Piketty examined U.S. income inequality over the past century. In particular, they looked at the changes in the share of total national income in the hands of the top 10 percent of earners.[2] In 2012, for example, that percentage included all families with an annual income above $114,000. They found that over the last three decades the top earners in the United States have accounted for a larger and larger share of overall income (see figure 3.1). In 1970 the top 10 percent of earners took home about one-third of total national income; by 2007 they accounted for *half* of total income. Not since 1928, when the country was on the brink of the Great Depression, have the top earners controlled such an immense share of economic resources. Even the Great Recession—the severe worldwide recession that erupted in 2008 with the American subprime mortgage crisis—had no calming effect on the steady increase in top-earner income shares and the rising gaps in family income.[3] In fact, just the opposite occurred: in 2012, four years after the start of the Great Recession, the top 10 percent of earners (families with an annual income above $114,000) accounted for *more than half* of the country's total income—the highest share in the last century.

The post–World War II era brought another dramatic change: the industrial restructuring of the economy and the labor market. Manufacturing employment in the United States peaked in the late 1970s, then declined steadily thereafter. In 1973 one out of four nonfarm workers worked in manufacturing. By 2007 this figure had dropped to only one out of ten. As high-paying manufacturing jobs rapidly disappeared, growth in employment in service-producing industries—such as financial services, hospitality, retail, health, human services, information technology, and education—accelerated. Today the service industry in the United States accounts for 68 percent of GDP, and for four out of five jobs.[4]

Together, the rise in economic inequality and the transformation of the

Figure 3.1 Top 10 Percent Income Share in the United States, 1917–2013

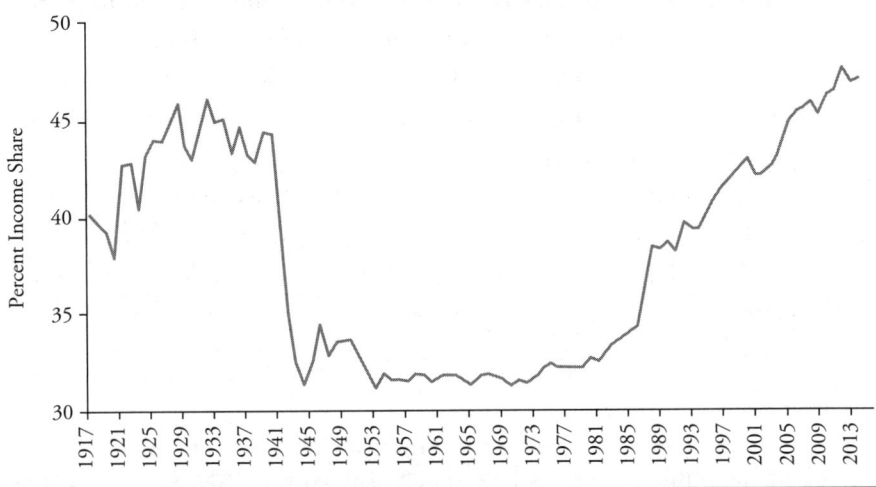

Source: Alvaredo et al.
Notes: Series based on pretax cash market income, including realized capital gains and excluding government transfers. In 2012 the top decile included all families with annual income above $114,000.

economy, especially the disappearance of good jobs in manufacturing, have led to declining social and economic mobility for most Americans. Not only do the affluent and the rest of the nation become more and more economically polarized, but those at the bottom—and even those in the middle—are finding it increasingly difficult to move up the economic ladder. Not surprisingly, Americans consider the gap between rich and poor to be the world's biggest problem, bigger than religious and ethnic hatred, nuclear weapons, pollution and the environment, and AIDS and other diseases.[5]

Declining Social and Economic Mobility

Not since Alexis de Tocqueville's visit to America has the topic of socioeconomic mobility been as popular in public and academic spheres as it is today. However, whereas Tocqueville celebrated the burgeoning country's relative equality of social conditions, which he believed was an essential component of a functioning democracy, today's discussion is about the derailment of the

American Dream. Recent magazine articles and policy briefs convey this state of affairs in their titles: "What Ever Happened to Upward Mobility?", "Harder for Americans to Rise from Lower Rungs," and "Economic Mobility: Is the American Dream Alive and Well?"[6] One article asks, "Does America Promote Mobility as Well as Other Nations?"[7] The answer, sadly, is no. In fact, today the United States has less social and economic mobility between the generations than do other industrialized countries, such as France, Germany, Canada, and the Scandinavian nations.[8] Canada is two and a half times more mobile than the United States, and Denmark is three times more mobile. Only in the United Kingdom, which still has an aristocracy and is infamous for being a very class-conscious society, can mobility chances be found that are similar to the United States. The America where a poor person, if he only worked hard enough, could enjoy endless opportunity is fading from view.

In 2012 the report "Pursuing the American Dream: Economic Mobility Across Generations," published by the Pew Charitable Trusts as part of its Economic Mobility Project, found that although the vast majority of Americans today have higher family incomes than their parents in absolute amounts, their relative standing in the economic hierarchy is not necessarily higher than that of their parents. For example, about 40 percent of Americans born at the bottom of the income and wealth ladders remained there as adults. This "stickiness" was also found at the top of the distribution: only 4 percent of those who started at the bottom as children made it to the top as adults. The prospects for blacks were even worse: not only were black adults more likely than whites to have been raised in families at the bottom of the income and wealth ladders, but they were also more likely to stay there. The numbers are staggering: 65 percent of blacks interviewed in 2009 were raised in families in the bottom income quintile. Half of them had remained in the bottom of the income distribution as adults, while an additional one-quarter had scrambled into the second quintile. Only one in four had made it into the top three quintiles, indicating steeper mobility.[9]

We would like to think that our class system is very different from a traditional caste system, in which one's caste is fixed by birth. Yet these statistics cannot help but make us wonder how big the difference really is between U.S. society and a traditional system, and whether the American Dream of boundless opportunity is just a mirage.

The Rise in the Economic Premium for a College Degree

Most people raised in the bottom income quintile in this country are unable to climb the economic ladder, but those who do somehow beat the odds are likely to have used a college diploma as their escape route from their parents' destiny.[10]

In 2006 two sociologists from Berkeley set out to examine how the United States has changed over the twentieth century in terms of nativity, residence patterns, family, education, work, living standards, religion, and culture. The researchers Claude Fischer and Michael Hout found that over the past one hundred years the differences among Americans have become defined less by race, gender, and place of residence and more by education level.[11] That is, America today is not a more equal nation than it was at the beginning of the twentieth century, but the "axes of difference" have changed. While the overall educational attainment of Americans rose dramatically over the last century, educational attainment also became a key axis of difference among Americans. Their education level—defined by the number of years of schooling and the type of degree attained—now determines their fortune, their marriage partner, their friends, and where and how long they will live. During the first half of the twentieth century the degree most responsible for the difference in life chances was a high school diploma. By the second half of the century it was a college diploma.

As manufacturing jobs began to dwindle in the 1980s, so did the chances of finding economic stability and social mobility without a college degree. As industrial restructuring required that workers upgrade their skills, the economic premium for being highly skilled, and especially for a college degree, rose. The premium continued to rise even as the supply of high-skilled workers greatly expanded, indicating that the demand for these skills was rising even further.[12] Not only have the past few decades been marked by a rise in the economic premium of attending and graduating from college, but college graduates have come to have more job opportunities than nongraduates.[13] In 2010, for example, among full-time, year-round workers age twenty-five and over, median earnings for male high school graduates were about $40,000, while bachelor's degree holders took home $72,000 (see figure 3.2). In other words, a male worker with a college diploma earned about 1.8 times more, on

Figure 3.2 Median Earnings of Full-Time, Year-Round Male Workers Ages Twenty-Five and Older, 1991–2010

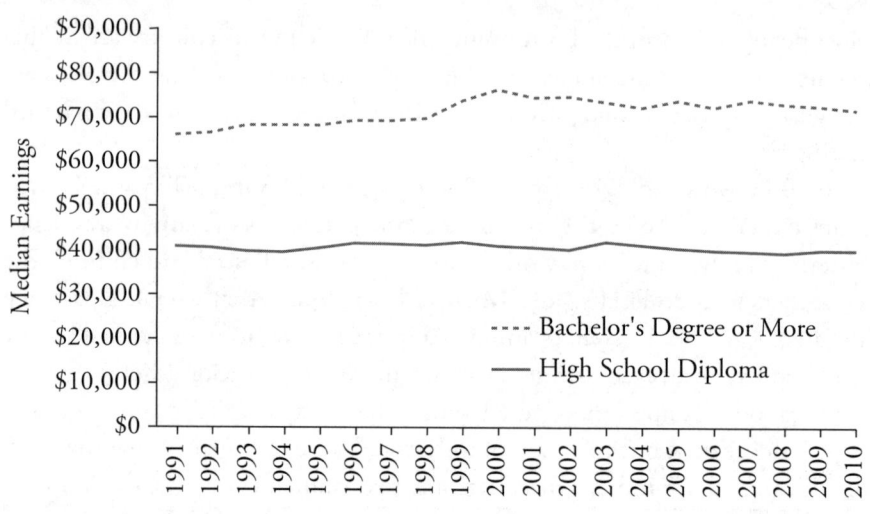

Source: U.S. Census Bureau 1991-2010. The data were compiled using the Recession Trends Dataverse, Version: 22, The Recession Trends initiative, a collaboration between the Russell Sage Foundation and Stanford University's Center on Poverty and Inequality.

average, than a male worker with a high school diploma. Back in the early 1990s, this ratio was around 1.6, indicating that the premium for a college degree has increased over time. Even the recent Great Recession did not erode the college economic premium: the ratio in 2010 was similar to that in the early 2000s.

In sum, after World War II, and especially during the last quarter of the twentieth century, the gap in living standards and lifestyles between those with and without a college degree widened immensely. In this new world, a college degree, once a privilege of the very few, became a must for economic stability and social mobility. A college diploma became the rope for climbing up the economic ladder.

The problem is that, while a college degree is the main engine of mobility today for people from every economic stratum, an individual's chances of entering college and attaining a degree depend quite a bit on the stratum that he or she starts off in. For example, if you were born between 1979 and 1982 to a family in the bottom quartile of the income distribution, your chances of entering college by the age of twenty-five (this cohort entered college around the millennium) were around 30 percent, and your chances of reaching graduation were only 10 percent.[14] But if you were born into the top quartile, your likelihood of entering college was 80 percent, and then you had a better than 50 percent chance of graduating. Socioeconomically disadvantaged high school graduates, even the high academic achievers among them, are much less likely to go to college than their privileged counterparts. The trends discussed in this chapter—rising income inequality, declining mobility, greater competition in college admissions, and escalating tuition costs—have made the transition from high school to college for today's youth even more difficult than it was several decades ago.

Today about 70 percent of high school graduates end up in college, up from 50 percent in 1970. Any college diploma will still secure greater life chances for you, but what seems to matter more today than in previous decades is the *type* of college you attend—that is, its prestige and quality. Indeed, a large body of research finds that economic returns are significantly correlated with college quality among those who attend four-year colleges. Attending a highly selective institution increases your graduation likelihood, occupational status, and future labor market earnings, above and beyond the general college premium.[15] One study, for example, compared the earnings of students from a selective, flagship state university who had just barely made the academic admission cutoff to students who had been just below the cutoff and, denied admission, had gone on to attend a less prestigious university.[16] Upon labor market entry, the former group earned about 20 percent more than the latter. Even scholars who are highly skeptical about the economic advantages of attending elite colleges, such as Stacy Dale from Mathematica Policy Research and Princeton economist Alan Krueger, have conceded that for black, Hispanic, and underprivileged students there are positive returns to attending selective schools.[17]

CHANGES IN THE AMERICAN HIGHER EDUCATION SYSTEM

As a result of all these forces, the demand for a college degree grew dramatically after the 1980s. Significant expansion of the postsecondary education system to accommodate this growth was accompanied by other changes: the stratification between institutions became more important, and the competition to gain admission to prestigious colleges intensified. These changes, in turn, changed how colleges and universities admit students and increased the costs of educating them.

The Expansion of the Higher Education System

The transformation of the labor market and the rise in the economic premium for a college degree set the stage for the academic and financial transformation of the American higher education system. Between 1955 and 2011, the total number of students enrolled in any type of degree-granting institution rose from 2.6 million to 21 million, and the college enrollment rate of high school graduates increased as well. In 1955, 45 percent of high school graduates attended college. By 2011, about 70 percent went to college (see figure 3.3).

The growth in demand for a college education was especially dramatic between 1955 and 1970, a period known as the "Tidal Wave." The number of eighteen- to twenty-four-year-olds in the general population grew by 60 percent, from 15 million to 24 million, reflecting the maturation of the first children of the baby boom and the entry of women, blacks, and certain immigrant groups into the education system.[18] In the fourteen-year period between 1955 and 1969, the absolute number of high school graduates doubled.[19] During that time, applications and enrollment swelled at colleges and universities across the United States.[20]

To accommodate the steep rise in demand for higher education, the postsecondary education system expanded dramatically in the 1960s and 1970s by increasing the capacity of existing institutions and adding new institutions, such as community colleges, regional universities, and additional branches of existing universities. This growth continued in the 1980s, although at a much slower pace, but stalled after the 1990s. Still, between 1955 and 2011 the number of institutions more than doubled, reaching 4,700 by 2011. The expansion of the higher education system was not uniform, however, across all tiers. Let's look at the growth in institutions according to school competitiveness level.

Figure 3.3 Percentage of Recent High School Completers Enrolled in College, 1960–2011

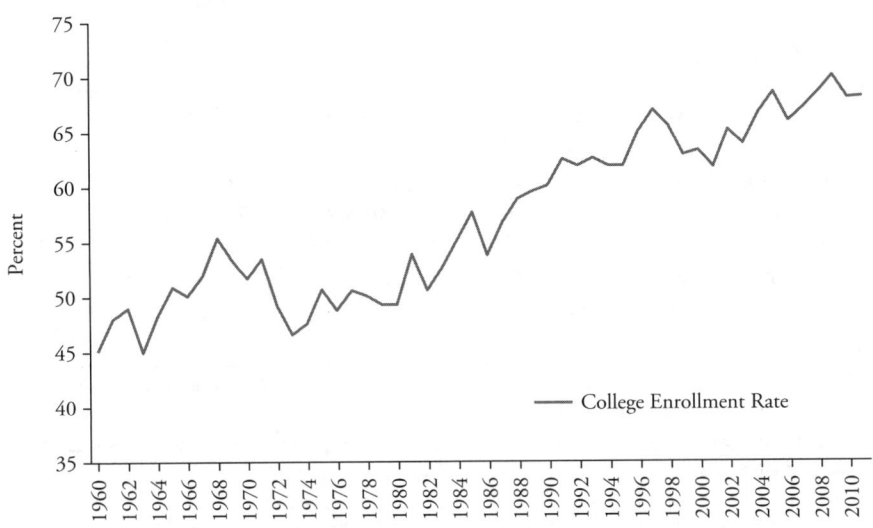

Source: National Center for Education Statistics 1960–2010. The data were compiled using the Recession Trends Dataverse, Version: 22, The Recession Trends initiative, a collaboration between the Russell Sage Foundation and Stanford University's Center on Poverty and Inequality.

The Growth in the Number of Selective Institutions

It is common to classify the competitiveness of four-year colleges and universities using one of the annual ranking reports, such as *Barron's Profiles of American Colleges* or the "Best Colleges" rankings issued by *U.S. News & World Report*. Because the *Barron's* ranking system is popular with researchers and its information can be integrated with data sets from the U.S. Department of Education, it is the ranking system I use for the investigations in this book. *Barron's* gives each college an academic rating (among other ratings) that indicates its competitiveness and selectivity, as determined by the academic profile of the freshman class. The academic rating is based on median SAT or ACT scores, high school class rank, mean high school GPA, and the

Table 3.1 *Barron's* Institutional Classification, by Freshman Characteristics, 1992

Rank	Name	Class Rank	Median SAT	% Applicants Admitted	% Freshmen in 1995–1996
1	Most competitive	Top 10 to 20%	625–800	Less than 33%	4%
2	Highly competitive	20–35%	575–625	33–50%	9%
3	Very competitive	35–50%	525–575	50–66%	22%
4	Competitive	50–65%	450–525	75–85%	41%
5	Less competitive	Top 65%	Less than 450	Top 85%	17%
6	Noncompetitive	Admit all high school graduates		—	7%

Source: National Center for Education Statistics, Beginning Postsecondary Students Longitudinal Study (BPS), 1996–2001; Schmitt 2009, table A-1.
Note: An additional category not included here were specialized programs such as professional schools of art, music, and theater arts.

freshman admission rate. Each school is put in one of six categories: 1 for "most competitive," 2 for "highly competitive," 3 for "very competitive," 4 for "competitive," 5 for "less competitive," and 6 for "noncompetitive."[21] (The classification is presented in table 3.1.) At less competitive schools (category 5), more than half of admits have SAT scores below 1,000. In comparison, the most competitive colleges (category 1) admit fewer than one-third of applicants on average. In 2008 their admits ranked in the top fifth of their high school class, and half had SAT scores above 1300 (or ACT scores above 29). The usual suspects—such as the Ivy League schools Harvard, Princeton, and Yale—are in this group, but so are dozens of other schools, including small private liberal arts colleges and large public state universities.[22]

Between 1972 and 1982, the number of less competitive (category 5) and noncompetitive four-year institutions (category 6) rose, thus increasing the capacity of the postsecondary system (see figure 3.4). However, this growth stalled after 1982, and after 1992 the share of such open-door schools declined dramatically. As for competitive institutions (category 4, not shown in figure 3.4), their number has remained stable at around 650 since the 1970s. For the more competitive schools the story is somewhat different. Since the 1970s, the number of very, highly, and most competitive colleges (categories

Figure 3.4 Postsecondary Institutions Listed in *Barron's Profiles of American Colleges*, by Admissions Competitiveness Categories, 1972–2008

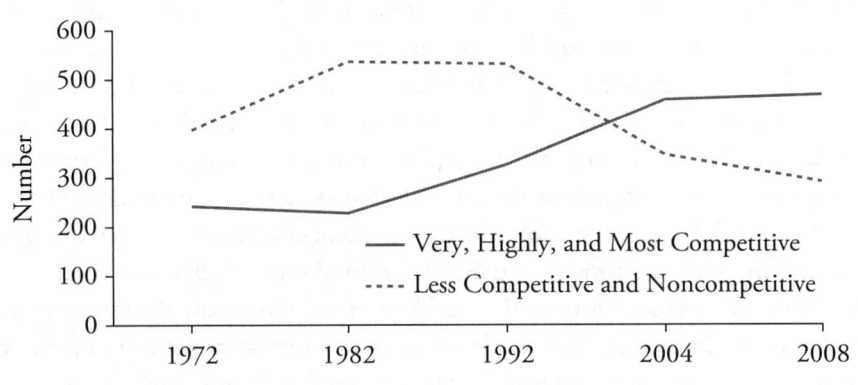

Source: Schmitt 2009, table A-1.

1–3) has ballooned. In 1972 there were 242 schools in the top three tiers. By 2008 that number was 468, with most of the growth occurring between 1982 and 2004. If only a small number of four-year postsecondary schools entered the education system after the mid-1980s, then how did we end up with so many more selective institutions?

Growing Competition in Admissions

After the mid-1980s, the stagnation in the supply of college seats, alongside the ever-increasing rate of college enrollment, created a bottleneck in the college pipeline. The growing demand for a college education, together with the stalled expansion of the postsecondary system, intensified the *competition* for slots in higher education.[23] Selective colleges in particular could not keep up with the heightened demand for seats, which resulted from the growing belief that a degree from an elite college yields higher economic returns than one from a less-selective school. Adding fuel to the fire was the publication in the early 1980s of annual college ranking reports, such as those from *Barron's* and *U.S. News & World Report,* which popularized and reinforced the college hierarchy. These reports, updated yearly, made the public more conscious about institutional stratification and, in turn, intensified the competition for slots at the most selective schools. High school graduates and their parents became very willing to put a great deal of money and effort into the pursuit of what they presumed to be a better college, with the expectation that this investment would pay off later in the labor market.

The process cascaded. The heightened demand struck colleges at the top of the hierarchy first, fueled by the higher economic premium for their degrees. In fact, the number of high school graduates applying to selective institutions has increased every year since the mid-1980s. But because the number of slots at these schools remains relatively fixed, their admission rates have plummeted, and they continue to drop. In 1990 Harvard University received about 12,000 applications for its incoming freshman class. By 2012, about 35,000 were applying. The problem, however, is that school capacity holds steady: 1,610 freshmen attended Harvard in 1990, compared to 1,660 in 2012. The squeeze is clear: the number of applicants rose nearly threefold while the number of seats barely budged. Consequently, the admission rate plunged by more than half, reaching 6 percent in 2012 (see figure 3.5). And Harvard is not alone. Other selective colleges experienced similarly dramatic drops in their acceptance rates. From 1992 to 2012, the undergraduate admission rate at Yale dropped sharply from 23 to 7 percent, and from 42 to 13 percent at the University of Pennsylvania.

But this is not the entire story. Other colleges were also affected. Applicants who knew that their chances of admission to the most competitive colleges were slim expanded their search and applied to institutions down the college hierarchy. When the demand for colleges that were once only moderately selective began to surge, their admissions officers were able to pick from among a surplus of high-quality applicants. As a result, many of these schools became more selective—that is, their selectivity level rose simply because of heightened demand, without corresponding changes in the quality of their faculty, resources, physical infrastructure, or core curricula.

Many institutions that were moderately competitive in the 1970s became more selective in the 1980s and thereafter. The growing competition in higher education was responsible for the increase in the number of colleges categorized as "more selective." However, we must keep in mind that not all institutions were affected in the same way. While some colleges were rejecting a growing number of prospective students and becoming more selective, others

Figure 3.5 Admission Rates at Harvard, Yale, Cornell, and Penn, 1959–2012

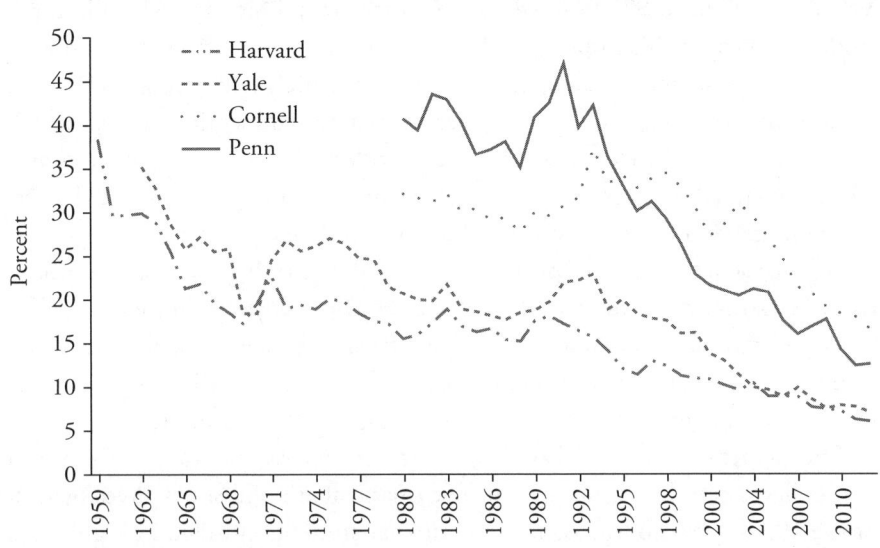

Source: Author's calculations from institutional data.

were struggling to lure applicants. This disparity reflects the growing gaps between four-year colleges in recent decades.

Institutional Stratification

Endowment Beyond variations in admission rates, colleges differ in their academic, social, and financial support of students. Let's begin with institutional wealth, where the disparities are stark. Consider, for example, two institutions that serve about the same number of students: Harvard University (category 1, most competitive), which today admits about 6 percent of applicants, and Washington State University (WSU) (category 4, competitive), the original and largest land-grant university in the state and a public research university that admits more than 80 percent of its applicants. Both schools served about 28,000 undergraduate and graduate students in 2012.

In 2012 Harvard's endowment was more than $30 billion, the largest endowment of any American college or university, while WSU's endowment of about $700 million came in at 100th place.[24] The endowment per student at WSU comes out to $25,000, while at Harvard it is more than $1 million per student.[25] Why is this important? Institutions use income from their endowments to supplement their operating budgets, which rely on and determine tuition and fees. Colleges with generous per-student endowments (which tend to be private universities) can offer a wide variety of academic programs and educational services, while a small endowment implies a restricted operating budget and less to spend on educating students.

Endowment size is an important factor in determining a school's competitiveness rating. According to *U.S. News & World Report*'s influential "Best Colleges" ranking system, an institution's financial resources per student determine 10 percent of its overall score.[26] Thus, schools with large endowments rank higher in this category than schools with smaller ones.

Endowment funds are also critical for another reason: they are the well that colleges can draw from to improve financial aid offers. My investigation of the 1995–1996 college cohort reveals that students enrolled in highly and very competitive schools (categories 2 and 3) received institutional grants that covered about one-third of tuition, compared to only one-quarter of tuition in category 4 and 5 schools. Clearly, institutional funds can mitigate both the financial burden of attending college and the disparities in price tags among schools.[27]

College Climate and Academic Integration   Endowment funds can also have dramatic effects on the college climate. They nurture the learning environment by enabling the college to attract the best faculty, maintain a small student-faculty ratio, and provide extra tutors and computer labs. They enrich the social environment by funding top-notch facilities, such as dining halls, dormitories, and gyms, and supporting student clubs, sports, and cultural activities. Students at better-endowed schools even exhibit greater academic and social integration on campus.

To illustrate, the U.S. Department of Education surveyed students who were freshmen in 1995–1996 about their overall level of academic integration during their first year of college.[28] Not surprisingly, the level of academic integration was directly related to the competitiveness and financial resources of their college: the more competitive and well-endowed the school, the higher the likelihood that a student had participated in a study group and had faculty contact outside of class (that is, had met with an academic advisor or talked with a faculty member about academic matters). For example, at the most competitive institutions almost all students reported some contact with faculty outside of class during their first year of college (95 percent), while one-quarter of students at noncompetitive schools had no such encounter throughout their college years.

The survey also asked students about their level of social integration on campus. The more competitive and well-endowed a school, the larger the share of students who reported involvement in school-related activities—namely, whether and how often they attended school-related fine arts activities; participated in intramural, nonvarsity, varsity, or intercollegiate sports and school clubs; and interacted socially with friends from school. The gap is glaring: at noncompetitive institutions, more than 60 percent of students did not participate in any school club during their first year of college, compared to only 14 percent at the most competitive schools.

Ann Mullen, an associate professor of sociology at the University of Toronto, interviewed students attending Yale University, an elite Ivy League school in Connecticut, and at Southern Connecticut State University (SCSU), a category 4 (competitive) school less than two miles down the road from Yale.[29] In 2012 the endowment funds at SCSU totaled around $14 million, or $1,200 per student. At Yale each student had $1.4 million in endowment funds. (Yale has the second-largest university endowment in the country after Harvard.) Mullen's findings show that the initial differences between the students at each school—Yale students, in general, were more prepared for college than those at SCSU—were compounded by the academic and social environments of their respective schools. For example, the vast majority of students at Yale resided on campus and thus had greater peer interaction and were more likely to develop strong friendships than their counterparts at SCSU, where most students commuted to school. Furthermore, Yale students had more opportunities to get involved in school-related social and organized activities, such as volunteer work, sports, school clubs, and other extracurricular activities. These aspects of college life shape the college experience, influencing both knowledge acquisition and personal growth.

Indeed, several studies confirm that the college experience of students at more competitive and prestigious schools is characterized by a wide spectrum of interactions, both inside and outside the classroom. The supportive academic, social, and financial climate at these schools prevents students from dropping out, even when the adjustment is difficult, and helps them persist until degree attainment. In fact, the graduation rate at elite schools is much higher than at less-selective schools. Half of the students who started college in the fall of 1995 at a category 4 school left the institution without a degree, while only one in ten did not graduate at the most competitive schools. Surely this divide partly reflects the initial gaps in student preparation for the academic rigor and financial burden of college, yet differences in school climate and resources also contribute to diverging graduation rates.

The marked disparities between colleges and universities help explain why so many strive for one of the few slots at elite institutions. In a land where all postsecondary institutions offer a similar college experience, it wouldn't matter where you attend college. The United States today, however, is not such a land. Attending an elite institution not only provides the opportunity for a high-quality education but also carries the promise of social and economic dividends throughout the life course, not to mention status and prestige. Given that selective institutions are the main implementers of affirmative action policy, the rising discontent with this practice since the 1990s is fundamentally a battle over who will get a seat at an elite institution.

ACADEMIC BARRIERS TO HIGHER EDUCATION

The "Shifting Meritocracy"

The growing competition for seats at selective schools has had another important effect: it has entirely reshaped the college admissions process. Today standardized tests are generally perceived as a legitimate mechanism for sorting high school graduates into colleges, but this was not always the case. Standardized tests became widespread as a screening instrument only in recent decades.[30] Before World War II, colleges did not rely heavily on standardized exams, although many institutions did stipulate entrance criteria. Ironically, standardized tests, such as the SAT, were originally designed to allow selective institutions to identify talented students from disadvantaged backgrounds. (In 1934 Harvard's representatives, seeking to screen candidates from the Midwest for a new merit scholarship, chose the SAT over other tests.)[31] In the 1950s, only a few hundred out of about 1,300 four-year postsecondary institutions considered test scores in their admission decisions. Today the majority of four-year schools do.

Standardized test scores started gaining in importance in the 1980s as admissions offices at the most sought-after colleges were bombarded with applications.[32] In an effort to ease the labor-intensive burden of evaluating a growing volume of highly qualified applicants, institutions began to rely on test scores more heavily.[33] Standardized scores were considered an objective and straightforward tool for appraising the college-readiness of students from diverse types of high schools. Meanwhile, other criteria perceived as less easily comparable, such as high school grades, declined in importance. This shift in how applicants are sorted and selected was a direct consequence of growing competition. In a paper published in the *American Sociological Review* in 2007, Marta Tienda and I refer to this transformation—that is, the increased reliance on test scores as a main screening tool in college admissions—as the "shifting meritocracy."[34]

Adaptation and the Widening Gaps in Academic Preparation

This rising emphasis on test scores in admissions triggered a reaction in prospective applicants. In a study published in the *American Sociological Review* in 2009, I exposed this response—what I called an "adaptation" process—and examined its consequences for equality of educational opportunity.[35] I focused on the crucial decade that began in the 1980s, when selective institutions started to put greater emphasis on test scores in their admissions decisions. Using two nationally representative samples of high school students —one of the cohort that graduated from high school in 1982, and the other drawn from 1992 graduates—I ranked all high school graduates, based on their test scores, on a scale ranging from 1 to 100. In each cohort, the top 1 percent of students (those with the highest test scores) were ranked at 100, while those in the bottom 1 percent were assigned the value of 1. I placed all the 1982 high school graduates into this percentile distribution and then examined what happened to the distribution a decade later. Of all the high school graduates, I tracked two groups in particular: those from low-socioeconomic-status (SES) families, and those with high-SES backgrounds. (SES was based on family income and parental education level.) I found that in 1982, before the competition for college slots intensified, high-SES seniors ranked, on average, at the sixty-fifth percentile on the test scores distribution (65 percent of their high school graduate cohort had lower test scores than the high-SES group). By 1992 this group had raised its relative standing to the seventieth percentile. They managed, within a period of ten years, to climb the test score ladder dramatically—by five percentile points!

Because this ranking system is relative, this considerable climb implies that not all high school graduates were able to follow suit. Those from the lower socioeconomic strata failed to keep up with their privileged counterparts in the test score race. In 1982, before the competition for slots intensified, low-SES seniors ranked, on average, in the thirty-eighth percentile in the test score distribution. This ranking is not surprising given that academic achievement tends to correlate with socioeconomic status. By 1992, however, their rank had plunged to the thirty-second percentile. Consequently, in 1992 the gap in test scores between rich and poor high school graduates was substantially wider than in 1982. Affluent students, as a group, were able to improve their position in the race to competitive colleges. As the college squeeze intensified from the 1980s onward, so did the class-based polarization in test scores.

How is it possible that affluent students, as a group, were able to improve their test scores relative to other test-takers? It appears that parents of middle and high financial means understood the college landscape and the competitive admissions process and became acutely aware of the rising importance of test scores in college admissions. They invested resources to promote their children's college options and targeted selective institutions. Indeed, the perception that high standardized test scores are the ticket to elite colleges prompted the vigorous use of expensive test preparation tools, including private courses, tutors, and books, and spawned a multibillion-dollar test preparation industry.[36] Put simply, high school graduates from middle- and upper-middle-class families adapted to the greater emphasis on test scores by *raising their test scores*.

The dramatic shifts in higher education over the past several decades, including the greater emphasis on test scores and the widening class-based polarization in test scores, led to growing class inequality in higher education. Privileged high school seniors benefited from these changes and climbed up the college ladder. Those at the bottom, however, saw their access to selective colleges diminish.

ECONOMIC BARRIERS TO HIGHER EDUCATION

During these years, another trend in higher education emerged in parallel with the greater emphasis on test scores, compounding the problem of inequality and further restricting poorer students' access to selective institutions: the rising costs of a college education and the shift of financial aid from a grant-based system to a loan-based one.

The Rising Cost of a College Education and the Decline in the Share of Financial Aid

After tuition at four-year colleges and universities stagnated during the 1970s, it began to soar in the mid-1980s (see figure 3.6). Colleges and universities invested more resources in their facilities, faculty, and services in order to ensure they could offer the kind of quality education that attracted applicants. In 1982 average tuition was about $7,500 at public four-year institutions and $17,000 at private ones. Between 1982 and 2012, average annual tuition rose by approximately 240 percent (in 2012 dollars), reaching $18,000 and $40,000 at public and private colleges, respectively. At Yale the 2012 undergraduate tuition was near $55,000 per year. With economic inequality continuing to rise, only the wealthy few can afford the growing price tag of an elite education in the United States, while more and more applicants need financial aid to finance an education at their dream school.

At the richest schools, most students with financial needs are awarded generous need-based grants. Half of Yale undergraduates, for example, receive scholarships and grants from internal sources—that is, endowment funds. Yet very few institutions in the United States have large enough endowment funds to be *completely* need-blind in admissions and to entirely cover their students' financial needs.

The problem is that while the total value of the financial aid distributed has increased, it has not kept pace with the sharp rise in tuition. As a result, the share of college expenses that families are expected to contribute has increased significantly, especially for students in the lower half of the income distribution. Grant aid in particular has failed to increase rapidly enough to fill the growing gap between the costs of attending college and the ability of

Figure 3.6 Average Tuition and Fees and Room and Board Charges in 2012 Dollars, 1972–2012, Selected Years

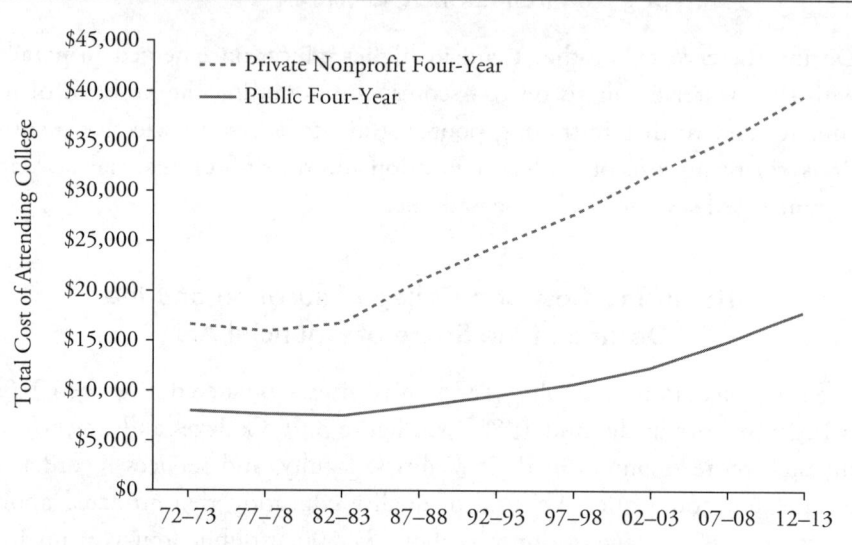

Source: College Board (2012a), table 2A.

students and families to pay those costs.[37] For example, the Pell Grant is the largest federal form of grant assistance to postsecondary students that is means-based. Yet from 1987–1988 to 2013–2014, the proportion of average expenses at a public college that the maximum Pell Grant could cover declined by 19 percentage points, from 50 to 31 percent.[38] Consequently, the ability of poor and middle-American families to pay for a college education stalled. What is more, as tuition levels spiked, state governments responded to political pressure from the affluent and middle classes by shifting funds away from need-based financial aid to merit-based assistance.[39] At the state level, aid is increasingly merit-based rather than need-based. Specifically, the proportion of state grants based on financial need declined from 91 percent in 1981–1982 to 74 percent in 2011–2012.[40]

Shifting Financial Aid from a Grant-Based to a Loan-Based System

In 1992 the average undergraduate student financed 65 percent of his or her college education using grant-based funds, while the rest was covered by loans and other means. By 2007 grant-based assistance had plummeted to 45 percent (although it had rebounded to 52 percent by 2012).[41] In essence, federal financial aid has shifted from a grant-based system to a loan-based one. Today only half the funds that students need to finance college are covered by money with no strings attached, while two decades ago two-thirds of college costs were covered by grants. About 60 percent of (nontransfer) bachelor's students in public and private nonprofit institutions who earned their degrees in 2011–2012 graduated with debt, borrowing an average of $26,500 each.

Any attempt to raise the share of college-educated individuals in the United States must begin with the population whose bachelor's degree attainment rates are especially low: high school graduates from the bottom half of the income distribution. Increasing their grant allocations can boost the share of college graduates among them and narrow the gap between them and their more affluent classmates. Hence, a more appropriate distribution of aid funds would be likely to facilitate the production of human capital among low-income students, widen the path of socioeconomic mobility, increase the share of bachelor's degree holders in the United States, and curb the reproduction of economic inequality.[42]

Recent trends in financial aid policy, however, have led to the opposite outcome. These trends include the shift from grant aid to loans, the shift from need-based aid to merit-based aid, and the inability of increases in financial aid to keep up with tuition hikes. Compared with high schoolers in the 1970s, today's poor high school graduates face a higher financial barrier to college access, and the help that they do receive comes mostly in the form of debt.

Given all of these towering economic and academic barriers, socioeconomically disadvantaged students have been falling behind in the race for seats at the best colleges in the country for several decades. It is not so surprising, then, that their chances for socioeconomic mobility have become so low.

THE STRUGGLE FOR A SLOT AT AN ELITE COLLEGE AND THE DISCONTENT WITH RACE-CONSCIOUS ADMISSIONS POLICIES

America has changed a lot since the 1970s. For a high school graduate back then, a college diploma was not necessary for climbing the economic and social ladder. Today high school graduates who aspire to economic well-being and social mobility have little choice: college is the gateway. Attending college has come to be perceived as the most important transition in the life course of youth from the middle and upper classes. If you graduated from high school in 1970, only half of your classmates went to college. Today almost three-quarters of high school graduates are college-bound.

Not only is a college degree a key asset in our era, but getting into college is a completely different game compared to three decades ago. The economic and academic changes in the postsecondary system have made access to selective and expensive institutions more difficult for minority and underprivileged high school graduates. The rising competition and growing emphasis on test scores benefit high school graduates from the top socioeconomic echelons because academic achievement and preparation are highly correlated with both race-ethnicity and socioeconomic status.[43] Rising college tuition and the decline in grant aid limit the college choices of poor and middle-class high school graduates, excluding them from the most expensive schools and thus widening the divide between them and their affluent peers.

It is no wonder, then, that applicants from socioeconomically underprivileged backgrounds are falling behind in the competition for slots at elite schools. They are no match for their well-off counterparts, who have ample resources at their disposal, such as better information about the college admissions process, better high schools and teachers, private tutors, college-educated parents, and money. Claire Vaye Watkins, an assistant professor of English at Bucknell, describes the difficulty of being the first in her family to go to college:

> Most parents, like mine, who had never gone to college, were either intimidated or oblivious (and sometimes outright hostile) to the intricacies of college admissions and financial aid. I had no idea what I was doing when I applied. Once, I'd heard a volleyball coach mention paying off her student loans, and this led me to assume that college was like a restaurant — you paid when you were done. When I realized I needed my mom's and my stepfather's income information and tax documents, they refused to give them to me. They were, I think, ashamed. Eventually, I just stole the documents and forged their signatures.[44]

Given the erosion of equality of educational opportunity in recent decades, few would question the need for some type of affirmative action policy at selective colleges. But as socioeconomic status becomes a more pivotal contour of inequality in the United States, many are asking whether affirmative action today should be based on race or on other aspects of disadvantage.

Thus, here in the widening class divide in higher education lies a clue as to why race-based affirmative action has been so controversial. There are other reasons, to be sure—and racism is surely still one of them—but the *rising* discontent with this practice is fueled by the fierce battle over the distribution of an increasingly scarce and ever more coveted resource: a seat at an elite college.

CHAPTER 4

Broad Diversity at Elite Colleges

Americans, more and more, are defined by class. For high school students today, the education and income levels of their parents will largely determine whether they will get a bachelor's degree and at what type of college, as well as their future position in the social hierarchy. During the same period that inequality in America began to climb, the notion that diversity is desirable and beneficial became deeply rooted in the national ethos, particularly within public and educational institutions. The belief is that a diverse society, by representing a wide array of viewpoints and perspectives, facilitates a fertile exchange of ideas. Campus diversity creates more opportunities for interaction with students from different backgrounds and thus increases students' tolerance for a wide range of viewpoints, enhances their cognitive and identity development, and prepares them for better citizenship and leadership in an increasingly diverse democratic society.[1] Educators, policymakers, and university leaders began to insist that having students with diverse backgrounds and viewpoints study together in a classroom would enhance the educational process, and the evidence confirmed this claim.[2] The nation's most selective colleges and universities—historically the most homogenous of the lot and the hardest to diversify—became committed to considering race in admissions since the 1960s. Their objective was to create student bodies that were more racially and ethnically diverse by including more underrepresented minority (URM) populations—namely, black and Hispanic students. Their efforts were not in vain: the share of minority students at "very," "highly," and "most competitive" institutions (*Barron's* categories 1 through 3) rose from 7 to 13 percent between 1972 and 2004.

The edge that affirmative action bestows lowered the academic barriers for URM compared to other applicants, making their admission to selective schools easier. As mentioned, the test score gap between blacks and whites admitted to elite institutions is in the ballpark of 170 to 200 points.[3] Thus, the structure of postsecondary opportunity at selective colleges varies by race, in that the affirmative action regime has, for black students, softened the blow of ever-increasing academic requirements. What is more, race-based affirmative action has also shielded black and Hispanic applicants from the full impact of rising college tuition and shrinking grant aid.[4] The more selective the school the greater its need for demographic diversity, and the greater its financial ability to provide an attractive aid offering in order to promote that diversity.

The diversity rationale is the only justification for the practice of race-conscious affirmative action in American higher education that has withstood Supreme Court scrutiny over time. Justice Powell first invoked this rationale in Regents of the University of California v. Bakke (1978), which is hailed as the landmark ruling in support of race-conscious admissions policies. All subsequent Supreme Court decisions on this issue—notably, Grutter v. Bollinger (2003), Gratz v. Bollinger (2003), and Fisher v. University of Texas (2013)—have reinforced the idea that diversity in colleges and universities is a compelling government interest.

What is often overlooked, however, is that in upholding the value of diversity in higher education, the Supreme Court has always been careful to endorse what I refer to here as "broad diversity"—that is, a diversity that includes many factors, not just race and ethnicity. Supreme Court Justice Powell, the architect of the diversity rationale, defined "diversity" in the Bakke ruling as follows:

> The diversity that furthers a compelling state interest encompasses a far broader array of qualifications and characteristics, of which *racial or ethnic origin is but a single, though important, element* . . . *ethnic diversity, however, is only one element* in a range of factors a university properly may consider in attaining the goal of a heterogeneous student body [emphasis added].[5]

Likewise, more than two decades later, Justice Anthony Kennedy wrote the following in his Grutter (2003) dissent:

> There is no constitutional objection to the goal of considering race as one modest factor among many others to achieve diversity, but an educational institution must ensure . . . that race does not become a predominant factor in the admissions decisionmaking.[6]

In interpreting the Grutter ruling, the Office for Civil Rights (OCR) in the U.S. Department of Education echoed this stand in its letter to postsecondary institutions in 2008, guiding them about the use of race in admissions: "The diversity sought by the postsecondary institution must be broader than mere racial diversity."[7]

If *broad* diversity is the kind of diversity that the Supreme Court has upheld since Bakke as an essential element in higher education and as the main justification for race-conscious admissions, then it is fair to ask: just how broad *is* diversity at elite colleges? If we are to truly embrace the Supreme Court's notion of broad diversity, then we must ask questions about other aspects of diversity as well, especially socioeconomic diversity. At a time when both income inequality and the class divide in higher education continue to widen in the United States, elite colleges, many contend, have not broadened their concept of diversity—and, accordingly, their admission practices—beyond demographic diversity. In this chapter, I examine the veracity of this claim and its implications for public sentiment about, and the future of, affirmative action policy.

SOCIOECONOMIC DIVERSITY AT ELITE COLLEGES

A 2011 article in *Time* magazine notes: "We can no longer blame the individual. We have to acknowledge that climbing the ladder often means getting some support and a boost."[8] This is exactly the role of affirmative action policy: it can intervene on behalf of disenfranchised groups and provide such a boost. The argument, however, that many advocates of affirmative action reform make is that today, given growing class inequality and its consequences, this statement rings most true for underprivileged youth. Are underprivileged kids free to "compete with all the others" for the precious slots at elite institutions? Do they have equal opportunity "to walk through those gates"?[9] The disadvantages of poor children are embedded in their homes and schools. Over the years, the effects of deficient academic preparation, inadequate support, and scarce resources accumulate, generating an achievement gap between rich and poor high school students.

During the same period that the share of URM at very, highly, and most competitive institutions almost doubled (1972 to 2004), the share of students from the bottom socioeconomic quartile decreased from 9 to 7 percent (see figure 4.1). By 2004 more than 70 percent of students at the most competitive four-year colleges in America hailed from families in the top quartile of the socioeconomic distribution, while students from the bottom quartile occupied fewer than 6 percent of seats (see figure 4.2). For youth from the bottom quartile, the most popular college destinations were noncompetitive schools, which lie at the bottom of *Barron's* classification system (category 6). This is also the case for high school graduates from the lower-middle quartile. And so, while the student bodies of elite institutions have become more ethno-racially diverse over time—largely owing to race-conscious admissions—they remain bastions of socioeconomic privilege. In fact, the representation of underprivileged youth at selective colleges has declined steadily since the 1970s.

However, most presidents of leading colleges and universities will insist, if asked, that their admission processes account for applicants' socioeconomic disadvantages, as William Bowen, Martin Kurzweil, and Eugene Tobin point out in their book *Equity and Excellence in American Higher Education*. They quote from a brief that several elite universities submitted to the Supreme Court in conjunction with the two cases brought against the University of Michigan in 2003, Gratz v. Bollinger and Grutter v. Bollinger:

> Admissions officials give special attention to, among others, applicants from economically and/or culturally disadvantaged backgrounds, those with unusual athletic ability, those with special artistic talents, those who would be the first in their families to attend any college, those whose parents are alumni or alumnae, and those who have overcome various identifiable hardships.[10]

How do admission officers select students for an incoming class? In general, there are two types of admission practices, and the choice between them

Figure 4.1 The Socioeconomic Status of Students Attending "Very Competitive," "Highly Competitive," and "Most Competitive" Four-Year Institutions, 1972–2004

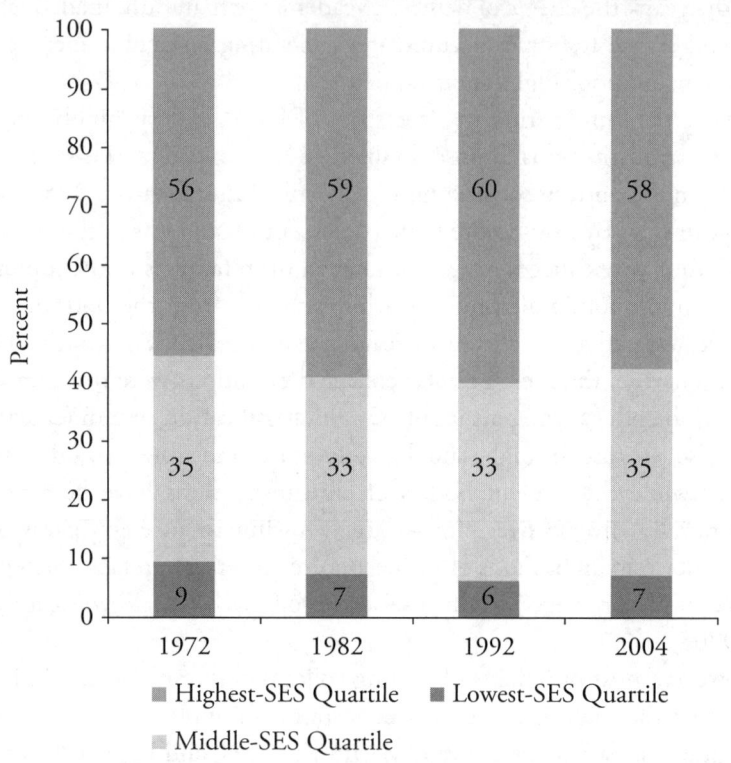

Source: Author's calculations using National Center for Education Statistics data sets: NLS:72, HS&B, NELS:88, and ELS:04.
Note: The data are for high school graduates from four cohorts (1972, 1982, 1992, and 2004). The estimates are weighted. "Very competitive," "highly competitive," and "most competitive" are the top three categories in *Barron's* classification scheme.

is usually dictated by application volume. Admissions at private colleges is generally a "holistic" process, while at public colleges it tends to be formulaic.[11] That is, because public colleges usually have small admission staffs relative to their large applicant pools, they tend to rely on objective formulas that draw heavily on high school grades and test scores. Applicants are ranked by

Figure 4.2 Students Attending "Most Competitive" and "Noncompetitive" Four-Year Institutions, by Socioeconomic Status, 2004

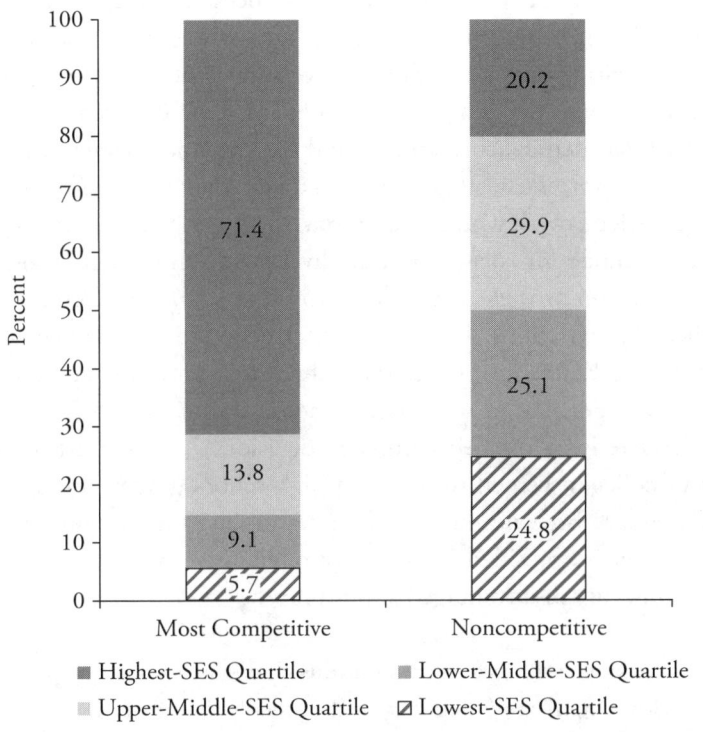

Source: National Center for Education Statistics, Education Longitudinal Study of 2004 (ELS:04).
Note: The data are for high school graduates from the 2004 cohort. The estimates are weighted.

academic achievement, and those with the highest achievement are selected. Private colleges, however, generally conduct a comprehensive full-file review, which also considers factors such as essays, writing samples, interviews, counselor and teacher recommendations, work experience, extracurricular activities, and information about obstacles in an applicant's life, if relevant. In the complex process of picking and choosing potential incoming students, these admission officers are "admitting the candidate who seems to offer something special by way of drive and determination, the individual with a set of skills that matches well the academic requirements of the institution, someone who will bring another dimension of diversity to the student body, or a candidate who helps the institution fulfill a particular aspect of its mission."[12] Schools that employ this nonmechanical admission process can assign value to a wide array of applicant characteristics, such as race-ethnicity and socioeconomic status, thus legitimizing their admission of some students with lower grades and test scores than the general threshold. This type of extensive, subjective evaluation of academic achievements and background characteristics is considered crucial for assembling a student body that is *broadly* diverse—the kind that Justice Powell would champion.

But the data about socioeconomic diversity at elite schools suggest that holistic admission processes have failed to increase the representation of underprivileged populations. Thomas Kane, an economist at the Harvard Graduate School of Education, notes that "there is little evidence that selective colleges used information on parental income, parental education, or high school characteristics in their admission decision. . . . The most selective 20 percent of colleges seemed to focus on high school grades, test scores, race, and little else."[13] Bowen and his colleagues discuss the misconception, held even by university presidents, that a comprehensive review process benefits socioeconomically disadvantaged applicants:

> What is striking is the juxtaposition of this clear statement of intent with the equally clear empirical finding that, at the schools in our study, there is absolutely no admissions advantage associated with coming from a poor family and only a very small advantage (about 4 percentile points) associated with being a first-generation college-goer; at least that was the case for the '95 entering cohort. We do not believe that this disjunction is due to any desire to be disingenuous or to "gild the lily." Rather, we believe it is due to a combination of a lack of data at the institutional level on the background characteristics of all applicants (data that are hard to assemble), financial aid constraints, a commitment to being need-blind (and therefore purposefully ignoring SES), and the lack of vocal champions for students from low-income families when tough choices are being made among a large group of very well-qualified candidates.[14]

Perhaps the best example of the failure of comprehensive review admissions to boost socioeconomic diversity is found in the University of California (UC) system. In 2002 six UC campuses began to implement a comprehensive review process in their fall admission cycle. The admissions evaluators were supposed to evaluate whether an applicant had faced hardships or unusual circumstances, and how he or she had responded to them. Other factors considered were linguistic background, parents' education, and other indicators of support available in the home. UCLA describes the process on its website: "All achievements, both academic and non-academic, are considered in the context of the opportunities an applicant has had, and the reader's assessment is based on how fully the applicant has taken advantage of those opportunities."[15]

If comprehensive review processes give an edge to applicants with socioeconomic hardships, then we would expect to see an increase in the share of poor students after an institution implements such a policy. Was there any growth in the share of poor students in UC schools after comprehensive review admissions were introduced in 2002? I decided to examine this question by tracking undergraduate students at UCLA and UC Berkeley (the two flagship institutions of the UC system) who received need-based aid from the government between 1998 and 2007 as an indicator of the share of low-income students (see figure 4.3). The trend over time reveals a flat line—that is, the comprehensive review process did not increase the share of low-income students at all. Although the share of students receiving federal grants did rise in 2008, this increase reflected a change in federal financial aid policy, which increased the number and size of aid awards.[16] Two other reports confirm this finding, one by the UC Berkeley sociologist Michael Hout and the other by the UCLA sociologist Robert Mare. Both researchers conclude that parents' education and income levels have had no effect on the admission chances of applicants at their respective universities.[17] Thus, the belief that comprehensive review processes at elite schools benefit underprivileged populations appears to be misguided.

In recent years some colleges have attempted to combat declining socioeconomic diversity by expanding need-based aid to poorer students in the face of rising tuition. For example, in the mid-2000s several elite schools announced changes in their financial aid policy to reduce the costs of attendance for low- and middle-income students. Harvard University describes its financial aid policy in its admission brochure:

> This is simple: anyone can afford Harvard. We have a long tradition of removing economic barriers for students who want to attend Harvard. Announced in

Figure 4.3 Receipt of Federal Grants by Full-Time, First-Time-Degree-Seeking Undergraduate Students, 1998–2010

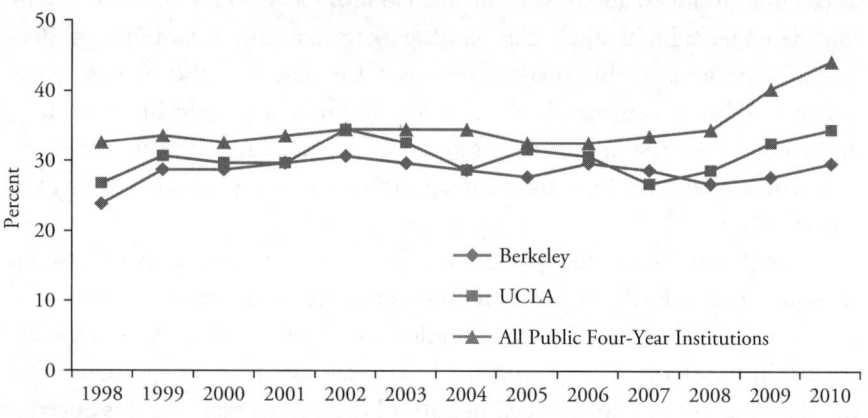

Source: National Center for Education Statistics, Integrated Postsecondary Education Data System (IPEDS).

Note: Federal grants (grants and educational assistance funds) include grants provided by federal agencies such as the U.S. Department of Education, including Title IV Pell Grants and Supplemental Educational Opportunity Grants (SEOGs); need-based and merit-based educational assistance funds and training vouchers provided by other federal agencies; and federally sponsored educational benefits programs in the Veterans Administration, U.S. Department of Labor, and other federal agencies.

2004, The Harvard Financial Aid Initiative (HFAI) is a continuation of this tradition and greatly expands financial aid to families who earn less than $80,000. And, if your family earns less than $65,000 per year, your parents pay nothing for you to attend Harvard. It is simply our effort to make sure you and your family know you can afford to attend Harvard.[18]

Given this shift in policy, why has the impact on the representation of low-income students been so marginal? The problem is that while these efforts are timely and commendable, this type of financial aid does not deal with the main barrier to admission: academic qualifications. The main academic barriers to entry—test score and grade requirements—have risen drastically in recent decades, but the admission offices of elite schools have done little to level the playing field for underprivileged applicants, giving no special consideration to their disadvantaged position. Financial aid only eases economic constraints *subsequent* to the admission decision—that is, it helps only applicants who have already gained admission, as opposed to giving poorer applicants an edge in admission. The high cost of getting an elite education is an important barrier for *enrollment,* and so it is encouraging that poor students admitted to Harvard can get an education there for free, but the problem is that there are very few high school graduates from poor families who have the perfect academic achievements and the wide-ranging experiences needed to be admitted to Harvard and other elite schools. Without an edge in *admissions,* they cannot exploit the free ride at these institutions. Consequently, students from poor families have fallen behind and the level of socioeconomic diversity at selective colleges in the country has declined. Elite institutions, despite their good intentions, have not opened their doors to students from all walks of life.

Thus, the rising academic and financial barriers to selective colleges have not affected all aspiring college students equally. For URM applicants, affirmative action policy in U.S. higher education has mitigated the effects of the growing exclusionary and homogenizing forces shaping entry to elite colleges; by so doing, it has expanded their chances for educational and socioeconomic mobility. This, in a nutshell, is the great triumph of race-based affirmative action. At the same time, poor white and Asian high school students were hit harder by these trends than were poor blacks and Hispanics. That is, race-based affirmative action slightly shielded URM from the consequences of the increasingly fierce competition in admissions, while poor applicants were not protected. Embedded in the very success of race-conscious admissions policies is the seed of discontent: in the absence of similar shields for the economically underprivileged, many Americans have fallen behind, including a large chunk of the middle class, especially those in the bottom echelons.

And so, while the legal ground for affirmative action in higher education promoted the need for broad diversity beginning in 1978, there has been no parallel shift in admissions practices, which have continued to focus on racial and ethnic diversity. Similarly, the public discourse and academic research on diversity in U.S. higher education in recent decades has focused almost solely on racial and ethnic diversity. Even when the term "broad diversity" is invoked, it is often as a synonym for racial and ethnic diversity.

Are colleges to blame for clinging to such a narrow definition of diversity? Yes, but they are not the only ones at fault. Despite the Supreme Court's mandate to focus on *broad* diversity, the Court has never been specific about how to achieve broad diversity—that is, what to do to ensure that different skills, talents, backgrounds, and opinions are represented in a student body. Even Justice Powell, who first outlined the diversity rationale in Bakke (1978), and Justice O'Connor, who stressed the importance of broad diversity in her Grutter (2003) decision, left the details vague. It is arguably inappropriate for the Court to come up with an admission formula—particularly given its deference to academic freedom. Yet the problem is that the narrow perspective on diversity adopted by elite colleges and universities does not match the broad approach endorsed by the Supreme Court.

But the greater consequence may be that the narrow focus on race-ethnicity is detached from the increasing class stratification in the United States and the eroding life chances of youth from the lower socioeconomic rungs. In hindsight, this narrow perspective may turn out to be a historic mistake—one that undermines the future of race-conscious admissions in higher education. That is, the frustration nurtured in some segments of the public by the neglect of socioeconomic circumstances may lead to a complete prohibition of race and ethnicity as factors in college admissions. Perhaps a clearer message from the Supreme Court could have been a wake-up call for selective colleges about the need to incorporate other aspects of diversity into their admissions formulas.

LINKING AFFIRMATIVE ACTION TO BROAD DIVERSITY

The consensus that diversity on campus is a good thing continues to hold, and affirmative action has been successful at boosting the representation of blacks and Hispanics at the top colleges in the nation. But these schools have been slow to respond to one of the greatest shifts in American society in recent decades: class inequality. Despite these trends, most colleges have not widened their view of diversity and continue to target race and ethnicity. The growing competition over seats at elite colleges has made many resentful of current policy, which has neglected to give a boost to other disenfranchised applicants in dire need of opportunities for social and economic mobility—namely, the underprivileged.

Affirmative action policy does have the potential to address multifaceted manifestations of inequality. In the United States, the search is on for race-neutral tools that can generate broad diversity and promote mobility and equality of educational opportunity for all segments of the population. To move forward with an analysis of current race-conscious admissions and their potential alternatives, we must expand and clarify the discussion of broad diversity. Specifically, there are three key aspects of the broad diversity issue that deserve further attention and will be explored in this book:

1. *What kind of diversity do we want in higher education?* With race-based affirmative action programs in higher education possibly heading for reform, we may be at a historical crossroads. If the goal of diversity is important to us as a society, then we need to devise admissions policies that are effective at generating it. But first we need clarity about the types of diversity we want at elite colleges. By illustrating different scenarios for student body diversity, this book will facilitate the deliberation process.

2. *Why is the Supreme Court vague about "broad diversity," and why have colleges snubbed the Court's arguments for breadth rather than narrowness in applying this concept?* The entire discourse about diversity in higher education is ambiguous with respect to "broad diversity": on the one hand, the objective of broad diversity is championed by everyone, while on the other hand, nobody dares make it more concrete. We need to understand why the Supreme Court has remained so elusive, despite having plenty of opportunities over the past three decades to clarify how to achieve broad diversity. Understanding why it is so difficult to provide a clear definition of broad diversity, as well as why selective institutions continue to adhere to a narrow view of it, is critical to an informed debate about the future of affirmative action. The empirical evidence presented in this book will provide insight into this deliberate act of obscurity.

3. *Can a different design of affirmative action policy achieve broad diversity at selective colleges?* The current controversy about affirmative action and the Supreme Court's legal responses to it are forcing colleges and universities to think more broadly about diversity and pushing them to do so with race-neutral tools. The obvious alternative to affirmative

action policies based on race are those based on class—that is, policies that give an edge in college admissions to the socioeconomically disadvantaged. The problem, however, is that we know very little about what class-based affirmative action in the United States might look like because it has never been implemented on a large scale. We also know almost nothing about the potential of class-based affirmative action to promote mobility for disadvantaged populations and diversity at selective colleges, relative to race-based policy. What we need—and are lacking—is a broad-spectrum evaluation of how various types of class-based affirmative action would measure up against race-based policies in two crucial respects: (1) the feasibility of implementation, and (2) the consequences for student body diversity, social and economic mobility, and the academic selectivity of selective schools. The goal of this investigation is to provide one such comprehensive evaluation. The first step in this journey is to obtain a more coherent understanding of class-based affirmative action as a conceptual and practical framework.

PART III

Class-Based Affirmative Action

CHAPTER 5

What Is Class-Based Affirmative Action?

In the United States, the term "affirmative action" has become synonymous with race-conscious admissions policies. In fact, this model of affirmative action, based on an ascribed trait, is the most common type of affirmative action policy found around the world. Today, however, owing to the controversy surrounding these policies and to recent Supreme Court rulings, affirmative action policy in U.S. higher education may be embarking on a new path. In Fisher v. University of Texas (2013), the Supreme Court affirmed the importance of diversity on college campuses but instructed universities to generate diversity using race-neutral solutions, allowing for the consideration of race and ethnicity in the admissions process *only after* race-neutral measures have been thoroughly exhausted. In light of the strict scrutiny that the Court has imposed on them—universities must present evidence of having explored race-neutral alternatives—the most selective colleges and universities in the nation will have to explore new means of generating campus diversity in the coming years.

The most likely alternatives to race-conscious admissions will be those based on class—that is, policies that give an edge in college admissions to the socioeconomically disadvantaged. The problem, however, is that the implications of replacing race with class in affirmative action are shrouded in ambiguity and misconceptions because, with the exception of sporadic experiments, class-based affirmative action has never been implemented in the United States. If Americans are serious about moving from race to class in affirmative action, then a comprehensive understanding of the available options and their implications is necessary. In this chapter, I shed light on what class-based affirmative action is and what it is not, and I methodically consider the various forms it can take. But first I outline the main arguments in favor of the class-based approach.

THE RATIONALE BEHIND CLASS-BASED AFFIRMATIVE ACTION

The idea of giving students of low socioeconomic standing a slight boost during college admissions has become popular in recent years, even more so after the Fisher v. Texas ruling in 2013. However, not all supporters of class-based affirmative action sound alike when explaining *why* we should implement it. Three distinct arguments among advocates can be identified.

Rationale 1: Use Class to Avoid Mismatch

The first camp of class-based affirmative action advocates is motivated mostly by an ideological opposition to race-conscious admissions. This group became especially vocal after the Fisher v. University of Texas hearings began in October 2012, with the goal of influencing that Supreme Court ruling. These advocates claim that by giving an edge in admission that is not based on meritocratic criteria but rather on group affiliation, race-based affirmative action runs counter to the core American values of individualism and egalitarianism, that it discriminates against whites and Asians, and that it benefits the "wrong people"—that is, it promotes "creaming" because only the most privileged among underrepresented minorities take advantage of it.

The main argument of this position is that race-conscious admissions set up minority students for failure. That is, by definition, the academic standing of affirmative action beneficiaries falls short of regular admission thresholds. This academic mismatch sets up the beneficiaries for failure in elite academic settings; thus, these minority students would be better served by attending less-demanding colleges. Perhaps the best spokesperson for this group is Richard Sander, a professor of law at UCLA and a long-standing opponent of race-conscious admissions policies. Sander and Stuart Taylor Jr. recently cowrote the book *Mismatch* about affirmative action in U.S. colleges.[1] Promoting the class-based road to affirmative action in place of race-conscious admissions, they maintain that class-based affirmative action will not produce the same problem of mismatch but do not explain why or how. The results reported in chapters 9 and 10 demonstrate that, indeed, the beneficiaries of class-based affirmative action are not destined for failure in elite academic settings—yet neither are the beneficiaries of race-based affirmative action.

Rationale 2: Use Class as a "Trojan Horse"

The second camp supports the move from race to class in affirmative action for practical reasons. They are not ideologically opposed to the use of race as a factor in college admissions and in fact endorse the use of class indicators in college admissions largely for the purpose of increasing racial and ethnic diversity.[2] Their reasoning is that, in the face of growing controversy about race-conscious admissions and the strict scrutiny imposed by the Supreme Court, the days of this practice appear to be numbered, and if this happens the share of blacks and Hispanics at elite colleges will inevitably drop. Experience shows that without the consideration of race in admissions, the level of racial and ethnic diversity will surely decline—the several states that have banned the use of race as a factor in admission decisions have already seen a sharp drop in the share of black and Hispanic students at selective institutions. The voices in this camp suggest that colleges consider other factors in admissions, such as family income and high school or neighborhood type, that are believed to approximate race; their assumption is that a large share of the students targeted with class-based indicators will be black or Hispanic. The motivation, then, is to cushion the expected dive in the share of URM by way of a race-neutral substitute for current race-based policy that can generate racial and ethnic diversity.

The strategy of using class as a "Trojan Horse" for race is not new. In fact, this thinking is even evident in the Fisher ruling, which mandates that institutions seek race-neutral ways of generating diversity before using race as a factor in admissions. This direction is rooted in the belief that certain race-neutral measures can act as a proxy for race. For example, suppose for a moment that all poor applicants (with qualifying academic records) seeking admission to elite colleges are also underrepresented minorities. In this hypothetical scenario, targeting applicants with low family income could achieve a level of racial and ethnic diversity similar to that of current race-based policy. Even if 80 percent of poor applicants are minorities, we would expect the resultant racial and ethnic diversity to approximate—but not match—the level produced by targeting race and ethnicity directly.

Perhaps the biggest supporter of the Trojan Horse logic is the U.S. government. In 2011 the Departments of Justice and Education copublished guidelines on how colleges and universities should go about generating racial and ethnic diversity.[3] The letter recommended five different admission procedures, the first of which is firmly rooted in the proxy rationale: "An institution could consider an applicant's socioeconomic status, first-generation college status, geographic residency, or other race-neutral criteria if doing so would assist in drawing students from different racial backgrounds to the institution." Technically speaking, this suggestion advocates for using class-based criteria that are race-neutral. But it is clear that a major goal of this approach is to generate racial and ethnic diversity. Institutions are urged to admit applicants from low socioeconomic backgrounds and districts and from low-performing schools only for the potential demographic dividends ("if doing so would assist in drawing students from different *racial* backgrounds to the institution" [emphasis added]). Socioeconomic and geographic diversity are not emphasized as valuable goals in and of themselves, and thus broad diversity, as delineated by the Supreme Court, is not the objective here. Although the means may be different—and more politically palatable[4]—the goal of this camp is very similar to that of advocates of race-conscious admissions: to boost racial and ethnic diversity.

The problem, however, is that class is not a good proxy for race and ethnicity because the majority of poor applicants are white. Thus, this strategy is unlikely to boost racial and ethnic diversity, as demonstrated in chapters 7 and 8.

Rationale 3: Use Class to Promote Socioeconomic Diversity

Only the third camp insists that advancing socioeconomic diversity and social mobility is a compelling goal in its own right. This group does not see class-based affirmative action as merely an indirect approach to promoting racial and ethnic diversity but as a way of expanding opportunity for all groups, thus promoting broad diversity, which they believe is beneficial both on campus and in society. Interestingly, the diversity rationale implemented in the

Supreme Court Bakke ruling—in particular the notion of broad diversity—laid the foundation for the possibility of class-based affirmative action.

Over time elite institutions have been able to enhance racial and ethnic diversity on campus by giving minority applicants special consideration during admissions, but socioeconomically deprived applicants have been given no similar edge that could help offset the depressing effect of home disadvantage on their test scores. Without any preferential treatment, the share of socioeconomically underprivileged students at selective colleges has remained low and has often declined. In their book *Equity and Excellence in American Higher Education*, Bowen and his colleagues ask: "Are the claims of equity really being met today by a policy that gives no positive weight to having come from a poor family—and having somehow overcome all of the attendant barriers in order to compete with a candidate from a very different background for a place in class?"[5] The rationale here is straightforward: class-based affirmative action is vital because it boosts much-needed socioeconomic diversity at elite institutions and promotes equal opportunity and social mobility.

Nonetheless, for these supporters class-based affirmative action does not have to be race-neutral. Class-based affirmative action could be implemented instead of race-based affirmative action or in addition to it; alternatively, race could be one of many factors considered within a framework of class-based policy. All options are on the table as long as they manage to boost socioeconomic diversity at the nation's most selective colleges and universities.

The Rationale Is Important

Each of these three rationales for class-based policy has a different goal: the first focuses on abolishing race-conscious admissions and preventing mismatch, the second on boosting racial and ethnic diversity, and the third on increasing socioeconomic diversity. One may think that the motivation for implementing a class-based policy is not important as long as the outcome is desirable, but this is not true for several reasons.

First, the logic and intentions behind a program are crucial for mobilizing and sustaining public support. How do the three rationales for class-based affirmative action compare in this respect? Advancing socioeconomic diversity and social mobility is valued in many societies, especially in the United States, while promoting racial and ethnic diversity is less universally valued and more controversial.[6] A class-based policy that is packaged to promote broad—with an emphasis on *socioeconomic*—diversity at America's bastions of privilege is likely to have strong public appeal (the third rationale).[7] Moreover, in pushing for socioeconomic diversity, the camp pushing for socioeconomic diversity is most attuned to the seismic shifts that have occurred in the United States in recent decades: rising economic inequality, stymied social mobility, and the growing class divide in higher education. Many Americans have firsthand experience with these shifts and are likely to support a policy that attempts to address them—even if the main beneficiaries would be black and Hispanic—as long as they agree with the rationale. They would not support a move from race to class in affirmative action just because there are problems with race-conscious admissions (as suggested by the first and second rationales) if such a move did not promote socioeconomic diversity as a strong raison d'être.

To illustrate this point, consider the race-neutral, class-based admissions policy implemented in Israel in the mid-2000s (discussed at length in chapter 6). Although Arab applicants to university benefit greatly from this policy, its goal is not to boost ethnic diversity, nor are applicants' disadvantages used simply as a proxy for ethnicity. If this were the case, there would be little support for the program. In fact, there is little opposition to the program because the diversity dividends of the Israeli policy are so broad (described in Chapter 7).

Second, the rationale for a class-based policy is important because it dictates how the program is set up to achieve its goals—that is, the rationale determines program *design,* and different rationales lead to different designs. For example, if the second rationale (the Trojan Horse) is the working rationale for implementing class-based policy, then the target design would be a race-neutral tool that yields the highest share of blacks and Hispanics. Let's say that we are deliberating between targeting students from high-poverty high schools (with a high share of poor students) and targeting those from poor families. Let's also say that 80 percent of students in high-poverty schools are underrepresented minorities, but that only 50 percent of students from poor families are minorities. If our main goal is to increase racial and ethnic diversity, then the choice is clear: the edge should be given to students from high-poverty schools. However, if the motivation is to boost socioeconomic diversity at elite colleges, then we would base the policy on the demonstrated disadvantages of individuals, and coming from a poor family would be one of them. Thus, different motivations behind class-based programs lead to different program designs that target different groups of applicants.

Finally, the rationale also determines how we evaluate a policy's success or failure. From a Trojan Horse perspective, class-based affirmative action is successful if it maintains the share of URM at the country's elite schools; such evidence will not suffice to determine whether the policy is successful if it was implemented to promote socioeconomic diversity. Thus, our perception of the success of class-based affirmative action is tied to the rationale for implementing it in the first place.

Thus, while the different rationales for race-conscious admissions—be it reparation, diversity, or equal opportunity—may lead to a similar program design (an edge in admission for minority applicants), different motivations for class-based policy can render very different designs. In other words, there is one way to implement race-based affirmative action, but there are multiple roads to class-based affirmative action. The rationale behind class-based policy is important for pinpointing goals, and having clear goals is essential for the proper design and evaluation of this policy (or any public policy for that matter). The ambiguity in the public debate about what type of diversity is needed at elite institutions is a prime example of unclear goals complicating the discussion of how best to design an effective affirmative action policy.

PROTOTYPES OF CLASS-BASED AFFIRMATIVE ACTION

Many assume that the shift from race to class in affirmative action policy would be relatively straightforward—that the only difference between class- and race-based policy would be the eligibility criteria. This belief is nurtured by the lack of hands-on experience with large-scale class-based programs in the United States and elsewhere. But class-based models are vastly different from race-based policy. Not only do race and class prototypes draw on different justice paradigms and generate different dividends for diversity and mobility, but there is also great variation among the class-based models themselves.

The race-based affirmative action policy currently in place in elite college admissions in the United States and several other countries is a prototype that adheres to the notion of macrojustice, in that the main criterion for eligibility is affiliation with a particular group, specifically, a racial or ethnic group. Under this paradigm, every individual who is part of a historically disenfranchised group is entitled to some compensation, regardless of individual experience; inequality and discrimination have been generated at the societal level, so the correction or redistribution must also occur at the macro level.[8] This model of affirmative action is also need-blind in that an applicant's economic standing is not considered in determining eligibility.

There is only one major prototype of race-based affirmative action, but there are several models of class-based policy. To clear some of the ambiguity surrounding the concept of class-based affirmative action, I suggest the following definition:

> For a policy to qualify as class-based affirmative action, it needs to give an *edge* in admissions to applicants from *underprivileged* backgrounds, defined by personal or contextual deprivation. Thus, the outcome of class-based affirmative action is a *boost* in the representation of *underprivileged* populations in a student body.

The term "underprivileged" here refers to circumstances in individuals' backgrounds—such as coming from a poor family, being the first in the family to go to college, residing in a poor neighborhood, or attending a low-performing high school—that are likely to have a depressing effect on their ability to exploit their own academic potential. There are several ways to characterize "underprivileged," and each leads to a different type of class-based affirmative action.

This section describes the three main prototypes of class-based policy. As we shall see, each adheres to a different justice paradigm, is based on different eligibility criteria, and may yield different diversity and mobility dividends. These prototypes also vary with regard to ease of implementation, but all are more difficult to implement than race-based policy. I consider some of the pros and cons of each model, the trade-offs between them, and the practical concerns that arise from each. Together, the race-based model and the three class-based models—four prototypes in total—are the pillars of affirmative action policy around the world. Table 5.1 presents the full typology of affirmative action policy and summarizes the characteristics of each class- and race-based model.

Prototype 1: Socioeconomic Affirmative Action

The most popular conception of class-based affirmative action is one in which eligibility depends on family income; some versions of this model also

WHAT IS CLASS-BASED AFFIRMATIVE ACTION?

Table 5.1 A Typology of Affirmative Action Policies

	Prototype			
	Race	Class		
		1: Socioeconomic	2: Structural	3: Multidimensional
Justice paradigm	Macro	Micro	Macro	Micro, macro
Group affiliation or individual attribute	Group	Individual	Group	Individual, group
Eligibility	Ascribed trait	Socioeconomic status	Structure	Socioeconomic status and structure
Selection criteria	Race, ethnicity, and caste	Parents' educational attainment and income	Neighborhood and school	Parents' educational attainment, income, neighborhood, and school
Ascribed characteristic	Yes	No	No	No
Race-neutral	No	Yes	Yes	Yes
Need-based	No	Yes	No	Yes
Consider opportunities for learning	No	No	Yes	Yes
Ease of implementation	Easy	Challenging	Easy	Challenging
Creaming	Yes	No	Yes	No
Expected diversity outcome	Demographic	Socioeconomic	School/geographic	Socioeconomic and school/geographic

Source: Author's calculations.

take parental education into account. Targeting family income alone would best be classified as *economic* affirmative action; if we also consider parental education, then technically we have *socioeconomic* affirmative action. In practice the term "socioeconomic affirmative action" is often used to refer to both of these models, and for the sake of parsimony I do the same in this book.

Both versions of this prototype draw from the same justice paradigm: microjustice. According to this outlook, individuals—not groups—suffer injustice. Thus, compensation should be based only on the demonstrated disadvantage of individuals.[9] This design is supposed to relieve the "creaming" problem—the grievance that race-conscious admissions benefit the most privileged among underrepresented minorities.

Despite its conceptual appeal, the most reliable simulations of this model suggest that socioeconomic affirmative action cannot match the level of racial and ethnic diversity produced by race-sensitive admissions.[10] Moreover, these policies may be limited by the small pool of applicants from socioeconomically disadvantaged backgrounds whose academic performance is close enough to the admission thresholds of selective colleges to qualify for affirmative action. The depressing effect of poverty on children's potential and academic achievements simply tends to be too big and too widespread. Even if we decide to go this route, the number of high-achieving yet socioeconomically underprivileged applicants may be too small for this policy to be practical. Race-based policies are less prone to such shortages because they draw largely on middle- and upper-class minorities, who are more likely to have high academic achievements. This is the flip side of the creaming problem. The comparative investigation in this book examines these problems.

Another challenge posed by this model is implementation: determining an individual's race is much more straightforward than measuring socioeconomic status. To implement a program that targets socioeconomic status, either alone or in addition to other characteristics, several questions must be considered, including:

1. *What are the relevant indicators for eligibility?* Should we use family income or parental education, or both? Should we include other indicators of poverty? Of wealth?

2. *What should be the thresholds for eligibility?* Family income of $50,000? Less? More?
3. *What should be the weight of each indicator?* For example, what is more important: family income or parental education?
4. *How do we collect the wide array of sensitive information and verify accuracy?* Self-reports of family income by applicants are generally considered neither accurate nor sufficient.

Determining an individual's race is based on a box checked at the application form, while determining an individual's socioeconomic status requires collection and verification of a large number of indicators about his or her underprivileged background, either personal or contextual. I elaborate on the feasibility and implementation of the various class-based models in the final chapter.

Prototype 2: Structural Affirmative Action

The structural prototype of class-based policy uses the deprivation in an applicant's surroundings—for example, a poor neighborhood or a low-performing or high-poverty high school—as the criteria for eligibility. This design is theoretically based in the long tradition of sociological research that links social structures, such as neighborhoods and schools, to youth achievement and educational outcomes.[11]

Neighborhoods vary in terms of their characteristics. There are differences in the strength and size of the local labor market, municipal services, child and family institutions, social organizations, and normative environments, as well as in poverty level, population composition, and marriage opportunities. These neighborhood characteristics affect overall school quality in that they are intimately tied to the financial resources of local schools, the quality of teachers, the learning environment, and school curricula and services. As a result, schools vary greatly in the learning opportunities that they provide their students, whose scholastic gains are shaped by the quality of those opportunities. Young people who reside in poor neighborhoods or attend bad schools also simply have fewer opportunities to excel compared to young people in more nurturing environments. This is called the "neighborhood effect."

In addition to directly targeting youth with structural disadvantages, the structural model of affirmative action also attempts to capitalize on the overlap between spatial boundaries and categorical inequality. Because poor neighborhoods and failing schools tend to be populated by many kinds of disadvantaged groups—including racial and ethnic minorities, recent immigrants, and the poor—targeting individuals with structural disadvantages indirectly targets blacks, Hispanics, the poor, and other disadvantaged groups.[12] Thus, to the extent that structural inequality overlaps other systems of inequality, this model could yield geographic and demographic diversity in addition to benefiting underprivileged applicants.

This logic underlies some of the recommendations by the Departments of Justice and Education in their recently published guidelines, which encourage colleges to give special consideration to applicants' structural disadvantages:

> *Example 2:* An institution could include in its admissions procedures special consideration for students who have endured or overcome hardships such as marked residential instability (e.g., the student moved from residence to residence or school to school while growing up) or *enrollment in a low-performing school or district* [emphasis added].
>
> *Example 4:* An institution could select schools (including community colleges) based on their demographics (e.g., their racial or socioeconomic composition), and grant an admission preference to all students who have graduated from those schools, regardless of the race of the individual student.[13]

Theoretically, structural affirmative action is similar to race-conscious admissions in that both models stress group affiliation rather than individual circumstances. The emphasis on group membership is consistent with a macrojustice perspective and facilitates implementation. That is, by focusing on the structure of opportunity instead of on individual adverse circumstances, this model bypasses the need for a complex mechanism of assessing disadvantage at the individual level (as is the case in prototype 1, the socioeconomic model). A key difference, however, is that the criteria for compensation in the structural model are not based on an ascribed trait (gender, race, ethnicity, or caste). This difference is crucial for the legal implications of such a plan and the public reaction to it.[14] I discuss these issues in greater detail in the final chapter.

Structural-type programs receive little attention in the United States. Elements of the structural rationale have been incorporated into affirmative action programs, however, in a few other countries, such as Brazil, France, and Israel. According to the Law of Social Quotas passed in 2012, Brazil's federal public universities (which are the selective universities) are required to reserve at least half of their slots for students from public high schools, which tend to serve a poorer population and to be lower-performing than the country's private high schools. This program is not strictly structural in that it also considers race and family income. Technically, then, the Brazilian program should probably be classified under the multidimensional prototype of class-based affirmative action (prototype 3) because it also includes individual criteria. Nonetheless, I mention the program here because its structural aspect is very strong.

In 2001 the Institut d'Études Politiques de Paris in France (known as Sciences Po) implemented a structural-type admissions program—specifically, a preferential treatment program for students from high schools serving disadvantaged areas in France.[15] Students from these schools were exempted from taking the competitive admissions exam and were asked to write an essay instead. The final selection was made following an interview, and those selected were given financial aid and tutoring. The program design is interesting, and the structural aspect is very strong, yet the small scale of the initiative (so far only 860 students have been admitted to Sciences Po through this admission program) makes it hard to determine its success.[16] Moreover, several main features of the design—the handpicking of beneficiaries, the guaranteed financial aid and tutoring, and the test waiver—limit its potential for replication on a large scale.

Finally, the affirmative action policy in place at the top universities in Israel is a paragon of the type of class-based policy that emphasizes structural disadvantages. Although certain individual hardships are also considered in this program, eligibility relies most heavily on high school type and neighborhood of residence. Moreover, it is an example of a class-based policy that is entirely race-neutral and need-blind. This policy is discussed in great detail in the next chapter.

Prototype 3: Multidimensional Affirmative Action

The third prototype of class-based affirmative action is the multidimensional prototype, which combines aspects of both the socioeconomic and structural models (prototypes 1 and 2). It targets both individual and structural disadvantages, thus combining the notions of microjustice and macrojustice. Proponents of this prototype argue that one-dimensional conceptions of class are insufficient to capture the complexity of what determines an individual's prospects and life chances. They contend that in order to identify what sociologists call the "truly disadvantaged," we must consider a wide array of factors, such as home environment (socioeconomic status and family structure) and structural effects (school composition, neighborhoods, and geographical region) as well as race, ethnicity, and gender.[17] (The term "truly disadvantaged" was introduced by the sociologist William Julius Wilson in 1987, in his book of the same name, to describe poor blacks living in American urban ghettos; the term is used here to describe groups and individuals with multiple aspects of disadvantage.)[18]

By taking into account both structures of opportunity (such as schools and neighborhoods) and a wide array of individual socioeconomic hardships (for example, family income, family wealth, and parental education), the multidimensional prototype targets many contours of inequality and addresses the complexity in determining a person's class status. Consequently, there are numerous possible designs for such a program. The Brazilian program is multidimensional because it accounts for high school type, family income, and race. The Israeli program can also be classified as multidimensional because it considers an array of individual hardships in addition to high school and neighborhood type.

In the United States, where there is talk about class-based affirmative action in college admissions but no hands-on experience with such models, some observers suggest that colleges consider all of the following in determining eligibility: parental income, wealth and net worth, parental education, family structure, language spoken at home, neighborhood poverty level, and high school share of minority students. This approach, what academics like to call the "kitchen sink approach," is promoted by The Century Foundation (TCF), a public policy think tank, in several reports published just before and after the Supreme Court's ruling in the Fisher case, including a report published in 2012 titled "A Better Affirmative Action."[19]

This approach, intuitively, seems promising. Richard D. Kahlenberg, a senior fellow at TCF, is an advocate for using a complex multidimensional model for determining eligibility for affirmative action. In fact, the main motivation for implementing such a complex scheme of admissions is to serve as a Trojan Horse for race-conscious admissions because family income, or any other socioeconomic indicator, is not a good proxy for race. He argues that a policy that incorporates an array of socioeconomic factors will be better at generating demographic diversity than one based solely on income. Kahlenberg, who authored several of the Century Foundation reports on the topic, writes that implementing such a design will help universities "equal or even exceed the racial diversity that they have achieved under racial affirmative action programs."[20] Unfortunately, these claims have never been tested. There is no evidence for whether the "kitchen sink approach" can boost demographic diversity while yielding wide-ranging diversity dividends, and if so, at what price.

Moreover, this approach to generating diversity has the same limitation as the socioeconomic prototype, only here the potential problem is even more severe: it requires finding enough truly disadvantaged applicants who are academically prepared for the rigor of selective colleges. Once again we must ask the critical question: how many applicants are there who fit this description and have somehow managed to beat the odds? How many high school students from poor families *and* poor neighborhoods *and* low-performing high schools have stellar academic achievements that put them near the threshold of the nation's most selective colleges? Chances are the answer is, not many. If this pool is indeed small, then this model's potential to boost diversity is low.

Finally, even more than the socioeconomic prototype, the multidimensional model is difficult to implement because it requires a wealth of information (especially if following the "kitchen sink approach") that must be verified.

These three prototypes of class-based policy are ideal types whose purpose is to orient the discussion about class-based affirmative action and help us understand its conceptual frameworks. But real policy designs are never as rigid as prototypes, nor should they be. Rather, they should draw from elements of several models. The exciting programs recently implemented in other countries, specifically in Israel and Brazil, suggest that between the two theoretical poles of micro- and macrojustice, and between the rival modes of race versus class affirmative action, there is a world of possibility—a spectrum in fact—for affirmative action policy in higher education. I revisit this notion later in the book after inspecting the evidence from both Israel and the United States.

MISCONCEPTIONS: WHAT IS NOT CLASS-BASED AFFIRMATIVE ACTION?

As the discourse about class-based affirmative action gains traction, so does the ambiguity surrounding the concept. Now that we have a general picture of what class-based affirmative action is, let's distinguish it from what it is not. For example, many construe percent plans, comprehensive review processes, and certain financial aid policies as class-based affirmative action even though they are not true examples of such. This confusion only impedes the design and implementation of true and effective class-based policies, and so it must be cleared up as we contemplate the move from race to class in affirmative action.

As mentioned in the beginning of this chapter, I hold that for a policy to qualify as class-based affirmative action it needs to give an edge in admission to applicants from underprivileged backgrounds. Thus, the goal of class-based affirmative action is to boost the representation of underprivileged populations in the student body. According to this definition, are percent plans, comprehensive review processes, and financial aid policy forms of class-based affirmative action?

Percent Plans

Since the 1990s, public referenda and lawsuits have led to prohibitions against using race as a factor in college and university admission decisions in several states. In Texas it was the Hopwood ruling in 1992, which affected the state's public universities. In California it was Proposition 209; passed by voters in 1996, it affects all state government institutions. Two years later, voters in the state of Washington passed Initiative 200, banning the consideration of race in college admissions. In 2006 Michigan voters approved Proposal 2, which outlawed affirmative action based on color, sex, race, or gender in public institutions.

After these laws went into effect, the share of blacks and Hispanics at selective colleges and universities in these states dropped sharply. For example, after California passed Proposition 209 in 1997, the share of black students at UC Berkeley declined by 52 percent, and the percentage of Hispanics by 43 percent.[21] In an attempt to recover the representation of URM at their flagship institutions, some of these states—namely, Texas, California, and Florida—decided to adopt admission policies that admit a fixed percentage of top students from each public high school in the state. These policies are often referred to as "percent plans." The expectation was that in states where high schools are highly segregated by race and ethnicity, large numbers of black and Hispanic students would qualify for the admission guarantee.[22]

The percent plan in California guarantees all high school graduates in the state who finish in the top 4 percent of their class admission to at least one university in the UC system, but it does not promise a particular campus. Similarly, the Talented 20 Plan in Florida guarantees public high school graduates who place in the top 20 percent of their class after completing required coursework admission to the University of Florida system, but not necessarily to their top school of choice. Under the Texas Top Ten Percent Plan, high school seniors who graduate in the top 10 percent of their class are guaranteed admission to their state university of choice.

Are percent plans a form of class-based affirmative action? To qualify as such, the first criterion is that it must give applicants from underprivileged backgrounds an edge in admissions. A key characteristic of percent plans, however, is that they are applied *uniformly:* by definition, the same rule of admission applies to rich and poor, to blacks and whites, to those from large metropolitan areas and those from small townships. Students from all schools are guaranteed admission as long as they pass the cutoff ranking. The most affluent students from the most privileged neighborhoods get the same consideration as every other student in the state, and applicants from underprivileged backgrounds or from the geographic periphery get no edge in admission compared to other applicants.

The second criterion for class-based affirmative action is that it must boost the share of underprivileged students on campus. Are percent plans successful at raising socioeconomic diversity? The numbers say no. In Texas, for example, the enactment of the Top Ten Percent Plan was not followed by a rise in socioeconomic diversity at the state's top state universities.[23] After the plan went into effect, the share of applicants and admits to UT Austin and TAMU (public flagships) from poor high schools in the state dropped.[24] The policy was successful, however, at broadening geographic diversity.[25]

In practice, students from affluent backgrounds are in a better position to take advantage of the program because they are more likely to rank at the top of their class and to have more knowledge about the workings of admission policies. Giving applicants from poor high schools an equal consideration in admission to that received by applicants from rich schools is not enough. A uniform admission regime cannot erase the depressing effect of studying in a poor high school on the ability to exploit one's own academic potential. Without an edge in admission or some kind of special treatment, the likelihood of boosting the level of socioeconomic diversity at elite schools is very low.

Thus, percent plans are not an affirmative action policy of any kind—they are neither race-based nor class-based. They are also not a type of geographic affirmative action because applicants from the periphery receive no special treatment in admissions. (A uniform admissions criterion is applied to both these applicants and applicants from strong neighborhoods.) Given that socioeconomically disadvantaged applicants receive no form of preferential treatment, it is not surprising that percent plans are unsuccessful at producing socioeconomic diversity.

Comprehensive Review Process

Comprehensive review (discussed in chapter 4) is another admission practice that is often mistaken for a kind of class-based affirmative action. Elite private colleges claim to use this "holistic" approach during admissions, meaning that they consider academic achievements in the context of applicants' previous life chances. Theoretically, comprehensive review can surely provide an edge to poor applicants if it is tailored to do so, in the same way that elite private colleges effectively use this process in race-conscious admissions. Nonetheless, the evidence shows that despite their potential to do so, comprehensive review processes, as practiced by elite colleges, do not give applicants from underprivileged backgrounds an edge in admissions and do not increase socioeconomic diversity. Thus, according to the definition, comprehensive review in and of itself is not a form of class-based affirmative action.

Financial Aid

Similarly, an institution's financial aid policy does not qualify as class-based affirmative action because it too does not give applicants from underprivileged backgrounds an edge in *admissions*. To be sure, financial aid is a form of class-based policy in that it is sensitive to a student's economic ability to pay for college, and it is conducive to raising the share of poor students at elite schools. Yet it is not a form of *affirmative action* because it eases financial constraints only for those applicants who have already gained admission and does not deal with the main barrier to college admissions: academic qualification. Generous financial aid is essential to ensure the success of affirmative action policy, yet without a policy that helps underprivileged applicants at the admission stage, its ability to boost socioeconomic diversity at bastions of privilege is quite limited.

In conclusion, none of the three policies—percent plans, comprehensive review, and financial aid—qualify as class-based affirmative action. They do not favor underprivileged applicants during the admissions process and thus are not effective tools to boost broad diversity.

CONCLUSION

This chapter has outlined the conceptual underpinnings of the three main models of class-based policy in college admissions. The question that naturally arises is what kind of outcomes would these class-based models yield in terms of both diversity and mobility, and how would these outcomes compare to race-based policies? The answers will help determine whether a shift from race to class in affirmative action in U.S. college admissions is desirable at this critical crossroads. The next step, then, is to move the discussion about affirmative action beyond the theoretical sphere and to start examining the evidence.

CHAPTER 6

Israel: Contours of Inequality, Higher Education, and Class-Based Affirmative Action at the Elite Universities

Israel and the United States are very different societies. They differ not only in geography, climate, and size but also in their history, political systems, demographics, labor market structures, and education systems. But what always amazes me, as one who has studied the two countries for many years, is that despite these disparities, the contours of inequality in the two countries are similar: race-ethnicity, class, and geography, the forces shaping inequality on the Israeli playing field, echo the forces aggravating inequality in the United States. Notorious among them are rising economic inequality, declining social mobility, and persistent racial-ethnic earnings gaps. The rising competition in admissions to the most selective institutions and fields of study has only deepened this rift because, in Israel as in the United States, education level and education type determine much of an individual's earnings potential. In both countries, youth from disadvantaged groups—be they Arabs in northern Israel or blacks in Detroit, poor high school students in southern Israel or their counterparts in Waco, Texas—are falling further and further behind.

In the mid-2000s, the four most selective universities in Israel adopted a class-based affirmative action policy that is both innovative and unique in that the program is race-neutral and need-blind: in evaluating the eligibility of applicants, the program considers neither their individual financial situation nor their ethnic origins. Although certain types of individual hardships are weighed, the program's main emphasis is on structural determinants of disadvantage: neighborhood socioeconomic status and high school socioeconomic status.

The Israeli policy stands in stark contrast to what is practiced in the United States, where the term "affirmative action" usually refers to admissions policies that consider race and ethnicity. But as the race-based model has come under increasing scrutiny over time, the idea of replacing it with an alternative has gained public support, and class-based policy is the most popular contender by far. With little experience with class-based affirmative action, the United States must look beyond its borders to observe it in action. Among the countries that have been experimenting with class-based policy in higher education, only Israel has a class-based program that is both old enough and large enough to be instructive, as the comparative investigation in this book will reveal. Most importantly, Israel is also the only country with *race-neutral* class-based affirmative action.

This chapter explores the key features of the unique hybrid design of the Israeli program; subsequent chapters examine the evidence of its dividends in terms of both diversity and mobility. That evidence taken together with similar evidence about the dividends of race-based affirmative action in the United States will lead us to new and more global insights about the potential of race-neutral public policy to promote equality in higher education. But we begin by asking the question that underlies any evaluation of such a program: why is it needed in the first place? To understand the motivation behind class-based affirmative action, we must first understand the major contours of inequality in Israeli society.

THE STRATIFICATION OF ISRAELI SOCIETY

As mentioned earlier, inequality in Israel looks very similar to inequality in the United States in that it is found along economic, racial-ethnic, and geographic dimensions. Here I consider each in turn.

Economic Inequality

In 2010 Israel become a member of the Organization for Economic Cooperation and Development (OECD), an international organization of high-income countries with market economies that is dedicated to promoting economic development and world trade. The OECD measures the degree of family income inequality within a given country using the Gini index, which works as follows: If one person earned all the income in a country, then the Gini index would equal 1. If all the income in a given country were distributed equally—that is, if everyone earned exactly the same income—then the Gini index for that country would be 0. The Gini index for most of the thirty-four OECD member countries clusters in the range of 0.25 to 0.33.[1]

In 2010, Iceland, Slovenia, and Norway scored lowest on the Gini index—all were below 0.250. Sweden and Germany were not far off, with scores of 0.269 and 0.286, respectively. Israel, however, was among the most unequal countries in the developed world, coming in at fourth place (0.376), right behind the United States (0.380), Turkey (0.417), and, the most unequal of all, Mexico (0.466). Even more troubling is that, according to OECD data, Israel is the country with the greatest rise in inequality over the past several decades: its Gini coefficient rose from 0.280 to 0.376 between 1975 and 2010. During the same period, the U.S. index rose from 0.320 to 0.380.

Another way to appreciate the change in Israel's level of income inequality is to compare the top earners with those at the bottom of the income distribution. In 1995 the income of the top 10 percent of earners was, on average, 8.6 times higher than that of the bottom 10 percent. At the time this was actually lower than the OECD average of 8.9. The economic gaps in OECD countries have widened over time, so that by 2010 the average ratio of top to bottom decile incomes was 9.8. In Israel, however, it was greater than the new average: 13.6. Unfortunately, we have no data on Israeli income ratios before the 1990s, but what we do have makes it clear that Israel, once one of the most equal countries in the world, has undergone a dramatic transformation. The "land flowing with milk and honey," as Moses envisioned and the Book of Exodus records, has indeed become more abundant, but this abundance is increasingly available only to those at the top.

What makes the picture in Israel even gloomier is that the prospects for economic mobility today are small. A recent study showed that an Israeli individual's chances of moving up the economic ladder from one year to the next (economic mobility) have declined over time. Between 2003 and 2009, the vast majority (92 percent) of earners in the top income decile remained in the top decile one year later, while the OECD average was about 80 percent.[2]

Among those in the top income decile in 2009, 11 percent worked in finance and 18 percent in the high-tech industry, the two most overrepresented sectors among top earners. Only 3 percent of bottom-decile earners worked in these two sectors.

Israel has changed a lot since the 1970s. A high school graduate back then did not need a college diploma to climb the economic and social ladder. Today college is the gateway to economic well-being and social mobility. Attending college, and especially attaining a degree in a professional field, determines the future position of Israeli youth in the social hierarchy. The question thus becomes: who gets access to the selective Israeli universities and the lucrative fields for which they prepare Israeli youth?

Ethnic Inequality

The total population of Israel today is about 8 million.[3] Since the state was founded in 1948, ethnic origin has been a major component of stratification in Israeli society: a clear hierarchy in educational attainment, occupational status, and earnings has persisted over the past sixty years. One cleavage is between Jews and the 1.6 million Israeli Arabs, who account for approximately 20 percent of the population. The second cleavage runs along ethnic lines within the Jewish population between Jews of European or American origin (Ashkenazi Jews, or Ashkenazis) and Jews of Asian or African origin (Mizrahi Jews, or Mizrahis). Ashkenazi Jews are at the top of the socioeconomic distribution, followed by Mizrahi Jews, while the Arab citizens of Israel are at the bottom.[4]

Ethnic Cleavage Among Jews Most of the Jewish population of Israel today originate from one of several immigration waves to the region. The first major wave began in 1882; the majority hailed from the Russian Empire, with smaller numbers arriving from countries in the Middle East, such as Syria and Yemen. By 1948 there were 650,000 Jews in Israel. The establishment of the state of Israel in 1948 brought with it massive new waves of Jewish immigrants, who continued to arrive throughout the 1950s. These waves consisted mainly of refugees from Europe and America (Ashkenazis) and from Asia and Africa (Mizrahis). To appreciate the magnitude of these immigration waves, consider the following statistic: in the three-year period between 1948 and 1951, 330,000 immigrants arrived from Europe. Between 1948 and 1957, more than half a million immigrants from Asia and Africa arrived.[5] The size of the Jewish population in Israel more than doubled in less than ten years. After the 1950s, immigrants continued to arrive, but in much smaller numbers and at a slower rate for the next three decades. That all changed with the arrival of 1 million Jews between 1989 and 1995, mostly from the Former Soviet Union (FSU). This wave represents 15 percent of the population today. There were also two small waves of immigrants from Ethiopia during this period.

The ethnic divide within the Jewish population of Israel is shaped by country of origin. The social and cultural assimilation of Ashkenazi immigrants into Israeli society was smoother, in general, than it was for Mizrahi immigrants. Consequently, a socioeconomic hierarchy was institutionalized among the Jewish population of Israel: Ashkenazi Jews are at the top, Mizrahi Jews are at the bottom, and Jews of mixed ethnicity occupy the space in the middle.[6] But with the passage of time since the major immigration waves of the late 1940s and 1950s, the share of third-generation Jews in the Israeli population is rising, especially among the college-age population. Today almost four out of ten Israelis in the age cohort of potential university applicants are third-generation Jews—that is, native-born Israeli Jews whose parents were also born in Israel.[7] This group is extremely heterogeneous, comprising many ethnic origins and combinations of ethnicities. Although the task of determining ethnicity is often not so clear-cut, it remains a strong indicator of economic and social prospects for the young Jewish population.

The Arab Minority   The Arabs who remained in Israel after the Arab-Israeli War of 1948 became citizens of Israel. But the socioeconomic status of these Arab citizens (today 20 percent of the population) has always trailed that of all Jewish groups.[8] Current data show that the poverty rate among Arab-Israeli families is 53 percent, while the rate among Jewish families is 14 percent. Male life expectancy is 76.8 years among Arabs and 80.4 years among Jews. In 2011 the average salary of male Arab workers was 60 percent that of Jewish workers, and fewer than one in three eighteen-year-old Arabs received a high school diploma granting eligibility to university, while one in two of their Jewish counterparts did.[9]

There are several reasons for this disparity. The first is spatial segregation (which I discuss in more detail later in this chapter). In general, Arabs and

Jews in Israel do not live in the same neighborhoods and do not send their children to the same schools. This is true even in Jerusalem, Haifa, and Tel Aviv, the three largest cities in Israel, all with significant populations of both Arabs and Jews. In fact, most of the Arab population of Israel (about 65 percent) reside in independent Arab localities, which tend to be small communities on the geographic periphery, far from the main economic and industrial hubs of Israel.[10] Most of these Arab towns are poor, partly owing to discrimination in the allocation of government funds and programs, but also because the local governments of Arab towns are reluctant to collect city taxes from their residents. Of the forty towns in Israel with the highest unemployment rates, thirty-six are Arab towns.[11]

Another key determinant of the differences in well-being between Jewish and Arab Israelis is the low level of labor force participation among Arab women. Only 27 percent of Arab women are employed, compared to 64 percent of Jewish women, while the disparity among men is only 4 percent (66 percent of Arab men were in the labor force in 2012, compared to 70 percent of Jewish men).[12] Still, among the employed there are gaps in earnings between Arabs and Jews because of insufficient employment opportunities in the vicinity of Arab towns, discrimination by Jewish employers, and competition with foreign workers in fields such as construction and agriculture.[13] But the inequality in earnings also stems from education gaps: the education level of Arabs is inferior to that of Jews in both duration and quality. Moreover, the majority of Arabs do not serve in the army; consequently, they are ineligible for many of the financial benefits that army service bestows, such as scholarships and housing loans.

The Ethnic Gap in Educational Attainment and Earnings The gap in educational attainment—as measured by mean years of schooling and share of population with a bachelor's degree—accounts for much of the persistent inequality in occupational status and earnings between Jews and Arabs, and between Ashkenazi and Mizrahi Jews. But this is only part of the story: the facts show that while the education gaps between the three major ethnic groups have actually narrowed over time, the *earnings* gaps have not.[14]

For example, the ratio of the share of native-born Mizrahi men with a bachelor's degree to their Ashkenazi counterparts climbed steeply between 1992 and 2001 (from 0.25 to 0.45), but the respective ratio of monthly earnings rose only slightly, from 0.64 to 0.68.[15] There are similar ethnic earnings

Figure 6.1 The Earnings Gap Among Workers Ages Twenty-Seven to Twenty-Nine Who Had Attended an Institution of Higher Education, 2005–2008

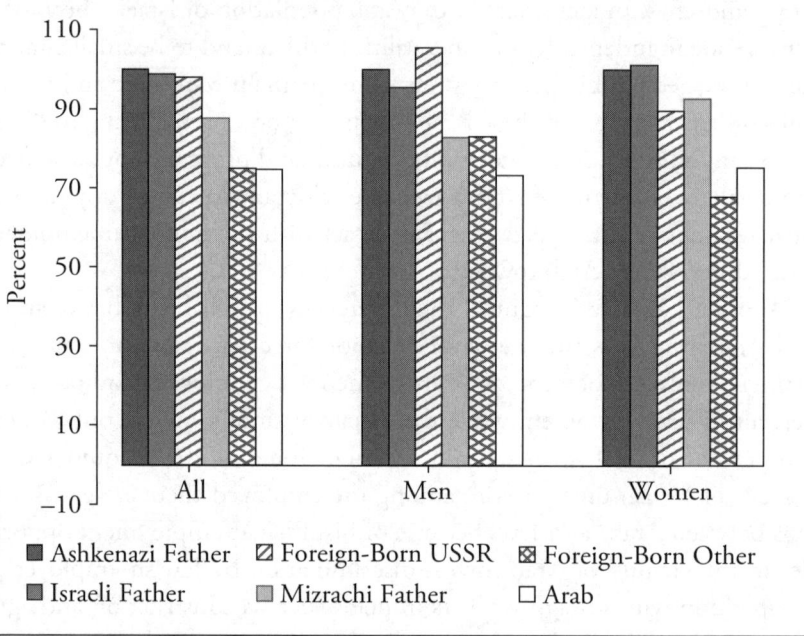

Source: Author's calculations from Israeli Income Surveys, 2005–2008 (see Alon 2015).
Note: Earnings of "Ashkenazi Father" = 100 percent.

gaps among bachelor's degree holders.[16] Between 2005 and 2008, second-generation Mizrachi men between the ages of twenty-seven and twenty-nine with some higher education earned a monthly salary that was 83 percent of that of similar second-generation Ashkenazi men (see figure 6.1).[17] Foreign-born men from the FSU enjoyed the highest pecuniary returns (106 percent that of Ashkenazi men), while recent male immigrants from other countries earned only 83 percent of what Ashkenazi men earned, and Arab men earned 73 percent.

There is clearly an earnings gap that is ethnicity-based even among recent cohorts of college-educated Israelis, and Arabs are still the most-disadvantaged group in terms of earnings. The overall increase in economic inequality in Israel during these years accounts for some of the mismatch between persistent ethnic earnings gaps amid narrowing education gaps. This trend is not unique to Israel: groups at the top of a hierarchy are better suited to take advantage of a rise in inequality while the position of those already at the bottom deteriorates. In addition, differences in the quality of education, including the type of degree attained by those who went to college, may also account for the persistent ethnic earnings gaps.

Spatial Inequality

Rich Versus Poor Communities In Israel, towns, cities, and localities vary greatly socioeconomically, and there is even further segregation at the neighborhood level. Poor people in Israel, as in other countries, tend to live in poor communities, and the rich tend to live among other wealthy people.

The Israel Central Bureau of Statistics classifies localities according to the socioeconomic level of their populations as determined by residents' financial resources, education levels, and employment profiles, as well as by the price of housing, the standard of living, various types of socioeconomic distress, and demographic characteristics. The index ranges from 1 (the lowest socioeconomic cluster) to 10 (the highest). The bottom four clusters represent deprived, or poor, localities, while clusters 8 through 10 are made up of the most-privileged, or wealthiest, localities.

Consider, for example, the towns of Shoham and Ofakim. Just before landing at Ben Gurion Airport, Israel's largest and only international airport, you can see Shoham from the air. It is a small town with a population of 20,000 residents.[18] Established in 1993, Shoham is twelve kilometers from Tel Aviv, the cultural and economic center of Israel. With its single-family houses and sprawling lawns, Shoham has a suburban feel. If you drive south of Shoham for about an hour, you will arrive at Ofakim, a town of about the same population, the majority of whom, as in Shoham, are Jewish.[19] This, however, is where the similarities end. Shoham and Ofakim differ in the socioeconomic levels of their populations, the services available to residents, and their distance from the economic center of Israel (the greater Tel Aviv area). Shoham is in the cluster 8 (wealthy), while Ofakim is in cluster 4 (poor).

As of 2010, only 9 percent of workers in places like Ofakim—the poor localities—held academic or managerial jobs, compared to over 40 percent in the wealthy localities—places like Shoham (see figure 6.2). This translates

Figure 6.2 Selected Characteristics of Local Authorities in Israel, by SES Cluster, 2010

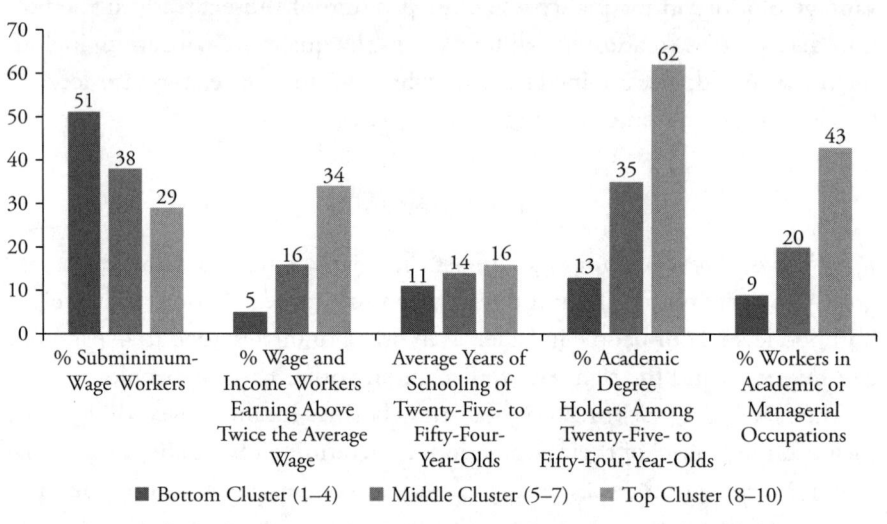

Source: Israel Central Bureau of Statistics (2010).

into huge discrepancies in income: the average monthly salary per capita in the deprived localities (the bottom four clusters) is only 23 percent of that in the wealthy ones. Half of the workers in the poor localities are what is referred to as the "working poor," meaning that their monthly salary is below the minimum monthly wage, while 34 percent of workers from the wealthy localities earn more than double the average monthly wage.

Underlying these income gaps are big differences in educational attainment. The average number of years of schooling in the deprived localities is eleven, compared to sixteen in the wealthy localities. Most people in the poor localities have only a high school education or less, while the vast majority of their counterparts in wealthy cities and towns have at least a bachelor's degree.

The Geographic Periphery Shoham and Ofakim also differ in their distance from the major metropolitan areas of Israel: Tel Aviv, Jerusalem, and Haifa. You do not see Ofakim as you land at the airport because it is about ninety kilometers from Tel Aviv. Because of Israel's small size, a distance of ninety kilometers from a major city is considered the geographic periphery.

Like several other towns in the geographic periphery, Ofakim is one of the "development towns" that the government established in the 1950s to absorb the massive influx of Jews—in particular, Mizrahis Jews—during those years. Between 1948 and 1957, more than half a million Jewish immigrants from Asia and Africa arrived in Israel. In 1951 alone, more than 100,000 immigrants arrived from Asia, and an additional 20,000 came from Africa. These immigrants, on average, were less educated than the Ashkenazi immigrants who had arrived before them. In a rush to find these Mizrachi immigrants a place to live, the government established twenty-seven new towns in just two years, between 1950 and 1951, and an additional twelve were founded by 1956. Most of these towns were built in the least dense parts of the country, either in the far south or the far north. In contrast, there was no settlement plan for the Ashkenazi immigrants who arrived from Europe in the years after 1948. They were mostly absorbed into existing cities and towns.

Over half a century later, most of Israel's development towns—indeed, 90 percent of them—lie in the bottom four clusters of the localities' socioeconomic cluster because of chronic neglect, the clustering of weak populations, and the scarcity of good jobs.[20] In this respect, their disadvantaged status has not changed much since the 1950s. More than half of the residents of the development town of Ofakim, for example, were eligible for government welfare benefits in 2010. Only one in three high school graduates had a diploma that met the requirements for university admission. Meanwhile, in Shoham, only 3 percent of residents were eligible for welfare, and 80 percent of high school graduates had a university-ready matriculation diploma. The demographic characteristics of development towns have also persisted. Even as late as 1995, more than half the residents of these towns were first- and second-generation Mizrahi Jews, who make up only about one-third of the general population.[21]

Living on the geographic periphery in Israel often translates into a life at the economic periphery, and it is a problem faced by Jews and Arabs alike. While development towns, populated largely by Mizrahi Jews, are concentrated in the south of Israel, the independent Arab localities tend to cluster in the north. Today about 43 percent of the Arab population (Muslim, Christian, and Druze) live in the northern part of the country, not including the city of Haifa.[22] In sum, Israel's development towns and Arab localities are a paragon of the overlap in geographic, ethnic, and economic systems of segregation.[23]

HIGHER EDUCATION IN ISRAEL

From the preceding review it should be clear that Israel is a country with persistent socioeconomic, ethnic, and spatial stratification, and its education system plays a key role in reproducing this inequality from one generation to the next. As in the United States, educational inequality in Israel begins with differences in the quality of K–12 education and extends to unequal access to postsecondary education. There are many important differences, however, between the structures of the postsecondary systems in Israel and the United States (see table 6.1), and the following section delineates some of them.

Differences Between Israeli and U.S. Postsecondary Systems

One difference between the two countries' higher education systems is governance. As in many European countries, the Israeli postsecondary system is centralized and funded by the state government. In the United States, conversely, state control of the system is indirect and often weak. In addition, the United States has a strong private sector for higher education that predates its public sector.

As of 2013, the Israeli higher education system consists of about seventy postsecondary institutions, which can be divided into two tiers. In the first tier are the six public research universities. The four most selective and internationally recognized among them are Tel Aviv University (TAU), The Hebrew University (HUJI), Ben-Gurion University (BGU), and The Technion (TECH). This book focuses on these four schools. The second tier includes many new "academic colleges," some of which are private, and most of which are the product of the massive expansion of the Israeli higher education system that began in 1995. The academic colleges grant bachelor's (and sometimes master's) degrees, but are not usually research institutions.[24] Admission to these colleges is substantially less selective than admission to the universities, and not surprisingly, the economic returns to their degrees are lower than the returns to degrees from the major universities.[25] Between 1994–1995 and 2012–2013, the total number of undergraduate students in Israel more than doubled, from 86,000 to 192,000 (see figure 6.3). This growth primarily

Table 6.1 Postsecondary Systems in Israel and the United States

	Israel	United States
Governance	• Centralized • Supervised by the Council for Higher Education • Mostly public	• Decentralized • State control - indirect and modest • Strong private sector
General characteristics	• Three years to attain a bachelor's degree • Low, standardized tuition (about $2,600 per year at public institutions) • No state financial aid	• Four years to attain a bachelor's degree • Varied and high tuition • Federal, state, and institutional financial aid
Application and admission	• High school graduates apply to majors (single/dual) • Professional education—undergraduate level • Mechanistic admission decision	• High school graduates apply to institutions • Professional education—graduate level • Mechanistic admission decision at large institutions • Holistic admission decision at small institutions
Stratification in kind	• Admission cutoff point is major-specific • Within-institution differences in selectivity	• Admission cutoff point is institution-specific • Between-institution differences in selectivity

Source: Author's calculations.

stemmed from the addition of second-tier institutions, but the number of undergraduates at the six universities also rose.

Another major difference between higher education systems in the two countries is that the duration of study for most bachelor's degrees in Israel is three years, as in most of Europe, as opposed to four years, as in the United States. Moreover, the tuition at Israeli public universities is relatively low (about $2,600 per year), and there is no state-funded financial aid. Tuition in the United States is much higher, and there is a strong infrastructure for financial aid, in the form of both grants and loans, at the federal, state, and institutional levels. The typical first-year bachelor's student in Israel is also

Figure 6.3 Number of Undergraduate Students in Institutions of Higher Education in Israel, by Type of Institution, 1980–2013

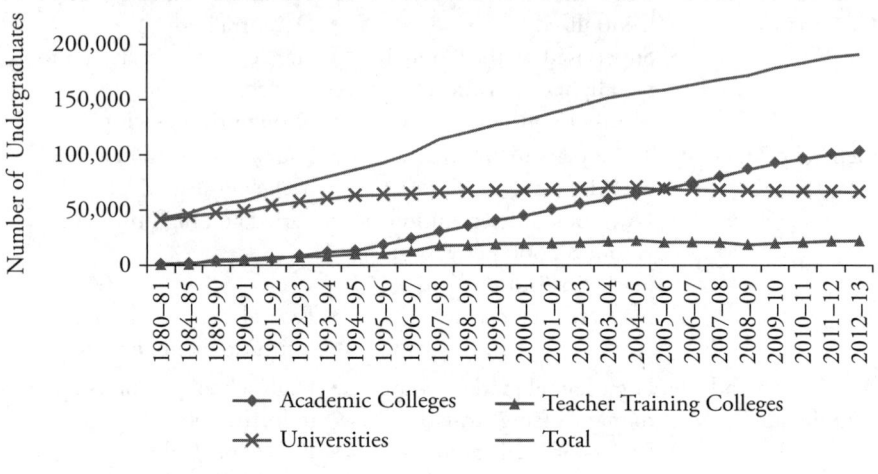

Source: Israel Central Bureau of Statistics 2014, "Table 1: Students in Institutions of Higher Learning, by Level of Degree and Type of Institution."

older than his or her American counterpart, with a median age of twenty-five; 67 percent of freshmen at four-year colleges in the United States are between fifteen and nineteen years old.[26] This difference is partly attributable to mandatory military service in Israel.

The admission mechanisms in the two countries are also very different. The selection process at the first-tier universities in Israel is entirely formulaic and based on an academic composite score, which is essentially a weighted mean of an individual's matriculation diploma grades and psychometric test score (similar to an SAT score). This mechanistic approach is actually somewhat similar to that of many large U.S. public universities and very different from the holistic comprehensive review processes that most private American colleges and universities favor.

The disparities between the countries in their admission processes go even deeper. In Israel, prospective undergraduate students apply to departments—to a specific major or field of study within the institution—and not to the institution generally. In the United States, prospective undergraduates commonly apply—and are admitted—to a college or university generally, not to a department within it (although applying to a department is common at the master's and doctoral levels). American undergraduates, then, usually do not have to choose their major or field of study until a year or two into their studies, while the admission decision in Israel is major-specific at the outset. This practice has led to departments being more or less selective within each Israeli institution. Inequality by field of study is an especially important factor in Israel because most professional degrees (law, medicine, accounting, and so on) are studied at the undergraduate level.[27] In the United States, by contrast, what matters more initially is the selectivity of the institution. Although U.S. universities and colleges are also organized according to academic disciplines, fields vary with respect to power, prestige, and economic payoffs in the labor market.[28]

Degrees in science, technology, and the professional fields pay off the most in the Israeli labor market, and as a result it is harder for prospective students to gain admission to these fields of study (see table 6.2).[29] Leading the pack in terms of both selectivity (measured by the annual admission rate of each major and the mean test scores of admits) and the starting monthly salary of recent graduates are various engineering programs, the computer sciences, medicine, the exact sciences, law, pharmaceutical studies, and economics. (Some of these degrees are not even offered at the second-tier academic colleges.) In the two most lucrative sectors of the labor market, finance and high-tech, most workers—especially those with the most lucrative jobs—hold a bachelor's degree from one of the selective universities. Degrees from these universities, especially from their most competitive departments, are key for economic and social mobility in Israel. At the bottom of the selectivity and earnings hierarchies are several fields in the humanities and social sciences.

Growing Competition in Admission

One would think that the spectacular expansion of the Israeli higher education system that began in the mid-1990s would have eased the competition for spots at the elite institutions and the most selective departments within them. In fact, the competition has only intensified over the last two decades as elite universities in Israel have become even more selective. All over the world, selective colleges and universities offer students a high-caliber educa-

Table 6.2 The Average Monthly Salary of Male University Graduates During Their First Two Years in the Labor Market, by Field of Study and University, 1999–2002

Major	Monthly Salary	Major	Monthly Salary
Electrical engineering	19,470 NIS[a]	History and philosophy	9,628
Medicine	19,139[b]	Biomedical engineering	9,243
Computer sciences	17,016	Communication	9,065
Industrial and management engineering	14,651	Accounting	8,100
Mathematics and computer science	13,815	Sociology	7,906
		Psychology	7,772
Mathematics	13,127	Geography	7,706
Physics	12,466	Chemistry	7,657
Chemical engineering	12,109	Architecture	7,576
Mechanical engineering	11,942	Nutrition sciences	7,438
Engineering—other	11,788	Art	7,328
Law	10,817	Agricultural sciences	6,984
Physiotherapy and occupational therapy	10,750	Regional studies and foreign languages	6,972
General studies (social sciences)	10,469	Social work	6,867
Management	10,145	Geology	6,844
Nursing	10,103	Molecular biochemistry	6,701
Statistics	10,089	Education	6,557
Pharmacy	10,032	Medical laboratory sciences	6,545
Political sciences and international relations	10,025	Biology	6,056
Economics	9,974	Hebrew, linguistics, and literature	5,647
Civil engineering	9,802	Jewish studies	5,591

Source: TAU, HUJI, BGU, and TECH administrative data.
Monthly salary of university graduates during their first years in the labor market following graduation, by field of study and by institution was obtained from the Israel Central Bureau of Statistics (draws from the administrative records of the state tax authorities) and was merged with the universities' administrative data (Israel Central Bureau of Statistics (2012c)).
[a]Salaries are given in 2004 new Israeli shekels (NIS).
[b]Based on information from Israel Doctors Association for the lowest rank, including pay for additional work.

tion in terms of faculty, institutional resources, exposure to cutting-edge research, and high-performing peers. This is no different in Israel, and university type does not go unnoticed by Israeli employers: in every field, the economic returns on degrees obtained from the top universities are higher than returns on those obtained from the second-tier colleges.[30]

The demand, then, by top students for admission to the top universities, especially in their most lucrative and selective fields, rose because of the economic premium of these degrees. Each year between 1999 and 2008 it became more difficult than the year before to get access to these schools. Thus, even as the system expanded with more seats and more institutions, the admission rates at the elite universities dropped. Between 1999 and 2003, for example, the aggregate admission rate at TAU, HUJI, BGU, and TECH dropped from 67 to 53 percent (although it partially rebounded afterwards, reaching 59 percent in 2008; see figure 6.4). Not only did the universities admit a smaller share of applicants, but the admitted applicants also had higher test scores. Between 1999 and 2008, the mean test score of admits to the top four schools rose by about 30 points, from 626 to 654 (scores range between 400 and 800; see figure 6.4). Given that the national distribution of test scores is standardized so that the mean is constant over the years, this finding suggests that the best applicants are more and more attracted to the elite universities, despite the emergence of new schools in the second tier. As a result of the growing demand for a university education, the departments at the top four universities have, on average, become more selective over time (measured by the annual admission rate of each major and the mean test scores of admits). The overall selectivity level of university departments (the selectivity index ranges from 0 to 1) rose from about 0.53 in 1999 to 0.61 in 2007 (see figure 6.4). Consequently, as in the United States, the growing volume of applicants seeking seats at elite schools allowed admissions offices to pick and choose from among the top applicants. This surely affected all applicants, but the most affected were underprivileged applicants—the poor, ethnic minorities, and those from deprived localities.

Variation Between Groups in Field of Study

Several groups are underrepresented at the top universities in Israel in comparison to their shares of high school graduates, especially within the most

Figure 6.4 Competition in Admission to TAU, HUJI, BGU, and TECH, 1999–2008

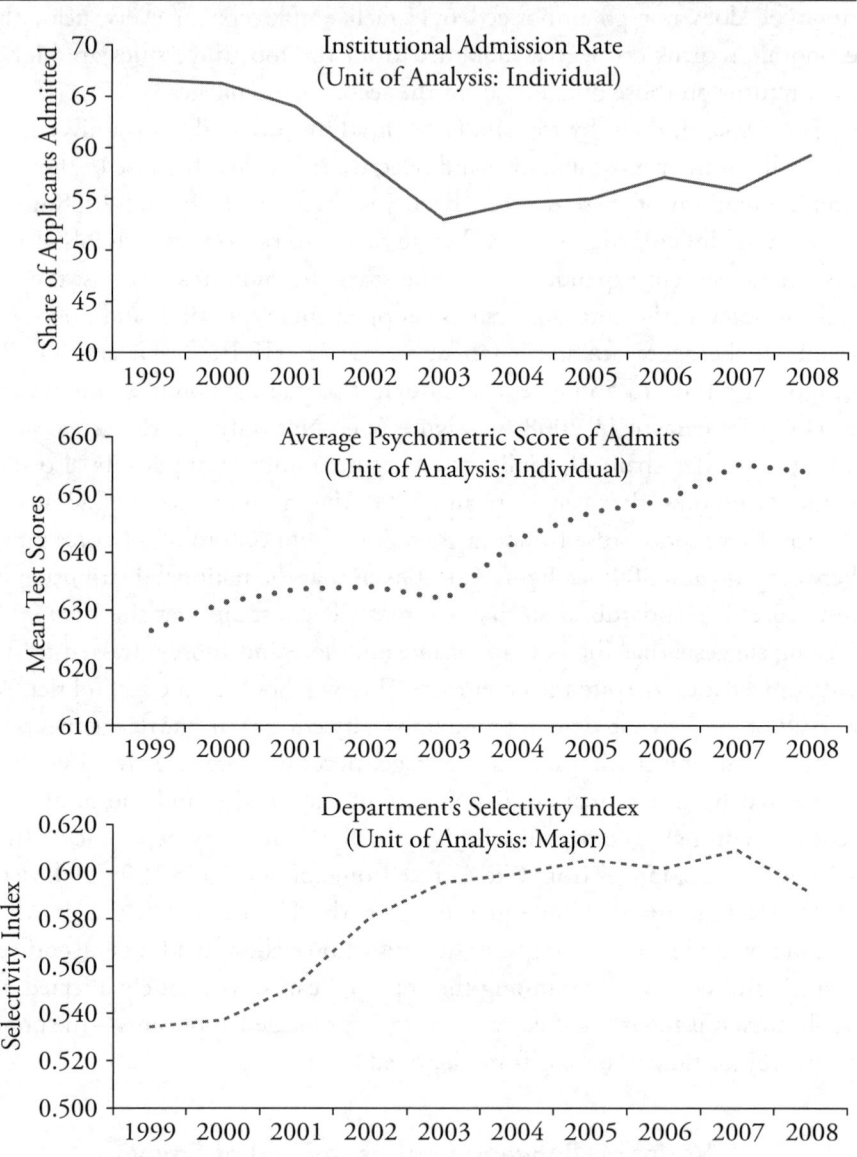

Source: TAU, HUJI, BGU, and TECH administrative data, 1999–2008.

selective, prestigious, and lucrative departments of these institutions. Among these groups are the country's ethnic minorities—namely, Arabs and Mizrahi Jews (though the latter are not a minority in size)—whose test scores and high school academic achievements trail those of Ashkenazi Jews. In 2006–2007, for example, Mizrahi university graduates were overrepresented in the humanities and social sciences but underrepresented in medicine, life sciences and mathematics, and engineering and architecture.[31] The main reason for this variation between ethnic groups was the disparity in K–12 academic preparation. For example, Jewish applicants whose parents both originated in Asia or Africa (second-generation Mizrachis) had the lowest average test scores among Jews of all other ethnic origins.[32]

This ethnic variation in fields of study ensures an ethnic gap in earning potential as soon as university graduates enter the labor market, owing to differences in the type of diploma attained. In a previous study, I examined the expected salary of Jewish university graduates by type of degree and ethnic origin group between 1999 and 2002.[33] Leading the pack were graduates who immigrated from the FSU, together with veteran Ashkenazi graduates (native-born Israeli Jews with one parent born in Europe or America and one native-born parent). Second- or third-generation Mizrachi graduates and second-generation Ashkenazi graduates were in the middle tier, with an expected monthly salary, by major, that was 95 to 96 percent that of their FSU-born counterparts for males, and 94 to 95 percent for females. First-generation male and female immigrants from other (non-FSU) countries were in the bottom tier; their expected salary, by major, was only 91 percent of that of their FSU-born counterparts.

The picture for the Arab population is more complex. Not only do Arab university applicants have lower test scores than Jews (Mizrachis and Ashkenazis), but their application pattern is very different from that of Jews, and much more skewed. Arab applicants demonstrate a very strong tendency toward the medical and health professions, at the expense of technology and engineering fields, compared to Jewish university applicants with similar academic backgrounds.[34] More than 20 percent of Arab university applicants between 1997 and 2008 ranked medical school, the most selective field, as their first choice, compared to only 10 percent of Jews. In contrast, 23 percent of Jews listed an engineering or computer science field as their first choice, while only 16 percent of Arabs did. Six percent of Arab graduates from the four universities during that period received a medical degree as compared to only 2 percent of Jews. Yet only 10 percent of Arab graduates obtained a degree in engineering or computer sciences as compared to only 16 percent of Jews.

Apart from ethnic groups, other types of groups are also underrepresented in selective universities and fields: youth from poor neighborhoods, remote towns, or poor families, as well as first-generation college students. This is still the case even after a decade of class-based affirmative action. Take, for example, the representation of students from poor localities (the bottom four clusters), where about one-third (36 percent) of the Israeli population resided in 2008.[35] Only one-quarter of the student body at the four selective universities came from a poor locality, and in the most selective majors only 15 percent did.[36] Students from the geographic periphery were also underrepresented: about one-third of the Israeli population resided in the northern and southern districts, but these residents made up only 17 percent of seats at the top four universities.[37] In the most selective fields, only 12 percent of students came from these two districts. Conversely, the Central and Tel Aviv districts were overrepresented, with 60 percent of admits, even though these districts accounted for only about 40 percent of the population. In the most selective majors, three out of four admits came from these two districts! Yet fewer than 1 percent of students in these selective fields came from development towns.

Thus, despite the great expansion of the Israeli postsecondary education system, the first-tier universities, especially their most prestigious departments, have remained out of reach for most high school graduates. Inequality of educational opportunity has become less about differences in "degree" (whether one attends college or not) and more about differences in "kind" (the type of institution one attends and the type of degree attained). Today in Israel, as in the United States, the key contours of inequality in higher education are institution type and field of study.

ISRAEL'S CLASS-BASED AFFIRMATIVE ACTION PROGRAM IN HIGHER EDUCATION

In an attempt to remedy the glaring underrepresentation of several population groups in their student bodies, Israel's top four universities implemented an affirmative action program during the early to mid-2000s: HUJI in 2001,

TAU in 2003, TECH in 2004, and BGU in 2006. Given the multiple contours of inequality in the country and the universities, several approaches to preferential treatment—class-, geography-, or ethnicity-based—could theoretically have served the purpose of expanding educational opportunity to disadvantaged groups. So which direction did the universities choose, and why?

A Brief History of Affirmative Action in Israel

The story begins in 1994, when the Buchmann Faculty of Law at Tel Aviv University wanted to embark on an experiment in affirmative action, under which twenty students whose academic composite score was lower than the general threshold for admissibility would be admitted.[38] The force behind this initiative was Menachem Mautner, a professor of comparative civil law and jurisprudence at the law school, who was influenced by the debate about affirmative action in American colleges. He looked around his contract law class and noticed that most of his mostly Ashkenazi students came from affluent neighborhoods in Tel Aviv and nearby cities. Missing from his class list were students from poor neighborhoods, poor localities, and development towns and Arab students.

Professor Mautner approached the admission committee of the law faculty with a proposal for a "special admission" program whose purpose would be to enhance diversity in the school's very homogenous student body, and the committee complied. They consulted with the Association for the Advancement of Education (AAE), a nonprofit organization that oversees boarding high schools catering to underprivileged youth and post–high school preparatory programs that help individuals meet the requirements for university entry. Until the 1980s, the selection criteria for the (limited number of) preparatory programs was ethnic: they were designed for Mizrachi Jews who had just completed their mandatory military service but did not have a university-ready high school diploma. As the programs expanded, the selection criteria changed and became focused on class. AAE now defined its target population as "eligible for advancement," which later became the name of the affirmative action program implemented by the universities.[39]

Building on AAE's long-standing experience with university preparatory programs, the law school's admission committee decided to adopt its mechanism for selecting high-achieving underprivileged youth. Professor Mautner explained later that in the deliberations about the main criteria for eligibility the committee members kept emphasizing that the main criterion for eligibility under the scheme should not be the individual hardship or adverse circumstances of the applicant. They wanted eligibility to focus on structural and spatial inequality.

When the plan was not approved by the Senate of Tel Aviv University, a fierce debate was ignited within academic circles, the media, and even the Knesset, the national legislature, or parliament, of Israel. Supporters of the university Senate's decision argued that universities "cannot jeopardize academic excellence," while opponents criticized the Senate for reinforcing the status quo of universities as "bastions of privilege." One-third of the Knesset—40 out of 120 members—signed a letter denouncing the decision and implicitly threatening to intervene in the matter. (The letter mentioned that the state budget financed a significant part of higher education.)

The TAU Senate decision clearly touched a nerve, exposing deep frustrations about the Israeli higher education system. As a result of the controversy, the Senate reconvened a few months after having rejected the plan to reconsider the decision. This time, minding public discontent and political pressure, the special admission program for the Buchmann Faculty of Law at Tel Aviv University was approved for a trial period of three years.

The first cohort to benefit from the special admission program began in the law school in the 1995–1996 academic year. In 1998 TAU decided to expand the special admission program to include the Faculty of Social Sciences, and in 2001 the Faculty of Exact Sciences. By 2003 the program was in place throughout the entire university. Other institutions followed suit: The Hebrew University of Jerusalem adopted the program in 2001, as did The Technion in 2004 and Ben-Gurion University in 2006. Not only did all four universities adopt the program in its original form, as first implemented at TAU's Faculty of Law, and use the same eligibility formula, as designed by AAE, but they also outsourced the sorting of applicants to AAE.

Like affirmative action programs in American higher education, the special admission program adopted by Israel's four flagship universities is entirely voluntary. In fact, in 2001 the Israeli Knesset's education committee considered proposing a bill that would impose affirmative action at the universities but decided that it was better to find a plan that was acceptable to the institutions rather than forcing one upon them. Moreover, as described in the next section, each university department has the discretion to pick and choose from among the applicants eligible for affirmative action consideration and can even reject them all.

The Design of Eligibility for Advancement

The Israeli affirmative action program is wildly innovative in its hybrid design:

1. It is class-based with an emphasis on structural determinants of inequality.
2. It is need-blind but considers some types of individual hardship.
3. It is completely race-neutral.
4. It relies on information that is available in the public record and easily verifiable.

Although the policy is class-based, it is not based on individual indicators of income or wealth. Rather, the notion of disadvantage is based on three parameters, all of which relate to the high school years only:

1. *Structure of opportunity:* Both neighborhood socioeconomic status[40] and high school socioeconomic status are considered.[41]
2. *Socioeconomic status:* Parents' education and the applicant's family size are taken into account.
3. *Individual hardship or adverse circumstances:* Also considered is whether an applicant is an orphan, an immigrant, a single parent, a divorced person or the child of divorced parents; suffers from a health disability or has a parent with a disability or chronic illness; or has experienced the death of a sibling. The parents' unemployment status is considered as well.

How is all this information measured and weighted? Each indicator is worth a set number of points, for a maximum of eighty-five possible points; the threshold for disadvantage-based eligibility is thirty points. The heaviest weight is given to the first parameter, the two structural factors: neighborhood of residence (twenty points) and high school attended (twenty points). Together, these two structural indicators account for almost 50 percent of all points and surpass the eligibility threshold. (The weighting algorithm is de-

Figure 6.5   Disadvantage-Based Eligibility for the Israeli Affirmative Action Program

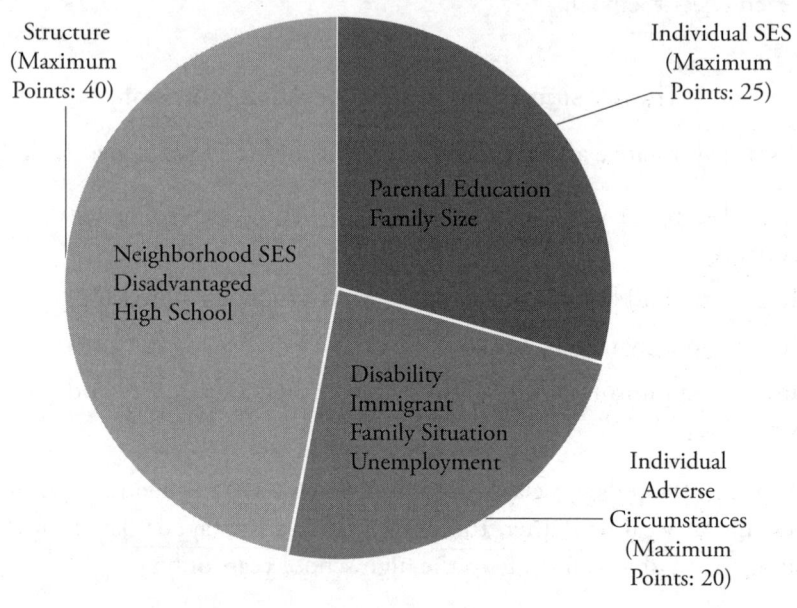

Source: Author's calculations.
Note: All data collected are from applicants' high school years only. The threshold score is thirty points, and the maximum score is eighty-five points.

picted in figure 6.5.) Substantially fewer points are granted for the second parameter, socioeconomic status: having a parent with no more than a high school education translates into five points (for each parent), while a parent with only an elementary school education equals seven points. Applicants with more than three siblings receive two points for each extra sibling.

As for the third parameter, each individual or family adverse circumstance is worth between five and fifteen points, for a maximum of twenty possible points in this category. This twenty-point cap is in line with the original desire of the program's founders at TAU's Faculty of Law that the program emphasize structural and spatial inequality rather than individual hardship or adverse circumstances. Thus, an applicant from a poor neighborhood who attended the only high school in the area is almost certain to pass the eligibility threshold, whereas it is almost impossible for an applicant without either structural disadvantage to make the cut.

To see this mechanism at work, consider Sarah, who applied for affirmative action when applying to university in the early 2000s.[42] Sarah was raised in a remote development town in southern Israel. The program's guidelines deem both her town and high school to be disadvantaged. She also had other hardships. Her parents, who immigrated to Israel from Morocco in 1956, were not college-educated. Moreover, her father died when she was a child, leaving her mother with the task of supporting Sarah and her four siblings as a single parent on a maid's salary.

Sarah passed the threshold for disadvantaged status based on the first two structural factors alone. Her other hardships, such as being the first in her family to attend college and being raised by a single parent, elevated her score further. Sarah's circumstances clearly illustrated the overlap between systems of inequality: those who grow up in poor neighborhoods and attend underprivileged schools are also likely to be poor and to suffer from other disadvantages. Yet, for the purpose of establishing her disadvantaged status, Sarah's additional hardships were redundant. The universities treat everyone whose score passes the cutoff point the same, so there is no extra advantage in having a score above 30.

The points garnered from disadvantaged socioeconomic status and individual circumstances—categories 2 and 3—can be significant, however, for those applicants with only one structural disadvantage (a poor school or neighborhood, but not both) or none at all. For example, consider Jacob, whose father died when he was a child and whose brother and unemployed mother both suffer from serious disabilities. No one in his family ever attended college. At the time of his application, his family lived in his grandmother's small apartment and subsisted on government welfare. Despite these setbacks, he graduated from high school and scored high on his standardized exams. Neither the neighborhood that Jacob lived in nor the high school he attended were classified as disadvantaged, so without either structural disadvantage, he was not likely to qualify as disadvantaged for the special admission program. But because Jacob had so many other hardships "working" for him, his points for socioeconomic status and adverse circumstances together (categories 2 and 3) were just barely enough to put him above the eligibility cutoff, with a score of 32.

Figure A6.2 illustrates how the eligibility score is calculated using the case stories of real applicants, such as Sarah and Jacob. I discuss these and other examples throughout the book.

The Stages of Implementation of the Class-Based Affirmative Action Program

The program is implemented in four stages (see figure 6.6):

Stage 1: Applying for Affirmative Action All prospective students can apply for affirmative action by submitting the standard application for preferential treatment, substantiated with documentation, along with their university applications. Applicants send the affirmative action application directly to the Association for the Advancement of Education. Thus, an applicant's eligibility for the affirmative action program is established outside of the universities.

Stage 2: Determining Affirmative Action Eligibility AAE examines all applications submitted for preferential treatment, verifies the information, and then assigns each applicant an index score of disadvantage by weighting the information provided. The organization then reports each applicant's score to the universities but does not reveal which determinants were used to calculate it. Scores range from 0 to 85, where the threshold for disadvantage-based eligibility is a score of 30, as determined by the universities. Once an applicant has passed the cutoff point, her score—that is, how disadvantaged she is and why—has no bearing on the admission decision (so a score of 85 would render no extra benefit over a score of 30). Applicants do not know the weighting algorithm used, nor whether they have met the thirty-point cutoff, when applying to university and selecting their majors.

Stage 3: Determining Academic Eligibility Passing the thirty-point threshold on the disadvantage-based index does not guarantee that an applicant will benefit from an edge in university admission. To be eligible for preferential admission, an applicant must also have an academic composite score that falls just below the admission cutoff of his or her desired field of study. Thus, in the third stage, academic eligibility is determined for those who passed the threshold for affirmative action eligibility. Academic eligibility is granted to those applicants with borderline achievements—that is, whose academic index score is around 0.5 to 1.0 standard deviation below the admission cutoff point of each major or department. Thus, the final pool of applicants eligible for preferential treatment in admissions consists of those applicants who have met the standards for both disadvantaged status and academic eligibility. Nonetheless, admission is not guaranteed even to those who pass all stages of eligibility.

Figure 6.6 The Stages of Implementation of Israel's Affirmative Action Policy

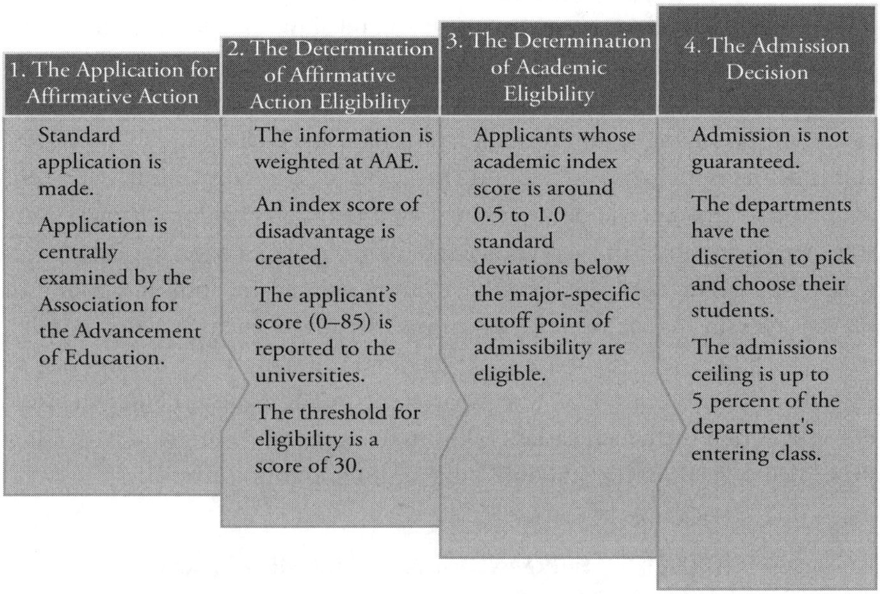

1. The Application for Affirmative Action	2. The Determination of Affirmative Action Eligibility	3. The Determination of Academic Eligibility	4. The Admission Decision
Standard application is made. Application is centrally examined by the Association for the Advancement of Education.	The information is weighted at AAE. An index score of disadvantage is created. The applicant's score (0–85) is reported to the universities. The threshold for eligibility is a score of 30.	Applicants whose academic index score is around 0.5 to 1.0 standard deviations below the major-specific cutoff point of admissibility are eligible.	Admission is not guaranteed. The departments have the discretion to pick and choose their students. The admissions ceiling is up to 5 percent of the department's entering class.

Source: Author's calculations.

Stage 4: Making the Admissions Decision   Even those who pass both stages of sifting—for example, an applicant who scored above 30 on the disadvantage-based index and whose academic index score is less than half a standard deviation below the major-specific admissions cutoff—are not guaranteed admission to their major of choice. To repeat, this special admission program is voluntary at both the university and department levels—all university departments have the discretion to pick and choose from among the applicants who are eligible for affirmative action consideration and are even free to reject them all. The departments are free to consider all the information available in an applicant's file, mainly matriculation diploma grades and psychometric test scores. While these two are used to form the composite academic score, a department may decide to give extra consideration to some components of this score. For example, a science department may give extra weight to the quantitative section of the psychometric test or to science grades in high school.

In sum, an edge in admission is only granted to applicants who pass the thirty-point cutoff for disadvantaged status *and* have an academic composite score very near a department's admission threshold *and* are chosen by the department. Out of the approximately 180,000 applicants to the four universities since the beginning of the program until 2008 (the year when the data for this investigation were collected), about 5 percent sought preferential treatment (receiving some score on the disadvantage-based index), and two-thirds of them met the thirty-point threshold for eligibility. Thus, 3 percent of all applicants met the disadvantage-based requirements for affirmative action (see figure 6.7). The acceptance rate of affirmative action applicants was about 55 percent, compared to 57 percent in the general applicant pool. (To prevent certain majors from being saturated with affirmative action admits, there is a 5 percent cap on the share of these admits in the entering class of each department, but only a few departments reach this cap.) Since the start of the program the beneficiaries of affirmative action in admission have comprised 3.6 percent of the student bodies at the top four universities.

ISRAEL'S AFFIRMATIVE ACTION PROGRAM: CHARACTERISTICS, RATIONALE, AND THE QUESTION OF DIVIDENDS

Theoretically speaking, the Israeli affirmative action program falls under the rubric of a multidimensional design (prototype 3) given that it considers and gives weight to both structural and individual disadvantages, thus combining both microjustice and macrojustice paradigms. In practice, however, structural factors dominate the eligibility algorithm with their heavy weight (twenty points each) and the program functions most like the structural model (prototype 2). The fact that information about individual financial circumstances is neither requested nor considered also puts the program in line with the structural prototype, in that group affiliation is more important than individual circumstances. In this sense, the Israeli design is similar to race-based models, which also emphasize group affiliation and a macrojustice rationale.

Even though a race-based program would be even easier to implement than one based on a structural model, there are several practical and political considerations that worked in favor of the Israeli model. First, the emphasis

Figure 6.7 Affirmative Action (AA) Status of Applicants to the Four Top Israeli Universities, from the Start of Each University's AA Regime to 2008

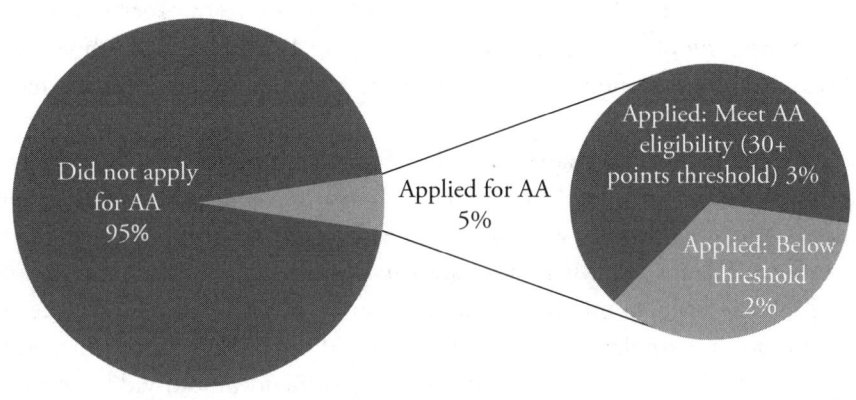

Source: TAU, HUJI, BGU, and TECH administrative data.

on group membership in the Israeli program, as in the American race-based model, simplifies the sorting mechanism and enhances its feasibility. The need-blind nature of the program allows it to steer clear of collecting information about an applicant's financial standing, which is difficult to verify, easy to manipulate, invasive of privacy, and often unreliable. The focus on structural inequality facilitates administration because information about an applicant's place of residence and high school is available in the public record and easily verifiable, as are documented life events. Second, while it is true that models based on group affiliation can lead to creaming, its severity is mitigated because, although they are not the dominant indicators, some socioeconomic and individual hardship indicators are also taken into account, unlike in the race-based and purely structural prototypes. Finally, being race-neutral allows this program to bypass the kind of criticism that basing eligibility on ascribed traits tends to provoke. Together, these two features, feasibility and race-neutrality, were decisive in pushing Israeli universities toward this unique affirmative action model.

Although this program is much easier to implement than any model that focuses on individual economic status, making implementation feasible is not a goal in and of itself. The objective of any affirmative action policy, whether based on race or class, is to diversify the student body of selective institutions and majors, to improve mobility, and to train the next generation of leaders, professionals, and role models. The question, then, is whether this kind of class-based program is truly able not only to promote the social and economic mobility of disadvantaged populations in Israel but also to boost demographic, socioeconomic, and geographic diversity at the country's most selective universities.

Perhaps the most fascinating question, however, is to ask how diversity and mobility would have fared in a program based on ethnic affirmative action instead. In other words, what would the diversity and mobility dividends have been if Arabs and Mizrahi Jews, the two ethnic groups at the bottom of the Israeli socioeconomic ladder, were given an edge in admission instead? This question is similar to the one at the core of the debate about affirmative action in the United States: how do the diversity and mobility dividends of current race-based policy measure up against those that could be advanced by a class-based policy? What diversity and mobility dividends would result from giving the edge in admission to students from poor high schools instead of to members of minority groups? Or to those from poor families? Or to those from both? These issues are at the heart of the comparative investigation in this book.

PART IV

Implications for Feasibility and Diversity

CHAPTER 7

The Feasibility and Diversity Dividends of Affirmative Action Policy in Israel

The contours of inequality in Israeli society are many. The ethnic and national cleavages—between Jews and Arabs, between Jews of different origins—have shaped Israel's stratification system and resulted in a clear hierarchy in educational attainment, occupational status, and earnings that has persisted over the last sixty years. In addition, economic inequality has been growing at an alarming pace, and spatial boundaries are as important as they were fifty years ago. People on the bottom rungs of the socioeconomic ladder see their chances for a better future declining from year to year. For them, as for their counterparts in the United States, a college degree is crucial for climbing the socioeconomic ladder. But the selective universities that offer the best chance for mobility remain bastions of privilege, despite the expansion of the Israeli postsecondary system over the last two decades.

The argument in support of affirmative action practices in admissions is that they can widen the gate to selective universities and selective fields of study for underrepresented populations. The policy route that the elite universities in Israel embarked on in the mid-2000s is focused on class, with a particular emphasis on structural determinants of disadvantage, in particular neighborhood socioeconomic status and high school rigor. (Some individual hardships are also weighed.) And yet the policy is completely need-blind—that is, the financial status of applicants is not a factor in eligibility. The policy is also entirely race-neutral in that the ethnic origins of applicants are ignored. It is precisely this unique race-ethnicity-blind and need-blind design that makes the Israeli program in the wake of the Fisher decision—which, by tightening the scrutiny on the consideration of race in U.S. college admissions amplified discussions about moving from race to class in affirmative action—a valuable example for American universities to consider, as well as a useful touchstone for this investigation.

There were many good reasons to choose this race-neutral model, and convenience was one of them: the design of the Israeli affirmative action program simply skirts the issue of the persistent ethnic rifts in Israel. Although this model of selection was already in use by the Association for the Advancement of Education in selecting underprivileged candidates for preparatory programs for universities studies when it was chosen as the model for the affirmative action program, the program architects' desire to avoid a sensitive political subject was surely another strong motivation to go in the direction of the class-based design. If such a discussion about affirmative action in Israeli higher education is ever held, it will most likely center on whether the universities should adopt a race-based policy, as has been done in the United States, India, and South Africa. However, any proposal for ethnic-conscious admissions—that is, special consideration for Arabs and Mizrachi Jews—would probably be controversial.

Echoing the "creaming" arguments against race-conscious admissions in the United States, some Mizrachi Jews, who comprise about half the Jewish population, would probably be labeled "undeserving" of admission because many among them are privileged, wealthy, and working in professional occupations. The same claim could be made against Arabs. Although, in general, Arabs are indeed the most-disadvantaged minority group in Israel in educational attainment and socioeconomic prospects, many are professionals (doctors, lawyers, architects) and businesspeople who hold lucrative positions and send their kids to private schools. Surely their offspring would be in the best position to take advantage of an ethnic-conscious admissions policy if it were implemented. In addition, there would most likely be a national outcry toward giving Arabs special treatment—either because they do not participate in many civic duties, such as military service, or because of racism. Still, the barriers to access to higher education faced by ethnic minorities, especially Arabs, are persistent. The Planning and Budget Committee (PBC), a subcommittee of the Council for Higher Education in Israel that oversees the higher education system, is "working to increase the accessibility of the Arabs,

Druze and Circassians in Israel's higher education system, and recently formulated a holistic program that handles complex barriers found throughout the continuum from high school to advanced degree attainment and labor market integration."[1]

Adopting a model of class-based policy allowed the Israeli universities to skirt a direct debate about the dividends of ethnic-conscious admissions. Thus, the question relevant here is one that was not asked: could an ethnic-blind program diversify the student body of elite universities successfully? How would the ethnic-blind program currently in place compare with a hypothetical program based on ethnic-conscious admissions in terms of diversity dividends? Which model of affirmative action—ethnic- or class-based—could produce higher levels of broad diversity along geographic, economic, and demographic lines within elite Israeli universities?

These questions are timely and extremely relevant not only for Israel but also for the debate in the United States and in other countries about the shift from race to class as the focus of affirmative action. The problem is that most of the discussion so far has been theoretical. Yet given how compelling this issue is, we need hard evidence regarding the diversity dividends of race- and class-based affirmative action programs.

To answer these questions, I conducted simulations that compared the actual class-based policy in Israel to a simulated ethnic-based alternative. The findings, based on extensive data and simulation exercises, provide valuable and intriguing (at times even surprising) insights into the debate about generating diversity using race-neutral tools. In this chapter, I focus in particular on the actual diversity dividends of the class-based policy currently in place compared to the diversity dividends that an ethnic-based alternative would potentially deliver.

DATA

As explained in chapter 6, the Israeli higher education system is a two-tiered system, and in the first tier are the four most selective and internationally recognized research universities: Tel Aviv University (TAU), The Hebrew University (HUJI), Ben-Gurion University (BGU), and The Technion (TECH). These four universities are the only schools that incorporated the class-based affirmative action plan throughout the 2000s, and the program is still in effect today at all four schools.[2] I obtained institutional administrative data directly from the admissions offices of these four universities.[3] This rich data set contains application information, admissions decisions, and student transcripts. The data cover the cohorts who applied to these schools between 1999 and 2008, but most of the analyses focus on the period after affirmative action policy was implemented at each university (hereinafter referred to as the "AA regime"). Under the AA regime, there were around 180,000 applicants and 100,000 admits.[4]

The university admissions process in Israel is different from that in the United States. As in most European countries, application and admission are major-specific: applicants state their major preference when filling out the application form, and admissions decisions are then made by the relevant department. What makes the Israeli data set so attractive for an investigation of affirmative action policy is the availability of both applicant transcripts and information about admissions decisions, by institution and per major. Moreover, it is possible to identify all affirmative action applicants, admits, and students. In contrast, it is difficult to identify affirmative action applicants and admits in U.S. data sets: studies on affirmative action in the United States generally use race or ethnicity as a proxy for affirmative action eligibility in determining admission likelihood given academic achievements.[5] Race and ethnicity, however, are not perfect indicators of affirmative action eligibility because not every minority applicant receives an edge in admissions. In particular, highly qualified minority applicants do not need an edge in admission, while minority athletes may be admitted because of preference for athletes, not because of race-conscious admissions.[6] In the Israeli data, there are no questions about the affirmative action status of each applicant.

The Israeli selection process for bachelor's admissions is formulaic, based entirely on an academic composite score, which is calculated by taking a weighted mean of the individual's matriculation diploma grades and psychometric test score. This formulaic admissions process is another advantageous aspect of the Israeli data, because it implies that we have access to all the information that determines admission. This level of certainty is difficult to obtain when studying elite American institutions, owing to the holistic nature of their admissions decisions. Even the most detailed empirical specifications cannot fully characterize an applicant's admissibility in the eyes of admissions officers in the United States.

Field-of-Study Stratification

Variation in the selectivity level of fields of study is a key contour of inequality in Israeli academia, since the admissions decision is major-specific within each Israeli institution. Altogether, there are 164 departments at the four elite institutions in Israel, representing approximately 13 disciplines or 50 general fields of study. To make sense of this variety, I characterized each department by its level of academic selectivity: the more selective the department, the more demanding its admission requirements and the more rigorous its academic environment. I then measured the selectivity level using two factors: the annual admissions rate of each major, and the mean test score of admits. I could then rank each department on an annual selectivity index ranging from 0 to 1, based on these two factors.

I classified the departments and majors in the top quintile of the selectivity index as "most selective." This category includes the medical sciences, engineering, computer science, architecture, and psychology—departments that tend to be associated with professional fields. Some of these programs—such as medicine, engineering, and architecture—require between four and six years of study, which is significantly longer than the typical three-year bachelor's program. The demand for these programs is high: about 43 percent of applicants in this study included at least one major from the top quintile of selectivity in their major choice set, but only 20 percent of the students studied in one of them. The mean test scores of admits to these departments was about 700, which is 160 points above the national average score of 540. Only 5 percent of the test-takers received a score above 700 (800 points being the maximum).

Consider, for example, the medical school at Tel Aviv University: it admitted about 15 percent of applicants between 1999 and 2008. Their average test scores was 740. The TAU computer engineering department admitted 22 percent of applicants, with an average score of 722. At The Technion, about one-third of applicants for a joint degree in electrical engineering and physics were admitted, with an average score of 730. To appreciate how selective these departments are, consider, for example, the TAU geography department, which admitted 70 percent of applicants (mean test score of 570), or the European studies department at The Hebrew University, which admitted 80 percent of applicants (mean test score of 580). Both these departments are in the bottom quintile of the selectivity index, representing departments that are not in high demand: fewer than 4 percent of applicants chose these departments, and only 10 percent of all university students enrolled in them. Still, the fact that the mean test scores of admits to these least selective departments were above the national average highlights how selective these Israeli universities are.

FROM CLASS TO RACE IN AFFIRMATIVE ACTION

The analyses compare the actual class-based policy in place to a simulated model of ethnic-conscious admissions. The simulations respond to the contours of persistent ethnic inequality in Israel: Ashkenazi Jews are at the top of the socioeconomic ladder, followed by Mizrachi Jews, while the Arab citizens of Israel are at the bottom. The simulations allow us to examine what the diversity dividends would have been if the slots that were granted to affirmative action admits under the current class-based scheme (hereinafter "class-based admits") had been allocated to the ethnic minorities in Israel instead—namely, Arabs and Mizrachi Jews—under an ethnic- or race-based scheme (hereinafter "race-based admits").

To assess this hypothetical scenario, I conducted simulations for the years of the AA regime. I identified all the applicants during those years and divided them into three groups by major. Later I juxtaposed and compared these groups, which include both real and potential admits:

1. *Class-based admits:* The beneficiaries of the actual class-based affirmative action program
2. *Race-based admits (simulated):* The beneficiaries of a hypothetical race-based affirmative action program
3. *Non-AA admits:* The admits who did not get an edge in admission (that is, who were not eligible for the actual class-based affirmative action)[7]

In the simulations, the slots filled in each major by class-based admits were reallocated to ethnic minorities who had applied but were rejected, according to the following procedure:

Step 1: Identifying actual class-based admits: I identified the beneficiaries of the program in each major, for every institution, in every year, exploiting the ability to single out all affirmative action applicants and admits. I then reassigned them to the overall applicant pool for their major, thus allowing the ethnic minorities among them to become candidates for the simulated ethnicity-based preferential treatment. I set aside the seats in each major occupied by the class-based admits for place holding and referred to them as "vacant slots."

Step 2: Identifying potential race-based admits: For each major and in every year, I identified applicants from the two ethnic minority groups (Arabs and Mizrachi Jews) who were rejected from the university departments and classified them as potential race-based admits. I conducted the main simulations for applicants who were *either* Mizrachi Jews or Arabs. To assess the implications of giving special consideration to only one of the two ethnic groups, I conducted additional simulations for each ethnic group separately: one for Mizrachi Jews only, and one for Arabs only.[8]

Step 3: Reallocating the vacant slots: I filled the vacant slots I created in step 1 in each major and in each year with applicants from the pool of potential race-based admits. I selected them based on their academic standing (academic composite score), proceeding from highest to lowest until all vacant seats were filled. This process mimicked the mechanistic admission process at Israeli universities.

To illustrate this process, consider the following example. In 2006 seven of the applicants admitted to the economics major at one of the elite universities were given an edge in admissions via the class-based affirmative action program. During the first stage of the simulation, I removed these class-based admits from the department and reassigned them to the non-AA pool, leaving seven empty seats in that major. In the second stage, I identified all of the rejected applicants that year to the department of economics who were either Arabs or Mizrachi Jews and classified them as potential race-based admits ($n = 337$). I also identified any of the seven original class-based admits who belonged to an ethnic minority as potential race-based applicants. I then selected the seven among the 337 ethnic minority applicants with the highest academic composite scores to fill the seven vacant slots in the economics department.

This procedure maintains the share of affirmative action admits in any incoming class. However, the beneficiaries of the edge in admission are now race-based admits instead of class-based admits.

To respond to the institution-major-specific nature of application and admission processes at Israeli universities, I conducted the simulations per institution per major per year, replacing every class-based admit in every major in which they were enrolled and including every minority applicant in the potential race-based applicant pool of all the departments to which they applied in a specific year. If, for example, a class-based admit was enrolled in both the economics and statistics departments in 2006, she was replaced with a minority applicant in both departments. Likewise, if an Arab applicant was originally denied admission to both the biology and chemistry departments in 2007, she would be included in the potential race-based applicant pool of both departments in that specific year.

THE DIVERSITY DIVIDENDS: CLASS-BASED (ACTUAL) VERSUS RACE-BASED (SIMULATED) AFFIRMATIVE ACTION POLICY

The simulations allow us to gauge which model of affirmative action—race- or class-based—can produce higher levels of broad diversity along geographic, economic, and demographic lines within elite Israeli universities. To compare the diversification effects of class-based policies versus race-based ones, I juxtapose and compare the real and potential pools of admits. As mentioned, the departments and majors within a given university in Israel vary greatly in selectivity level: the more selective the department, the more demanding its admission requirements and academic environment. Given the differences in selectivity level between departments, it is especially important to assess whether the diversity dividends reach the more-selective programs, where student demand and academic requirements are high and disadvantaged groups are consequently most underrepresented. To examine the reach of the diversification effects—that is, to determine whether the most selective departments experience a boost in diversity—I present two sets of figures in the following subsections: one set reflects the entire body of admitted students at the flagship institutions, and the other focuses only on the most-selective departments.[9]

Academic Selectivity

One of the allegations against race-conscious admissions in U.S. college admissions is that these policies, by promoting the access of minority applicants with low academic achievements, lower academic standards at elite universities and damage their institutional standing. By default, the average test scores of students admitted via affirmative action programs, whether race- or class-based, are lower than those of the non–affirmative action pool of admits. Yet the results of the Israeli simulations reveal that shifting from the actual class-based policy to a hypothetical race-based one would not lower the degree of academic selectivity at Israeli universities. In fact, race-based admits have higher average test scores than do class-based admits (see figure 7.1).

Specifically, class-based admits score, on average, forty-six points lower than do non–affirmative action admits. Given that test scores range from 400 to 800, this is a gap of about 10 percent. The gap between race-based admits and the non-AA pool (those not eligible for the current class-based policy) is smaller: twenty-seven points, or about 7 percent. Nonetheless, additional simulations conducted separately for each ethnic group reveal that ethnic-conscious admissions designated to benefit only Arabs would yield a substantially weaker student body. In other words, race-based admits are academically stronger than class-based admits because of the high test scores of Mizrachi Jews.

The story is somewhat different when it comes to the most-selective departments, such as medicine and several engineering and computer science departments. Here race-based admits have higher average test scores than both the non-AA and class-based admits. Why did applicants with such high test scores need preferences in admissions (class-based admits) or find themselves denied admission altogether (race-based admits)? The answer lies in the major-specific admission system: highly qualified applicants can be rejected from an extremely selective major—medical school, for example—but probably could have been admitted to another less-selective major. The higher scores of class-based and race-based admits compared to non-AA admits reveal that these applicants applied to extremely selective majors—more so than the general pool of applicants—and highlight the fact that the beneficiaries of affirmative action are highly qualified students.

In sum, whether race-based affirmative action in Israel would produce a stronger student body than class-based policy *depends on which minority groups are considered*. The student body generated by a race-based policy that draws from both ethnic minority groups (Arabs and Mizrachi Jews) would be academically stronger than the student body generated by the class-based

Figure 7.1 Mean Test Scores of Actual and Simulated Admits to Israeli Universities, AA Regime

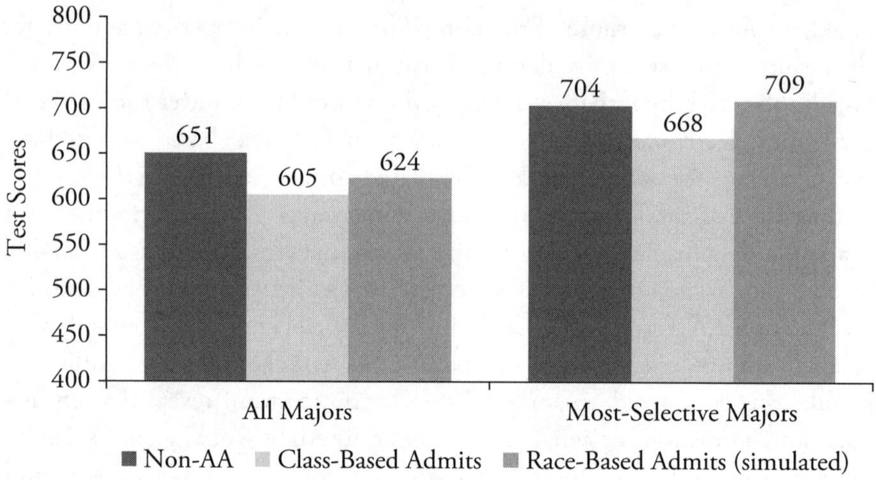

	All Majors	Most-Selective Majors
Non-AA	651	704
Class-Based Admits	605	668
Race-Based Admits (simulated)	624	709

Source: TAU, HUJI, and BGU administrative data, AA regime.

policy currently in place. Thus, *race-based affirmative action would strengthen, rather than weaken, the academic standing of elite universities compared to the current class-based policy. However, the opposite would be true if the race-based affirmative action were to target the Arab population only.*

DEMOGRAPHIC DIVERSITY

In Israel demographic diversity reflects not only different ethnic origins but also residents' immigration status, as separately considered in this section.

Ethnic Origin

All (simulated) race-based admits, by default, are ethnic minorities—either Arabs or Mizrachi Jews. Class-based affirmative action, by contrast, draws from all races and ethnicities and thus would never be able to achieve the level of ethnic diversity generated by race-conscious tools. The level of ethnic diversity, then, would be significantly higher under a race-based regime than

Figure 7.2 The Share of Arabs and Mizrachi Jews Among Actual and Simulated Admits to Israeli Universities, AA Regime

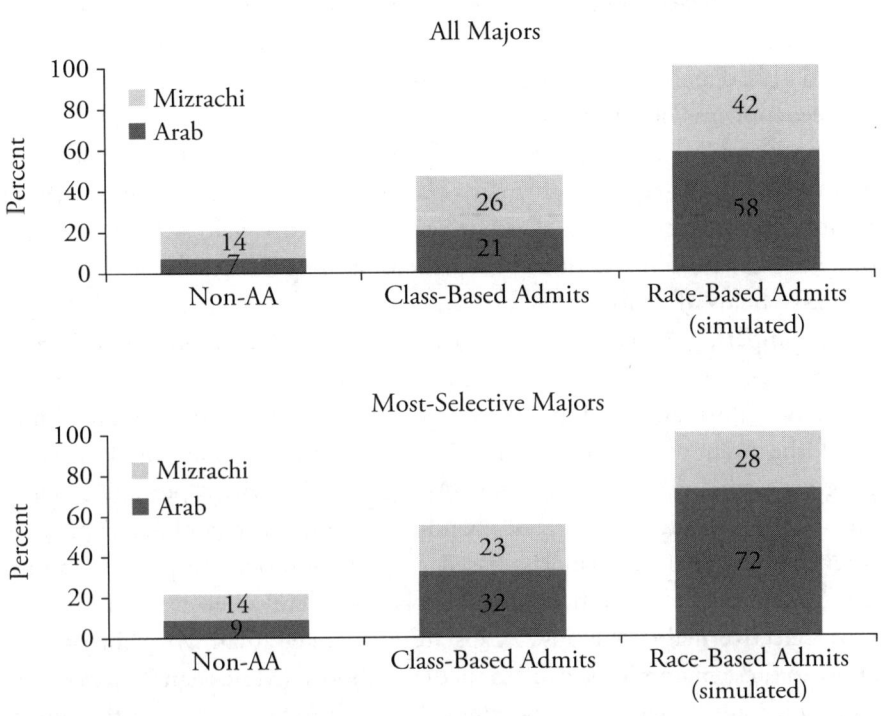

Source: TAU, HUJI, and BGU administrative data, AA regime.

under the current class-based one. Nonetheless, given the race-neutral nature of class-based policy, it is quite remarkable that about half of all class-based admits are ethnic minorities (see figure 7.2). Clearly, a policy that addresses spatial and school inequality stretches the diversity dividends to include national and ethnic origins as well. The ethnic diversification effect is especially strong within the most-selective majors: 55 percent of class-based admits were ethnic minorities, compared to only 23 percent among non-AA admits (figure 7.2).

Take, for example, the electrical engineering department at Tel Aviv University, which is considered one of the most selective university departments in Israel, given that fewer than one in three applicants is admitted.

The percentage of ethnic minorities among non-AA admits was only 17.2 percent, which is much lower than the share in the entire student body (22 percent). The class-based policy increased their share in this department to 17.7 percent. If the policy had been race-based, the share of ethnic minorities in this department would have grown to 18.4 percent. Given that a degree from this department is one of the most lucrative in the labor market and provides access to the booming high-tech sector in Israel, it is noteworthy that both types of affirmative action open the gate to more ethnic minorities, who are typically underrepresented in this field. Chapter 9 elaborates on the mobility dividends of widening the path to such selective and lucrative fields of study.

In comparing the two ethnic groups, Arabs would gain more than Mizrachi Jews from race-based affirmative action. Under a hypothetical ethnicity-race-based affirmative action regime, 58 percent of affirmative action admits would be Arab, compared to only 21 percent under the current class-based program and 7 percent among non-AA admits. Forty-two percent of race-based admits would be first- and second-generation Mizrachi Jews, compared to 26 percent in the actual class-based program and only 14 percent among non-AA admits. The Arab edge is especially evident when we consider the most-selective majors, because Arabs are more likely than Mizrachi Jews to apply to these majors, especially to medical schools. (More than 20 percent of Arab applicants ranked medical school as their first choice; this was the choice of only 10 percent of Jews.) Arabs also benefit more than Mizrahi Jews from the current class-based program, mainly owing to the level of residential and school segregation between Jews and Arabs in Israel. Arabs and Jews do not generally live in the same neighborhoods and do not send their children to the same schools. Even in Jerusalem, Haifa, and Tel Aviv–Jaffa—the three largest cities in Israel, all with significant numbers of both populations—Arabs and Jews tend to reside in different neighborhoods. In fact, most of the Arab population (about 65 percent) reside in independent Arab localities.[10] This issue is discussed further in the next section.

Although Arabs are one of the groups that have benefited from the current class-based program in Israel, they would benefit even more from a race-based program. The question, however, is whether ethnic-conscious admissions could garner the necessary public support in Israel. The extra dividends in terms of ethnic diversity might come at the price of stigma and controversy. Thus, the question is not only about the potential racial-ethnic diversity dividend of the program but also about its ability to mobilize and sustain public support. After all, as argued in chapter 5, the motivation behind affirmative action policy is important for its survival. Without strong public support, the diversity dividends would be short-lived.

In sum, *affirmative action limited to ethnic minorities produces a higher level of demographic diversity than race-neutral affirmative action.* By focusing on class, the current policy realizes half of this potential demographic diversity.

Immigration Status

Dmitry immigrated to Israel with his parents in 1990 at the age of twelve from the Former Soviet Union (FSU). That same year Marina immigrated from the Ukraine with her parents, at the age of fifteen.[11] A decade later, both applied to selective departments at one of the top four universities. Did Dmitry and Marina benefit from the class-based affirmative action program in place? If so, how and to what extent?

The representation of first-generation immigrants is another parameter of demographic diversity in higher education. Under current program guidelines, immigration status is considered a criterion of disadvantage, but it has very little weight—immigration status points alone bring an applicant nowhere near the eligibility threshold. Moreover, the pool is limited to only the most recent of immigrants because only those who immigrated within seven years of applying to university are eligible for the few points based on immigration status. The problem is that very few such new immigrants are able to acquire enough Hebrew and the proper academic qualifications within seven years to even consider applying to one of Israel's most selective universities. Thus, the program is not geared at promoting eligibility based on immigration status, and this is mainly because first-generation immigrants, on the whole, are not underrepresented at the flagship schools. Fourteen percent of all admits to Israeli universities under the AA regime are foreign-born, and the majority of them are from the FSU (65 percent).[12] This is impressive given that the share of foreign-born in that age group (ages fifteen to twenty-four) in the Jewish population is 13 percent.[13]

And yet, despite this, the findings demonstrate that a large share of affirmative action beneficiaries are first-generation immigrants, accounting for 20

Figure 7.3 The Share of Immigrants Among Actual and Simulated Admits to Israeli Universities, AA Regime

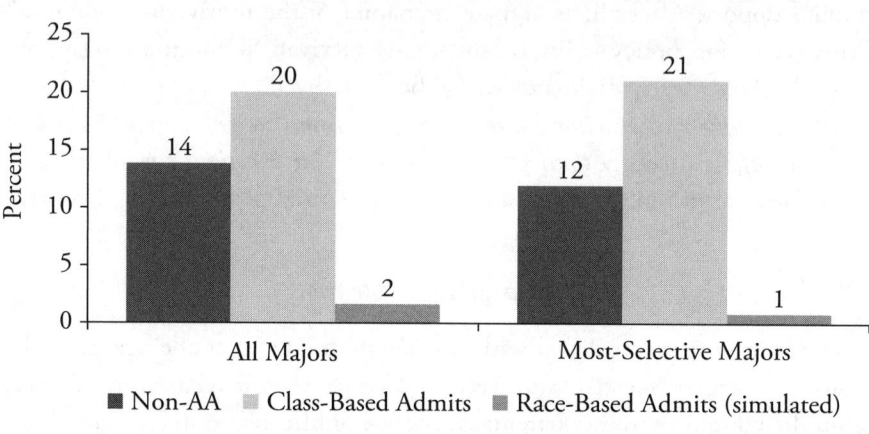

Source: TAU, HUJI, and BGU administrative data, AA regime.

percent of class-based admits (figure 7.3). This overrepresentation is even more striking when we consider the alternative: under race-based affirmative action, only 2 percent of affirmative action admits would be foreign-born. That is, the largest group of recent immigrants to Israel—Jewish immigrants from the FSU—would not benefit from an affirmative action program based on race or ethnicity because such a program would be likely to target only Arabs and those with origins in Asia or Africa. But the question remains: how is it that so many immigrants gain from the class-based program, given that immigration status is a relatively minor factor with limited eligibility?

It is likely that class-based admissions policy benefits recent immigrants by tapping into their residential and school segregation, in addition to other types of disadvantage. In other words, with regard to affirmative action, first-generation immigrants seem to benefit more from their structural disadvantages than from their immigration status. On the one hand, FSU immigrants, as a group, tend to be highly educated, to value education, and to be highly motivated. In another study, I show how these tendencies translate into an ambitious major choice set when they apply to the universities studied here.[14] FSU immigrants have high aspirations and a predilection for applying to the STEM (science, technology, engineering, and mathematics) fields, which are typically more selective and lucrative. The most lucrative field in the major choice set of about 35 percent of male FSU immigrants was engineering, which tops the list of starting salaries. This percentage is high relative to other male applicants: about 30 percent of veteran Ashkenazi and only 20 percent of immigrants from non-FSU countries had an engineering field in their major choice set. Eventually, based on the major of graduation, FSU immigrants lead the pack among university graduates in terms of expected salary.[15]

On the other hand, FSU immigrants have difficult circumstances that are related to being uprooted from their country. They may not get many points for their immigration status, but they tend to have other kinds of hardships—broken families, single-parent households, parents with health issues, bad neighborhoods—that elevate their eligibility score for the affirmative action program.[16] The results reported in this section suggest that many of these ambitious immigrants are served well by a policy based on class and structural hierarchies. They benefit from the program not as we would necessarily expect (immigration status) but rather from a mix of other disadvantages. This is another example of how the policy works in indirect and unexpected ways by tapping into the overlap between different realms of underprivilege.

Indeed, both Dmitry and Marina were eligible for class-based affirmative action because both resided in the poor neighborhoods of larger cities during high school. Marina also received points for being the first in her family to go to college, and Dmitry, despite having attended one of the best high schools in the country and having two parents with bachelor's degrees (from the FSU), received extra points on account of his mother's disability. With this slight edge in admission, both were admitted to selective university departments.

In sum, *foreign-born university applicants in Israel—most of them from the Former Soviet Union—benefit from class-based affirmative action much more than they would from a race-based program, in large part because of their structural disadvantages and other socioeconomic hardships, not solely because of their immigrant status.*

SPATIAL DIVERSITY

Although Israel is a small country (about the size of New Jersey), there is substantial variation among the cities and towns. Some localities are affluent, and some are poor. Some are close to economic centers and can provide ample employment and good jobs; others are "abandoned" on the geographic and economic periphery. Even within towns and cities there is variation between neighborhoods, sometimes just a block apart: simply crossing the street can reveal the difference in life chances between neighborhoods.

The opportunities of youth and adults are shaped to a large extent by where they live. The structure of opportunity for all residents is shaped by levels of poverty, crime, and pollution, the quality of schools, labor market opportunities, and the marriage market—all of which overlap. With segregation and low levels of residential mobility, what the sociological literature calls the "neighborhood effect" tends to endure.[17] Thus, place plays a major role in the development of a child's potential. Spatial stratification embodies the overlap between geography, ethnic inequality, educational and occupational opportunities, and other disadvantages. In this section, I examine the student body representation of students from poor communities, geographically remote locales, and development towns—the last of which exemplify the overlap of systems of segregation.

Poor Communities

In the previous chapter, I documented substantial disparities between localities in Israel in terms of the socioeconomic level of their populations, as determined by financial resources, employment profile, educational attainment, and the demographic characteristics of their residents. There are ten clusters on this index: the bottom four clusters represent deprived, or poor, localities, and the top clusters 8, through 10, contain the most privileged, or wealthy, localities. To illustrate the differences in life chances for residents in these different localities, consider the following: the average monthly per capita salary in the poor localities is only 23 percent (less than one-quarter) of the average salary in the wealthy localities. These income gaps are linked to disparities in education levels: the average number of years of schooling in the deprived localities is eleven, compared to sixteen in the wealthy ones. Thus, it should come as no surprise that youth from poor localities are underrepresented in the student bodies of Israeli universities. Thirty-six percent of the Israeli population resided in poor localities in 2008, yet only one-quarter of university student bodies came from poor localities; in the most-selective majors, only 15 percent did (figure 7.4).[18]

The question at hand is this: is the class-based affirmative action program

Figure 7.4 The Share of Actual and Simulated Admits to Israeli Universities from the Bottom Cluster (1–4) on the Localities Socioeconomic Index, AA Regime

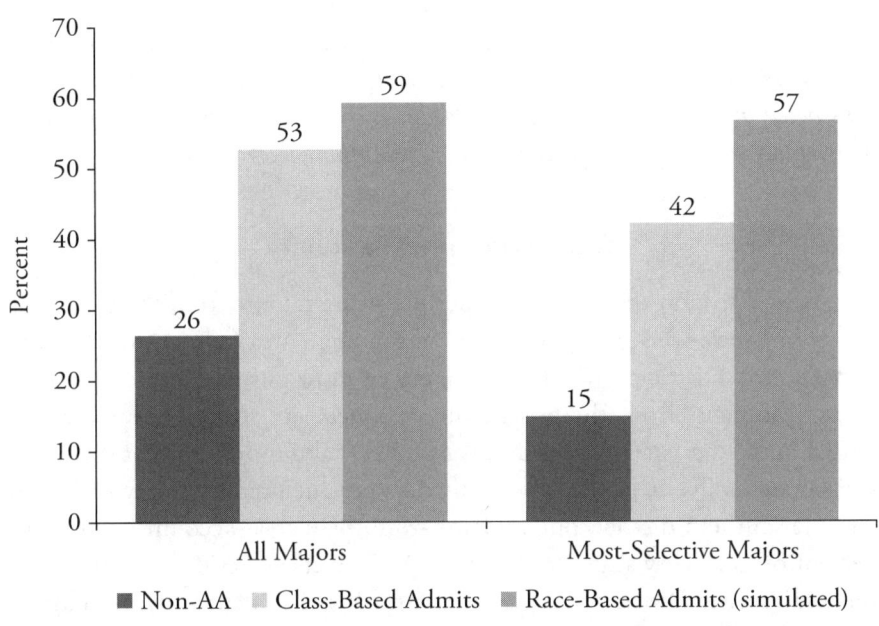

Source: TAU, HUJI, and BGU administrative data, AA regime.

at the elite universities effective in drawing talented youth from poor localities? The answer is yes. The program enhances the level of sociospatial diversity not only at these institutions but also in their most-selective departments. About 53 percent of all class-based admits were from poor localities, as were 42 percent of class-based admits in the most-selective departments. Nonetheless, it appears that a race-based program could do this even better: nearly 60 percent of the simulated race-based admits came from poor localities.

Given geographic segregation and its overlap with ethnic and national divides, it makes sense that ethnic-conscious admissions would bring applicants from poor localities to the fore. Eighty percent of independent Arab villages and towns rank in the bottom third of the socioeconomic index, and most development towns and many poor neighborhoods are populated with Mizrachi Jews.[19] Yet ethnic-based policy would benefit only the members of the ethnic minority group who reside in poor localities; their next-door neighbors who are not Arabs or Mizrachi Jews would be excluded from the assistance of such an affirmative action program.

In sum, *the class-based model of affirmative action enhances sociospatial diversity at selective universities, and in the selective majors within them, but a race-based model would do so even more effectively. The difference is that under the class-based model all residents of poor localities could potentially benefit from the preferential treatment policy, regardless of their ethnic background.*

The Geographic Periphery

Israelis who live on the geographic periphery are remote from the economic center of Israel—the greater Tel Aviv metropolitan area (namely, the Central and Tel Aviv Districts), which is the locus of most business and cultural activities. Students from the geographic periphery are strikingly underrepresented in the top Israeli universities: as of 2011, about one-third of the country's residents live in the northern district (not including the city of Haifa) and the southern district, but students from these areas account for only 17 percent of university seats (see figure 7.5). Conversely, residents of the Central and Tel Aviv Districts are overrepresented in the student body, accounting for 60 percent of admits, even though these districts are home to only 40 percent of the population. Moreover, in the most-selective majors, three out of every four admits come from these two districts! (see figure 7.6).

How does affirmative action policy fare when applied to students from the geographic periphery? It appears that both the actual class-based and the simulated race-based programs are successful at infusing elite universities, especially the most-selective departments, with students from the geographic periphery. About 40 percent of AA admits, under both class- and race-based schemes, come from Israel's southern and northern regions. Thus, admits from the geographic periphery are overrepresented in both pools of affirmative action admits, not only relative to their meager numbers among non-AA admits (17 percent) but also compared to their share in the general population (32 percent). The effect of geographic diversification is even more pronounced in the most-selective departments. Yet, while the class-based affirmative action program draws students from the southern and northern districts of Israel equally, the race-based model strongly favors admits from the north-

Figure 7.5 The Districts of Residence of Actual and Simulated Admits to Israeli Universities Relative to the General Population, All Majors, AA Regime

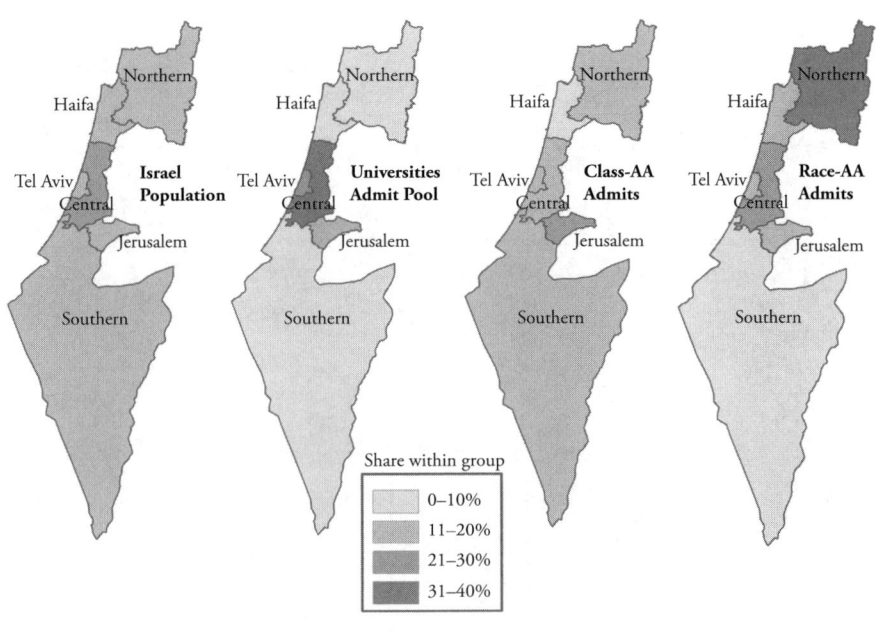

Source: Population figures from ICBS (2011a); TAU, HUJI, and BGU administrative data, AA regime.

ern district. This is because Arabs, who are concentrated in the northern region, benefit from race-based affirmative action more than Mizrachi Jews. Thus, the geographic diversity generated by the class-based model is more balanced, and it also opens the gates of the elite universities to applicants from the southern part of Israel. Therefore, although the level of geographic diversity generated by the class-based and race-based models is similar, the reach of the class-based affirmative action is more evenly widespread geographically.

In sum, *both the actual class-based and the simulated race-based affirmative action programs bring more students from the geographic periphery to Israel's elite universities—including their most-selective departments—than would otherwise be the case, but the geographic diversity generated by the class-based model is more widespread than that generated by the race-based model.*

Figure 7.6 The Districts of Residence of Actual and Simulated Admits to Israeli Universities Relative to the General Population, Most-Selective Majors, AA Regime

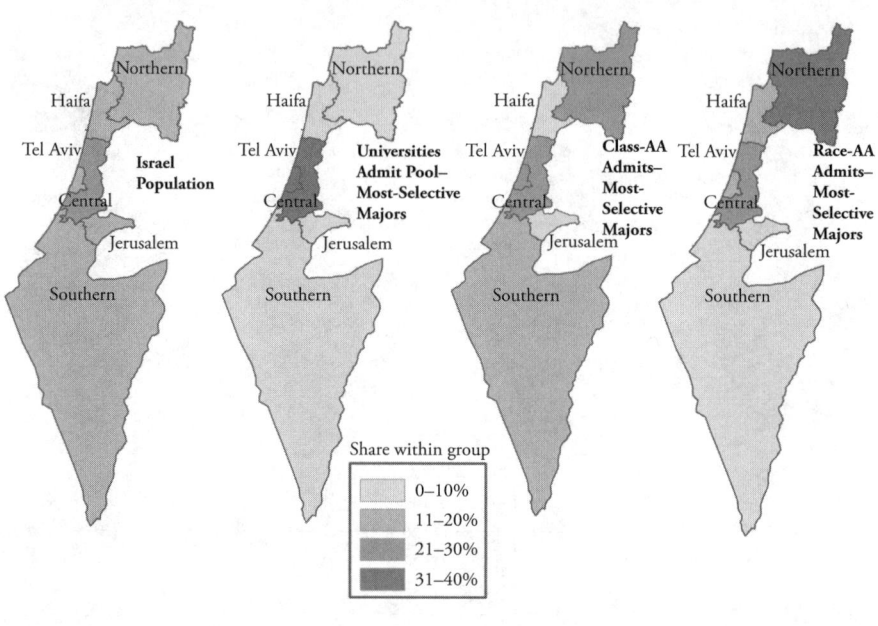

Source: Population figures from ICBS (2011a); TAU, HUJI, and BGU administrative data, AA regime.

Development Towns

The development towns epitomize the overlap of geographic, ethnic, and economic systems of segregation in Israel.[20] Established by the Israeli government to absorb the massive influx of Mizrachi Jewish immigrants during the 1950s, they are located on the geographic periphery and home to a socioeconomically weak population. For example, in Ofakim, the small development town in the southern part of Israel discussed in chapter 6, only one in four eighteen-year-olds had a high school matriculation diploma that met the basic requirements for university admission in 2010. It is not surprising, then, that youth from development towns such as Ofakim are underrepresented in Israeli universities.

Figure 7.7 The Share of Residents of Development Towns Among Actual and Simulated Admits to Israeli Universities, AA Regime

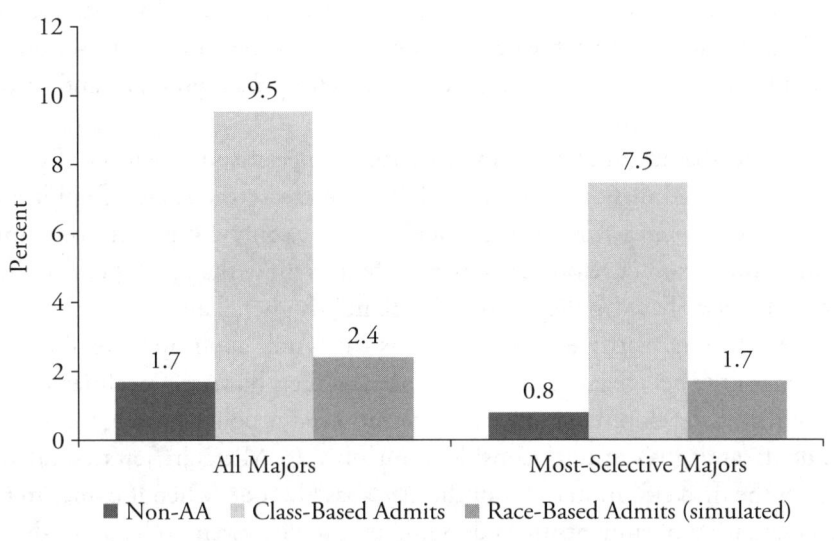

Source: TAU, HUJI, and BGU administrative data, AA regime.

In the last chapter, we met Sarah, a university student who was raised in Ofakim. Both her town and high school are classified as disadvantaged in the class-based affirmative action program guidelines. These two factors alone gave her enough points to pass the eligibility threshold for affirmative action when she applied to university in the early 2000s. She was the first in her family to go to college, despite the tough circumstances at home. (Recall that her mother supported Sarah and her four siblings on a maid's salary after Sarah's father died when she was young.) At the elite universities in Israel, students like Sarah are few and far between. Only 1.7 percent of students come from development towns (figure 7.7), and in the most-selective fields of study fewer than 1 percent do. Are affirmative action programs capable of drawing in students from development towns considering their stark under-representation in Israeli universities?

If we focus on the actual class-based program, we find that the almost 10 percent of class-based admits under the AA regime came from development towns (7.5 percent in the selective majors). Sarah was one of them. Despite her difficult circumstances, she graduated from high school with high test scores and a university-level matriculation diploma. This against-the-odds achievement was almost, but not quite, good enough to gain entrance to a leading law school. With the edge in admission that her affirmative action eligibility granted, however, she was accepted, achieved a high GPA, and graduated with a law degree.

The race-based simulations indicate that a special consideration of ethnic minorities in admissions would do little to increase the share of applicants from development towns. Under such a scheme, only 2.4 percent of admits would come from development towns, which is more than a 75 percent drop from the class-based policy and only slightly higher than the share among non-AA admits. Partly explaining this is that Arab applicants are about 60 percent of the beneficiaries of the race-based policy, but Arab localities are not classified as development towns. However, even a policy that ignores Arab students and gives special consideration only to Mizrachi Jews could not match the diversification effect of the class-based model when it comes to the representation of students from development towns. Even under a race-based model for Jews only, only 5 percent of the simulated race-based admits (all Mizrachi) would come from development towns, and this would drop to only 2 percent in the most-selective majors. Thus, the Mizrachi applicants who would benefit from race-based affirmative action would tend not to come from development towns.

In sum, *a policy that spotlights spatial and school inequality is more effective at expanding educational opportunity for high school graduates from development towns than a program that gives special consideration to ethnic minorities.* This effect is even more pronounced in the most selective fields of study.

SOCIOECONOMIC DIVERSITY

One of the arguments against race-based affirmative action in higher education admissions is that the most privileged among underrepresented minorities take advantage of these policies, a phenomenon known as "creaming." One of the hopes for class-based affirmative action is that it will benefit individuals with demonstrated disadvantages. Basing eligibility for preferential treatment on family income will surely target poor applicants and enhance the economic diversity of student bodies. This effect is not guaranteed, however, under the Israeli model because, with its heavy emphasis on two structural elements (high school and neighborhood type), eligibility does not depend on family income and parents' education level.

The evidence so far has demonstrated that the Israeli class-based policy opens the gates for applicants from ethnic minority groups, the geographic periphery, and poor communities. But are these class-based admits actually poor? Did we widen the path for socioeconomic mobility for applicants whose parents never went to college? Or, alternatively, did the offspring of affluent and college-educated parents, who just happen to reside in poor or remote places, take advantage of the special consideration in admission? In other words, did creaming occur? This section answers the question of how successful the Israeli class-based model is in boosting socioeconomic diversity at elite universities.

Socioeconomic diversity has been a great challenge for the bastions of privilege in Israel, as it has been for elite colleges in the United States. At Tel Aviv University during the AA regime, only 7 percent of general pool admits (admits not eligible for the current class-based program) had a father who was either unemployed or out of the labor force (figure 7.8).[21] Was the class-based affirmative action program, which is strictly need-blind, able to tap into this disadvantaged group? The answer is yes: 22 percent of class-based admits had an unemployed father.[22] The race-based simulation was less effective at reaching out to this particular population: only 13 percent of the simulated race-based admits fell into this category.

Another indicator of family socioeconomic standing is parents' occupational prestige, which is commonly measured by the Socioeconomic Index (SEI). The SEI is a composite of occupational prestige, income, and education, ranging from 0 to 100, with 100 representing the highest possible occupational prestige. For example, university professors, mathematicians, engineers, and mayors score above 95, while porters, seamstresses, and unskilled workers in kitchens and laundries score below 10. On average, non-AA admits at TAU had fathers with the highest occupational prestige of all groups (SEI = 59), while the class-based admits had fathers with the lowest (SEI = 39; see figure 7.9). The score for the simulated race-based admits is closer to that for non-AA admits (SEI = 51).

The best indicator for being poor is receiving financial aid. In Israel, there

Figure 7.8 The Share Among Actual and Simulated Admits to Israeli Universities with a Father out of the Labor Force or Unemployed, AA Regime

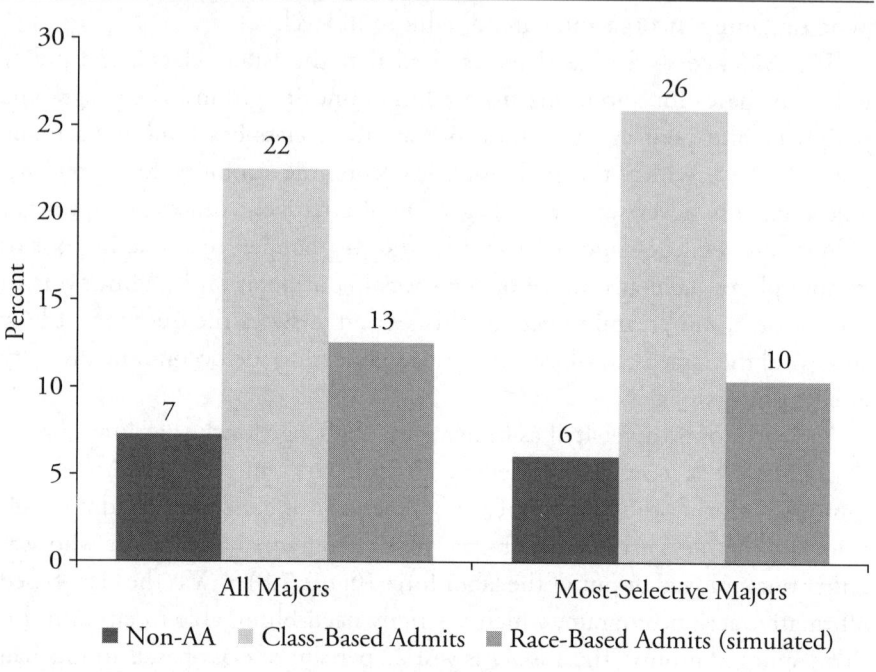

Source: TAU, HUJI, and BGU administrative data, AA regime.

are no direct financial aid provisions by the state, such as the Pell Grant in the United States, but some aid is allocated by the institutions themselves.[23] The universities in Israel determine eligibility for institutional need-based grants only after students enroll. Within each institution in a given year, the allocation of grants is solely need-based and thus distinguishes between more and less needy students. Moreover, decisions about eligibility for affirmative action are unrelated to those that determine financial aid. They are made by different organizations at different times: the eligibility score for the class-based affirmative action program is need-blind and determined by the Association for the Advancement of Education, a nonprofit organization outside of the universities, *before* the admissions decision, whereas financial aid eligibility is determined by the universities *after* an applicant has been admitted

Figure 7.9 The Mean SEI Score of Father's Occupation for Actual and Simulated Admits to Israeli Universities, AA Regime

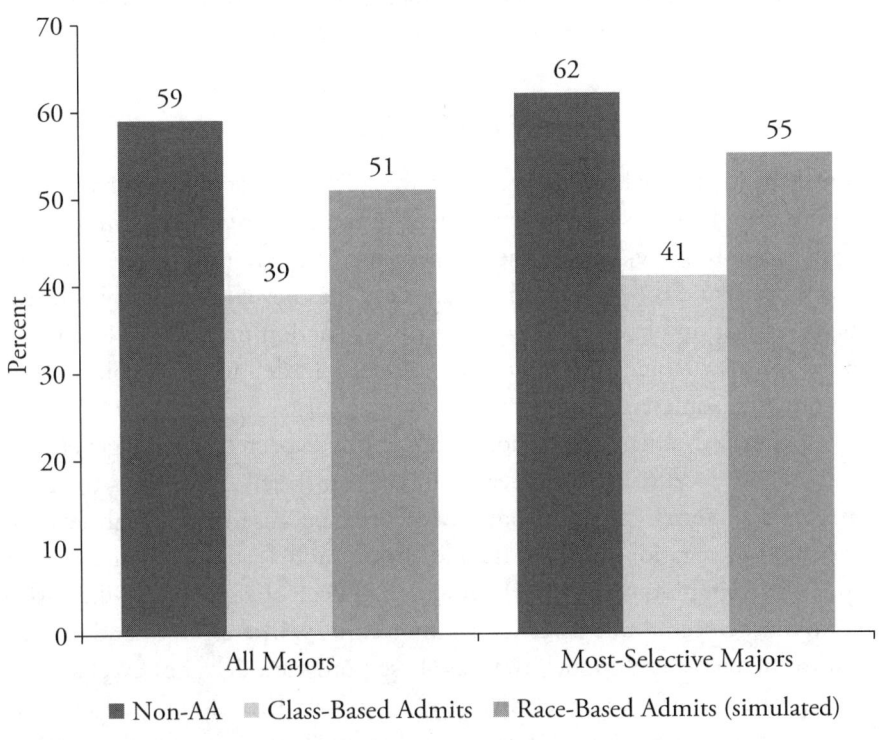

Source: TAU, HUJI, and BGU administrative data, AA regime.

and has decided to enroll. In my investigation, 52 percent of class-based admits received need-based grants in their freshman year, whereas 41 percent of potential race-based admits would have received these grants; this is also a high figure when compared to those not eligible for the class-based program, non-AA admits, of whom only 15 percent received this type of assistance.

It appears that the class-based program, despite being strictly need-blind, does a good job of admitting students with economic hardship who would otherwise be less likely to be admitted. Its diversifying effect is strongest in the most-selective majors, where students from such populations are rare. Ethnic-conscious admissions would also elevate the socioeconomic diversity at these flagship schools, but to a lesser extent than the class-based program does.

In sum, *the class-based affirmative action policy generates a higher level of socioeconomic diversity than a potential ethnic-based policy.*

BROAD DIVERSITY

Here is the dilemma: how can we ascertain which model of affirmative action, race- or class-based, is best for generating broad diversity? This is a challenging question because, despite the frequent use of the notion by the U.S. Supreme Court and the public, "broad diversity" has never been clearly defined. The investigation of the class-based affirmative action program in Israel presented in this chapter underscores the difficulty in defining this concept but also provides some insight into it.

A race-based affirmative action program, as expected, would generate a much higher level of ethnic diversity in the top Israeli universities than the current race-neutral program does. Moreover, because of the high level of residential segregation in Israel, the race-based model would enhance certain types of geographic diversity. However, the effect of race-based affirmative action on socioeconomic diversity is rather limited. Interestingly, and in contrast to the race-based model, the class-based program does not excel at promoting one particular type of diversity. Rather, its hybrid and multidimensional design targets several aspects of disadvantage simultaneously, so its diversity effects are more widespread. In addition to its effect on spatial diversity, the class-based program also enhances the representation in elite universities of ethnic minorities, new immigrants, poor individuals, and individuals from poor localities. *Perhaps the key insight for broad diversity is that, compared to the race-based model and other models, this type of class-based program does not create the highest level of diversity in any one aspect but generates a more diverse package overall.*

Is "a little bit of everything" a good definition of broad diversity? If so, then what determines a program's potential to yield broad diversity is its ability to tap into the overlap between systems of inequality—that is, between racial-ethnic, school and neighborhood, and socioeconomic segregation. On one side of the range we have an extremely segregated society in which residents of poor neighborhoods are poor ethnic minorities. The overlap between

Table 7.1 The Characteristics of Arabs and Mizrachi Jews in the Class-Based and Race-Based Admit Pools of Israeli Universities, AA Regime

	% Race-Based Admits	% Class-Based Admits
New immigrant	2	4
Locality: low-SES cluster	59	60
Development town	2	10
Father out of labor force or unemployed	13	27

Source: TAU, HUJI, and BGU administrative data, AA regime.

systems of inequality is perfect. On the other side of the spectrum there is no overlap at all since the ethnic profile of poor neighborhoods mimics that of affluent ones and poor individuals live in both places. None of these extreme situations exist, and so the empirical question is this: which model of affirmative action better taps into this overlap, if such indeed exists? The answer to this question varies from country to country and may change over time.

One especially intriguing question arises in this context: what is the extent of overlap between ethnicity and privilege under the race- and class-based models? The answer is especially pertinent to the current debate in the United States about the shift from race to class in affirmative action in college admissions. We need to go back to the Israeli data and look at the evidence from a different angle.

Let's focus only on the ethnic minorities (Arabs and Mizrachi Jews) who were admitted with the help of either the actual class-based or the simulated race-based programs. Under class-based affirmative action, one in two class-based admits was an Arab or Mizrachi Jew, while the share in the race-based pool, by definition, was 100 percent. However, the ethnic minorities in the class-based pool were, on average, more disadvantaged than those in the race-based pool. For example, among race-based admits, only 2 percent were first-generation immigrants, while this share was double among ethnic minorities in the class-based admits (see table 7.1). Only 13 percent of race-based admits had a father not in the labor force, compared to 27 percent of ethnic minorities admitted under the class-based scheme. Ten percent of ethnic minorities among the class-based admits came from a development town, whereas only 2 percent of race-based admits did. It is only in the overlap between race and deprived localities that the two models match. Overall, *the overlap between ethnicity, spatial segregation, and socioeconomic hierarchy is more pronounced among the class-based admits than among the beneficiaries of ethnic-conscious admissions.*

But while the class-based program in Israel has created a comprehensive and wide-ranging diversity package, it has done so at the price of less ethnic diversity (compared to a hypothetical race-based program). *A race-based model would reveal a mixture of disadvantages, but its focus is tilted toward ethnic diversity, and the scope of diversity dividends tends to be much narrower.* This is usually the result of creaming, because the most privileged among Arabs and Mizrachi Jews are the ones most likely to take advantage of such an edge in admissions.

CREAMING

Creaming has provoked opposition toward affirmative action policies based on ethnicity and race in the United States, and if such a policy were implemented in Israel or other countries, it would be likely to rouse similar controversy. The argument would be that both Mizrachi Jews and Arabs are "undeserving" of special consideration in admissions because many among them are privileged and wealthy. Although these groups in Israel are disadvantaged in terms of educational attainment and socioeconomic prospects, the elite among them are more likely to take advantage of an edge in admission, a notion supported by simulation results. Thus, even before national antagonism toward giving Arabs special treatment—either because they do not participate in many civic duties, such as military service, or because of racism—enters the discussion, it seems that the problem of creaming would turn most away from ethnic-conscious admissions policies.

The focus on structural determinants of disadvantage, not on individual hardships, makes the Israeli class-based affirmative action program susceptible to creaming. Theoretically, the Israeli program is similar to race-conscious admissions in that *group* affiliation is emphasized rather than individual circumstances—that is, both models adhere to a macrojustice perspective. The emphasis on group membership in the Israeli program simplifies sorting and implementation, but as happens with race-based policy, it can lead to creaming because the offspring of the privileged among the groups, who are generally better prepared academically and more aware of admission policies at the universities, are better positioned to exploit the program.

Neta is one example of the creaming that occurs under the class-based program because of its reliance on group indicators. She grew up in a poor city not far from Jerusalem, yet was raised in a big house in an affluent neighborhood. The high school she attended was on the list of disadvantaged schools, and that contributed, along with having four siblings and a mother without a college degree, to her affirmative action eligibility score of 31—just one point above the cutoff. This score helped her get a seat at a selective university department. Both her parents were employed, and she suffered from no other adverse circumstances. In fact, her father was the elected mayor of the city where the family lived.

Maya, another beneficiary of preferential treatment, had an eligibility score that was way above the threshold. She grew up in a development town in the north of Israel and attended the local high school. However, her mother was a high school principal; she not only had a bachelor's degree and good, stable employment but also an excellent understanding of the education system and how to prepare her children for higher education. Suzanne, another student, also made the cutoff for the affirmative action program. She was an Arab from a poor village in the north, yet she attended a private Christian high school considered one of the best high schools in Israel. Moreover, her father had a bachelor's degree and her mother a teaching certificate. When Suzanne applied to university, three of her four sisters were in college. (The fourth was still in high school.)

Clearly, all three girls came from socioeconomically strong families. Nonetheless, the use of structural indicators—neighborhoods and high schools—helped them gain an edge in admission to selective majors. This is creaming, for sure, but is it really unjustified, wrong, or unwarranted? Were Neta, Maya, and Suzanne undeserving of the edge in admission they got? We cannot be sure. After all, these three girls came from poor towns and two of them attended a deprived high school; those structural factors most likely had a depressing effect on their academic potential and aspirations because local resources, their learning environment, and the quality of teachers, curricula, and services were all limited relative to what was available to other Israeli high school students. If these girls had grown up in a more nurturing environment, they might have been higher-achievers and more ambitious. Moreover, there are very few students like these three girls in the Israeli elite universities, especially in the selective fields of study. Thus, their presence in class, with their different backgrounds and perspectives, created opportunities for interaction with students from diverse backgrounds and broadened students' range of viewpoints, thus surely enriching the educational process.

To be sure, the findings regarding socioeconomic diversity suggest that *the class-based affirmative action model in Israel, with its emphasis on structural indicators, leads to creaming, but it does so to a lesser extent than the race-based model does. In other words, the creamy layer generated by focusing on high schools and neighborhoods is thinner than what ethnic-based affirmative action would produce.* Students who were eligible for this class-based program were indeed needier financially than those who would have benefited from ethnic-conscious admissions. After all, affluent people do not typically reside in bad neighborhoods and send their children to failing schools. In sum, creaming is more widespread in race-based affirmative action than in programs that focus on structural indicators.

CONCLUSION

So which model of affirmative action is better suited for diversifying selective universities in Israel? Unfortunately, there is no silver bullet answer. Israeli universities need to answer a more fundamental question: which diversity outcome is most desirable? Is demographic or socioeconomic diversity more important for enriching students' learning experiences and increasing their tolerance for a wide range of viewpoints? Unfortunately, we cannot have both kinds of diversity.

Putting the question another way, are the selective institutions in Israel willing to pay the price associated with enhancing ethnic diversity—that is, lower levels of socioeconomic and geographic diversity? This dilemma is further illuminated by the results of the U.S. simulations presented in the next chapter.

CHAPTER 8

The Feasibility and Diversity Dividends of Affirmative Action Policy in the United States

In recent decades the competition over selective colleges and universities in the United States has become fierce. The disparities between four-year institutions, especially since the mid-1980s, have increased as admission rates to elite schools have decreased and less-selective institutions have struggled to lure applicants. In the discussion of the stratification of colleges and universities in chapter 3, we saw differences in terms of the share of applicants admitted, the academic preparation of incoming students, financial resources, academic and social climates, graduation likelihood, and earning potential. These disparities help explain why so many strive for one of the few slots at elite institutions. In a nation where all postsecondary institutions offer a similar college experience, it would not matter so much where students attend college. But this is not the case in the United States.

In the race for slots at elite institutions, minority applicants and those from socioeconomically underprivileged backgrounds have been falling behind. They just cannot match the preparation of their well-off counterparts, who have ample resources at their disposal, such as better information about the college admission process, better high schools and teachers, private tutors, and college-educated parents who can guide them and offer advice. Consequently, access to the more invigorating learning environments of elite institutions—with their financial resources and supportive academic and social climates—is not equally distributed among race and class groups.

One result is that colleges differ not only in selectivity levels but in the diversity levels of their student bodies. To increase their representation of minority students, elite colleges and universities started to give black applicants (and later also Hispanic applicants) an edge in admissions in the late 1960s. With no similarly special consideration for students from underprivileged backgrounds, however, the level of socioeconomic diversity at elite institutions did not get a boost, and that is why many now support the idea of moving from race to class in affirmative action in college admissions. The most pressing question in this debate is this: which model of affirmative action—class-based or race-based—can generate higher levels of broad (geographic, socioeconomic, and racial-ethnic) diversity at the most selective schools?

To answer this question I conducted simulations that are similar in logic to the Israeli simulations, but with the circumstances reversed. In the American simulations, the real beneficiaries of *racial and ethnic* affirmative action at elite schools were replaced with students who attended less-selective four-year institutions and would have been eligible for *class-based* affirmative action had such a program existed. The potential diversity dividends of the simulated class-based policy were then compared with the real diversity dividends of actual race-based policy.

In this investigation, I used a cohort who began college in 1995–1996.[1] This is an especially interesting cohort to track because it was the last to start college before affirmative action was banned in several states, as it was in Texas and California in 1996, in Washington in 1998, in Florida in 1999, in Michigan in 2006, in Nebraska in 2008, in Arizona in 2010, and in New Hampshire and Oklahoma in 2012. The data set contains information about more than 12,000 students attending any type of postsecondary institution; about 8,400 of them (roughly 70 percent) attended four-year colleges and universities. Of those attending a four-year institution, only a minority attended one that I deem in this book an "elite" or "selective" college—that is, an institution with an academic rating of 1 (most competitive) or 2 (highly competitive) in *Barron's Profiles of American Colleges*.[2]

The focus on elite colleges and universities is pertinent for this study because only these institutions give some kind of preferential treatment in admissions to black and Hispanic applicants, as previous studies have found.[3] Naturally, colleges that admit a much higher percentage of black and Hispanic applicants do not need to rely on race-conscious admissions policies because they are able to achieve racial and ethnic diversity without it. How do we know which institutions implement affirmative action in their admission decisions? We compare high school students with similar test scores and high school achievements, given that these indicators typically predict college admission chances, and examine whether black and Hispanic students are more likely to gain admission than whites and Asians.[4] The data for the 1995–1996 cohort confirms this conclusion. When comparing applicants with similar test scores, high school grade point average, number of Advance Placement (AP) courses, AP course GPA, and number of honors courses, a clear pattern emerges: only institutions at the top of the hierarchy (categories 1 and 2) gave an edge in admissions to minorities in 1995.[5] This edge was not evident in other colleges. To illustrate, black and Hispanic applicants were three times more likely than their white and Asian counterparts with similar academic achievements to attend a category 1 college in 1995–1996. In short, elite institutions are where all the "action" in "affirmative action" occurs.

Of all the students at *any* type of postsecondary institution in 1995–1996 (including two-year community colleges and all four-year schools), 25 percent were black and Hispanic—a slightly lower share than the share of blacks and Hispanics in the school-age population (ages five to twenty-four) that year. These minority students were concentrated, however, at two-year schools, where every third student was either black or Hispanic. Despite the race-conscious admissions policies at elite schools, only 16 percent of their student bodies were black or Hispanic; blacks and Hispanics were still underrepresented at category 1 and 2 colleges compared to their numbers in the general student population (herein the source of the term "underrepresented minorities"). Nonetheless, this representation would have been even lower *without* race-conscious admissions.

FROM RACE TO CLASS IN AFFIRMATIVE ACTION

The race-based affirmative action programs at selective institutions have been successful at promoting the racial and ethnic diversity they urgently needed (although blacks and Hispanics are still underrepresented at the top), but at the price of growing controversy. At the same time that race-based policies have come under attack, the growing socioeconomic divide in higher education—such as the tightening link between family income and the academic outcomes of high school seniors—has highlighted the need for taking socioeconomic background into account in admission decisions. Although class-based affirmative action has never been tested in the United States, supporters hope that it could foster socioeconomic diversity at elite schools by giving an edge in admissions to underprivileged applicants.

In the absence of an actual class-based policy to observe, we must rely on statistical simulations of hypothetical class-based policies in order to evaluate their potential effects. In the past decade, both William Bowen and his colleagues and Thomas Espenshade and Alexandria Radford have conducted simulation studies in this vein.[6] Both teams reached the same unambiguous conclusion: if class-based affirmative action were to replace the current race-based model, racial and ethnic diversity at elite colleges would decline substantially. These scholars concluded that class-based affirmative action cannot substitute for race-conscious admissions in generating racial and ethnic diversity because race and socioeconomic status are not good substitutes for each other. First, not all blacks and Hispanics are poor or from the first generation going to college. Second, blacks and Hispanics represent only a small fraction of all low-income youth, and an even smaller fraction of high-achieving low-income youth.[7]

These simulation studies have been criticized, however, for employing a narrow definition of socioeconomic status.[8] Bowen and his colleagues, for example, use family income as an indicator for class in their simulations, but some argue that wealth is a better proxy for race than income.[9] Less wealth has accumulated in the black community over the generations owing to the legacy of slavery, the history of land and property seizure, and discrimination in the home mortgage market.[10] As the sociologists Melvin Oliver and Thomas Shapiro put it in their book *Black Wealth/White Wealth,* blacks were "locked out of the greatest mass-based opportunity for wealth accumulation in American history" because they were excluded from the suburbanization of America that occurred from the 1930s through the 1960s.[11] As for Hispanics, most Hispanic immigrants came to the United States without assets and have yet to accumulate wealth.

Indeed, the Century Foundation, a public policy think tank, is a proponent of the claim that family wealth is the best possible proxy for race—that is, that using wealth as an indicator of class in class-based affirmative action will ensure the representation of underrepresented minorities:

> A wide body of research finds that standard indicators of socioeconomic status provide an inadequate measure of economic well-being and underestimate the ways in which African Americans tend to be economically disadvantaged compared with whites. Three factors in particular stand out: differences in *concentrated poverty*, differences in *wealth or net worth*, and differences in *family structure* . . . using the right set of economic criteria in class-based affirmative action programs can help capture—and counteract—past and current instances of racial discrimination. . . . Most powerful of all, because wealth is accumulated over generations, the nation's steep wealth inequality reflects in some important measure the legacy of slavery and segregation as well as ongoing discrimination in the housing market. *Smartly structured economic affirmative action programs* can address these instances of discrimination indirectly, without conflicting with our legal system and public perceptions of fairness [emphasis added].[12]

The analyses in this chapter examine whether diversity can be boosted by alternative prototypes of affirmative action, to what extent it can be boosted, and what type of diversity responds to alternative programs. To address these issues, I conducted simulations that replaced the current race-based policy with various models of class-based policy. When devising the simulations, I aimed to create "smartly structured economic affirmative action programs" that would take into account various definitions of disadvantage. I then implemented and compared three types of class-based affirmative action policy in the simulations, in accordance with the three prototypes developed in chapter 5 (see table 8.1).

Types of Simulation, by Prototype

Race-Based Affirmative Action   This is the current model of affirmative action implemented by elite institutions in the U.S. All the class-based models are compared to this prototype.

Prototype 1: Class-Based Affirmative Action: Socioeconomic Models   This prototype focuses solely on an individual's socioeconomic circumstances. There are two versions of this model in the simulations: (a) economic affirmative

Table 8.1 Types of Simulation of Class-Based Affirmative Action Policy, by Prototype, 1996–2001

Prototype	Type	Definition	% Among Four-Year Students in 1995–1996
Race	Race and ethnicity	Blacks or Hispanics	13.2
Class: economic-socioeconomic	(a) Economic	(a) EFC bottom quartile	14.1
	(b) Socioeconomic	(b) EFC bottom quartile + parents' education less than BA degree	8.8
Class: structural	High school economic level	High school with poor student body: 40 percent eligible for free or reduced lunch	4.5
Class: multidimensional	Socioeconomic + high school economic level	EFC bottom quartile + parents' education less than a BA degree + high school with poor student body	1.4

Source: National Center for Education Statistics, Beginning Postsecondary Students Longitudinal Study (BPS), 1996–2001.

action, in which eligibility is based solely on family economic standing, and (b) socioeconomic affirmative action, which is almost identical to version (a) except that it also includes parental education level.

A. *Economic affirmative action:* The best way to ascertain students' economic standing is to look at their Expected Family Contribution (EFC). Colleges use the EFC to determine eligibility for federal, state, local, and institutional aid. The EFC is based mostly on the information reported on the Free Application for Federal Student Aid (FAFSA), which all students who seek financial aid from the federal government are required to submit. (Some of this information is provided directly by the Internal Revenue Service.)

The key advantage of the EFC is that it includes wealth and assets in addition to family income and other financial resources, while adjusting everything by family structure. The formula takes into account family taxed and untaxed income, assets, benefits (such as unemployment and Social Security), family size, and the number of family members who will attend college that year.[13] The EFC is an attractive measure because it is already available in student records, which eliminates the need to collect and verify information about the economic standing of each applicant. If the determination of EFC and financial aid were moved to an earlier stage of the admissions process, as has been suggested in the past in order to help families know which institutions they can afford, then colleges could also use the EFC as a criterion for affirmative action eligibility.

I divided all the students in the 1995–1996 cohort into four quartiles according to their EFC. Forty-two percent of all students at two-year institutions were in the bottom EFC quartile, but they accounted for 14 percent of the student bodies at four-year institutions. Less than 10 percent of the student bodies at elite colleges were in the bottom EFC quartile (this includes the minorities who benefited from affirmative action). In the simulation analysis, students at four-year institutions in the bottom quartile, whose families could contribute the least to financing their education, became eligible for an edge in admission.

B. *Socioeconomic affirmative action:* In this model, the definition of class is expanded to include parental education levels. Having college-educated parents is another important indicator of advantage, not only because a college degree is a precursor to economic well-being in today's economy and labor market, but also because parents who attended college better understand the college preparation and application processes and are better able to help their children. While 50 percent of students attending four-year non-elite schools in 1995–1996 were first-generation college students—students whose parents did not have college degrees—this was true of only 20 percent of students at elite schools (including URM who got an edge in admission). The vast majority of students at elite schools had at least one college-educated parent.

This model of affirmative action considers both parental educational attainment and economic status, as defined earlier. Only students from the bottom EFC quartile whose parents do not have college degrees would be eligible for affirmative action consideration under this policy. Nine percent of students at four-year institutions met this criteria in 1995–1996. I used this group in the simulation applicant pool for socioeconomic affirmative action.

Prototype 2: Class-Based Affirmative Action: Structural Model This prototype uses structural disadvantages, such as residing in a poor neighborhood or attending a high-poverty high school, as the basis for class-based affirmative action. The simulation here used high school economic level as the criterion for eligibility. Applicants from high schools with concentrated poverty (at least 40 percent of students were eligible for a free or discounted lunch) met the criteria for this program. Under this simulation model, about 5 percent of all four-year college students in 1995–1996 were eligible for affirmative action.

Prototype 3: Class-Based Affirmative Action: Multidimensional Model This model is an amalgam of the socioeconomic and structural prototypes and is popular among many of the prominent voices in the current debate about affirmative action. Its allure stems from the belief that by focusing on several indicators of disadvantage, a policy has a good chance of targeting those who are truly disadvantaged and avoiding creaming. Students at four-year institutions who were in the bottom EFC quartile *and* were the first in their family to attend college *and* who attended a high school with concentrated poverty are eligible for affirmative action under this simulation model. Thus, this simulation takes both socioeconomic status and high school poverty level into account. Fewer than 2 percent of students at four-year institutions in 1995–1996 had all of these disadvantages.

Implementation of the Simulations

Data Requirements Implementing this ambitious simulation framework requires a wealth of reliable information about students' socioeconomic status. I use data from the restricted-use Beginning Postsecondary Students Longitudinal Study (BPS), which is linked to the National Postsecondary Student Aid Study (NPSAS). Given its rich, detailed, and accurate information, this data set is ideal for determining applicants' eligibility for various class-based affirmative action prototypes. In comparison to previous simulation studies that relied on student self-reports about family financial standing, these data draw from rich information provided in the FAFSA, which is more reliable than self-reported measures. The data include the Expected Family Contribution (EFC) for each student, which is especially useful for simulations in which affirmative action is based on socioeconomic status because it is a composite measure: it considers not only income but also wealth, other financial resources, and family structure. The data set also contains several features that are pertinent for the simulation process, such as detailed information about students' social, economic, and academic backgrounds, parents' educational attainment, type of high school and postsecondary institution attended, and the trajectory of the postsecondary years, including transfers, dropouts, academic outcomes, and attainment.[14]

Another advantage of this data set is that it identifies underprivileged applicants, regardless of whether they applied to elite colleges. This is especially important because there is no shortage of high school graduates from low-income households who are high achievers. In fact, Caroline Hoxby and Christopher Avery estimate that about 17 percent of high achievers—those with scores in the top decile of the ACT/SAT distribution and a high school grade point average of A or higher—are in the bottom quartile of the family income distribution.[15] The problem, however, is that the vast majority of these high-achieving, low-income students *do not apply to selective colleges.* This is an important point because, to date, simulation-based research on class-based affirmative action has focused on the current pool of applicants to elite colleges.[16] These simulations have therefore included only the small percentage of high-achieving underprivileged students who apply to elite schools. With the vast majority of qualified underprivileged candidates not even applying to elite colleges, a large source of high-achievers has been ignored in the simulations conducted to date.

The inherent flaw in these studies is that the implementation of class-based affirmative action policy would most likely alter the application behavior of this group of underprivileged applicants. If socioeconomically disadvantaged students believe that they will receive an edge in admissions, they will be more likely to apply to elite colleges. As Bowen and his colleagues acknowledge, "It is likely that the applicant pools would change under this admissions policy—most notably, the number of bottom-quartile applicants would probably rise to take advantage of the new admissions preferences. This is an important consideration, which potentially could be addressed by using a weighted sample of the national pool of SAT-takers as a 'predicted' applicant pool."[17] Thus, even they concur that their findings, which cast doubt over whether class-based admissions can match the level of racial and ethnic diversity generated by a race-based policy, apply only to the first years of a new admission scheme—before the pool of potential college applicants has had time to adjust their behavior.

Consequently, in order to approximate a situation in which low-income students have had time to adjust their application behavior, such studies must draw from the *potential* applicant pool, rather than the *current* applicant pool, to elite colleges. The simulations in this book are able to do so by using data from a national sample of students attending any four-year institution. This strategy advances the literature on class-based affirmative action by considering the entire pool of high-achieving underprivileged youth and by taking into account potential changes in application behavior.

The Simulation Process The simulations replace the beneficiaries of race-based affirmative action with students who attended less-selective four-year institutions and are deemed eligible for class-based admissions, according to the prototype used. The site of the simulations is limited to the colleges that *Barron's* classifies as "most competitive" and "highly competitive"—the top two categories, 1 and 2—because these are the institutions that grant an edge in admissions to URM applicants. A scheme of the simulation process is provided in figure 8.1.

1. *Identifying the race-based admits.* First, the beneficiaries of race-based preferential treatment at elite institutions must be identified, because not all the URM who attended a category 1 or 2 college in 1995–1996 benefited from preferential admission. The URM at each institution who fell below a certain academic threshold in terms of their SAT or ACT scores are assumed to have benefited from an edge in admission; hereinafter, I refer to these students as "race-based admits." I set two thresholds, one for the most competitive (category 1) institutions and one for highly competitive institutions (category 2). The chosen threshold for each institutional category is the twenty-fifth percentile of test scores among non-athlete white and Asian students (which means that only one-quarter of non-athlete white and Asian students scored below this cutoff point).[18] URM with test scores lower than these thresholds are flagged for replacement in the simulation process. About half of the URM at category 1 and 2 schools scored below the thresholds.

Figure 8.1 The Process of Simulating Class-Based Affirmative Action

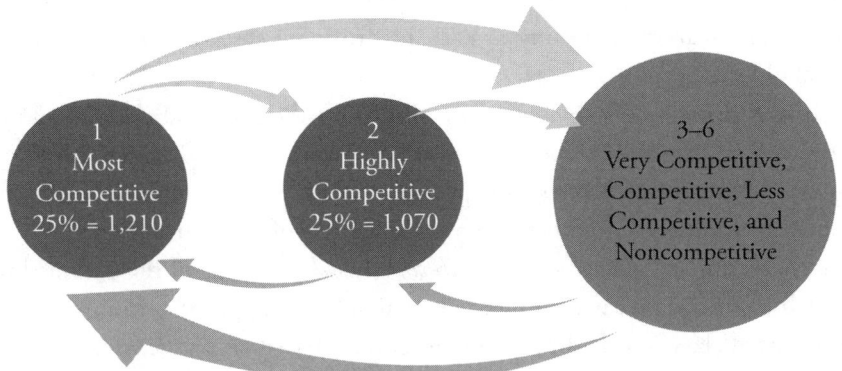

Identifying and Reassigning Current Race-Based Admits
The threshold is the bottom 25% of the test scores distribution
for whites and Asians (excluding athletes).

Identifying and Selecting Class-Based Admits
The "vacant slots" are reallocated (by prototype), and
selection is based on academic standing (SAT).

Source: Author's calculations.

Thus, in the main simulation, URM are treated as beneficiaries of affirmative action only if their test scores were in the bottom quarter of the student body test score distribution for each category of elite colleges. For the purpose of sensitivity analysis, I repeat the simulations using two additional thresholds: (1) at the fiftieth percentile (URM are identified and replaced if their test scores fell into the bottom half of the test score distribution), and (2) with no threshold (a scenario in which all URM at elite colleges are assumed to have received an edge in admissions and thus all are subject to simulated replacement via class-based affirmative action). In all simulations, URM can be reselected if they qualify for the class-based prototype being tested.

2. *Assigning race-based admits.* After identifying the beneficiaries of race-conscious admissions, I reassign them to institutional categories in a cascading process. I start with the most competitive (category 1) colleges and then move to the highly competitive (category 2) ones. Those at category 2 colleges are reassigned to the general applicant pool (*Barron's* categories 3 to 6)

and are thus included in the potential applicant pool for class-based affirmative action. Those at category 1 colleges are reassigned either to a category 2 college, if their test scores are above the relevant threshold, or to the general pool. The race-based admits plucked out can be reselected by class-based admissions if they qualify for the particular class criterion at hand in each prototype. The seats they occupy in each institutional category are replaced by placeholder "vacant slots."

3. *Identifying the class-based admits.* I identify the potential class-based applicants from the general pool of students at four-year institutions based on their eligibility for each respective prototype, be it economic status, socioeconomic status, high school type, or a combination of these prototypes.

4. *Replacing race-based admits with class-based admits.* I fill the vacant slots in each institutional category created in step 2 with applicants from the pool of potential class-based admits. The selection is based on test scores, proceeding from highest to lowest until all vacant seats are filled. These admits are hereinafter referred to as (simulated) "class-based admits." This process ensures that the share of affirmative action admits in the student body is maintained—but now they are class-based admits instead of race-based admits—and that the best-performing applicants are admitted. The full results of the simulation (including all varieties) are presented in tables A8.1–A8.3.

THE DIVERSITY DIVIDENDS: RACE-BASED (CURRENT) VERSUS CLASS-BASED (SIMULATED) AFFIRMATIVE ACTION POLICY

The simulations allow us to gauge which model of affirmative action—race- or class-based—can produce higher levels of broad diversity along geographic, economic, and racial-ethnic lines within elite American universities. In each section, there are two types of figures. The first juxtaposes and compares three groups:

1. *Race-based admits:* Beneficiaries of the current race-based AA program
2. *Class-based admits (simulated):* Beneficiaries of a hypothetical class-based AA program under different prototypes, including economic-socioeconomic, structural, and multidimensional

3. *Non-AA admits:* Students at elite colleges who did not get an edge in admission (that is, who were not eligible for the current race-based admissions)

The second figure in each section compares pre- and post-simulation student body compositions—that is, it shows the current body of students at elite colleges (with race-conscious admissions) alongside the student body that would have existed had these schools implemented class-based affirmative action instead.

Academic Selectivity

For elite colleges, the basis of their reputation is their academic standing, which attracts applicants and donors while reinforcing their prestige and ranking. Lowering academic standards could depress graduation rates by promoting the admission of students who might be unprepared for the level of academic rigor at these institutions. Thus, it is unlikely that elite institutions will compromise their current level of academic demands to accommodate class-based admissions any more than what they do for race-conscious admissions.

The good news is that this would not be a problem with most types of class-based policy. Although the academic achievements of class-based admits from socioeconomically deprived backgrounds and from high-poverty high schools fall behind those of admits who do not benefit from affirmative action, the test scores and high school GPAs of class-based admits are higher, on average, than those of current race-based admits (see top panel of figure 8.2). For example, the mean test scores of admits under socioeconomic affirmative action and structural affirmative action would be 1,130 and 1,100, respectively, compared to 950 among race-based admits (versus 1210 for non-AA students). Economic affirmative action would yield the strongest group in terms of test scores and stock of Advanced Placement courses. Overall, the student body that economic, socioeconomic, and high school–based affirmative action would generate at elite colleges would be academically equivalent to, or even stronger than, the current student body in terms of test scores, grades, and number of AP courses. (See bottom panel of figure 8.2 for a comparison of pre- and post-simulation student body compositions.) The simula-

Figure 8.2 Pre- and Post-Simulation Test Scores (Mean) at Elite U.S. Universities, 1995–1996

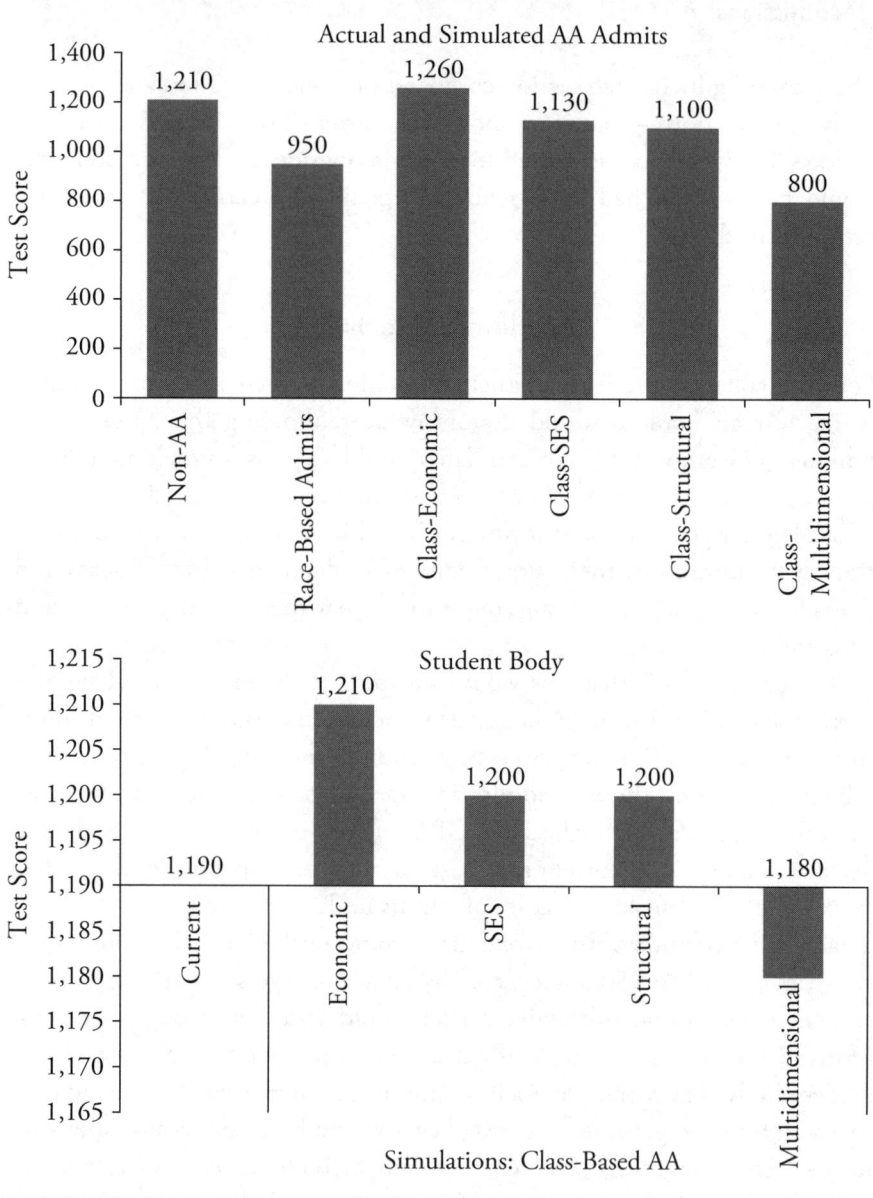

Source: National Center for Education Statistics, Beginning Postsecondary Students Longitudinal Study (BPS), 1996–2001.

tions support the claim that there is no shortage of high-achieving, underprivileged high school graduates. Although they do not typically apply to elite schools, it is plausible that a class-based edge in admission would alter their application behavior and encourage them to do so.

The results are less rosy, however, when we consider the multidimensional prototype, the model that targets high school students with multiple disadvantages. This group of high school students trails furthest behind the others, including behind race-based admits, in all measures of academic preparation. Their GPAs are lower, they take fewer AP courses in high school, and their test score mean is around 800, which is 150 points lower than that of race-based admits. Targeting students with as many disadvantages as possible is fair and politically correct, but given that elite institutions are likely to admit only the highest-achieving among this group, the diversifying potential of such a policy is limited by the short supply of extremely disadvantaged high-achieving students to draw from. I revisit this option later in the chapter.

In sum, *the academic selectivity of elite institutions will not be jeopardized if affirmative action shifts from race to class, except in the case of a class-based policy that targets multiple disadvantages (the multidimensional prototype).*

RACIAL-ETHNIC DIVERSITY

In the 2013–2014 academic year, less than 8 percent of Princeton's undergraduate student body was black, and a similar share was Hispanic.[19] Princeton's level of racial and ethnic diversity is similar to that of other institutions in this echelon and has not changed much over the last decade. What would have been the share of minority students at this distinguished university and others, with the opportunities they provide to thrive and excel, if class-based affirmative action had been implemented instead of race-sensitive admissions?

The current level of racial and ethnic diversity at elite institutions was partly achieved by giving an edge in admission to some URM applicants, at the price of rising controversy. Without any type of affirmative action, however, the share of URM at competitive colleges would drop sharply. Given that race and ethnicity are still key contours of inequality in the United States and that black and Hispanic youth do not have equal access to these colleges, the question of whether class-based affirmative action can maintain the racial and ethnic diversity at elite institutions is critical. Many proponents of class-based admissions promise that such programs would yield levels of racial and ethnic diversity similar to current programs, and this idea has spread throughout the public sphere. For example, a recent report by the Century Foundation maintains that "some universities may be able to equal or even exceed the racial diversity that they have achieved under racial affirmative action programs if they provide a sufficiently large boost to socioeconomically disadvantaged students."[20]

Almost all the evidence, however, indicates otherwise. One of the few experiments with class-based admissions in the United States, conducted at UCLA Law School (and discussed in chapter 11), had very mixed success in preserving racial diversity (the experiment lasted only a year before being greatly scaled back).[21] Simulation research has yielded similar conclusions: the level of racial diversity at elite colleges would substantially decline if class-based policies replaced race-based ones.[22] It seems that socioeconomic status is not as good a substitute for race because blacks and Hispanics represent only a small fraction of all low-income youth and an even smaller fraction of high-achieving low-income youth.[23] However, these simulations used a narrow definition of socioeconomic status: family income and sometimes also parental education. The question is whether class-based programs could match the level of racial-ethnic diversity produced by a race-based policy if they relied on different eligibility criteria, such as wealth and assets in addition to family income.

The answer is no. If we replace race-based affirmative action with socioeconomic affirmative action, the share of minority students falls dramatically. The estimate for the 1995–1996 cohort is that it would have declined by nearly one-third, from 16 percent to around 10 percent, which is similar to the estimates in previous simulation research.[24] (See bottom panel of figure 8.3 for pre- and post-simulation comparisons of the share of URM in elite colleges.) This is not surprising because there is little evidence to support the notion that the overlap between wealth and race is greater than that between income and race.[25]

Moreover, if the real share of URM who got an edge in admission is greater than what the simulations assume, then a shift from a race- to a socioeconomic-based policy would lead to an even steeper decline in the number of minorities at elite colleges. The share of URM declines even further, to 7 percent, when we replace the URM admits in the bottom half of the distribution (using the fiftieth percentile as a threshold) with students who are socioeco-

Figure 8.3 The Pre- and Post-Simulation Share of Underrepresented Minorities at Elite U.S. Universities, 1995–1996

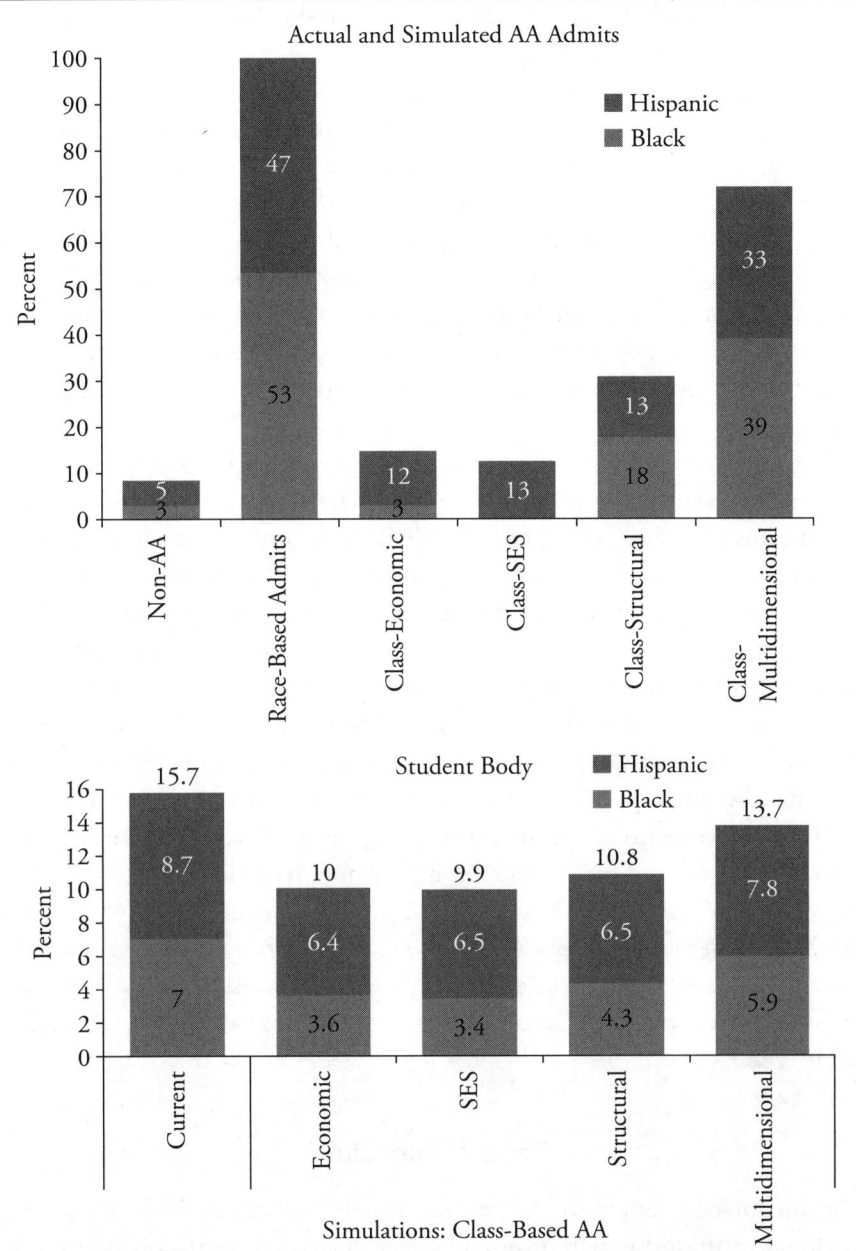

Source: National Center for Educaton Statistics, Beginning Postsecondary Students Longitudinal Study (BPS), 1996–2001.

nomically disadvantaged. Finally, if we assume that all URM are beneficiaries of admission preferences, then under socioeconomic affirmative action the share of blacks and Hispanics at elite schools would shrink to 4 percent of the student body. This trend is similar in all class-based prototypes.[26]

Plans that focus on individually determined socioeconomic circumstances (prototype 1)—even if they are based on an elaborate eligibility scheme that considers wealth, assets, family income, family structure, and parental education levels—end up targeting applicants who are mostly white and Asian. Only 13 to 15 percent of affirmative action admits under such model plans are black or Hispanic (see top panel of figure 8.3). The simulations predict that such race-neutral socioeconomic models would be especially detrimental for the representation of blacks, whose share at elite institutions would be cut by as much as 50 percent (compared to a 25 percent cut for Hispanics).[27]

Notably, admissions based on structural disadvantages (prototype 2) have greater potential to approach the level of racial and ethnic diversity at elite institutions than those based on individual socioeconomic attributes. Thus, a model for class-based affirmative action that targets applicants from high schools with concentrated poverty provides a better starting point for generating broad diversity. Targeting students with multiple disadvantages (prototype 3) yields the most racially and ethnically diverse student body among all class-based options, but the results are still less diverse than those generated by race-based admissions. However, if elite colleges capped the number of truly disadvantaged applicants in order to maintain their academic admission levels, then the racial and ethnic diversity generated by such a policy would match that produced by focusing on high school type alone.[28]

In sum, *the student bodies of elite colleges would be substantially less diverse racially and ethnically under all types of class-based affirmative action relative to current race-based policy. Admissions that focus on structural disadvantages generate more racial and ethnic diversity than those that target individual socioeconomic status.*

Race Within Class

The unequivocal conclusion is that the current level of racial-ethnic diversity at elite institutions, now buttressed by race-conscious admissions, cannot be sustained by any class-based affirmative action policy that is race-neutral, regardless of its design. Given this caveat, a policy shift from race to class might have to include some special consideration for an applicant's race or ethnicity within the general framework of class-based affirmative action. A class-based model that is also race-sensitive would guarantee an edge in admission to minorities, specifically the socioeconomically disadvantaged among them, while also benefiting underprivileged nonminority applicants. To assess this possibility, the simulations also examine a hybrid design that integrates race and ethnicity as an element in class-based affirmative action. To this end, I replicated the simulations of class-based admissions, but gave URM a small edge—specifically, a 100-point test score advantage—when selecting admits.

If such a "race within class" model were implemented, the share of URM at elite colleges would be one or two percentage points higher than that predicted by the race-neutral, class-based models. For example, inserting a race-conscious element into class-based affirmative action would increase the share of blacks and Hispanics from 10 to 11.6 percent under the socioeconomic framework (prototype 1), and from 11 to 12 percent under the structural framework (prototype 2), which gives preferential treatment to applicants from high-poverty high schools (the results are reported in table A8.2). There are other notable advantages to a race-conscious, class-based model. First, the increase in the level of racial diversity is achieved without jeopardizing academic selectivity.[29] Second, the level of socioeconomic diversity remains intact compared to race-neutral class-based admissions, because each affirmative action candidate, including URM, must meet certain class criteria. Finally, under the "race within class" model, students of different racial groups might be more likely to have some commonality across social class regardless of race.[30]

In sum, *the level of racial and ethnic diversity generated by nesting race preferences within class-based affirmative action approaches the current level, while also benefiting underprivileged nonminority applicants. The price of this outcome is the abandonment of race-neutrality.*

SOCIOECONOMIC DIVERSITY

In this section, I compare the four prototypes of affirmative action in terms of their potential to generate socioeconomic diversity at elite colleges in the United States through the lens of two indicators: family economic standing and parental education levels. I take this approach because poor and first-generation college students (that is, neither parent has a college degree) are underrepresented at elite schools. Affirmative action plans that target such applicants will, by default, promote socioeconomic diversity. The question, however, is whether plans that target socioeconomic factors are better at achieving socioeconomic diversity than need-blind policies, whether based on race or high school poverty level.

Let's first focus our attention on poor students at elite colleges. Race may not be a good proxy for low-income status among high school graduates, but in the context of elite colleges there is substantial overlap between race and low income. Of all the URM at elite colleges, 18 percent are poor (in the bottom quartile of the EFC distribution) compared to only 7 percent of white and Asian students (see table A8.5), and 25 percent of the race-based admits. Thus, in the educational bastions of privilege, black and Hispanic students, especially those who received an edge from affirmative action, are less affluent, on average, than their white and Asian counterparts. *Accordingly, race-conscious admissions do infuse elite schools with* economically *underprivileged populations.* Put differently, *without race-based affirmative action, the level of economic diversity at elite institutions, minimal as it is, would be even lower.*

In fact, it appears that the class-based structural policy (prototype 2), which focuses on high school type, cannot exceed the level of economic diversity produced by the race-based policies currently in place (see figure 8.4).[31] Thus, the potential of high school–based structural affirmative action to increase economic diversity above and beyond what race-based admissions already accomplish is limited. Nonetheless, a design that takes other indicators of structural disadvantage into account, such as neighborhood economic level, may be able to better pinpoint socioeconomically disadvantaged applicants. *Only admissions sensitive to applicants' economic status, either alone or including parental education levels, are able to dramatically boost economic diversity at elite colleges*—from the current 9 percent up to 14 percent.

Next, let's consider first-generation college students: this group accounts for only 21 percent of the student body at elite colleges but for half of the student body at other four-year institutions. This underrepresentation is not surprising, because college-educated parents understand the postsecondary educational system better and can better help their children navigate the multistep pathway to getting into a selective college.

Figure 8.4 Pre- and Post-Simulation Expected Family Contribution, Elite U.S. Universities, 1995–1996

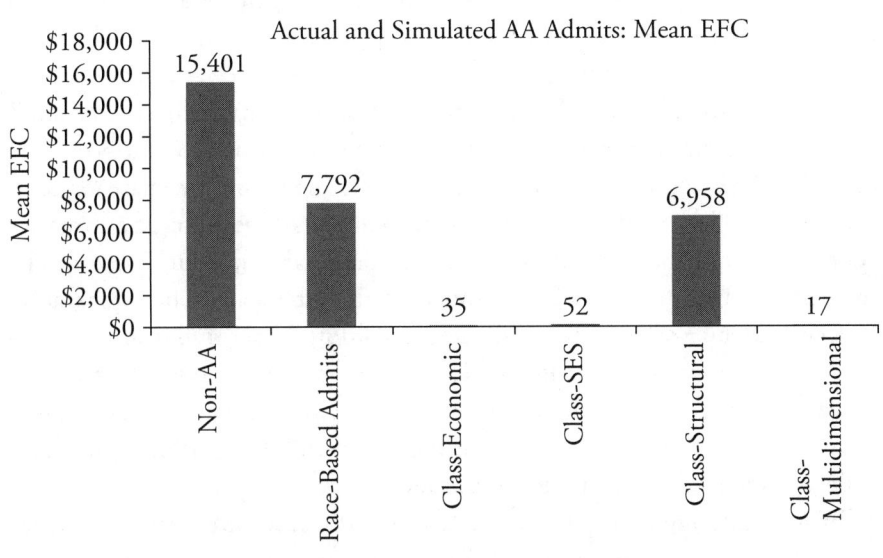

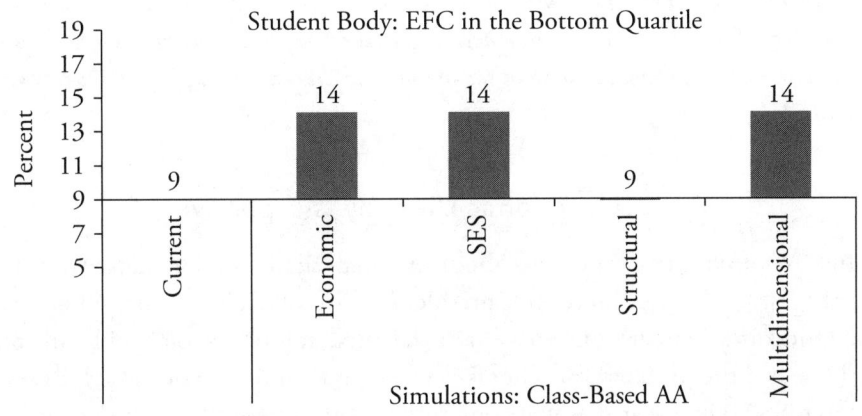

Source: National Center for Education Statistics, Beginning Postsecondary Students Longitudinal Study (BPS), 1996–2001.

My findings show that current race-conscious admissions policies increase the share of first-generation college students at elite schools: the share is only 17 percent among white and Asian students, but 38 percent among all URM (see table A8.5). Moreover, among the URM who benefited from affirmative action (race-based admits), half were first-generation college students (see figure 8.5). Hence, *the level of social diversity at elite institutions would be much lower without race-conscious admissions.* Structural affirmative action that focuses on high school poverty can just about maintain the share of first-generation college students in the student body. If socioeconomic affirmative action, targeting both family income and parental education, were implemented in lieu of race-conscious admissions, then the share of first-generation college students within elite institutions would probably rise, from 21 to 24 percent.[32] The multidimensional model yields similar results. Remarkably, however, purely economic affirmative action yields a negative diversity dividend in terms of parental education levels, and the share of first-generation college students drops from its current level.

In sum, although race-conscious admissions infuse elite institutions with poor and first-generation college students, *admissions that target the socioeconomically underprivileged can boost socioeconomic diversity at these bastions of privilege. Structural affirmative action based on high school type is expected to generate roughly the same level of socioeconomic diversity as race-conscious admissions do.*

Socioeconomic Diversity Is Expensive

In a *New York Times* interview about the small share of poor students at elite colleges, Catharine Bond Hill, president of Vassar College, said, "Talented, low-income kids are out there, and talented middle-income kids are out there. But the problem for schools is when you admit one of those kids, you forgo $50,000 a year that you could use for other things."[33]

There you go. Shifting from race-based to socioeconomic-based admissions policy is costly. The cost of providing financial aid to a larger number of needy students, as well as additional support services, is immense. In their book *Equity and Excellence in American Higher Education,* Bowen and his colleagues estimate that such a shift would require increasing grant aid funds by approximately 12 percent.[34] Moreover, a less wealthy student body resulting

AFFIRMATIVE ACTION POLICY IN THE UNITED STATES 181

Figure 8.5 The Pre- and Post-Simulation Share of Students at Elite U.S. Universities Who Have Parents Without a College Degree, 1995–1996

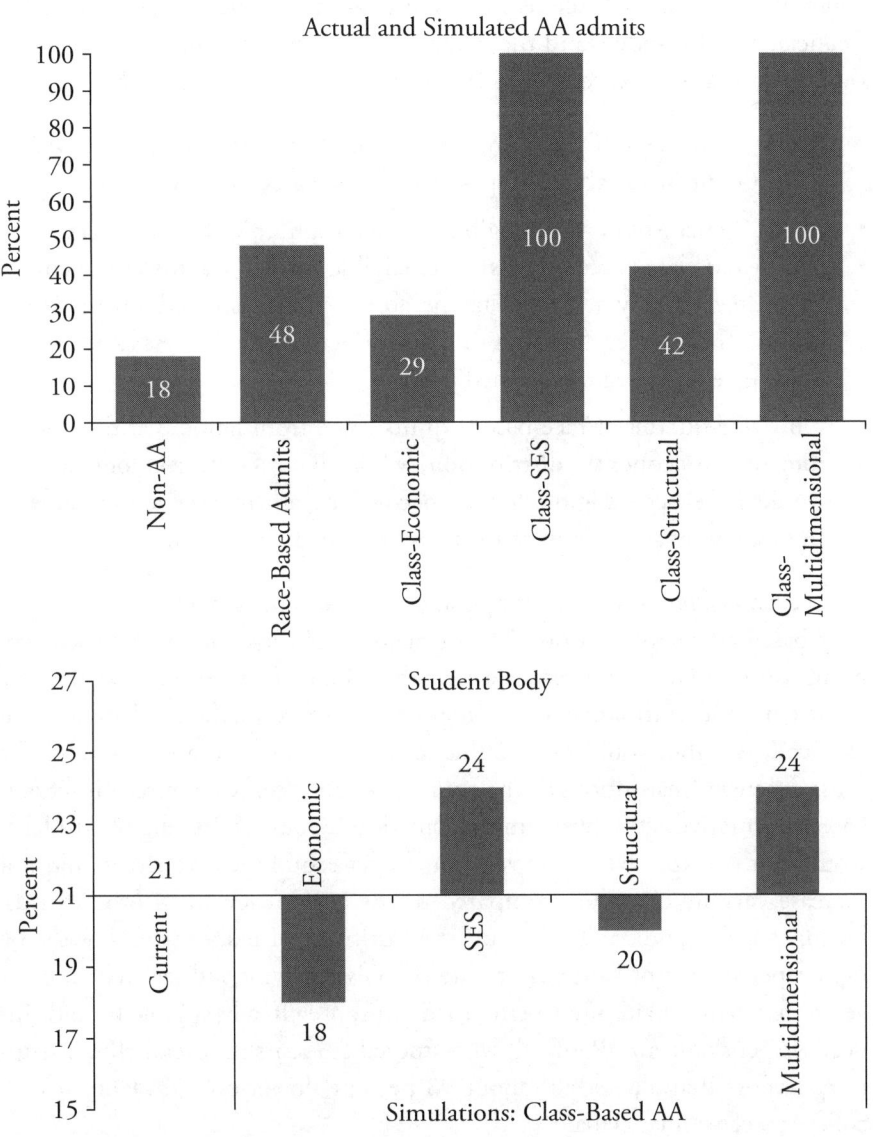

Source: National Center for Education Statistics, Beginning Postsecondary Students Longitudinal Study (BPS), 1996–2001.

from class-based affirmative action is associated with an additional cost: reduced future donations. In contrast, race-based affirmative action is less expensive than a class-based approach because, with wealthy minorities also benefiting from race-conscious admissions, less money needs to be devoted to financial aid. To understand the magnitude of this problem, let's go back to the cohort that started college in 1995–1996 and consider a few facts:

- About 14 percent of the overall student body at elite colleges received a Pell Grant, while about 40 percent of race-based admits did.
- About 75 percent of those eligible for socioeconomic affirmative action (simulated class-based admits) were eligible for Pell Grants at the colleges they actually attended, in the absence of class-based affirmative action. These colleges are not only less selective but also less expensive than the elite colleges examined here.
- Only one-quarter of race-based admits came from families at the bottom of the economic distribution, while, by default, everyone who would have been eligible for socioeconomic affirmative action came from a family at the bottom of the economic distribution.

So even *before* the simulated upgrade to more expensive colleges as part of class-based affirmative action, the vast majority of those eligible for socioeconomic affirmative action received need-based aid. It is certain that under a socioeconomic affirmative action regime, the share of the student body at elite colleges who would require financial aid in order to attend one of the most expensive institutions in the country would rise. (Conversely, if school-based affirmative action were implemented, the share of Pell-eligible students would not be expected to rise very much, yet economic diversity would not increase very much either, compared to the current level). In other words, having poorer candidates move up the institutional ladder would lead to a higher percentage of students at elite schools receiving aid, as well as more generous financial aid offers being made to those already eligible for aid. Indeed, Espenshade and Radford, who studied students at several elite institutions, report that almost all (about 98 percent) lower-class students at elite colleges receive financial aid.[35]

Need-based grants come from three main sources: the federal government, institutions, and state governments. Pell Grants are the largest source of means-tested federally financed grant aid to postsecondary students, but the grant amounts are small and insufficient for covering students' financial needs during college, especially at institutions with high tuition. They are supplemented by need-based grants from states, institutions (the college or university attended), and other sources. Institutional grants are the main source of need-based aid, making up roughly half of the need-based grant package, while federal and state sources contribute about 20 percent each.[36] Institutional grants covered more than half of tuition costs for the beneficiaries of race-conscious admissions at elite institutions in 1995–1996. This fact implies that increasing socioeconomic diversity would rely heavily on institutional commitment, specifically on the ability to augment financial aid budgets so that underprivileged admits not only could afford to enroll but also would not drop out owing to lack of funds. *A shift from race to class in affirmative action would put added pressure on the financial aid budgets of elite colleges.*

Thus, the dividends of socioeconomic affirmative action programs, as predicted by the simulations in this book, would depend on the financial resources that colleges dedicate to the cause. When Vassar College president Hill was asked why a college would expand its financial aid budget instead of spending the money on other causes, such as new and improved buildings, state-of-the-art labs, or faculty salaries, she replied: "We are being supported by the federal government and the state government as a nonprofit. They're doing that because of our nation's commitment to equal opportunity and social mobility, and part of our obligation is living up to making that more of a reality in the United States."[37]

The question, then, is this: how willing and financially able are elite institutions to commit themselves to increasing the share of low-income students in campus?

GEOGRAPHIC AND HIGH SCHOOL DIVERSITY

Among the 2013–2014 freshman class at Harvard College (excluding international students), about 45 percent came from two regions on the East Coast of the United States, New England and the Middle Atlantic.[38] This regional overrepresentation is similar to what we find among all elite schools in the 1995–1996 cohort: nearly 40 percent of students hailed from these

Figure 8.6   The Geographic Region of Actual and Simulated AA Admits to Elite U.S. Universities, 1995–1996

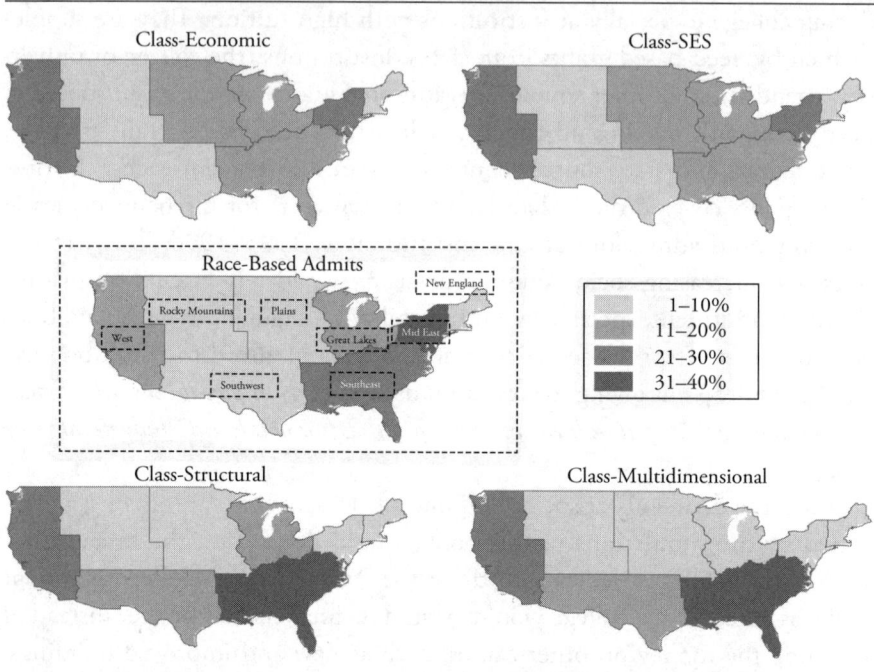

Source: National Center for Education Statistics, Beginning Postsecondary Students Longitudinal Study (BPS), 1996–2001.

two regions, where just 20 percent of all U.S. eighteen- to twenty-four-year-olds lived that year. This pattern is not surprising given that critical masses of high-achieving high school students and most of the wealth in the United States are concentrated in these areas.[39] The majority of elite institutions are located in these regions, and so are their traditional feeding populations. Overall, the geographic distribution of the student bodies of selective schools is far from representative of the general college-age population in the United States, and this is true for URM as well (see the maps in figure 8.6). Affirmative action policy that targets youth from disadvantaged high schools is expected to create the highest level of geographic diversity: under this model, only 6 percent of the simulated class-based admits are from the East Coast, compared to 36 percent of race-based admits and about 25 percent of class-based admits under economic or socioeconomic affirmative action.

The resources available to youth as they make their way through the education system are determined to a large extent by the economic strength of their towns, neighborhoods, and schools and the socioeconomic level of their neighbors and classmates. Not surprisingly, graduates of high schools with a high share of poor classmates are underrepresented at elite colleges and universities. Yet their share would be even lower without race-conscious admissions: 12 percent of race-based admits are from poor high schools compared with only 1 percent of white and Asian students at these elite institutions. Interestingly, the individual-level socioeconomic model *does* increase regional diversity, but *does not* infuse elite institutions with students from disadvantaged high schools.

In sum, *class-based affirmative action, if implemented, would most likely draw high-achieving applicants from outside of the East Coast region and thus might enhance geographic diversity at elite colleges. Affirmative action policy based on the structure of opportunity is better suited for enhancing both geographic and high school diversity than policy based on individual socioeconomic status.*

BROAD DIVERSITY

The rationale behind any affirmative action policy is important. If the main consideration is increasing the share of minority students, then race-based affirmative action is the best bet because it creates the highest level of racial and ethnic diversity. If, on the other hand, the motivation is to increase socioeconomic diversity, then socioeconomic affirmative action should be implemented because it is best suited for achieving this goal. However, the Supreme Court has consistently emphasized *broad* diversity as essential, and the public seems to concur. Elite colleges value racial and ethnic diversity, but they also want socioeconomic diversity. How can they achieve both goals?

The prescription for boosting one type of diversity is straightforward, but it is more difficult to say which prototype would produce the best combination of diversity effects, mainly because there is not much overlap between race, class, and neighborhood in the pool of high-achieving college-bound students. For example, if a substantial share of all poor students with qualifying academic records seeking admission to elite colleges were underrepresented minorities, first-generation college students, from regions outside of the East Coast, and from poor neighborhoods (or some combination of these factors), then we would think that basing admissions on economic status might create broad diversity. Alas, the findings in this chapter demonstrate that this is not the case.

Economic affirmative action, for the most part, generates only economic diversity, because the overlap between the economic divide, race-ethnicity, and geography among high-achieving college students is relatively small. That is, poor students who could make the academic cut at elite colleges and universities are not concentrated in one racial or ethnic group, one type of high school, or one geographic area. Keep in mind that this conclusion is pertinent only for high-achieving students at four-year colleges—a very selective group that is *not* representative of the entire population. Within the general population, the possible overlap between income inequality and other facets of stratification is more substantial, but this is not the population targeted by affirmative action policy at elite institutions. Consequently, the main potential strength of economic affirmative action policy is in fact promoting economic diversity. Of all the prototypes considered, even a "smartly structured" economic affirmative action program that takes wealth, assets, and family structure into account yields the smallest stock of all other diversity dividends. Thus, because of its narrow focus, economic affirmative action falls short of realizing the goal of broad diversity. Considering parental education levels and parents' economic status—that is, *socioeconomic* affirmative action—somewhat broadens the focus, but this model would still dramatically reduced the share of URM at elite schools.

In stark contrast, the multidimensional model taps into the overlap between the realms of inequality more precisely. Its elaborate definition of disadvantage considers multiple factors, drawing a circle small enough to capture a high degree of overlap between contours of inequality. The problem, however, is that the population inside this circle does not contain enough high-achieving students. Very few individuals who are poor *and* who attended a high school with a poor student population *and* who have parents with no college degree overcome these hurdles to the extent that they qualify for the country's most elite colleges. In the end, both these approaches toward class-based affirmative action—the socioeconomic model (prototype 1) and the multidimensional model (prototype 3)—miss the mark of broad diversity.

Affirmative action based on high school type (prototype 2) also does not create broad diversity, in that it creates less socioeconomic diversity compared to socioeconomic affirmative action. Nonetheless, this model is the best Trojan Horse for race and ethnicity because there is considerable overlap between race-ethnicity and high school type: 30 percent of (simulated) school-based admits were either black or Hispanic, and 12 percent of URM who benefited from affirmative action policy attended a high-poverty high school.

Perhaps the best route to generating broad diversity is a race-within-class model, which nests racial preferences within a class-based program. Under this model, the decline in racial and ethnic diversity is expected to be smallest relative to all the alternatives to existing race-conscious admissions, while the level of socioeconomic diversity would match that of race-neutral class-based policy. Such a plan, with both race-sensitive and class-based measures, has the greatest potential to yield broad diversity at elite colleges, but it is not race-neutral.

This, ultimately, is the major insight of this chapter: *Although race-based affirmative action does not produce broad diversity, a race-neutral model would also fall short of achieving this goal. Within the current college admissions framework, there is a trade-off between broad diversity and race-neutrality when it comes to affirmative action policy. We cannot have both.*

There is at least one more alternative: can institutions have both broad diversity and race-neutrality if they radically reform their admissions practices—that is, if they stop preferential treatment in admissions for other types of applicants, including athletes and the offspring of alumni, professors, celebrities, and donors? I explore this option in chapter 11.

PART V

Implications for Academic Outcomes and Mobility

CHAPTER 9

The Academic Outcomes and Mobility Dividends of Affirmative Action Policy in Israel

Yusuf and Bashir grew up in the same Arab agriculture-based village, where all residents are Muslim. It is located in the northern part of Israel, where half of all Israeli Arabs live, and is ranked in the second decile at the bottom of the localities' SES Index. The salary of almost 60 percent of the employed was below the monthly minimum wage in 2009, and fewer than 40 percent of high school seniors graduated with the matriculation diploma required by the universities. Both Yusuf and Bashir came from large families: Yusuf had six siblings and Bashir had nine. They graduated from the local high school—already an indicator of mobility relative to their parents, who never attended high school. Both wanted to go to college and hoped to get a professional degree, such as medicine, dentistry, engineering, computer science, law, architecture, or accounting. However, their chances of getting into such a department were slim, because their grades qualified them only for admission to less-selective fields of study, which do not lead to lucrative occupations. Nonetheless, because Yusuf and Bashir were eligible for class-based preferential treatment, both gained admission to a university department granting a professional degree and eventually graduated.

The affirmative action program certainly improved Yusuf's and Bashir's life chances and enabled them to climb up the economic hierarchy. Moving beyond stories and anecdotes, in this chapter I examine the mobility dividends of the Israeli affirmative action policy. Widening the path to socioeconomic mobility is more important than ever because the rate of economic inequality in Israel today is one of the highest in the developed world, and Israel is the country with the greatest rise in inequality.[1] Moreover, as the haves and have-nots have become increasingly polarized in recent decades, the chances of moving up the economic ladder have been declining. Education is a big part of this story in that educational opportunities shape the life chances of Israelis in terms of employment, career advancement, earnings, personal growth, and character development. As of 2012, the employment rate for twenty-five- to sixty-four-year-olds with a postsecondary education was 85 percent, compared to 47 percent for adults without one, a difference of more than 30 percentage points![2] The economic premium of a college education is also evident in the earnings gap: a postsecondary degree translates into 52 percent higher earnings compared to a high school degree. It is almost impossible to earn a salary at the top of the income distribution without a bachelor's degree. A college degree is the engine for social and economic mobility.

The addition of many second-tier colleges in Israel since the mid-1990s has generated optimism about future mobility. The dramatic increase in the capacity of the higher education system has certainly succeeded in increasing the share of the population with a bachelor's degree. In 2012 Israel ranked fourth among OECD countries for postsecondary attainment among twenty-five- to sixty-four-year-olds: 46 percent had a postsecondary degree, compared to the 33 percent OECD average.[3] As access to degree-granting institutions rose, however, so did the significance of education *type*. Elite universities offer a higher-quality education because of their institutional resources, their research orientation, and the caliber of their faculty and peers. Consequently, attending a selective college or university became more important for occupational status and wage prospects as the Israeli higher education system expanded, in that in every field the economic premium for diplomas from elite universities was higher than that for diplomas from the second-tier academic colleges.

What became most critical for determining employment and economic prospects was a degree from a selective field of study, many of which are not even offered at second-tier colleges. A degree in science, technology, or a professional field, especially a degree from one of the top universities, pays off well in the labor market and thus is a guarantee of economic and social well-being. For example, among the top earners in Israel—those with salaries in the top 10 percent of the income distribution—we mostly find workers in the finance and high-tech industries, many of whom have degrees in these fields.

The inequality in income trajectories and life chances explains the fierce competition for seats at the top universities, especially in the most lucrative fields of study. Between 1999 and 2008, only 60 percent of applicants to the top four universities were granted admission. Some departments were more difficult to get into than others: the most-selective departments admitted 23 percent of their applicants, on average, while the least-selective departments accepted more than 70 percent.

The rising competition in admissions and the underrepresentation of several populations in the first-tier universities in Israel, especially in the most-selective departments, prompted the four most-selective universities to implement an affirmative action admissions program in the early to mid-2000s. The program is race-neutral and class-based, with an emphasis on structural determinants of disadvantage—namely, neighborhood socioeconomic status and high school socioeconomic status. (Some individual hardships are also weighed.) In chapter 7, I demonstrated that this policy infuses the elite universities, including their most-selective departments, with the disadvantaged populations underrepresented at these bastions of privilege. That is, this policy increases several types of diversity in the student bodies of these institutions. But what about mobility? What was the effect, down the road, of the edge in admission on those who benefited from it?

This chapter examines the mobility dividends that the Israeli affirmative action policy yields for its beneficiaries. There are two ways in which special admissions can affect mobility prospects. First, the program provides some applicants with increased chances of attending an elite university instead of a second-tier college or none at all. Second, it gives some applicants an edge in admission to a more-selective field of study within an elite university. Both of these effects can fundamentally change the life course of applicants, who would have otherwise attended a less-selective institution or gained admission to a less-competitive field. Such a policy, then, allows its beneficiaries to enjoy the economic premium of a degree from an elite institution or a more prestigious, more lucrative, and more professionally oriented field.

For instance, David, who was born in Iran and emigrated to Israel with his parents in 1983, at the age of six, grew up in a poverty-stricken neighborhood of a major metropolitan area in the central district of Israel. David's parents died when he was young; he and his sisters were sent to boarding schools. He was drafted at age eighteen into a combat unit of the Israeli Defense Force (IDF) for his mandatory military service but was eventually released so that he could support himself financially. (The salary of soldiers during mandatory service years is nominal.) He was admitted to a selective and prestigious field of study in one of the universities and completed his degree. David was the first in his family to attend college.

The most straightforward way to evaluate mobility would be to compare the admission and academic outcomes of class-based admits (like David) to the outcomes that would have resulted if the policy had not been in place. The "what if?" question cannot be assessed directly, however, because we do not know what the admission and academic outcomes would have been if the class-based admits had not been selected for preferential treatment. We only know their destinations after being given the edge in admission. But there are other ways of gauging the mobility dividends of affirmative action. Fortunately, the unique features of this natural experiment and the simulations are useful for assessing the effect on its beneficiaries. In this chapter, I assess the mobility dividends in three different ways: in terms of period effects, simulation effects, and threshold effects.

PERIOD EFFECTS

We can get a sense of the class-based policy's effect on mobility chances by analyzing the admissions data before and after the plan went into effect. Specifically, I compared the admission chances and chosen majors of groups of disadvantaged applicants who benefited from the class-based affirmative action policy (those from poor localities) before and after the affirmative action program was implemented. A finding of better admission outcomes in the second period (relative to others) suggests that the affirmative action policy improved the mobility chances of underprivileged applicants.

Admission

The expansion of the higher education system, which began in 1995, continued throughout the period of this investigation, 1999 to 2008. In this decade, the number of seats systemwide grew from 126,000 to 172,000. Despite this growth, the four top universities became increasingly competitive, and each new cohort of applicants faced a higher admissions barrier than the one before it. In 1999, 67 percent of applicants to the top four universities were admitted. By 2007 that rate had dropped to 56 percent.

Figure 9.1 Admission Rates Before and During the AA Regime, by Locality SES Cluster, 1999–2008

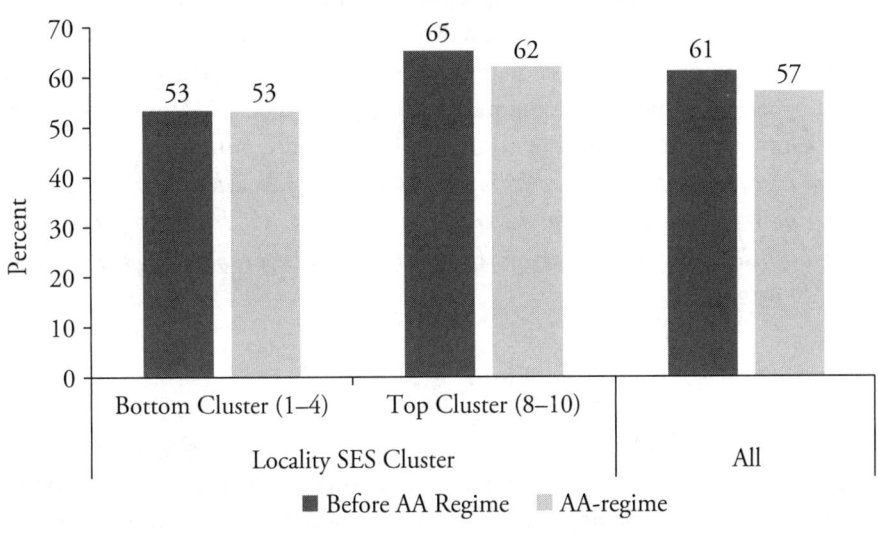

Source: TAU, HUJI, BGU, and TECH administrative data, 1999–2008.

Youth from poor localities, including both Jews and Arabs, have always been underrepresented at the four elite universities, particularly in their most-selective departments. We would expect, then, that this group, being one of the most disadvantaged in Israel, would have been the first to suffer from growing competition, which has had this effect in other countries, including the United States. But the universities also implemented the preferential treatment policy during this decade, in the early to mid-2000s. How, then, did applicants from this disadvantaged group fare during the decade-long trend of tightening admissions? Did the preferential treatment policy balance the detrimental impact of rising competition on individuals from poor localities? The data reveal that the admission rate of applicants from poor localities in the years before the implementation of affirmative action remained stable in the years after, at an average rate of 53 percent (see figure 9.1). During this period, however, applicants from the most-affluent localities saw their admission rate *drop*, from 65 to 62 percent. Without the affirmative action program, it is likely that poor applicants would have fallen behind their more-privileged peers.

In sum, the chances of individuals from poor localities gaining access to the country's most prestigious universities have *improved* since the class-based program was implemented, *relative to* applicants from affluent localities. As a result, the level of inequality at Israel's first-tier universities has decreased: the gap in admission rate by locality narrowed from 12 percent before the policy was implemented to 9 percent after. Although these effects cannot be linked directly to the policy, they are nonetheless indicative of *the positive effect of the policy on the mobility of disadvantaged groups. It seems that the class-based affirmative action program shielded applicants from poor localities in Israel from the full impact of increased competition in university admission.*

Field of Study

Department Selectivity Although admission to a top university in any field is a significant marker of future labor market success, it is also important to observe whether affirmative action helped applicants from disadvantaged groups gain access to fields of study associated with prestigious and well-paid careers. Altogether, the universities in this investigation had 164 departments, representing approximately fifty fields of study, or thirteen disciplines. As explained in chapter 6, each department was characterized (annually) by its level of academic selectivity, based on the supply of seats relative to demand and the cutoff test score. For every year of the investigation each department received a selectivity score, ranging from 0 to 1, that indicated how difficult it was to gain admission to said department in said year. On average, the departments in the four schools became more selective over time, from about 0.53 in 1999 to 0.61 in 2007. Thus, in every year within the observation period it was more difficult to get access to all majors, on average, than in the previous year. This declining access surely affected all applicants, but the question here is whether the edge in admission was enough to help applicants from poor localities keep up the pace in this race.

To examine this issue, I assigned each admit to the four universities a number that reflected the selectivity level of the most-selective field to which he or she was admitted. Not surprisingly, in the period before the preferential treatment program, there was a gap in the average level of selectivity by admits' locality-socioeconomic standing. The average selectivity score of admits from

Table 9.1 Admits' Fields of Study Before and During the AA Regime, by Locality SES Cluster, 1999–2008

	Locality SES Cluster			
	Bottom (1–4)		Top (8–10)	
Admits' Field of Study	Before AA Regime	AA Regime	Before AA Regime	AA Regime
Selectivity score[a] (mean)	0.548	0.600	0.613	0.660
Professional field[b]	33	31	39	38
Expected salary[c] (mean, in new Israeli shekels)	8,854	8,388	9,708	9,388

Source: TAU, HUJI, BGU, and TECH administrative data, 1999–2008.
[a]The department's selectivity index based on competitiveness and academic rigor (year-specific).
[b]Medicine, dentistry, engineering, computer science, law, architecture, and accounting.
[c]The average monthly salary of the department's graduates in their first years in the labor market following graduation.

poor localities was 0.55, whereas that of their counterparts from wealthy localities was 0.61 (see table 9.1).[4] Under the AA regime, there was a ten-percentage-point increase in the mean selectivity level of admits from poor localities, to 0.60, while the upsurge for those from the strongest localities was more moderate, increasing eight percentage points, to 0.66. In sum, the rise in the mean selectivity level for those from poor localities was larger than that of admits from wealthy localities.

Professional Fields Obtaining a degree in a professional field—such as medicine, dentistry, engineering, computer science, law, architecture, or accounting—is key for social and economic mobility in Israel because the prestige and economic returns to these degrees are higher than in other fields; these benefits are especially significant for high-performing minority students. This advantage holds even after taking test scores and high school grades into account, suggesting that the economic premium of professional fields is not just the result of a crop of better admits in the first place.[5] These fields in Israel tend to be studied at the undergraduate level, which provides us with the opportunity to examine the access of disadvantaged groups to these avenues for social and economic mobility.

The rising competition at the four elite universities made it especially difficult to get into the sought-after fields: the share of applicants admitted to the computer sciences, engineering, medicine, law, and accounting departments during the AA regime, compared to the preceding period, experienced an across-the-board decline. This was true even for applicants from the most-affluent localities, where the vast majority of residents attained a bachelor's degree and 40 percent of workers were in academic or managerial occupations. The admission rate of this group to professional fields went from 39 percent before the AA regime to 38 percent afterward (see table 9.1).[6] Remarkably, their counterparts from poor localities—where only 9 percent of workers held academic or managerial occupations and the average years of schooling was eleven—experienced a similar decline, from 33 to 31 percent. In other words, they were not hit harder than their wealthier peers in this respect.

Why is it surprising that applicants from poor localities were not losing ground relative to their affluent peers? One reason is that youth from socioeconomically strong backgrounds are steered toward fields that lead to "good" jobs and lucrative careers from an early age. The research from the United States (and this pattern surely applies elsewhere) tells us that parents from high socioeconomic echelons devote considerable effort to cultivating the academic currency of their offspring in order to ensure their access to elite institutions and fields of study.[7] These parents understand the postsecondary landscape and the competitive admission processes better than others and are more aware of the dramatic transformation of the economy and labor market. They convey their postsecondary expectations to their young children, are heavily involved with their academic activities, and track their progress throughout high school. They invest in resources to promote college attendance, be it a math tutor in high school or private classes for test preparation. These adaptation strategies improve the grades and test achievements of privileged high school students and put them in a better position to gain admission to high-status and lucrative fields of study in college and university.

So while it is true that the rising competition made it difficult for the underprivileged group to find seats in the professional fields of study, it is reasonable to assume that the drop would have been steeper than it was. That this was avoided seems to indicate that, to a certain extent, the class-based affirmative action policy sheltered applicants from poor localities from the growing competition in admissions. To illustrate this point, take Joel, who was admitted to one of the top law schools in Israel in the mid-2000s. Joel grew up in a development town in the northern part of Israel, graduated from a local high school, and was the first in his family to go to college. His home was in a disadvantage locality: in 2009 about 40 percent of the employed earned less than the monthly minimum wage. He was classified as a Mizrachi Jew because his father immigrated to Israel from Tunisia in 1958. (His mother was born in Israel.) Joel's parents were divorced, and there were several health and disability problems in his immediate family. Not surprisingly, his affirmative action eligibility score was very high (70), considerably above the thirty-point threshold.[8]

In the development town that Joel grew up in, most high school students did not go to college. In 2009 only 40 percent obtained a university-ready matriculation diploma, while the remainder either did not graduate from high school or obtained a lesser diploma, one not accepted by the universities. Joel was one of a small group of high school seniors in his town to receive a full matriculation diploma, with a GPA of 94 (out of 100) and a high standardized test score. These academic achievements were very close to, but not sufficient for, the general admission threshold at the competitive law school he wanted to attend, which admitted only one in three applicants on average. Nonetheless, with the edge in admission that his class-based disadvantage provided, Joel was admitted to this department and graduated with a law degree a few years later.

The affirmative action program certainly improved Joel's life chances and economic well-being. But these programs also tend to have spillover effects: Joel and others like him—future doctors, engineers, computer scientists, lawyers, and architects—are important role models for other youth residing in localities where there are very few professionals and where most of them have never set foot in an institution of higher education. This is the far reach of mobility dividends.

Expected Salary The rising competition in admissions, especially in the professional fields, implies that it is getting more and more difficult for students to enter fields that lead to lucrative occupations. How, then, have the economic mobility prospects of admits from poor localities changed over time?

To assess this question directly, I obtained pay data on the average monthly salary of each department's graduates during their first two years in the labor market for four cohorts of university graduates (2000 to 2003).[9] I obtained this earnings information from the Israel Central Bureau of Statistics (ICBS), which provides the tax authorities' administrative records for salaried workers, by major and institution. Each admit to the four universities was assigned the expected wage of the most lucrative field he or she was admitted to. For example, the data tell us how much graduates of TAU's electrical engineering department earned upon labor market entry and how much TECH graduates in the same field earned. This information yields the pecuniary market value of each department and offers a glimpse into the economic prospects of graduates from each field of study, at least at the outset of their careers.

The results reveal a gap, by place of residence, in the market value (in terms of monthly salary) of the departments to which applicants were admitted (see table 9.1). Before the affirmative action program was implemented, that gap between students from poor versus affluent localities amounted to about 900 NIS (8,800 versus 9,700 NIS, respectively).[10] As access to the fields that lead to lucrative professions tightened over time, all groups lost ground in the market value of the fields to which they were admitted. Although universities were expanding, they were mostly adding seats in the less-lucrative fields, while the capacity of the most-lucrative fields stayed the same. During the AA regime, applicants from both poor and affluent localities were admitted to less-lucrative fields, on average, compared to the period before the affirmative action was implemented. The decline in expected salary experienced by admits from the most-affluent localities was smaller than that for those from poor localities, but the difference was not big (three and five percentage points, respectively).

There may be several reasons for why applicants from disadvantaged backgrounds managed, against the odds, to (almost) keep pace with their privileged peers during a phase of tightening competition, and the preferential treatment policy implemented in the mid-2000s is probably one of them. By providing a protective shield from the increasing competition in admissions, the program has been able to promote economic mobility for some underprivileged groups.

In sum, the evidence in this section suggests that *the class-based affirmative action program at the four most-selective universities in Israel has helped youth from underprivileged groups maintain, and sometimes even augment, their access to a top education, especially in fields of study leading to prestigious and lucrative occupations, at a time when most other students have been losing ground.* Without this policy, individuals from underprivileged groups would probably have fallen further behind.

SIMULATION EFFECTS

In chapter 7, I reported the results of the simulation analyses of the comparative investigation, in which the actual class-based beneficiaries of the Israeli affirmative action program were replaced by the theoretical beneficiaries of a simulated race-based program. The latter would draw from the pool of applicants representing the two ethnic minority groups, Arabs and Mizrachi Jews. Given this context, another way to capture the mobility dividends of the class-based regime is by comparing the actual versus the simulated admission chances and outcomes of the simulated race-based admits. That is, we can examine the actual admission outcomes of this group without ethnic affirmative action in place, relative to their possible destinations if a race-based policy had been implemented. Can one's chances for mobility be transformed by an edge in admission? The evidence says yes.

About 55 percent of the minority applicants flagged as simulated race-based admits had been denied admission to the elite universities. For these applicants, a race-based affirmative action program would have opened the door to an elite education, boosting the admission rate of Arabs and Mizrachi Jews.[11] For admits who did enroll in the universities, we can juxtapose the field-of-study assignments with and without the hypothetical race-based program. The results suggest that such a policy would have elevated this group's chances of getting into more-selective fields. The real data show that race-based admits ended up in departments with an average selectivity level of 0.62 (on a scale of 0 to 1). (If it were not for the class-based regime, this figure would actually be lower, because 20 percent of minority applicants qualified for both the actual class-based and the simulated race-based programs.) Under race-based affirmative action, the average department selectivity level corresponding to these ethnic minority admits would have climbed to 0.65 (see table 9.2). Such a jump can translate, for example, into a move from chemistry to mechanical engineering, or from sociology to statistics, at one institu-

Table 9.2 Fields of Study of Individuals Who Were Eligible for the Simulated Ethnic-Based Affirmative Action, AA Regime

Admits' Field of Study	Without Ethnic-Based Affirmative Action: Before Simulation	With Ethnic-Based Affirmative Action: After Simulation
Selectivity score[a] (mean)	0.618	0.654
Professional field[b]	28	30
Expected salary[c] (mean, in new Israeli shekels)	7,935	8,608

Source: TAU, HUJI, and BGU administrative data, AA regime.
[a]The department's selectivity index based on competitiveness and academic rigor (year-specific).
[b]Medicine, dentistry, engineering, computer science, law, architecture, and accounting.
[c]The average monthly salary of the department's graduates in their first years in the labor market following graduation.

tion. At other universities it meant moving from economics to structural engineering, or from history to political science. Race-based affirmative action would have increased the share of ethnic minorities in professional fields by about 9 percentage points (from 28 to 30 percent). This edge would have resulted in more lucrative occupations, in which the starting monthly salary was 8 percentage points higher, on average, than the actual level (7,900 NIS versus 8,600 NIS, respectively). Over the course of an individual's career, this differential can mean a huge pecuniary gain.

In sum, *a race- or ethnic-based affirmative action policy would have given Arabs and Mizrachi Jews greater access to elite universities and the more-selective fields of study that lead to professional occupations and greater economic gains.* The class-based regime that the Israeli universities actually implemented was able to accomplish similar mobility gains, but for different groups and individuals.

THRESHOLD EFFECTS

In chapter 6, we met Jacob, whose dream was to enroll in a selective field at an elite university, even though his composite academic score was not high enough to guarantee admission. He submitted a standard application for preferential treatment and just passed the thirty-point cutoff for disadvantage-based eligibility with a score of 32. This was surprising given that neither his neighborhood nor his school qualified as disadvantaged. With no structural disadvantages, it is almost impossible to pass the threshold for preferential treatment. Nonetheless, Jacob had several hardships and adverse circumstances that together gave him just enough points to qualify: his father had died, his mother was unemployed, she and his brother both suffered from serious disabilities, his family lived in his grandmother's small apartment on government welfare support, and no one in his family had ever attended college. With the edge in admission that he received, Jacob was admitted to a very selective and lucrative field of study. Out of the sixty-two departments in his university, his department ranked twelfth in terms of the expected salary of its graduates.

What would have been Jacob's fate if his score was 29 instead of 32? How does he compare to other applicants who applied for preferential treatment but did not qualify? Such a comparison would allow us to answer the "what if?" question and to appreciate the mobility dividends of affirmative action policy from yet another angle. These are known as "threshold effects." This particular analysis focuses on applicants who are just above and just below the cutoff—plus or minus ten points—because there are few systematic differences in grades, test scores, motivation, or aspirations between applicants within a narrow range of the thirty-point threshold for disadvantage-based eligibility. The main difference between them is just a few points on their affirmative action eligibility score, which could indicate that only one circumstance, or even a "stroke of luck," sets them apart. Can one such difference determine one's destiny?

To compare these two groups I exploit the explicit formulaic method that is used to determine disadvantage-based eligibility. Those who scored above 30 on the index were eligible for preferential treatment, but they were not necessarily admitted. I tracked the applicants who fell just above and just below the thirty-point cutoff in order to observe whether passing the threshold set better admission opportunities in motion. The results suggest that the answer is yes. Fifty-eight percent of applicants who qualified as disadvantaged (just above the threshold) were admitted to the four universities, compared to 53 percent of those who fell just below the threshold (see figure 9.2). These

Figure 9.2 Admission and Enrollment Outcomes of Individuals Who Fell Just Above and Just Below the Affirmative Action Threshold of Eligibility, AA Regime

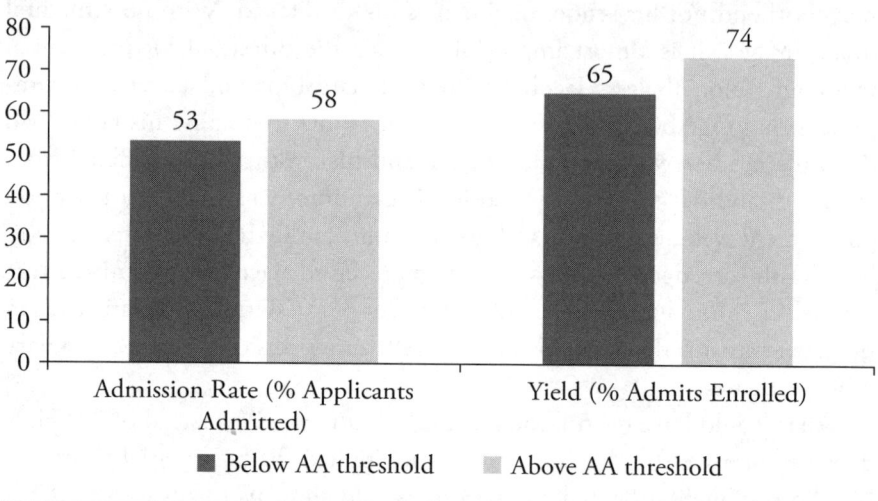

Source: TAU, HUJI, BGU, and TECH administrative data, AA regime.
Note: Just above and just below the affirmative action threshold of eligibility is defined as plus or minus ten points around the thirty-point cutoff.

numbers are remarkable in part because university departments *are not required* to admit any of the students deemed eligible for affirmative action. Granting an edge in admission is at the complete discretion of each department, and there are no quotas to fill, which means that these departments have voluntarily decided to become more inclusive.

This decision has implications for enrollment behavior, in that the enrollment yield of admits (the share of admits who actually enroll) was greater among those admits just above the threshold of eligibility for affirmative action (74 percent) than among those who fell just below (65 percent).[12] It seems that the greatest motivation for an admit to enroll in a field of study was gaining admission to the field that he or she found most desirable; the eligible ones were more likely to have gotten what they wanted than those who failed to meet the threshold for eligibility. For example, although individuals from both groups were just as likely to apply to professional fields of

Table 9.3 Fields of Study of Admits Who Fell Just Above and Just Below the Affirmative Action Threshold of Eligibility, AA Regime

Admits' Field of Study	Below AA Threshold	Above AA Threshold
Selectivity score[a] (mean)	0.601	0.625
Professional field[b]	26	30
Expected salary[c] (mean, in new Israeli shekels)	7,959	8,179

Source: TAU, HUJI, BGU, and TECH administrative data, AA regime.
Note: Just above and just below the affirmative action threshold of eligibility is defined as plus or minus ten points around the thirty-point cutoff.
[a]The department's selectivity index based on competitiveness and academic rigor (year-specific).
[b]Medicine, dentistry, engineering, computer science, law, architecture, and accounting.
[c]The average monthly salary of the department's graduates in their first years in the labor market following graduation.

study, those above the eligibility cutoff were more likely to gain admission (30 percent) than those below it (26 percent).[13] Applicants who made the cut for affirmative action were also admitted to departments whose selectivity level and expected salaries were higher than the selectivity and expected salaries in the departments to which applicants just below the threshold applied (see table 9.3). The edge in admission, then, sets the two groups apart, and it translates into clear mobility dividends, because admission to such fields implies better labor market prospects and higher economic returns.[14]

Of course, we do not know what Jacob's fate would have been without the edge in admission. But the results here strongly suggest that he would have enrolled in a less-selective field of study, with lower returns. In other words, while Jacob had many disadvantages working against him in life, he did benefit from having a disadvantage index score of 32 rather than, say, 29. A small difference in eligibility score can translate into a big difference in fortune.

In sum, the findings indicate that *students who just barely passed the disadvantage cutoff for the voluntary class-based policy in Israel had a significantly higher probability of admission and enrollment relative to otherwise similar students who were just below the cutoff.* They also were more likely to be admitted to more-selective and more-lucrative fields of study. Thus, this edge translated into entry into the fields of study that pave the way for social and economic mobility. These results reinforce the conclusion that the class-based affirmative action program in Israel cultivates better life chances for some disadvantaged individuals.

ATTAINMENT, ACADEMIC OUTCOMES, AND THE "MISMATCH" HYPOTHESIS

The story of mobility dividends does not end with determining the quality of the college or university attended and the potential economic returns to a field of study. To realize the mobility potential afforded them by affirmative action policy, students must persist in university until graduation. Affirmative action in college admissions is futile if those who benefit drop out. A bachelor's diploma is a quintessential marker of mobility, and without it access to an elite education is an empty promise of mobility. Grades in college also have a powerful and independent effect on mobility, as there is a premium associated with doing well academically, even among graduates of elite schools.[15] Research suggests that grades are influential in securing a job and determining initial pay.[16] In Jacob's case, the opportunity was not wasted because he eventually graduated with a degree in a professional field, and with a good GPA. But is this typical? How does affirmative action affect students' persistence and academic outcomes? In studying the mobility dividends of any affirmative action policy, we must also consider graduation likelihood and grades.

Critics of race-conscious admissions in American higher education have charged that affirmative action sets up minority students for failure because these students are ostensibly unprepared to succeed in elite academic settings.[17] This claim is known as the "mismatch hypothesis,"[18] which suggests that the beneficiaries of race-based affirmative action are not well matched with the institutions that they end up attending. The rationale is that "when students are given a preference in admission because of their race or some other extraneous characteristics, it means that they are jumping into a competition for which their academic achievements do not qualify them and many find it hard to keep up."[19] Presumably, mismatched minority students become demoralized, underperform, and ultimately fail to graduate.[20]

Most of the evidence, however, does not substantiate the mismatch hypothesis. Several studies have shown that not only do minority students thrive at selective colleges, but they are also more likely than minority students attending less-selective schools to graduate, pursue an advanced degree, and earn well later in life.[21] Despite the lack of support for the mismatch claim, opponents of race-conscious admissions continue to use it to promote the move to class-based affirmative action. For example, in their recent book *Mismatch*, Richard Sander and Stuart Taylor advocate for class-based affirmative action as a means of dodging the mismatch problem associated with race-based affirmative action.[22] However, even if we assume that minority students are harmed by the special treatment in admissions—despite all the evidence to the contrary—this fundamental question remains: *if mismatch is such a problem for students of color, then wouldn't it also be a problem for beneficiaries of class-based affirmative action?* The authors do not address the logical problem with their position. As Joyce Sterling and Catherine Smith, the editors of a special issue of the *Denver University Law Review*, put it: "Sander needs to do a better job explaining why he thinks low SES students, once they have gained admissions preferences, will do better than have students of color once they arrive on the campuses of our nation's most elite law schools. What is it about these students that frees them of the 'mismatch' dangers that so concern him with students of color?"[23]

The fact is that the authors cannot answer this question because, as class-based affirmative action has never been implemented in the United States, it is an empirical question that has never been examined. That being said, with all the administrative data on Israel's class-based affirmative action program, this investigation has allowed me to probe into whether the beneficiaries of a class-based policy are indeed mismatched. Can we argue that the beneficiaries of the Israeli affirmative action program would be better off had they enrolled in less-selective institutions or fields of study? After all, they did gain admission to departments more selective than those they would have qualified for otherwise. Do the beneficiaries of class-based affirmative action in Israel experience a mismatch problem that is detrimental for their academic success in terms of grades and graduation likelihood?

To determine whether the AA admits found it hard to keep up after enrollment, I compared the academic outcomes—grades and graduation chances—of class-based admits whose affirmative action eligibility score was just above the cutoff to the outcomes of admitted students who had applied for prefer-

Table 9.4 Various Academic Outcomes of Students Who Fell Just Above and Just Below the Affirmative Action Threshold of Eligibility, AA Regime

	Unadjusted Gap			Adjusted Gap[a]		
	Below AA Threshold	Above AA Threshold	Difference	Below AA Threshold	Above AA Threshold	Difference
Freshman GPA[b] (person-major)	77.5	77.1	-0.4	81.5	81.5	0.0
Graduation likelihood[c]	67.2%	67.6%	0.5%	70.0%	70.7%	0.7%
Final GPA[d] (person-major)	83.0	83.5	0.5	79.3	79.8	0.5

Source: TAU, HUJI, BGU, and TECH administrative data, AA regime.
Note: Based on OLS and logit regression models; full results are in table A9.1. Just above and just below the affirmative action threshold of eligibility is defined as plus or minus ten points around the thirty-point cutoff.
[a]Control for student's academic composite score and major's fixed effects.
[b]For 2003–2007 (TAU), 2006–2007 (BGU), 2001–2008 (HUJI), and 2004–2007 (TECH).
[c]For 2001–2005 (HUJI).
[d]For 2001–2005 (HUJI).

ential treatment but whose eligibility score was just below the cutoff. This comparison is actually biased in favor of the group that fell below the affirmative action threshold—that is, who did not benefit from affirmative action—and thus had lower admission chances than those above the threshold. Because fewer of these applicants were admitted to elite institutions—and probably the best among them were accepted—they are a more-selective group of students than the class-based admits. Moreover, they were admitted to less-selective majors, which are ostensibly easier, and were less likely to enroll. In this context, it is reasonable to expect that the gap in academic outcomes, if it exists, will favor those with an eligibility score below the program's threshold.

The results prove this expectation wrong. The beneficiaries of class-based affirmative action whose eligibility score was above the cutoff had similar grades in their first year in college (in each major studied) to the grades attained by students whose eligibility score was below the cutoff (see table 9.4).

The average GPA of both groups was around 77. Overall, class-based admits were more likely to graduate and did so with slightly higher grades relative to those admits just below the affirmative action cutoff.

It can be argued that the students just below and just above the threshold differ in two important ways: (1) they have different academic credentials (test scores and high school grades), and (2) they study in different majors, with different academic climates and grading norms. Because both of these factors can shape grades in college and graduation chances, we must be sure to compare "equivalent" students—or as we say in the professional jargon, that we netted out the effect of both of these factors in estimating academic outcomes. When we net out composite academic scores and the grading norms of majors, we get the same result: the GPAs of first-year admitted students on both sides of the AA threshold were almost identical.[24] Thus, *class-based admits with an affirmative action eligibility score just above the cutoff had similar academic outcomes in college, on average, compared to outcomes for students who applied to the program but did not reach the thirty-point threshold.* Put simply, *the beneficiaries of class-based affirmative action were not falling behind academically.*

Moreover, the advantages that class-based affirmative action bestows upon beneficiaries at the admission stage persist until graduation. To illustrate this further I tracked a group of applicants at one institution, The Hebrew University, from application until graduation, comparing those just above and just below the threshold. At each stage along the college pipeline, I tracked the selectivity and salary levels of the fields of study of both groups. The results show that the advantage gained at the admission stage from affirmative action in terms of both selectivity and expected salary was not lost at degree attainment (see figure 9.3). *The beneficiaries of affirmative action graduated from fields of study that are more rigorous, prestigious, and lucrative than those of their counterparts just below the eligibility cutoff.*

This pattern is confirmed in the study my colleague Ofer Malamud and I conducted recently, which implemented regression discontinuity (RD) design, a more sophisticated way of assessing the differences in academic outcomes between admitted students who fell just above and just below the affirmative action threshold of eligibility.[25] We found that AA admits were more likely to graduate, and to graduate with higher GPAs, although the gaps were not large. We confirmed that the beneficiaries of affirmative action did

210 RACE, CLASS, AND AFFIRMATIVE ACTION

Figure 9.3 Tracking Fields of Study from Application to Graduation for Individuals Who Fell Just Above and Just Below the Affirmative Action Threshold of Eligibility, AA Regime

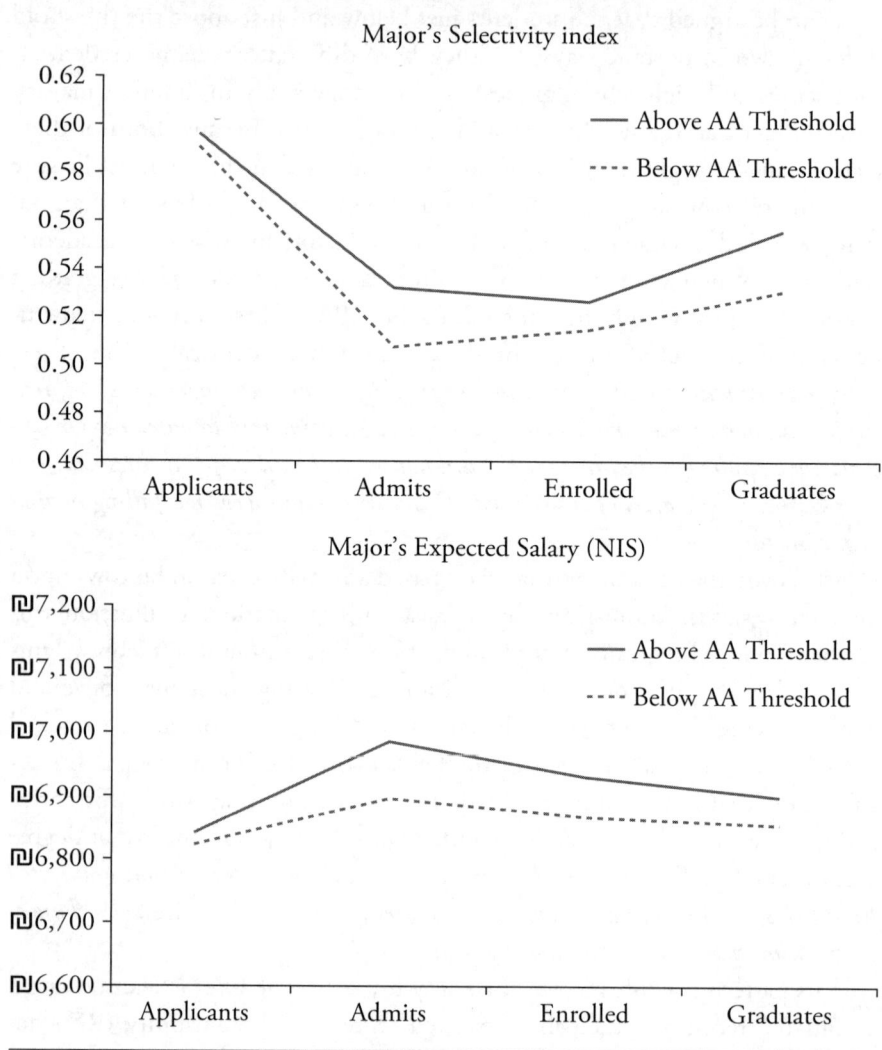

Source: HUJI administrative data, AA regime, and person-major data, 2001–2005.
Note: Just above and just below the affirmative action threshold of eligibility is defined as plus or minus ten points around the thirty-point cutoff.

just as well academically as other students, if not better. We also examined the graduation likelihood from selective majors—an important outcome because it tells us whether the beneficiaries of affirmative action who graduated were able to maintain their GPAs only because they switched from the academically rigorous fields of study that they initially enrolled in to easier majors. Our study concludes that AA-eligible students were also more likely to graduate from selective majors compared to students who fell just below the AA threshold of eligibility.

It seems, then, that the students whose stories have been told here—David, Jacob, Joel, Yusuf, Bashir, Sarah, Neta, Suzanne, and Maya—were not alone. In fact, most students who received an edge in admission under the Israeli class-based affirmative action program persisted in college until graduation and obtained good grades. These results are consistent with previous U.S. research that negates the mismatch hypothesis.[26]

In sum, *eligibility for class-based affirmative action is associated with neither subpar academic performance in courses taken during university nor failure to graduate. The beneficiaries of affirmative action do just as well academically as other students, and sometimes better. The mismatch hypothesis is refuted: the beneficiaries of the Israeli affirmative action program would not be better off without an edge in admission.*

Richard Sander and Stuart Taylor's claim that the beneficiaries of class-based affirmative action will not find it hard to keep up with their classmates at elite institutions is correct. Yet the findings in the next chapter reveal that their assumption that minority students are harmed by race-conscious admissions to American colleges and universities is utterly wrong.

THE MOBILITY DIVIDENDS OF AFFIRMATIVE ACTION POLICY

In examining the issue from different perspectives, I was able to corroborate the hypothesis that the affirmative action policy in Israel yields social and economic mobility dividends for its beneficiaries. Because attending an elite university and getting a degree from a selective field of study in Israel yields advantages with respect to educational achievements, occupational status, and wage prospects, I focused on whether the program widens the path to elite institutions, especially to the fields of study that are most lucrative and selective. As I followed the beneficiaries of the policy throughout the college pipeline, from application to graduation, I was also able to test the merit of the most vociferous claim against affirmative action policy: that its beneficiaries fall behind academically.

Taken together, the findings from the three sets of analyses (period, simulation, and threshold effects) unequivocally establish that benefiting from an affirmative action policy is not detrimental to one's success in college or labor market prospects. Quite the reverse is true: getting an edge in admission allowed Israeli applicants from disadvantaged backgrounds to improve their chances at the admission stage in access to both elite universities and selective majors. The evidence suggests that the beneficiaries of affirmative action fully exploit the opportunity it opens up by converting the advantage they gain at the admission stage into a prestigious and lucrative college degree. In an era of growing economic inequality, the beneficiaries of affirmative action are able to translate access to an elite education into social and economic mobility. The conclusion is straightforward: *Israel's class-based affirmative action program expands the access of academically borderline applicants from disadvantaged backgrounds to a quality education and thus widens the avenue to mobility for groups at the bottom of the hierarchy.*

The class-based regime that the Israeli universities implemented has huge mobility dividends. A race- or ethnic-based affirmative action program could accomplish similar mobility gains for different groups and individuals. Given these sizable mobility dividends, the question of who is eligible for special consideration in admissions takes on new meaning. At stake is not just *what type* of diversity can be boosted at elite institutions by affirmative action, but *who* can be boosted. Who will have their lives transformed for the better, and who will not?

CHAPTER 10

The Academic Outcomes and Mobility Dividends of Affirmative Action Policy in the United States

> The University admits minorities who otherwise would have attended less-selective colleges where they would have been more evenly matched. But, as a result of the mismatching, many blacks and Hispanics who likely would have excelled at less elite schools are placed in a position where underperformance is all but inevitable.[1]
> —Justice Clarence Thomas

> Maybe affirmative action places a stigma on its recipients. I would guess that if we asked most recipients, they would shrug, and say that stigma is nothing compared to where they might have been without it.[2]
> —Berneta Haynes, law student at the University of Iowa

Today in the United States, only 4 percent of children living in families at the bottom of the income ladder will ever make it to the top. It is no wonder, then, that when comparing the economic standing of adults to their parents, the United States trails all other industrialized countries in economic mobility between generations.[3] Even more alarming perhaps is that very few Americans attain a higher level of education than their parents.[4] Among those who do move up the economic ladder—the upwardly mobile population—90 percent have a college degree.[5] The good news is that a large proportion of adults in the United States do have a university-level education. The Organization for Economic Cooperation and Development (OECD) ranked the

United States fifth in the percentage of adults with a postsecondary education, just after Israel. The bad news is that this rate is increasing much faster in many other countries. The large proportion of college-educated individuals in the United States speaks mainly to the success of past generations; our fifth-place ranking will fall as other countries catch up. Indeed, we already have a glimpse of the gloomy future: the younger U.S. population comes in at eleventh in the percentage with a university-level education, compared to other industrialized nations.

Because of its economic value in the labor market, a college diploma is especially important for those at the bottom looking for a way out. The gains in the labor market are significant: about one-third of American adults with a college education earn more than twice the national median income, while half of those without a degree earn less than half the median.[6] In fact, the United States is the industrialized country with the largest economic premium for a college diploma. Among the college-educated, the chances for economic mobility and the size of the economic premium depend on institution type and field of study. But access to the most-prized institutions varies considerably according to race-ethnicity and socioeconomic status. For minority and socioeconomically disadvantaged applicants, climbing the economic ladder is difficult because their chances of attending an elite college or university are low.[7] In this capacity, affirmative action policy has the potential to increase access to an elite education for applicants who would benefit from it most and thus to promote their social and economic mobility.

The mobility dividends of affirmative action policy begin with the college experience, because beneficiaries reap the labor market benefits of having attended an elite college only if they persist until they earn a degree. It is true that whether or not a student graduates is already largely determined by the time he or she begins college by factors such as level of preparation for the academic rigors of college, the academic level of peers, and the ability to adapt academically and socially to college life. Nonetheless, as discussed in chapter 3, the odds of attaining a bachelor's degree are also affected by an institution's resources for promoting learning. For example, selective colleges with large endowments offer greater financial aid and contact with faculty, as well as academic and social environments that are conducive to learning and personal growth, all of which has a positive effect on persistence and degree attainment. Affirmative action, in pushing some eligible applicants up the institutional ladder to colleges with more supportive and stimulating learning environments, may also be making it more likely that they will graduate.

Mobility dividends are at the heart of the mismatch hypothesis—the claim that affirmative action sets up minority students for failure because they are assumed to be unprepared to succeed academically in elite academic settings. Presumably, mismatched minority students become demoralized, underperform, and ultimately fail to graduate and thus would be better off having attended a less-selective college.[8] The notion that the beneficiaries of affirmative action would be better off without it has managed to penetrate the halls of the Supreme Court. For example, in his concurring opinion to the 2012 Fisher decision, Justice Clarence Thomas posits:

> The University admits minorities who otherwise would have attended less-selective colleges where they would have been more evenly matched. But, as a result of the mismatching, many blacks and Hispanics who likely would have excelled at less elite schools are placed in a position where underperformance is all but inevitable because they are less academically prepared than the white and Asian students with whom they must compete. Setting aside the damage wreaked upon the self-confidence of these overmatched students, there is no evidence that they learn more at the University than they would have learned at other schools for which they were better prepared. Indeed, they may learn less.[9]

In this chapter, I explore whether affirmative action in U.S. college admissions contributes to the social and economic mobility of its beneficiaries or whether, as Justice Thomas suggests, they would be better off attending less-selective schools. I assess both the mobility dividends and the mismatch hypothesis by chronicling the benefits—in terms of academic and social integration, degree attainment, and field-of-study choices—that stem from an edge in admission. What is the impact of moving up the institutional ladder? How would URM students have fared without affirmative action? How would high-achieving students of low socioeconomic status have fared if class-based affirmative action had been in place? This "what if?" question cannot be answered directly in that we cannot know what the outcomes would have been if the beneficiaries of affirmative action had not received an edge in admissions. Nonetheless, the simulations that I conducted in the comparative investigation allow me to examine this issue while bypassing this analytical hurdle.

SIMULATION EFFECTS: MOVING UP THE INSTITUTIONAL LADDER

The simulations mimic current race-based affirmative action by moving the potential beneficiaries of a hypothetical class-based policy up the institutional ladder. That is, actual race-based admits are replaced by simulated class-based admits, so that students of low socioeconomic status or from high-poverty high schools move from the less-selective schools in which they actually enrolled to elite colleges ("highly competitive" and "most competitive," *Barron's* top two categories). In chapter 8, I showed that preferential treatment, whether based on race or on class, infuses elite universities with disadvantaged and underrepresented populations. But what is the effect of the edge in admission on those who benefit from it?

I use the results of the simulation to examine what it means to move up the institutional ladder. Specifically, I compare the *actual* admission and attainment outcomes of two groups of students:

1. *Class-based admits:* Those students who most likely would have benefited from class-based affirmative action if it had been implemented at elite colleges. These are students from deprived socioeconomic backgrounds who would have been eligible for at least one prototype of class-based affirmative action, be it economic, socioeconomic, or structural (high school–based).[10]
2. *Race-based admits:* Those students who benefited from race-based affirmative action and attended elite colleges.

In essence, this is a comparison of the *actual* admission and attainment outcomes of high-achieving students from deprived socioeconomic backgrounds (that is, class-based admits without any preferences in admissions, before simulations) to their *potential* outcomes under a class-based affirmative action policy (that is, the actual outcomes of race-based admits, before simulations). The results capture the potential mobility dividends of class-based affirmative action, but they can also be perceived as the mobility dividends of race-based affirmative action.

What makes this comparison valid is that both groups of high school graduates—both race- and class-based admits—had *similar academic starting points before college* in terms of test scores, number of AP courses taken, and grades.

In fact, the test scores and high school GPAs of the (simulated) class-based admits were *higher,* on average, than those of the race-based admits. For example, the mean test scores of class-based admits under socioeconomic affirmative action was 1,130—and 1,100 under structural affirmative action—compared to 950 among the race-based admits. Nonetheless, because the actual road taken in affirmative action was race-based, not class-based, the (simulated) class-based admits ended up at schools that were less selective than those attended by race-based admits. Had class-based policy replaced the current policy, the race-based admits would have attended less-selective schools, and the socioeconomically deprived class-based admits would probably have attended more elite schools.

What were the actual college destinations of the class-based admits—the high-achieving students who would have benefited from class-based affirmative action (and been eligible for at least one model) had it been adopted by elite institutions? Without an edge in admission, only 12 percent of these academically well prepared students from deprived socioeconomic backgrounds made it to a highly competitive institution (category 2; see figure 10.1) in 1995–1996, the year the comparative investigation focuses on, while 70 percent enrolled in category 3 or 4 schools. (The few underprivileged students attending the most competitive [category 1] institutions in the country are not classified here as "class-based admits" because they would not have benefited from class-based affirmative action, since they were already at the top of the institutional hierarchy.) What is more, 17 percent of these high-achieving students entered category 5 or 6 four-year colleges (the bottom two *Barron's* categories). The simulations reassigned all of these students to category 1 and 2 colleges, which captures the typical magnitude of an edge in admissions: an upgrade of one or two categories.[11]

And so, if class-based affirmative action had been in place, class-based admits would have attended schools whose endowment funds per student are six times higher[12] and where about 80 percent of students graduate (as opposed to about 50 percent at all other four-year schools). But what would this upgrade have really meant for these students? What impact would it have had on their mobility chances later on? To answer this question we turn to a discussion of how the differences in institutional climate and resources affected the college experience, degree attainment, and field-of-study choices of race-based admits and their class-based counterparts.

Figure 10.1   The College Destinations of Individuals Eligible for the Simulated Class-Based Affirmative Action, 1995–1996

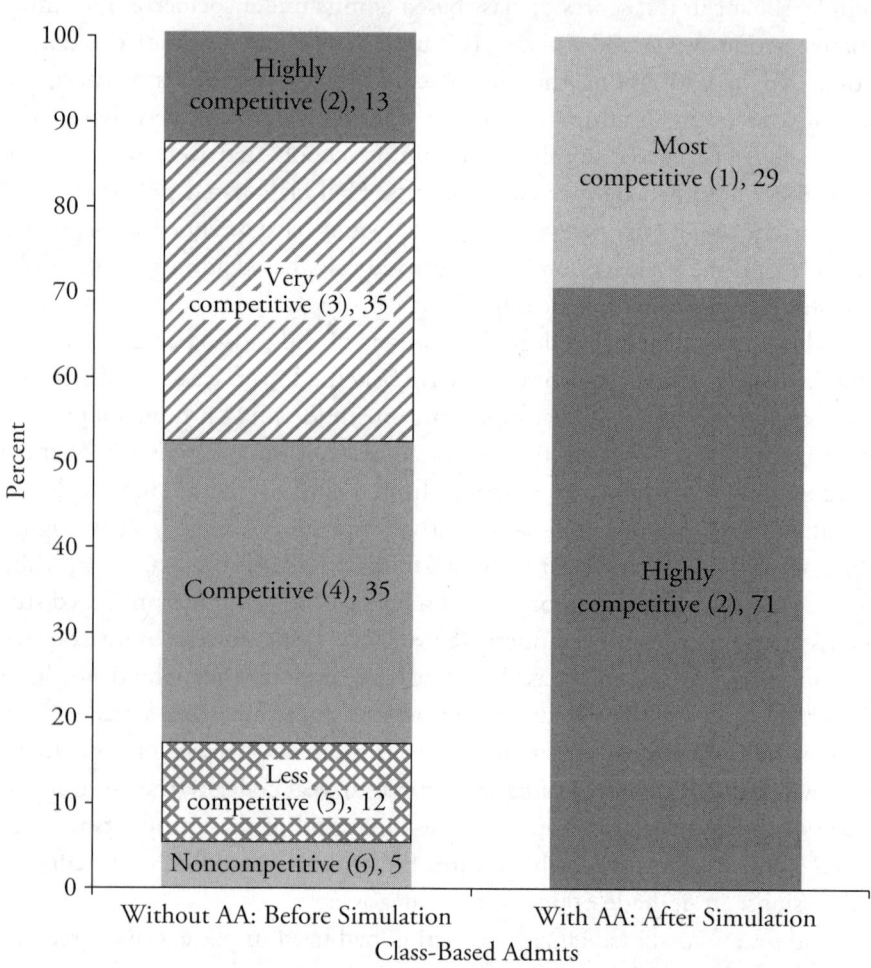

Source: National Center for Education Statistics, Beginning Postsecondary Students Longitudinal Study (BPS), 1996–2001.
Note: The few underprivileged students attending category 1 institutions are not class-based admits because they attended the most competitive institutions in the country without any edge in admissions. They would not have benefited from class-based affirmative action.

Academic and Social Integration

Academic and social involvement in college affects students' chances of persisting until degree attainment. For example, research has shown that the more students interact with each other and with faculty, the more likely they are to stay in college and graduate.[13] Such interactions are especially important for students from socioeconomically disadvantaged backgrounds, particularly first-generation college students. What does an upgrade to an elite school mean in terms of students' ability to interact with faculty and students on campus? I answer this question by comparing the college experience of the class-based admits to that of the race-based admits.

The U.S. Department of Education surveyed students who were freshmen in 1995–1996 about their overall level of academic and social integration on campus during their first year of college in terms of how often they had participated in various activities.[14] Forty percent of race-based admits reported that they participated in study groups often during their first year, while only about 20 percent of class-based admits did so (see figure 10.2).[15] Moreover, 22 percent of class-based admits *never* participated in a study group. About one-third of the beneficiaries of race-based affirmative action reported that they met with an academic adviser often as freshmen and that they had often spoken with a faculty member about academic matters outside of class. The potential beneficiaries of class affirmative action were less likely to have contact with faculty as freshmen: only 13 percent met with an academic adviser often, and only 23 percent spoke with a faculty member about academic matters outside of class. When the responses for all questions pertaining to academic integration were tallied according to the Department of Education's scale, race-based admits scored an average of 214 (out of a maximum of 300 points), while class-based admits scored 195.[16] Overall, the academic integration of race-based admits attending elite colleges was much higher than that of their class-based counterparts at less-competitive schools, in spite of the fact that both groups began with similar academic qualifications.

The race-based admits at elite schools also reported being more socially involved relative to the class-based admits at less-selective schools: they attended fine arts activities, participated in sports (either intramural, nonvarsity or varsity, or intercollegiate) and school clubs, and went out with friends from school. Although the gap in social integration is not as large as the gap

Figure 10.2 The Academic Integration of Students at the First Institution They Attended During the 1995–1996 Academic Year, by AA Status

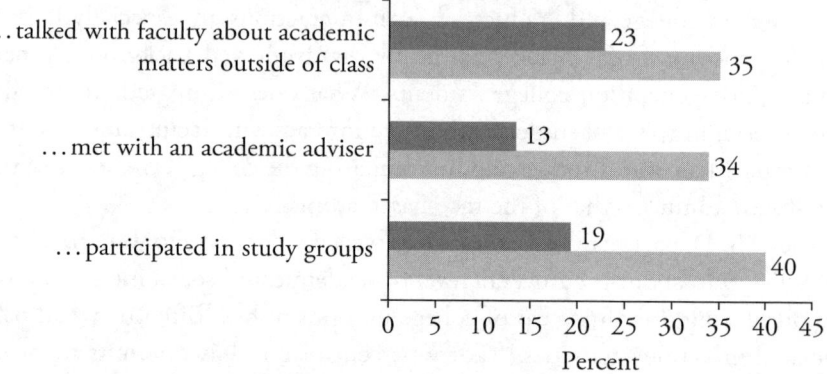

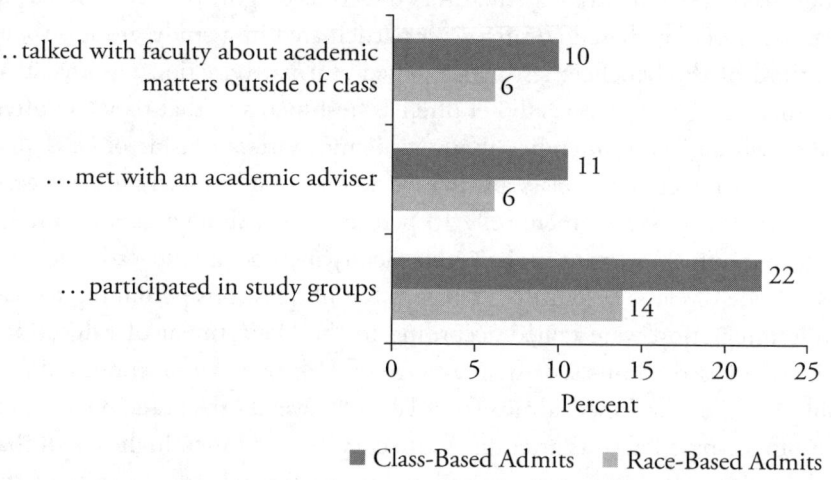

Source: National Center for Education Statistics, Beginning Postsecondary Students Longitudinal Study (BPS), 1996–2001.

in academic integration, it is still significant. For example, 42 percent of class-based admits never participated in a school club as freshmen, compared to only 30 percent among race-based admits.

Taken together, these results demonstrate that *the beneficiaries of race-conscious admissions at elite institutions are better integrated academically and socially by the end of their first year in college compared to their counterparts from socioeconomically underprivileged backgrounds at less-selective schools.* Given that the students from the two groups had similar academic credentials when they began college, the gap in academic integration that emerges toward the end of the first year captures the effect of the institutional environment on students' prospects for academic success, above and beyond their own potential. By allowing students to attend a more-competitive school, affirmative action policy enhances their academic and social integration in college and contributes to their chances of academic success. Whether this gap materializes into a gap in graduation chances is examined in the next sections.

Degree Attainment

The disparity in academic climate associated with race-based versus class-based admits during the first year of college sets the stage for what happens down the road. With less guidance and support from professors and peers, the class-based admits were less likely than their race-based counterparts to return to college the next fall (87 versus 90 percent, respectively; see figure 10.3), despite their similar performance in high school and on standardized tests. The gap widens over time, so that by the fall of junior year, only 78 percent of the class-based admits matriculated, compared to 89 percent of their race-based counterparts. Eventually, only 65 percent of class-based admits attained a bachelor's degree from the non-elite institution in which they first enrolled in the fall of 1995, compared to 73 percent of the race-based admits at elite institutions.

Interestingly, the graduation rate of class-based admits at the college they entered as freshmen was higher, at 65 percent, than the institutional average, at 52 percent. This is not surprising given that this was a group of students with high academic potential to start with—that is, they were the creamy layer at their less-selective schools. Moreover, some of the high-achieving students from socioeconomically disadvantaged backgrounds regrouped after dropping out of the first institution they attended and transferred to, and

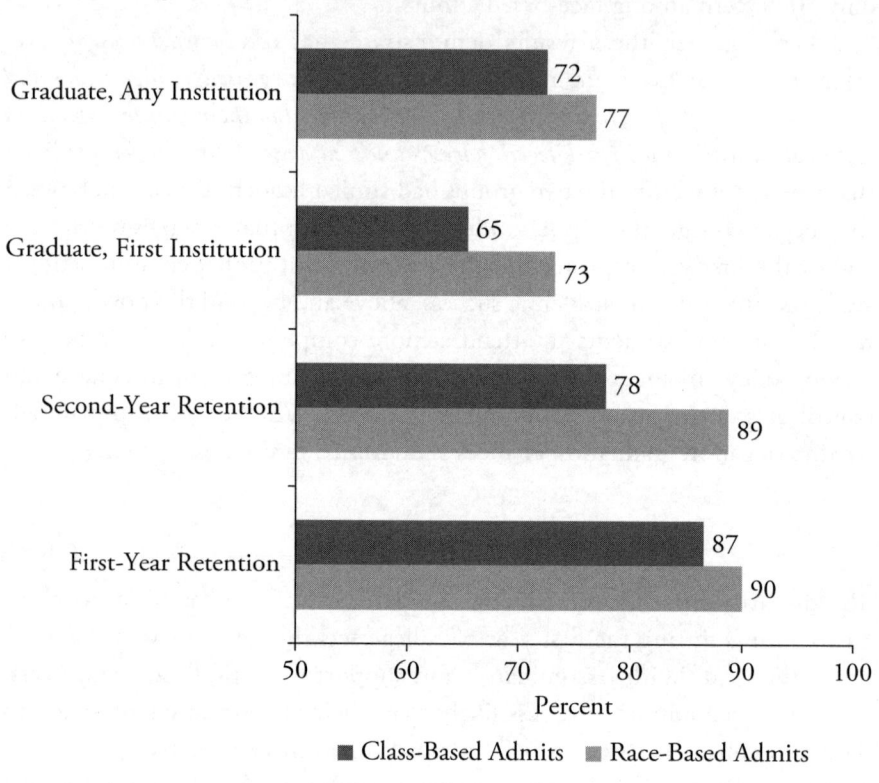

Figure 10.3 Persistence Toward a Degree of Students Who Enrolled During the 1995–1996 Academic Year, by AA Status

Source: National Center for Education Statistics, Beginning Postsecondary Students Longitudinal Study (BPS), 1996–2001.

graduated from, another institution. Nonetheless, the divide between the two groups in degree attainment persists.

In sum, *the beneficiaries of race-conscious admissions at elite institutions in the United States are more likely to attain a degree than socioeconomically underprivileged students with similar credentials at less-selective schools.* Thus, the former group benefits twice from attending an elite institution: first, the edge in admission increases their chances of degree attainment; and second, their diplomas are more valuable in the labor market.

These results capture the potential mobility dividends of class-based affirmative action: if such a policy were in place at elite colleges and universities, the chances of socioeconomically underprivileged students attaining a degree would be significantly higher.

Fields of Study

The field in which a degree is obtained is also important, in that it determines career opportunities, initial salary, wage trajectory, and the likelihood of acquiring an advanced degree.[17] Students attending elite institutions have a different profile of degree attainment and field of study than those at non-elite schools.[18] This was also true for the cohort that began college in the fall of 1995.

With regard to the elite profile (institutions in categories 1 and 2), the majority (64 percent) of freshmen in 1995 ended up with a bachelor's degree in the social sciences, humanities, and STEM fields (science, technology, engineering, and mathematics), all of which are launching pads for pursuing advanced degrees (see figure 10.4).[19] In the non-elite profile (all other four-year institutions), about half of freshmen in 1995 did not graduate at all. About one-quarter obtained a degree in the social sciences, humanities, or STEM fields, while one-quarter graduated with a degree in a vocational field, such as education, business, or the health professions. Vocational fields, while strongly linked to the labor market, generally lead to less-prestigious jobs compared to STEM fields and have a relatively flat earnings trajectory. Most of the graduates in vocational fields did not go on to pursue advanced or professional degrees.

This disparity is not surprising. Elite institutions offer a wide selection of courses in the liberal arts and science fields, but very few in applied fields. Elite colleges tend to emphasize the value of intellectual exploration and the pursuit of knowledge more than other schools do, thus orienting their students toward a broad education, not a practical occupation.[20] Their students are more likely to obtain bachelor's degrees in the liberal arts, which do not lead to specific occupations or lucrative careers. Nonetheless, these students tend to go on to graduate and professional schools, where they attain degrees that offer job opportunities that are far better than the ones available to those with a bachelor's degree in a vocational field.

The structural and educational environment of elite colleges and universities influences the field-of-study choices of everyone on campus, including the beneficiaries of race-conscious admissions. Consequently, the field-of-

Figure 10.4 Field of Study of Students Who Started College in 1995–1996 upon Graduation (When Last Enrolled) from First Institution, by Institution Type and AA Status

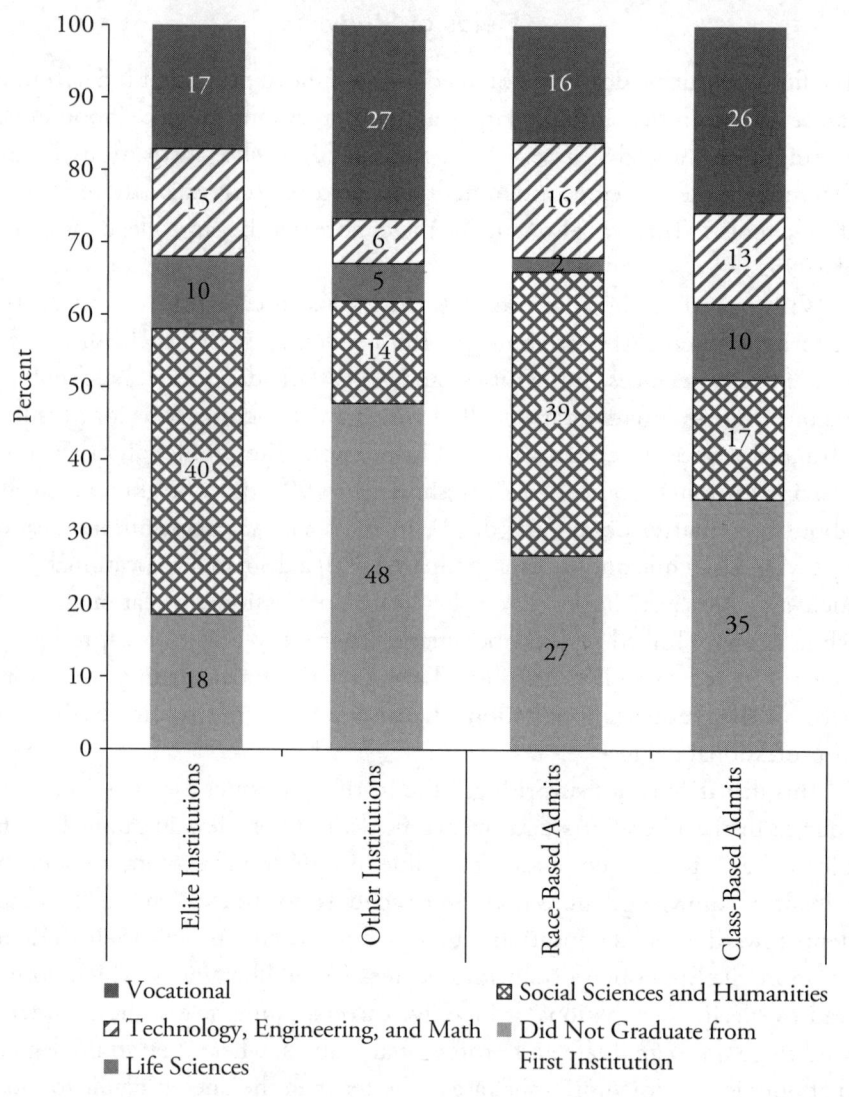

■ Vocational
☒ Social Sciences and Humanities
▨ Technology, Engineering, and Math
■ Did Not Graduate from First Institution
■ Life Sciences

Source: National Center for Education Statistics, Beginning Postsecondary Students Longitudinal Study (BPS), 1996–2001.

Note: "Technology" includes computer and information sciences and physics. "Vocational" includes education, the health professions, business, and other vocational fields.

study profile of racial and ethnic minorities who got an edge in admission to elite colleges is not very different from that of their classmates. About 60 percent of race-based admits graduated with a bachelor's degree in the social sciences, humanities, or STEM fields (see figure 10.4). These types of degrees were attained by only 40 percent of class-based admits—that is, high-achieving students from underprivileged backgrounds who attended less-selective colleges. Interestingly, the share of degrees in the social sciences, humanities, and STEM fields was larger among the class-based admits than among their classmates at non-elite schools. Then again, this is not surprising given that they had been the highest-achieving high school students before they enrolled at these less-selective four-year schools. Nevertheless, there is disparity between their field-of-study outcomes and those of the beneficiaries of affirmative action at elite schools.

These results point to the power of institutional influences on individual pathways, from the choice of field of study to persistence until graduation. Unfortunately, the data at hand do not allow us to evaluate and compare the advanced degree and labor market trajectories of race- and class-based admits, but the evidence from other studies strongly suggests that their distinct patterns in bachelor's degree attainment also lead to different occupations and earnings.[21] A degree from an elite school opens doors in graduate school and the labor market and thus leads to a more prestigious and lucrative career.

In sum, *the high-achieving class-based admits were more likely than race-based admits to either drop out of college or earn a degree in a vocational field.* Given that the beneficiaries of race-conscious admissions and high-achieving socioeconomically disadvantaged students enter college with similar academic credentials, *the degree-type profile of each is very much a reflection of the type of college they attend.* Elite institutions create environments that are more conducive to learning, personal growth, persistence, and degree attainment.

THE MOBILITY DIVIDENDS OF AFFIRMATIVE ACTION POLICY AND THE MISMATCH HYPOTHESIS

The findings in this chapter support the notion that for disenfranchised students—be they racial and ethnic minorities or socioeconomically disadvantaged youth—affirmative action is a key vehicle for mobility. The mobility dividends of affirmative action policies at elite U.S. colleges kick in during the first year of college. The edge in admissions allows URM to attend institutions that not only provide a wider spectrum of experiences but also facilitate and support the learning process and academic attainment. In this investigation, the black and Hispanic freshman beneficiaries of race-conscious admissions at elite schools were better integrated on campus, both academically and socially, compared to students at other colleges with similar academic starting points. Having more contact with faculty and peers contributed to their ability to navigate hurdles during their first year in college, and they were more likely than their counterparts at less-selective schools to continue into their second year and to graduate. They were more likely to obtain degrees in the social sciences, humanities, and STEM fields, all of which are launching pads for graduate and professional schools. In other words, the edge in admission helped race-based admits translate their academic potential into valuable college credentials and to fully realize their potential. If class-based affirmative action policy were in place, students from deprived socioeconomic backgrounds could fully realize their potential too.

Common sense dictates—and the findings in this chapter confirm—that the mobility dividends of affirmative action in college admissions are huge. But not everyone agrees. As mentioned, some argue that the URM recipients of affirmative action are destined for academic failure because they are unprepared for the level of academic rigor in elite academic settings. This logic implies that the beneficiaries of race-conscious admissions would be better off attending less-selective colleges.

This claim stems from gaps in academic outcomes between minority and other students at elite colleges. Consider, for example, the graduation gap at elite colleges in the 1995–1996 cohort: 73 percent of race-based admits graduated from the elite institution that gave them an edge in admissions, while the average graduation rate at these schools was 82 percent. Clearly, when compared to other students at elite schools, URMs were not faring so well in that their graduation rate was lower than the institutional average. But there is a more relevant question: would their chances of persistence have been better had they attended a less-selective college instead, as Justice Thomas suggests? If we consider the graduation data from a different angle, we notice that while 73 percent of race-based admits graduated from the elite institution that gave them an edge in admissions, only 65 percent of potential class-based admits graduated from the non-elite college in which they first enrolled. Contrary to the mismatch hypothesis, the graduation likelihood of the beneficiaries of race-conscious admissions was much higher than would probably have been the case at "schools for which they were better prepared." Moreover, all the evidence suggests that they would not have learned more at less-selective schools. Minority students are better off attending more-selective institutions even if their graduation rates there are below the institutional average. As a matter of fact, any student would benefit from a more supportive and enriching environment, including high-achieving students from deprived socioeconomic backgrounds.

What we see here are two approaches to assessing the simple question of whether minority students benefit from an edge in admission when it comes to academic outcomes and graduation rates. Supporters of the mismatch hypothesis compare the academic outcomes of race-based admits to those of their classmates at elite schools because this is the available comparison group. But this is not a fair comparison, because their classmates had a better starting point academically and a more-privileged upbringing. What the supporters of the mismatch hypothesis are complaining about, in essence, is that the recipients of affirmative action at these bastions of privilege did not turn out to be identical to their affluent white peers. Clearly, this is an unreasonable expectation.

It does make sense, however, to compare the race-based admits at elite colleges with their high school peers at less-selective ones. As mentioned earlier, the problem with finding this comparison group is that it involves asking the "what if?" question: what would have been the academic outcomes of race-based admits if they had enrolled at less-selective institutions instead? Alternatively, how would high-achieving students of low socioeconomic status have fared if class-based affirmative action had been in place? Although these questions are typically difficult to answer, the comparison of race-based to class-based admits presented in this chapter allows us to ask these "what if?" questions.

Given this more suitable comparison, we can reevaluate the claims of the mismatch hypothesis:

1. Are the achievements of the beneficiaries of affirmative action in admissions lower than those of their classmates in elite schools? *Yes.*
2. Would they be better off attending less-selective schools? *No.*
3. Do they benefit from affirmative action? *Yes.*

These conclusions are in line with the evidence from Israel (described in chapter 9), as well as with the vast majority of research that plainly refutes the mismatch hypothesis. A large body of literature based on robust evidence shows that there is no merit to the mismatch hypothesis when it comes to minority students, contrary to the claims. Despite their disadvantaged starting point, minority students thrive at selective colleges, which bestow many advantages upon all their students, such as a higher likelihood of persisting until graduation, attending graduate or professional school, and higher earnings later in life.[22] For example, I conducted a study with Marta Tienda of Princeton University (published in 2005) that showed that the graduation likelihood of black and Hispanic students increases as college selectivity level rises. Others have shown that shifting minority students from more- to less-selective institutions—as happened in California after the ban on race-conscious admissions following the passage of Proposition 209—harms their educational and employment opportunities.[23] The conclusion drawn from the evidence in this chapter is no different.

The beneficiaries of preferential treatment in U.S. college admissions thrive at elite schools. They are not harmed by the edge in admission, and they would not be better off attending a less-selective school instead. Rather, they benefit tremendously from the opportunity granted to them. The results in this chapter make it clear that an edge in admission enriches the college experience and expands the pathway to a degree. Race-based affirmative action has put black and Hispanic students in a more academically and socially stimulating environment where the support and resources available increase the chances that they will not drop out of college, as so many less-fortunate students do at non-elite colleges that lack support mechanisms. Ultimately, race-based affirmative action improves the life chances of black and Hispanic students.

A law student at the University of Iowa, Berneta Haynes, described in an essay for *Inside Higher Ed* what she gained from affirmative action:

I'm not ashamed to admit that without affirmative action, I'm not certain I would be on the precipice of the law career that I'm at right now. As an African-American woman from a poor family, I have little doubt that affirmative action helped me get into college, earn a degree, and enroll in law school.

Affirmative action policies made it possible for me to achieve more than my family had before. The possibility that Fisher could undo affirmative action has left me wondering where I would be if affirmative action didn't exist.

In fact, affirmative action policies that allowed me access to college helped minimize the social stigma of my childhood and helped me appreciate the strength and insight my life gave me. Affirmative action helped me find freedom from the constraints of my background. What's more, it has allowed me access to the tools and knowledge I can use to help those like me free themselves from the constraints of their own racial and economic backgrounds.

Maybe affirmative action places a stigma on its recipients. I would guess that if we asked most recipients, they would shrug, and say that stigma is nothing compared to where they might have been without it.[24]

Clearly, there are mobility dividends for beneficiaries of affirmative action policy, regardless of whether the road taken is race-based or class-based, but the beneficiaries of these dividends are different. Currently, black and Hispanic students benefit from affirmative action, in that it changes their lives and puts them on the road to prosperity. If a class-based policy were implemented, the life chances of many socioeconomically underprivileged high-achieving students would improve as well.

There is no question that affirmative action yields huge mobility dividends. The question is: who should enjoy them? No wonder that the debate about who deserves such a gift is so fierce. As mentioned in chapter 9, at stake here is not just the type of diversity that affirmative action can boost at elite institutions, but whose lives will be transformed for the better—and whose will not.

PART VI

Insights from a Comparative Outlook

CHAPTER 11

Race, Class, and Affirmative Action

> The greatness of America lies not in being more enlightened than any other nation, but rather in her ability to repair her faults.[1]
> —Alexis de Tocqueville, *Democracy in America* (1835)

In the 1960s, in the wake of the civil rights movement, several elite colleges and universities in the United States began to give black applicants an edge in admissions. This practice was perfectly aligned with the reparation rationale of the time: affirmative action in higher education was one attempt to redress historical discrimination at a time of massive racial inequality, rising consciousness, and a changing society. Since then, selective colleges have become even more committed to promoting racial and ethnic diversity, which is still undoubtedly a necessary and important objective. But they have been slow to respond to one of the greatest shifts in American society: class inequality.

The growing economic inequality and industrial restructuring of recent decades have eroded the potential of underprivileged youth to climb up the socioeconomic ladder and led to a society polarized by social class. Today attaining a college degree has become one of the most important determinants of one's position in the social hierarchy. And yet the class divide in higher education, especially at the more-selective schools, is larger than ever. Escalating competition in admissions and rising tuition costs have made it very difficult for a talented high school senior from an underprivileged background to aspire to one of the best colleges in the country. And for their part, elite institutions have done very little to extend to underprivileged applicants access to their invigorating learning environments, with their financial and academic resources. Nonetheless, as a consequence of recent Supreme Court rulings and rising public discontent with race-conscious admissions in college admissions, elite colleges and universities in the United States may be forced to embark on a class-based road. Shifting affirmative action from race to class in college admissions, however, is not a simple proposition.

This study was motivated by the pressing need for evidence-based assessments of the effectiveness, feasibility, and implications of shifting the focus of affirmative action practices from race to class. I have taken the perspective that much can be learned about the feasibility and suitability of the class-based road for college admissions in the United States from other nations' battles with inequality and from how they have dealt with the obstacles posed by class-based affirmative action. This investigation has tried to answer some of the most pressing questions regarding the shift from race to class in affirmative action by focusing on two countries, the United States and Israel, and on two types of affirmative action policy, race- and class-based. More generally, the evidence from within- and between-country comparisons of the two types of policies has allowed me to develop new and more universal insights about how race-neutral public policy promotes equality of educational opportunity at selective postsecondary institutions.

In this chapter, I take the insights from this comparative outlook on affirmative action and revisit the key issues plaguing the debate. I start by considering the similarities and differences between the two types of affirmative action and discuss what makes both policies effective and successful. Then I review the mobility dividends of affirmative action policy and the implications for the mismatch hypothesis. I move on to a discussion of the politics of ambiguity that surrounds the goal of broad diversity and how it stifles efforts to devise an effective affirmative action policy. I also address one of the most sensitive and controversial issues in this debate—whether affirmative action in U.S. college admissions should be race-neutral or race-conscious. Finally, I consider the implications of a general reform in admissions—including the elimination of legacies and other preferences—for broad diversity at elite colleges. Throughout this chapter, I convert these insights into practical advice regarding the design of affirmative action policy in college admissions.

My hope is that the insights in this chapter will inform the debate around this issue and help several constituents—including American policymakers, university administrators and leaders, and the general public—seriously consider whether we should embark on the road not taken in affirmative action policy in American higher education.

TWO ROADS TO AFFIRMATIVE ACTION: ELEMENTS OF SUCCESS

Israel and the United States are very different countries—in land size, population size, demographic contours, and history. They also differ in the structure and size of their postsecondary systems and in their college application and admission processes and tuition costs. But there are also similarities. For one, in both Israel and the United States a college education is the engine of mobility and prosperity for youth of every economic stratum. Moreover, both postsecondary systems, like those in many other countries, face a major challenge today: underprivileged youth in both countries are largely underrepresented at selective colleges and universities, even though educational access has increased greatly in recent decades as both systems expanded. Because they dispatch so many graduates into high-rung professional, government, and leadership positions, it is essential that elite colleges and universities serve youth from all walks of life.

Amid rising expectations that the flagship colleges and universities in both countries should not only strive for excellence but also promote equality of educational opportunity and diversity, these institutions have come under pressure to expand access to socioeconomically underprivileged populations. In both countries, affirmative action policy is used by elite colleges to promote the representation of disadvantaged populations in their student bodies and to boost these students' chances for social and economic mobility. But Israel and the United States originally embarked on two very different roads to affirmative action.

The road taken by the United States, as well as by several other countries, has been race-based; specifically, black and Hispanic students have been given an edge in admissions. This type of preferential treatment is based solely and specifically on an individual's affiliation with a particular racial or ethnic group. Israel, on the other hand, has taken the road less traveled. In the mid-2000s, four of the country's most-selective universities adopted a class-based, race-neutral affirmative action policy. Eligibility is based on three parameters of disadvantage, all of which refer to an applicant's high school years: the structure of opportunity (neighborhood of residence and high school attended); family socioeconomic status (parental education and family size); and individual or family adverse circumstances. The architects of this program did not deem all three parameters equally important: structural factors are given the most weight, in that neighborhood and high school attended account for about 50 percent of applicants' eligibility score. In sum, while the program pays attention to certain individual hardships, it is mostly based on structural disadvantage.

Still, the Israeli and American affirmative action programs have much in common. A few key factors account for the success of both policies in boosting diversity at elite institutions and widening the path to social and economic mobility for their beneficiaries.

Affirmative Action Programs Are Voluntary

In both countries, the use of admission preferences is entirely voluntary. There are no laws mandating the implementation of these preferences and no quotas to fill. This is in utter contrast to Brazil's Law of Social Quotas and India's mandatory reservation system. It is important to note that, without a law in place, higher education in both countries had the option of adopting these voluntary policies on no more than a symbolic level. For example, Israel's universities could have decided to limit affirmative action to their least-selective majors, and American schools could have decided to consider race in admissions in theory but to give it very little weight in practice. Nonetheless, the findings in this book show that both class-based affirmative action in Israel and race-based affirmative action in the United States have had very real results. That the impact of both policies has been significant and widespread seems to indicate a genuine desire on the part of American and Israeli elite colleges and universities to diversify their student bodies.

From a sociological perspective, the question of why elite colleges and universities in both countries adopted affirmative action policies voluntarily is intriguing. There were probably two major forces at play. The first was administrative pragmatism: institutions on both sides of the ocean were attuned to public sentiment and political pressure regarding rising inequality. The rapid change of heart at Tel Aviv University following the outcry in response to its initial rejection of the special admissions program (described in chapter

6) demonstrates this point. The same was true across the ocean, where elite American colleges embraced race-based affirmative action without being forced to do so. With the democratic ideals of mobility, equal opportunity, and diversity infiltrating the public discourse on race, pressure mounted on elite schools, which did not want to be seen as rich white relics of another age.[2] Now, similar pressure can lead to adopting a class-based affirmative action policy.

The second force at play was what sociologists call "isomorphism"—the tendency of organizations to imitate the policies of other institutions. To illustrate, once several faculties at Tel Aviv University had adopted the special admissions program, other universities followed suit. In the United States, too, top schools did not adopt affirmative action simultaneously, but rather, it spread from one institution to another.

However compelling the forces of administrative pragmatism and isomorphism, it is nonetheless true that *in both countries institutions preferred adopting these policies voluntarily, which leaves room for flexibility, rather than being compelled by law.*

The Criteria for Eligibility Are Simplicity and Group Affiliation

Another similarity of note is that both the Israeli class-based program and the American race-based model adhere to the notion of macrojustice in their design, in that the major criterion of eligibility is affiliation with a particular group. In the United States, the admission decision takes into account an ascribed trait—specifically, race or ethnicity. In Israel, eligibility is determined by an applicant's environment—specifically, residence in a poor neighborhood or attendance at a high-poverty high school. The major advantage of any prototype that relies on a macrojustice rationale, whether based on race or neighborhoods, is that the emphasis on group membership facilitates implementation.

Indeed, *a key insight from this investigation for anyone interested in class-based affirmative action is to keep it simple, which in practice means relying on group affiliation more and on individual circumstances less.* It is not surprising that the two models of class-based affirmative action currently being implemented, in Israel and Brazil, base eligibility at least partly on group affiliation. At the same time, it is troubling that the most popular conception of potential class-based policy for elite U.S. colleges is one that involves a wide array of indicators—including parental income, wealth, and net worth, parental education levels, family structure, language spoken at home, neighborhood poverty level, and high school share of minority students—given that such a complex design seems destined for failure.[3]

Consider, for example, UCLA's short-lived experiment with a class-based program. In 1995 the Regents of the University of California passed a resolution that banned the consideration of race in admissions in the state's public universities. Given this limitation, UCLA's School of Law decided to try a class-based admissions program, which it implemented two years after the ban. The school's faculty came up with a sophisticated multidimensional design that assessed eligibility by supplementing academic criteria with socioeconomic and structural factors. This admissions mechanism weighed family income and net worth, parental education levels, neighborhood of residence, and high school type.[4] This combined index was used to rank *all* applicants—thus, each applicant to UCLA's law school in 1997 was evaluated not only by his or her academic achievements, as is typically the case, but also by these additional factors.

The outcome of this experiment at UCLA confirmed the results of my simulations in the comparative investigation presented in this book—namely, that class-based policy, even models that consider multiple indicators of disadvantage, cannot match the level of racial and ethnic diversity generated by race-based programs. Although this admissions program did increase socioeconomic diversity at the law school, "the enrollment of blacks and American Indians fell by more than 70 percent from the levels typically achieved under the old race-based system."[5]

But this was not the reason that the program was terminated after only one year. (The law school did continue using a class-based system, but in a much more limited and discretionary form.)[6] Rather, it was the difficulty of implementation. It turns out that determining indicators of eligibility and then collecting, verifying, and weighting a wide array of sensitive information is a thorny undertaking. Richard Sander, the UCLA law professor mentioned in chapter 5, describes the problem candidly:

> Whatever else can be said for it, class-based affirmative action is not simple. Applicants cannot be asked to check boxes corresponding to "lower class," "working class," or "middle class and above," with the various classes routed to

appropriate decision rules. For many years, our admission process had officially taken "socioeconomic background" into account, but this was done chiefly in extraordinary circumstances, where an applicant's personal essay described social and economic challenges so compelling as to give some intangible boost to the candidacy. This is sensible enough; but if one wants to move towards a more systematic use of socioeconomic background as a serious admissions factor, the next defensible step is a long one.[7]

In other words, the key issue with this theoretically attractive model is feasibility. Sander maintains, however, that although the administrative challenges of class-based affirmative action are not trivial, they are solvable.[8] Nonetheless, it is hard to imagine a mechanism for determining multidimensional eligibility that can be easily integrated into the admission processes of large institutions.

Thus, the key impediment to a form of class-based affirmative action based on individual factors (family, economic, and social resources), either with or without a structural component (high school and neighborhood type), may be something that the statistical simulations altogether ignore: implementation. In the race-based prototype, eligibility is simple to determine and implementation is easy. Group membership determines eligibility, which is easy to ascertain. Thus, every minority applicant near the academic threshold can get an edge in admission. Determining high school type, as in structural-based programs, is also relatively straightforward. In socioeconomic affirmative action, however, eligibility is based on individual disadvantages, each of which must be demonstrated and verified—a much more arduous process.

The experience of Brazilian universities with various types of affirmative action is telling. The Law of Social Quotas, enacted in 2012, was the climax of efforts to increase diversity and enhance equal opportunity at Brazil's most-selective universities. Before the law went into effect, many universities had already established some sort of affirmative action program. Most of these programs were hybrid in that they targeted more than one beneficiary group, including public high school students, Afro-Brazilians, and low-income and rural youth.[9] Michelle Peria and Stanley Bailey, two sociologists from the University of California–Irvine, aptly describe the difference between determining whether an applicant is black or attended a public high school and determining whether she comes from a poor family:

In the large majority of cases, racial status has been combined with a class criterion (public school attendance or low-income status), with only the class criterion requiring corroborating documentation. Nonetheless, there has been some criticism that universities reserving slots for low-income students require families to undergo a prohibitively involved process to verify family income. By contrast, neither public school attendance nor indigenous status has attracted criticism as a criterion or in terms of verification.[10]

Clearly, determining race or high school or neighborhood type is more straightforward than measuring socioeconomic status. The task of establishing socioeconomic eligibility is taxing and requires a complex sorting mechanism. This is a key, but often overlooked, functional caveat of any policy that conforms to the microjustice approach and targets the demonstrated disadvantages of individuals. The complexity of implementation also increases as more indicators for establishing socioeconomic eligibility are used, while the pool of academically qualified applicants shrinks. This is not to say that this model is entirely impractical, but rather that implementing it warrants difficult decisions and quite a lot of work.

Why, then, do such complex models dominate the discussions about moving from race to class in affirmative action in the United States? A common justification for this type of model is that it can serve as a proxy for race and thus can also promote racial and ethnic diversity on elite college campuses. The comparative investigation reveals that there is merit to this claim. Targeting students with multiple disadvantages yields a more racially and ethnically diverse student body relative to all other class-based options (although this student body is still less racially diverse than that generated by race-conscious admissions). However, these gains are theoretical, because the actual pool of high-achieving high school students who fit the profile of multiple disadvantages is too small to draw from. In sum, the results do not justify the trouble that such an intricate model demands.

Creaming Is Unavoidable

One of the main criticisms of race-based affirmative action is that, by overlooking individual hardships, it tends to benefit the most privileged among minorities, and not the truly disadvantaged. This problem is referred to as "creaming." A popular claim about class-based affirmative action is that it can eliminate the creaming problem because it targets those with demonstrated socioeconomic disadvantages. My findings defy this notion, however, in that they show that the class-based affirmative action program in Israel is not creaming-free. Thus, what American race-based and Israeli class-based policies also have in common is that both induce creaming. Thus, as the findings in this book suggest, it may be time to refine the creaming debate.

First, creaming is a matter of degree, and it exists in all types of affirmative action programs, including those based on class. Policies that adhere to a macrojustice perspective, such as race-based affirmative action, will naturally induce creaming by stressing group affiliation rather than individual circumstances. Class-based policies are not immune to this problem, especially those that use the criteria of high school or neighborhood type—as the programs in Israel and Brazil do—because these are also types of group membership. There is no doubt that the most privileged of students at a poor high school are in a better position to benefit from a class-based policy than others. However, this is not to say that the magnitude of the creaming issue is the same under racial and structural affirmative action. Focusing on ascribed characteristics, such as race, may create more creaming than targeting applicants from disadvantaged neighborhoods and schools. This happens because, whereas race-conscious admissions can benefit extremely privileged minority populations, focusing on spatial and school inequality is more likely to produce a creamy layer of moderately disadvantaged populations, given that the number of affluent families who reside in bad neighborhoods and send their offspring to failing schools is limited.

Creaming can even occur in socioeconomic affirmative action, which does not rely on group affiliation, depending on where we set the bar for eligibility. For example, if we base eligibility on family income—say, on an annual family income below $50,000—then those at the upper end of the income distribution (between $40,000 and 50,000) will be better suited to take advantage of this opportunity than those from poorer families, given the correlation between income and academic achievements. If, instead, we consider only applicants with a yearly family income below $40,000, we will have less creaming, and if we set the bar at $30,000, then creaming will be reduced even further. Thus, lowering the income threshold from $50,000 to $30,000 reduces the likelihood that individuals who are not really poor will exploit the policy.

Creaming can also be minimized by taking a wide array of factors into account, such as home environment (socioeconomic status and family structure) and structural effects (school composition and geographical region), as in the multidimensional prototype. As we add more disadvantages in determining eligibility and set the bar higher for each of them, we become better able to target the "truly disadvantaged" and have less of a creaming problem.

Minimizing creaming and focusing on the truly disadvantaged, however, introduces two new problems: the pool of truly disadvantaged individuals with adequate academic credentials is extremely small, and the financial burden for elite colleges increases, given that the truly disadvantaged, by default, require more financial aid to bear the costs of attending college. Thus, raising the eligibility bar for class-based affirmative action will limit the pool of academically qualified applicants to choose from and push up costs for colleges. In response to both of these problems, selective colleges and universities will admit fewer disadvantaged students, consequently curbing the potential of class-based policy to boost their diversity.

In the end, we must acknowledge that creaming also occurs under class-based policy and, more importantly, that a moderate amount of creaming is essential for the success of any affirmative action policy, in terms of its potential to boost diversity. It is unrealistic and counterproductive to focus only on those with multiple disadvantages; this puts too much pressure on institutional finances and academic standards. A creaming-free policy is academically and financially unfeasible, while a moderate level of creaming ensures diversity and does not compromise social and economic mobility. Thus, *any affirmative action program, whether based on race or on class, must rely to some extent on the creamy layer within each target group.* It may seem counterintuitive, but a socioeconomic-based program is actually more likely to succeed overall with an annual family income threshold of $50,000 rather than $30,000.

These three elements—voluntary implementation, a simple design that focuses on group affiliation, and a moderate amount of creaming—are necessary ingredients for any successful affirmative action policy, whether race- or class-based. These elements have made the Israeli and American programs effective at promoting both diversity at elite institutions and mobility for the beneficiaries. Nonetheless, the findings from my comparative investigation reveal significant differences in the mobility and diversity dividends of the two policies.

MOBILITY DIVIDENDS

One of the rationales behind affirmative action in admissions to elite colleges and universities is to boost the representation of disadvantaged groups in academia, business, government, and the professional sphere. The findings in this book demonstrate that *affirmative action at elite institutions in Israel and the United States meets this objective: it is a key vehicle of mobility for disenfranchised students, whether they are racial and ethnic minorities or socioeconomically disadvantaged.* It allows them to attend schools that provide a wider spectrum of experiences, facilitate and support the learning process, and lead to better labor market outcomes.

The class-based affirmative action program in Israel gives certain underprivileged and academically borderline applicants from high-poverty schools and poor neighborhoods the chance for a better future by opening the gates of elite institutions. This edge translates into a degree in a field of study with better labor market prospects and higher economic returns. Likewise, the beneficiaries of race-based affirmative action at elite American institutions are better integrated academically and socially by the end of their first years in college compared to their counterparts from socioeconomically underprivileged backgrounds who attend less-selective schools, and they are also more likely to complete their bachelor's studies. The findings reinforce a large body of literature that shows that despite their disadvantaged starting point, minority students prosper at selective institutions, which bestow certain advantages—such as a higher likelihood of persisting until graduation, attending graduate or professional school, and earning a good income later in life—on all of their students.[11]

Clearly, affirmative action programs pave the way for social and economic mobility. Nonetheless, the notion that the beneficiaries of preferences would be better off without them has taken hold in many sectors of society. Opponents of race-conscious admissions continue to use the mismatch hypothesis—the claim that affirmative action sets up its beneficiaries for failure because they are ostensibly unprepared to succeed academically at elite colleges—to support the move to class-based affirmative action.[12]

The findings from both countries, when taken together, unequivocally establish that *benefiting from an affirmative action policy, be it class- or race-based, is not detrimental to one's success in college nor to one's labor market prospects.* To the contrary, the beneficiaries of preferential treatment in college admissions in Israel and the United States thrive at elite colleges and in selective fields of study. They are not harmed as a result of the edge they received in admission, nor would they have been better off attending less-selective colleges instead. Put simply, *American colleges and universities may decide to move from race to class in affirmative action, but the mismatch claim does not hold up as a rationale for this move.*

BROAD DIVERSITY AND THE POLITICS OF AMBIGUITY

In an era of growing economic inequality, the beneficiaries of special consideration in admissions in both Israel and the United States are able to translate access to an elite education, bestowed by affirmative action, into social and economic mobility. There is no question that affirmative action policy yields huge mobility dividends. The question is: who should benefit from them?

The Supreme Court has repeatedly ruled that the diversity sought by postsecondary institutions must be broader than racial and ethnic diversity. The desire to assemble a student body with diverse talents and perspectives at elite schools, the training ground for leadership and professional positions, is the main rationale for affirmative action policy in college admissions in the United States and has been its legal foundation since the Supreme Court Bakke ruling in 1978. Campus diversity creates more opportunities for interaction with students from different backgrounds and thus increases students' tolerance for a wide range of viewpoints, enhances their cognitive and identity development, and helps them become better citizens and leaders in an increasingly diverse democratic society.[13]

All subsequent Supreme Court rulings on affirmative action have reinforced the notion of broad diversity, endorsing it as a compelling governmental interest. Elite colleges, however, in implementing affirmative action policies that focus almost solely on race and ethnicity, have largely overlooked other aspects of diversity. They have been slow to respond to the growing polarization of American society by social and economic class and have not broadened the scope of their diversity efforts. This is one reason for the attacks on race-based affirmative action and the growing support for moving from race to class.

But what is the potential for a race-neutral class-based affirmative action program to generate broad diversity at elite schools? To answer this question I set up a series of simulations and used them to compare several prototypes of class-based affirmative action with the race-based model. The findings were conclusive: *there is no silver bullet for generating broad diversity at elite institutions. All of the prototypes of affirmative action that were tested fell short of achieving broad diversity, both in Israel and the United States.* The strengths of each model are easily detected, but so are the weaknesses. *Diversity is about trade-offs: gains in one aspect of diversity are losses in another. This makes broad diversity a difficult target.*

In anticipation of the recent Supreme Court Fisher decision, the *Chronicle of Higher Education* reported on Applications Quest, data-mining software designed by Juan Gilbert, chairman of Clemson University's human-centered computing division.[14] The *Chronicle* explained that this software, which automates the evaluation of applications, "allows users to assign equal weight to various attributes, such as an applicant's race, gender, geographic location, and intended major," and that "admissions offices can build more-diverse student populations by using sophisticated software." This software may help in the weighting of indicators, but it does not solve the feasibility problem—we still need to collect and verify the information from applicants.

Yet the main problem is even more fundamental. If broad diversity were just the sum or average of all aspects of diversity, then maybe we could use software to weigh family income, parents' education, race, ethnicity, high school type, and so on, equally. We would only have to decide which aspects of diversity to include. But in reality, some aspects of diversity are more socially important than others, so they are given extra weight. Thus, we would have to determine not only the contours of diversity but also the importance of each contour. For example, if we decided that racial and ethnic diversity is indispensable, then the weight would shift in that direction while other aspects of diversity played a more minor role. If, alternatively, we determined that socioeconomic diversity is a crucial feature of the student body at elite schools, then some racial and ethnic diversity would have to be forfeited. Diversity is a zero-sum game: one attribute prevails at the expense of others.

Diversity-generating software is futile if we do not know which aspects of diversity to consider and how we will weight each aspect. No software can save us from having a serious public discussion about our societal and educational priorities for student body diversity at elite colleges and universities. There is no way around it: we have to start removing the smoke screen around the concept of diversity by addressing several complicated questions, the answers to which will help social scientists, policymakers, and university leaders design admissions policies attuned to the most pressing societal concerns about inequality while still fulfilling the educational mission of elite institutions:

1. What is the rationale behind implementing affirmative action policy in elite colleges and universities? Why do we need it, and what goals do we expect to achieve?
2. What are the most desirable diversity outcomes for our society?
3. What aspects of diversity are most conducive to enhancing the educational process and students' tolerance for a wide range of viewpoints?
4. Are we willing to pay the price associated with any chosen solution?

Besides these questions, there is one overarching question: what is "broad diversity"? Given the high profile of the debate about affirmative action, it may seem odd that this concept has remained so elusive, but I argue that the conceptual and empirical ambiguity around the notion of broad diversity serves a purpose: it thwarts disagreement about the kind of diversity (and equality) that we, as a society, want to promote. In an article published in 1988, Christopher Jencks, a professor of social policy at Harvard University, argues that the ideal of "equal opportunity" continues to command broad support precisely because its definition is blurry. He claims that because equal opportunity "is an ideal consistent with almost every vision of a good society," it is "one of the few ideals a politician can safely invoke on all occasions."[15] The ideal of broad diversity, like that of equal opportunity, also enjoys widespread consensus, from Supreme Court justices to university presidents. All concur that broad diversity serves a compelling educational interest and has enormous value in educational settings. *Invoking the term "broad diversity" blurs the lines of disagreement about what aspects of diversity should be maximized and disguises the fact that different constituents have different definitions of diversity.*

Once we are forced to define "broad diversity," the concept will lose much of its appeal. In a zero-sum situation, in which trade-offs are unavoidable, there are sure to be clashes about what type of diversity is most desirable, fitting, and fair. One camp will argue that socioeconomic diversity at elite colleges and universities is most important, given rising class inequality, while another will claim that race and ethnicity is still a critical contour of inequality in American society, independent of one's economic position, and that we must ensure the representation of certain minorities at elite schools. This will not be an easy deliberation process.

In considering the role of the politics of ambiguity in this debate, it is not difficult to understand why the Supreme Court, supported by the media and academia, champions the broad diversity rationale for affirmative action without specifying what it means and how to achieve it. The problem is that this vagueness also hinders the development of an admission policy that can effectively generate broad diversity—that is, a student body with different skills, talents, backgrounds, and opinions. Now that the continuation of race-based considerations in admissions is under severe threat, it is imperative that we conduct a serious discussion about the kind of diversity that we seek to achieve so that we can spell out clear expectations regarding the diversity dividends of both race- and class-based policies. Obviously, one of the most contentious issues in such deliberations is whether race and ethnic diversity is crucial in higher education. Related to this issue is the question of whether we are willing to settle for a lower level of socioeconomic diversity in order to maintain a higher level of racial-ethnic diversity.

Race-Neutral or Race-Conscious?

Despite the great achievements of the civil rights movement, including the introduction of affirmative action in higher education and the workplace, blacks, who are 12 percent of the U.S. population (as of 2012), still suffer the ramifications of centuries of discrimination and the accumulated burden of their imposed inferiority. This is manifested in high rates of poverty, crime, discrimination, racism, and racial profiling by police. Hispanics, who as of 2012 made up 17 percent of the U.S. population, are also a disadvantaged minority group with high poverty rates. Nearly 40 percent of Hispanic youth and 34 percent of black youth (under age eighteen) were poor in 2012; the rate among whites was about 14 percent.[16] Contributing to this pattern is the disparity in unemployment rates: in 2012 the rate for blacks (14 percent) was double the rate for whites (7 percent), and it was 1.4 times greater among Hispanics (10 percent).[17] There are gaps even among the employed: the median household incomes of black and Hispanic families were only 60 and 70 percent, respectively, of the median household income of white families ($56,000).[18] Most striking, perhaps, are the differences in wealth: in 2010 the average wealth of American white families was about $632,000, compared to about $100,000 for black and Hispanic families.[19] The wealth gap is especially important because of its persistence: as assets and possessions pass from one generation to the next, they determine the mobility chances of individuals and families.

The persistent gaps in educational attainment between these groups surely contributes to this economic inequality and restricts the mobility chances of minorities. For example, the share of twenty-five- to twenty-nine-year-old whites with a bachelor's degree was more than double the share among blacks and Hispanics in 2013.[20] Moreover, black and Hispanic youth who pursue a postsecondary education are more likely to do so at two-year or nonselective four-year colleges compared to whites.[21] As discussed in previous chapters, the type of four-year college one attends is a key determinant of life chances, and whites overall have better chances of getting into the elite colleges. In 2004, 17 percent of white four-year students attended an elite institution (*Barron's* categories 1 and 2), while only 7 percent of black four-year students did. Almost one-third of Hispanic four-year students attended institutions at the bottom of the college hierarchy (categories 5 and 6).[22]

Race and ethnicity are still good predictors of the quality of the higher education that we will get and of the life chances and opportunities available to even the youngest among us. This explains, at least partly, why increasing the representation of blacks and Hispanics at elite colleges and universities, the training ground for leaders, cannot be accomplished without concerted effort. But can this goal be achieved using race-neutral means?

Some have suggested that the "Trojan Horse" tactic can do the trick—that is, that we can achieve racial and ethnic diversity with race-neutral tools if we use indicators that correlate strongly with race and ethnicity. Nonetheless, the results from both Israel and the United States suggest that the potential of this strategy is quite limited. Structural disadvantages may be a better proxy for race and ethnicity than socioeconomic status, but they are still not a *good* substitute. Unfortunately, *no race-neutral model of preferential treatment can match the level of racial and ethnic diversity achieved by race-based affirmative action.* If the main goal of Trojan Horse approaches is to maintain the share of blacks and Hispanics in the student body, then we should stick with current race-based policy, given that it is the most effective and transparent way of achieving this goal. The problem, however, is that race-based affirmative action does not produce enough socioeconomic and geographic diversity. Given rising economic inequality and growing discontent with current policy, race-based affirmative action may not hold up as a viable option for much longer. In this context, a fresh way of thinking about affirmative action policy is warranted.

If the goal is to boost broad diversity at elite institutions—that is, to see students from all walks of life at bastions of privilege, including both the socioeconomically underprivileged and underrepresented minorities—then one promising option is to base eligibility for affirmative action on both race and class. The Brazilian model, for example, uses a hybrid design that embeds the consideration of race within class-based affirmative action: the public universities in Brazil are required to reserve at least half of their slots for students from public high schools, which serve a poorer population and perform worse overall than the country's private high schools, and half of these reserved slots are set aside for low-income students. Additionally, the allocation of all reserved slots must match the racial makeup of each state. Although this particular type of hybrid design would not translate well to the American context (because quotas are unconstitutional in the United States), we can find inspiration in some elements of this design, which focuses on high school type, income, and race simultaneously. The program defines its target group as "poor black students" rather than black students in general.[23]

The simulations conducted with U.S. data, presented in chapter 8, tested the outcomes of a model that nests racial preferences within class-based affirmative action. The results of this "race-within-class" model predicted that under this scheme racial and ethnic diversity would decline the least among all alternatives to existing race-conscious admissions, while the level of socioeconomic diversity would match what race-neutral class affirmative action could generate. Such a hybrid plan, which entails both race-sensitive and class-based measures, has the greatest potential to yield broad diversity at elite schools. Moreover, this model could create socioeconomic diversity within race and ethnic groups, which is important to achieve if racial stereotypes are to be broken down and double balkanization across race and class lines prevented. Thus, this model is the one most likely to narrow the social distance between whites and minority groups and enhance healthy intergroup relations.[24]

The race-within-class model of affirmative action is not race-neutral, however, and so it may not quell the controversy and legal battle around the use of race in admissions. If the Brazilian case is any indication, the discontent is not likely to abate, even if race is only one factor among mostly socioeconomic ones. In 2003, nearly a decade before the Law of Social Quotas was enacted in Brazil, Rio de Janeiro's two state universities[25] implemented an affirmative action model that was very similar to what the Law of Social Quotas would later require: it gave preference in admissions to students from public high schools and to racial minorities.[26] Soon after the admissions outcome of the first cohort was made public, more than 200 lawsuits were filed against the universities, mostly by white students seeking admission to the faculties of medicine and law. These lawsuits, as some scholars point out, mainly took issue with the use of race, not class.[27]

Although a race-within-class model would probably provoke more opposition than an entirely race-neutral design, it would still be met with less resistance than current race-based affirmative action because *it would also benefit underprivileged white and Asian applicants and because, with only poor minorities getting an edge in admissions, it would reduce creaming*. Moreover, such a policy would ensure both demographic and socioeconomic diversity better than any purely race- or class-based design.

A CASE FOR REAL REFORM: CLASS-BASED AFFIRMATIVE ACTION IN A WORLD WITHOUT LEGACIES AND OTHER PREFERENCES

We know that race-conscious admissions is failing to generate a sufficient level of socioeconomic diversity at elite institutions, and so it is not a good candidate if our goal is to generate broad diversity. Many hope that class-based affirmative action could do the trick instead, but the findings in this investigation suggest that it is difficult to achieve broad diversity at elite schools with race-neutral class-based measures. The implication is that a trade-off between broad diversity and race-neutrality must be accepted, but is this really the case? Institutions could achieve broad diversity with race-neutral tools *if they radically reformed their admission practices.* In this section, I discuss the most radical option for an admission policy, one that can not only maintain the current level of racial and ethnic diversity at elite colleges and universities but also increase it.

I begin with the thoughtful comment of someone self-identified only as Hunter56 in a talkback response to a 2013 article in *The Economist* entitled "Time to Scrap Affirmative Action":

> I chair the Admission Committee at a leading liberal arts college. We accept students with a fairly narrow range of high academic achievement. When building a class, we give preference to many plus factors: academic excellence, ethnicity, geography, gender, legacy, donor potential, ability to pay, arts or athletic talent among others. We do not believe that our educational goals are served by having everyone be basically identical. The world they will enter isn't like that.
>
> I am struck, however, how controversial is any preference for students of color, while the myriad preferences that favor white males are accepted, yea, even celebrated. The most glaring example: If my college or any similar school chose solely on academic achievement, our student body would be 70% female and 30% male. We admit many "less qualified" males over "more qualified" females, and no one says a thing. On the contrary, it is actively encouraged and celebrated. We accept "less qualified" rich kids over "more qualified" middle class kids sometimes because of the former's potential as major donors. This favors whites as there are more wealthy whites than blacks. We give preference to the children of alumni, which again favors white kids, as fewer blacks attended such colleges in the past.
>
> All of these preferences are common in college admissions, and rarely questioned, never challenged or changed. So be careful what you wish for. If colleges were somehow restricted to using only academic achievement in their admissions decisions, many more privileged white males would have much more to whine about, as their preferential treatment, which greatly outweighs affirmative action, would disappear.[28]

It turns out that Hunter56 is right. Elite colleges give an edge in admissions to many groups and individuals *besides* racial and ethnic minorities, including athletes and the children of alumni, professors, celebrities, and wealthy parents.[29] Consider, for example, the academic trajectory of the children of former vice president Albert Gore: all four were admitted to Harvard University, an institution that admits fewer than 10 percent of applicants with stellar credentials. His three daughters were outstanding students, but his son, Albert Gore III, was not. This and other cases are discussed in Daniel Golden's 2006 book *The Price of Admission: How America's Ruling Class Buys Its Way into Elite Colleges—and Who Gets Left Outside the Gates*, a comprehensive investigation of the pervasive preferential treatment practices at elite colleges that are *not* race-based. For example, Princeton University admitted high school senior Harrison Frist in 2001 despite the fact that his grades and test scores were far below the university's standards. Harrison's father, Bill Frist, a former U.S. senator and Republican leader, is a Princeton alumnus and former trustee who donated $25 million to the university in order to build the Frist Campus Center. Margaret Bass was admitted to Stanford University in 1998. Her father, Texas oil magnate Robert Bass, had given $25 million to Stanford in 1991. Nine students from her private high school in Groton, Massachusetts, applied to Stanford that year, but she was the only one admitted, despite the fact that her grades and test scores were well below those of seven of her rejected classmates. It seems that even a $250,000 donation can pave the way to admission. Paul Zofnass, a financial consultant, donated between $250,000 and $500,000 to Harvard University, and both of his daughters were admitted to the university in 2004 and 2005. They were the third generation in his family to attend Harvard.[30]

What is the effect of being a legacy (that is, being the offspring of alumni) on admission decisions? Thomas Espenshade and Chang Chung report that 3 percent of applicants to several elite schools in 1997 had legacy status and 46 percent of them were admitted.[31] This was a much higher admission rate than that of applicants with no connection to the school, which was only 21 percent. The benefit of legacy status is actually even higher, because nonlegacy applicants have better academic credentials than legacy applicants. When this is taken into account, the odds of admission for the children of alumni are three times higher than the odds for nonlegacy applicants. For example, at Stanford only 5 percent of about 40,000 applicants were admitted in 2013, whereas the admission rate of alumni children was three times higher. Stanford's alumni magazine reports that when an applicant indicates that he or she is a legacy, the admissions office checks with the school's alumni association, not just to confirm the applicant's status but also to determine whether the alumnus/a in question has maintained his or her connection to the school.[32] While each application is read once, every legacy application is read twice. (In fact, William Fitzsimmons, the dean of admissions and financial aid at Harvard College, told Daniel Golden that he personally reads all applications from alumni children.) Stanford's alumni magazine went on to state that "one of Stanford's biggest priorities, as it is at most universities, is the bond of legacy."[33]

There is also affirmative action for celebrities. Brown University, a private Ivy League research university in Providence, Rhode Island, made a name for itself as "the school for glamour."[34] One college adviser told Golden that at Brown celebrity status is worth 100 SAT points in admissions.[35] What's in it for the institution? Prestige and publicity, which boost application numbers. Moreover, Ivy League schools sponsor athletic activities considered "rich people's sports," such as crew, golf, polo, rowing, fencing, and lacrosse. These sports are favored by alumni and donors and are rarely played by minorities.[36] The colleges accept borderline athletes in these high-status sports whose parents can donate to the school and boost its reputation and desirability. Another group enjoying an edge in admission includes the children of faculty members. Free or reduced tuition for the children of faculty was originally intended as a fringe benefit for university employees, but it has turned into a full-blown system of admission breaks.[37]

Although this elaborate system of preferences has long been deeply established at elite colleges and universities, the debate about preferences in college admissions is overwhelmingly focused on race-based preferences. This is strange given that the number of applicants who benefit from preferential treatment because they are the children of celebrities, athletes, faculty, alumni, or donors is far greater than the number who benefit from race-based affirmative action. Logic would seem to dictate that if we end the consideration of race-ethnicity in admissions, as some suggest, then we should also eliminate preferences for other groups. In the context of this investigation, it seems fair to ask: what would the diversity dividends of class-based affirmative action be if all other preferences in admissions were eliminated? Moreover, can institutions have both broad diversity and race-neutrality if they radically reform their admission practices?

Simulations

To examine the implications of this possibility, I conducted one more simulation with the U.S. data used in chapter 8. In the main simulation there, URM were considered beneficiaries of affirmative action if their test scores fell in the bottom quarter of the student body test score distribution, for each category of elite colleges. In fairness, however, there were other (nonminority) students at the bottom of the distribution, but they were not labeled beneficiaries of affirmative action. Why not question their admissibility credentials for elite colleges? Some of what we find in this bottom quarter segment are students who received an edge because of their family connection to the school or potential donor status. In fact, *all* students in the bottom 25 percent are likely to be the beneficiaries of some kind of special treatment, whether due to their legacy status, family connections, athletic prowess, or race or ethnicity. So I conducted another simulation. This time I replaced all the students at elite schools in the bottom quartile, including whites and Asians, with class-based admits. As before, every student could be reselected if he or she qualified according to the class-based prototype being tested.

The diversity dividends of class-based affirmative action under an admission regime with *no* preferences (for legacies, athletes, or minorities) are presented in figure 11.1. I compare these results, which I call "reform," to the results of two other regimes (in which legacies are preserved) reported in chapter 8: class-based affirmative action that replaces race-conscious admissions, and race-within-class admissions. For each admission regime (class-based affirmative action, race-within-class, and reform) I report the results for the two class-based prototypes that are the most likely candidates for future implementation: the socioeconomic and structural (high school) models.[38]

It turns out that if elite institutions eliminated race-based affirmative action in addition to other types of preferences—not just URM but also legacies, children of donors, athletes, and so on—they could achieve broad diversity using a race-neutral class-based affirmative action policy. In fact, under these conditions, race-neutral class-based affirmative action could not only replicate the current level of racial and ethnic diversity at elite institutions but even increase it. For example, if we substitute for legacies and all other prefer-

Figure 11.1 Pre- and Post-Simulation Student Body Characteristics Under Three Regimes for Class-Based Affirmative Action at Elite U.S. Universities: Class, Race-Within-Class, and Reform, 1995–1996

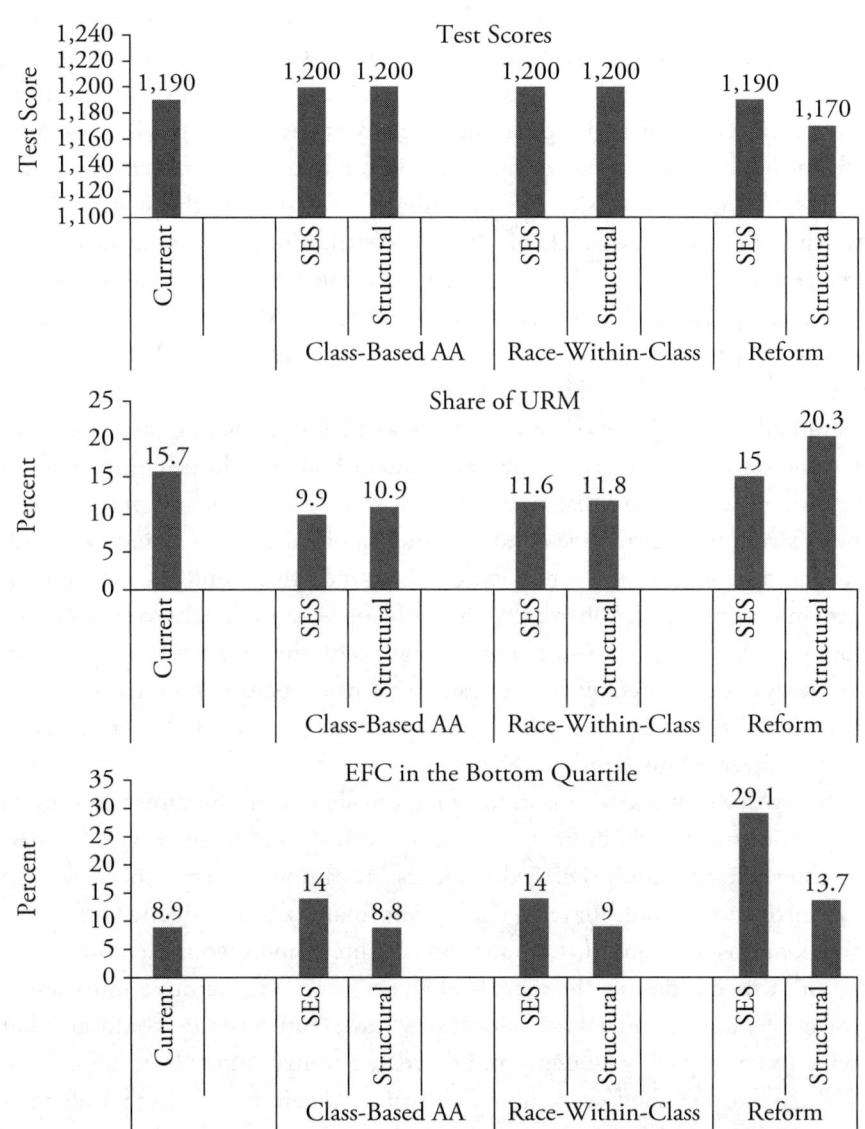

Source: National Center for Education Statistics, Beginning Postsecondary Students Longitudinal Study (BPS), 1996–2001.

ences, including preferences given to URM, with socioeconomic affirmative action the share of minority students remains almost intact. In the estimate for the 1995–1996 cohort, the share would decline slightly from around 16 percent (under race-conscious admissions) to 15 percent (with socioeconomic affirmative action). This is much higher than what the class-based model could generate without a reform in admissions, which is around 10 percent.

At the same time, class-based affirmative action could also significantly boost socioeconomic and geographic diversity at bastions of privilege under a reform in admissions. For example, socioeconomic affirmative action would increase economic diversity at elite colleges dramatically: the share of poor students (the bottom quartile of the EFC distribution) rises from the current 9 percent to 29 percent! Thus, if elite institutions revamped their admission policies and ceased giving special treatment to URM as well as to legacies, celebrities, and athletes, then class-based affirmative action plans would be better at generating broad diversity.

And all this could be done without jeopardizing academic selectivity—in fact, the test score average of the new student body would be comparable to the current average. Similarly, in a world without legacies and other preferences, structural affirmative action (high school–based) might increase both racial and socioeconomic diversity, but here the price would be a decline in academic selectivity. Apparently, the pool of very high-achieving students from poor high schools is not large enough to fill the slots left by eliminating legacies and other preferences. A design that fuses socioeconomic status with structural disadvantages in the eligibility formula would probably yield the optimal diversity dividends.

The major obstacle to this kind of large-scale reform in admission criteria is that it would require dramatic changes in tuition and financial aid. Increasing the share of underprivileged students on campus is very expensive, and elite institutions would have to triple their financial aid budgets. Under this model, at least one out of three students at elite schools would require financial aid, which is double the share under current race-conscious admissions.[39] Not only would financial aid allocations surge, but revenue would also fall owing to fewer paying students and decreased contributions from donors.

These findings shed even more light on the dilemma of whether affirmative action policy should be race-neutral or race-conscious. If the current framework of admissions remains intact without reform, *then a class-based policy will require a race-conscious component in order to maintain the current level of racial diversity at elite schools*. If legacies and other types of preferences are eliminated as part of a vast reform scheme in admissions, tuition, and financial aid, *then race-neutral class-based affirmative action can generate broad diversity, including racial and ethnic diversity, and widen the path to socioeconomic mobility without lowering academic standards*.

The question is whether elite institutions are ready to contemplate such bold reform, and whether they have sufficient resources to make it happen. Given how deeply institutionalized preferences such as legacies are in the culture of elite colleges, and given their reliance on donation money, it is very unlikely that such reform will take place in the near future. This being the case, we need to lower our expectations regarding what race-neutral class-based affirmative action can achieve.

Taken together, the evidence in this book demonstrates that broad diversity and race-neutrality are conflicting goals. Since enhancing broad diversity at elite colleges and universities is a compelling societal interest, the Supreme Court, in its future rulings on the issue, should urge institutions to demonstrate that their admissions practices generate broad diversity—that is, demographic, socioeconomic, and geographic diversity—rather than insisting that their practices be race-neutral. There is no point in expecting them to achieve both goals.

CONCLUDING REMARKS

There are two types of affirmative action policy that can promote equal opportunity, social mobility, and diversity in higher education: class-based and race-based. Each road leads to a different destination in terms of the type of diversity it generates and whose life chances are transformed. Regardless of whether American colleges and universities decide to stick with race-based affirmative action or embark on the road not taken—namely, class-based policy—*we need to set realistic goals for what affirmative action policy can, and cannot, accomplish*. This book's broad-spectrum evaluation of various types of preferences demonstrates that even though class-based affirmative action is a solid alternative to race-conscious admissions in U.S. college admissions, lamentably, it is not a problem-free or superior alternative.

No one prototype—neither the race-based model nor any of the class-based models—is particularly well suited for generating broad diversity. Each prototype is good at boosting one type of diversity, but the focus on one aspect of disadvantage limits the potential of tapping into other aspects because of the relatively low degree of overlap between class, racial, and spatial inequality in the pool of high-achieving college-bound students.[40] The expectation that we can have the maximum level of diversity in every aspect is an illusion.

This means that if we wish to infuse elite college campuses with students from diverse backgrounds and perspectives, then the design of preferential admissions must target multiple criteria simultaneously. If we are willing to define broad diversity as "a little bit of everything," then hybrid designs of affirmative action—that is, crossbreeds that incorporate elements from several different prototypes—have greater potential than any one prototype to generate wide-ranging diversity. Such hybrid programs do not create the highest level of diversity in any one aspect, but they do generate a more diverse package overall.

New and innovative affirmative action designs that have been implemented around the world demonstrate that between the two poles of the micro- and macrojustice paradigms, and between the rival models of race-based and class-based policies, there is a wide range of possibility—a spectrum, in fact—for affirmative action policy. *Thus, reforming affirmative action in college admissions is not about choosing between the race and class models, but about determining what aspects we should target to achieve the broadest and most desirable diversity dividends.* Given that a race-neutral admission policy would almost certainly decrease racial and ethnic diversity at elite institutions, and that race and ethnicity are still important determinants of life chances in the United States today, the question of whether race should be one of the factors embedded in a hybrid design is pressing and unavoidable in this debate.

University leaders, admission officers, and public policy makers in the United States and elsewhere should harness the empirical evidence presented in this book and the insights of its comparative outlook to design a creative and feasible model for affirmative action policy in college admissions. They need to find the most effective policy that can boost broad diversity at elite institutions and widen the avenue to social and economic mobility, while being attuned to the specific needs of American society. This is a big challenge, but it is surely a worthwhile investment in our future.

APPENDIX

Figure A6.1 The Distribution of Disciplines and Admits to Israeli Universities, 1999–2008

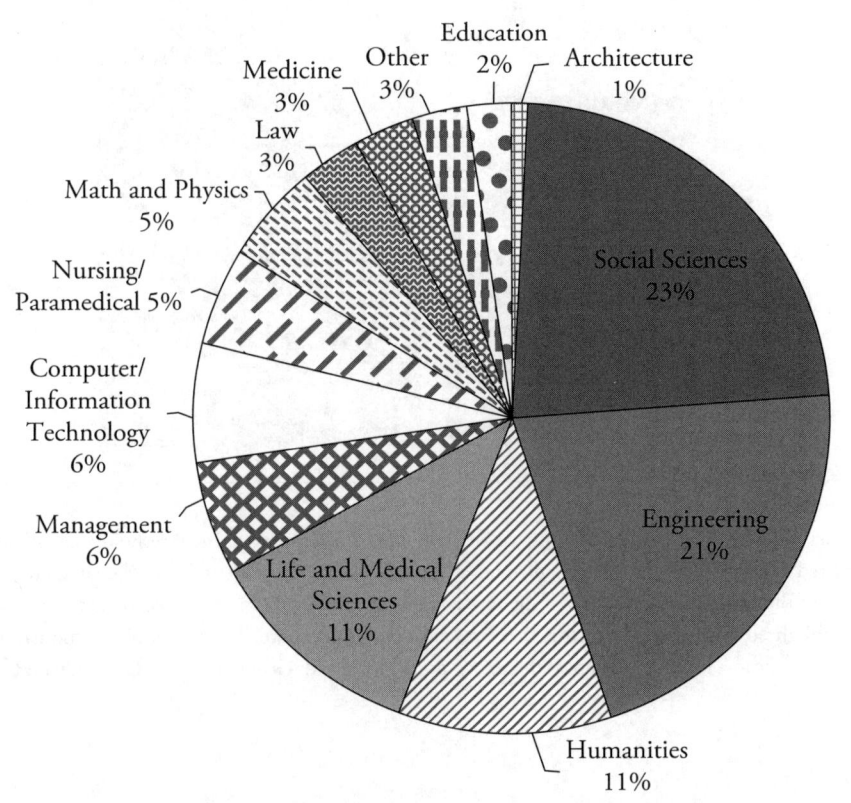

Source: TAU, HUJI, BGU, and TECH administrative data, 1999–2008.

Figure A6.2 The Components of the Disadvantage-Based Eligibility Scores of Applicants Admitted Under the Class-Based Affirmative Action Plan in Israel

Joel	David
• Resided in a **development town** in the northern part of Israel that is on the list; studied in a **high school on the** list	• Resided in a poor **neighborhood** on the list in a town in the central district of Israel; studied in a "Yeshiva" **high school** on the list
• Father immigrated to Israel from Tunisia in 1958 and had a **high school education**; Israeli-born mother had **vocational training**	• Mother had a **high school education; three siblings**
• **Had divorced parents**, suffered from a health disability, and had a **parent with a disability** and a **family member with chronic illness**	• Born in Iran, **immigrated** to Israel with parents in 1983; **parents died**; released from the IDF because of financial problems
• DISADVANTAGE SCORE: 70	• DISADVANTAGE SCORE: 69
• Neighborhood and high school attended: 20 + 20 = **40**	• Neighborhood and high school attended: 20 + 20 = **40**
• Family socioeconomic status (parental education and family size): 10 + 0 = **10**	• Family socioeconomic status (parental education and family size): 5 + 4 = **9**
• Individual and/or family adverse circumstances: **20 (maximum)**	• Individual and/or family adverse circumstances: **20 (maximum)**
• GPA of high school matriculation diploma: 94; psychometric score: 661	• GPA of high school matriculation diploma: 95; psychometric score: 631

Source: Author's calculations.

Notes: These real cases of applicants whose score passed the thirty-point threshold were all admitted under Israel's class-based affirmative action plan to one of the selective departments in one of the top four institutions of higher learning, and all of them graduated with this major. Highlighted in bold are the factors that contributed to their score. These examples demonstrate that it is almost impossible to pass the thirty-point threshold without a structural disadvantage.

Figure A6.2 (continued)

Sarah	Jacob
• Resided in a **development town** in southern Israel on the list; studied in a **high school** on the list	• Resided in a town in the central district of Israel
• Parents immigrated to Israel from Morocco in 1956; father had **high school education**; mother had **elementary school education; four siblings**	• Both parents were born in Israel; father had a **high school education**; mother had **vocational training; father died; two siblings**
• **DISADVANTAGE SCORE: 56**	• Family lived in the grandmother's small apartment; **mother had a disability; brother had a disability; received government support**
• Neighborhood and high school attended: 20 + 20 = **40**	
• Family socioeconomic status (parental education and family size): 14 + 2 = **16**	• **DISADVANTAGE SCORE: 32**
• Individual and/or family adverse circumstances: **0**	• Neighborhood and high school attended: **0**
• GPA of high school matriculation diploma: 100; psychometric score: 625	• Family socioeconomic status (parental education and family size): 10 + 2 = **12**
	• Individual and/or family adverse circumstances: **20 (maximum)**
	• GPA of high school matriculation diploma: 91; psychometric score: 629

Joel, David, and Sarah (pseudonyms) got the maximum number of points for residing in a disadvantaged neighborhood and graduating from a disadvantaged high school. Jacob is the exception because he (barely) passed the threshold without a structural disadvantage but with a daunting set of family hardships. The term "on the list" refers to the set of criteria to qualify for the class-based affirmative action program.

Table A7.1 Characteristics of Actual and Simulated Admits to Israeli Universities: General Admit Pool, Class-Based Admits and Race-Based Admits, All Majors, AA Regime

	Non-AA	Class-Based Admits	Race-Based Admits (Arabs + Mizrachi Jews)	Race-Based Admits (Mizrachi Jews)	Race-Based Admits (Arabs)
Academic achievements					
Mean test score (psychometric)	651	605	624	634	587
Matriculation Diploma Grades	102	99	106	100	108
Standardized Academic Composite Score	55	42	61	50	56
Locality characteristics					
Development town	2	10	2	5	1
Share of students in locality	17	13	12	15	8
Locality SES cluster					
Bottom cluster (1–4)	26	53	59	39	93
Middle cluster (5–7)	38	32	27	41	6
Top cluster (8–10)	36	16	13	19	1
Geographic region					
Jerusalem	15	21	10	21	1
North	7	19	32	7	59
Haifa	9	7	15	6	24
Center	32	19	23	30	14
Tel Aviv	27	17	12	21	1
South	10	18	8	15	0
Immigration status					
New immigrant	14	20	2	4	0
Origin					
Arab	7	21	58	0	100
Mizrachi	14	26	42	100	0
Other	78	53	0	0	0
Parents' SES status					
Father's occupation rank (TAU)	59	39	51	51	48
Mother's occupation rank (TAU)	50	32	38	44	28
Father out of labor force (TAU)	7	22	13	13	12
Mother out of labor force (TAU)	15	40	32	19	50
N person-major[a]	127,240	4,353	4,298	4,127	4,002

Source: TAU, HUJI, and BGU administrative data, AA regime.
Note: The general applicant pool and the class together make up 100 percent of the presimulation population. The race group is made up of applicants who were not admitted.
[a] Number of persons times the number of majors they were admitted to. If a person is admitted to two majors then he or she contributes two observations to the sample.

Table A7.2 Characteristics of Actual and Simulated Admits to Israeli Universities: General Admit Pool, Class-Based Admits and Race-Based Admits, Most Selective Majors, AA Regime

	Non-AA	Class-Based Admits	Race-Based Admits (Arabs + Mizrachi Jews)	Race-Based Admits (Mizrachi Jews)	Race-Based Admits (Arabs)
Academic achievements					
Mean test score (psychometric)	704	668	709	702	688
Matriculation diploma grades	108	107	114	108	114
Standardized academic composite score	81	71	94	82	91
Locality characteristics					
Development town	1	7	2	2	2
Share of students in locality	18	14	12	16	9
Locality SES cluster					
Bottom cluster (1–4)	15	42	57	24	82
Middle cluster (5–7)	38	35	30	49	17
Top cluster (8–10)	47	23	14	27	1
Geographic region					
Jerusalem	6	5	2	8	1
North	7	26	44	6	64
Haifa	8	8	18	8	23
Center	39	23	22	37	12
Tel-Aviv	36	22	12	29	0
South	5	16	3	11	0
Immigration status					
New immigrant	12	21	1	4	0
Origin					
Arab	9	32	72	0	100
Mizrachi	14	23	28	100	0
Other	77	45	0	0	0
Parents' SES status					
Father's occupation rank (TAU)	62	41	55	55	53
Mother's occupation rank (TAU)	52	32	40	48	34
Father out of labor force (TAU)	6	26	10	11	11
Mother out of labor force (TAU)	13	41	31	15	40
N person-major[a]	18,796	469	469	465	468

Source: TAU, HUJI, and BGU administrative data, AA regime.
Note: The general applicant pool and the class together make up 100 percent of the presimulation population. The race group is made up of applicants who were not admitted.
[a] Number of persons times the number of majors they were admitted to. If a person is admitted to two majors then he or she contributes two observations to the sample.

Table A7.3 Characteristics of Actual and Simulated Admits to Israeli Universities (Including TECH): Class-Based Admits and Race-Based Admits (Arabs Only), All Majors, AA Regime

	Class-Based Admits	Race-Based Admits (Arabs)
Academic achievements		
Mean test score (psychometric)	607.3	590.6
Matriculation diploma grades	99.9	108.1
Standardized academic composite score	42.6	56.2
Locality characteristics		
Development town	9.5	0.5
Share of students in locality	12.7	7.9
Locality SES cluster		
Bottom cluster (1–4)	54.2	92.8
Middle cluster (5–7)	30.9	6.0
Top cluster (8–10)	14.9	1.2
Geographic region		
Jerusalem	19.2	0.8
North	22.0	60.7
Haifa	7.7	23.5
Center	18.2	13.5
Tel Aviv	15.9	1.0
South	17.0	0.5
Origin		
Arab	22.5	100.0
Mizrachi	24.7	0.0
Other	52.8	0.0
Parents' SES status		
Father's occupation rank (TAU)	38.6	48.4
Mother's occupation rank (TAU)	32.3	27.6
Father out of labor force (TAU)	22.5	12.2
Mother out of labor force (TAU)	39.9	50.2
N person-major[a]	4,632	4,279

Source: TAU, HUJI, BGU, and TECH administrative data, AA regime.

[a] Number of persons times the number of majors they were admitted to. If a person is admitted to two majors then he or she contributes two observations to the sample.

Table A7.4 Characteristics of Actual and Simulated Admits to Israeli Universities (Including TECH): Class-Based Admits and Race-Based Admits (Arabs Only), Most-Selective Majors, AA Regime

	Class-Based Admits	Race-Based Admits (Arabs)
Academic achievements		
Mean test score (psychometric)	670.1	691.6
Matriculation diploma grades	107.3	114.5
Standardized academic composite score	71.4	90.5
Locality characteristics		
Development town	7.3	1.9
Share of students in locality	13.2	8.9
Locality SES cluster		
Bottom cluster (1–4)	46.5	86.9
Middle cluster (5–7)	32.7	12.7
Top cluster (8–10)	20.8	0.4
Geographic region		
Jerusalem	4.7	0.5
North	30.2	64.1
Haifa	9.0	23.7
Center	21.4	11.5
Tel Aviv	20.1	0.2
South	14.4	0.0
Origin		
Arab	36.7	100.0
Mizrachi	20.0	0.0
Other	43.3	0.0
Parents' SES status		
Father's occupation rank (TAU)	40.7	52.9
Mother's occupation rank (TAU)	32.3	34.3
Father out of labor force (TAU)	25.9	11.4
Mother out of labor force (TAU)	41.3	39.6
N person-major[a]	529	528

Source: TAU, HUJI, BGU, and TECH administrative data, AA regime.
[a] Number of persons times the number of majors they were admitted to. If a person is admitted to two majors then he or she contributes two observations to the sample.

Table A8.1 Simulations Results: Characteristics of AA Admits to Elite U.S. Universities, by Prototype, 1995–1996

	(1)	(2)	(3)	(4)	(5)	(6)
			Simulations: Class-Based Affirmative Action			
	Non-AA	Race-Based Admits	Class-Economic	Class-SES	Class-Structural	Class-Multidimensional
Test scores (mean)	1,210	950	1,260	1,130	1,100	800
High school GPA (mean)	5.7	5.3	5.4	5.4	5.8	4.5
AP courses taken (mean)	2.0	0.9	1.4	0.8	1.1	0.5
Black	3.0%	53.4%	2.9%	0.0%	17.6%	39.1%
Hispanic	5.4	46.6	11.8	12.5	13.2	32.8
Asian	14.6	0.0	16.2	18.1	19.1	9.4
Other	1.1	0.0	0.0	1.4	0.0	0.0
White	75.9	0.0	69.1	68.1	50.0	18.8
% URM	8.4	100.0	14.7	12.5	30.9	71.9
% Immigrants	12.1	10.6	19.4	22.1	15.9	16.7
Black	3.3	28.6	0.0	0.0	0.0	0.0
Hispanic	9.8	71.4	25.0	26.7	10.0	30.0
Asian	58.7	0.0	66.7	66.7	80.0	50.0
Other	0.0	0.0	0.0	0.0	0.0	0.0
White	28.3	0.0	8.3	6.7	10.0	20.0
Parents, high school degree or less[a]	11	34	18	61	23	80

Parents, some college education[b]	7	14	11	39	19	20
Parents, bachelor's degree[c]	27	24	47	0	34	0
Parents, advanced degree[d]	56	27	24	0	23	0
Family income (mean)	$87,245	$55,773	$18,796	$15,837	$57,801	$12,072
Expected Family Contribution (EFC) (mean)	$15,401	$7,792	$35	$52	$6,958	$17
Quartile 1 (bottom)	7.6%	24.7%	100.0%	100.0%	20.6%	100.0%
Quartile 2	15.5	24.7	0.0	0.0	30.9	0.0
Quartile 3	25.4	23.3	0.0	0.0	27.9	0.0
Quartile 4 (top)	51.6	27.4	0.0	0.0	20.6	0.0
% of poverty level	516	346	159	125	315	92
% Pell grantees	11.5	39.7	76.5	76.4	25.0	93.8
High poverty high school[e]	2.2	12.3	1.5	2.8	100.0	100.0
Region						
East	36.9	35.6	25.0	22.9	5.9	9.4
Midwest	18.9	16.4	23.5	32.9	13.2	10.9
South	27.6	31.5	23.5	21.4	51.5	53.1
West	16.6	16.4	27.9	22.9	29.4	26.6

Source: National Center for Education Statistics, Beginning Postsecondary Students Longitudinal Study (BPS), 1996–2001.

[a] Both parents have a high school diploma or less.
[b] A parent with the highest education has some college education.
[c] A parent with the highest education has a bachelor's degree.
[d] At least one parent has an advanced degree.
[e] A high school in which at least 40 percent of students were eligible for a free or discounted lunch.

Table A8.2 Pre- and Post-Simulations Results: Characteristics of the Student Bodies of Elite U.S. Institutions, by Prototype, 1995–1996

	(1)	(2)	(3)	(4)	(5)
		Basic Simulations			
	Current	Economic	SES	Structural	Multi-dimensional
Test scores (mean)	1,190	1,210	1,200	1,200	1,180
High school GPA (mean)	5.6	5.6	5.6	5.7	5.6
AP courses taken (mean)	1.9	1.9	1.9	1.9	1.9
Black	7.0%	3.6%	3.4%	4.3%	5.9%
Hispanic	8.7	6.4	6.5	6.5	7.8
Asian	13.5	14.3	14.3	14.8	14.1
Other	1.0	1.0	1.0	1.0	1.0
White	69.9	74.7	74.8	73.4	71.2
% URM	15.7	10.0	9.9	10.9	13.7
% Immigrants	12.0	12.4	12.6	12.3	12.3
Black	5.1	2.9	2.9	2.9	2.9
Hispanic	14.1	11.8	12.5	9.8	11.8
Asian	54.5	58.8	58.7	60.8	57.8
Other	0.0	0.0	0.0	0.0	0.0
White	26.3	26.5	26	26.5	27.5
Parents, high school degree or less[a]	13.0	11.0	14.0	12.0	16.0
Parents, some college education[b]	8.0	7.0	10.0	8.0	8.0
Parents, bachelor's degree[c]	27.0	28.0	25.0	27.0	25.0
Parents, advanced degree[d]	53.0	54.0	51.0	53.0	51.0
Family income (mean)	$84,747	$82,532	$82,265	$85,204	$82,004
Expected Family Contribution (mean)	$14,797	$14,327	$14,327	$14,805	$14,325
Quartile 1 (bottom)	8.9%	14.0%	14.0%	8.8%	14.0%
Quartile 2	16.2	14.5	14.5	16.4	14.5
Quartile 3	25.2	23.5	23.5	25.3	23.5
Quartile 4 (top)	49.7	48.0	48.0	49.5	48.0
% of poverty level	502	491	488	501	485
% Pell grantees	13.7	16.2	16.0	12.6	17.4
High poverty high school[e]	3.0	2.4	2.5	9.0	9.0
Region					
East	36.8	35.9	35.8	34.8	34.9
Midwest	18.7	19.2	19.9	18.5	18.2
South	28.0	27.3	27.5	29.4	29.5
West	16.6	17.6	16.8	17.3	17.3

Source: National Center for Education Statistics, Beginning Postsecondary Students Longitudinal Study (BPS), 1996–2001.
[a]Both parents have a high school diploma or less.
[b]A parent with the highest education has some college education.

(6)	(7)	(8)	(9)	(10)	(11)	(12)	(13)
Race with Class				Reform			
Economic	SES	Structural	Multi-dimensional	Economic	SES	Structural	Multi-dimensional
1,210	1,200	1,200	1,180	1,220	1,190	1,170	1,190
5.6	5.6	5.7	5.6	5.6	5.5	5.6	5.5
1.9	1.9	1.9	1.9	1.9	1.9	1.9	2.0
3.7%	4.0%	4.7%	6.3%	4.3%	5.4%	9.2%	8.6%
6.8	7.6	7.2	8.0	8.2	9.6	11.1	11.0
14.3	13.9	14.6	14.0	13.7	13.0	12.6	12.0
1.0	1.0	1.0	1.0	0.9	1.0	0.9	0.9
74.1	73.5	72.6	70.7	72.9	71.0	66.2	67.5
10.5	11.6	11.8	14.3	12.5	15.0	20.3	19.6
12.7	12.1	12.3	12.2	13.3	12.3	12.1	11.6
2.9	4.0	2.9	3.0	3.6	4.9	3.0	3.5
14.3	13.0	10.8	13.9	18.0	16.5	19.8	17.6
57.1	57.0	59.8	57.4	55.0	54.4	53.5	50.6
0.0	0.0	0.0	0.0	0.0	0.0	0.0	0.0
25.7	26.0	26.5	25.7	23.4	24.3	23.8	28.2
11.0	14.0	12.0	16.0	14.0	23.0	17.0	18.0
7.0	9.0	8.0	8.0	10.0	14.0	9.0	9.0
28.0	25.0	27.0	25.0	27.0	19.0	25.0	22.0
54.0	51.0	53.0	51.0	50.0	44.0	48.0	50.0
$82,501	$82,266	$85,108	$82,072	$74,563	$73,115	$79,291	$80,921
$14,327	$14,327	$14,761	$14,325	$12,398	$12,398	$13,571	$14,127
14.0%	14.0%	9.0%	14.0%	29.1%	29.1%	13.7%	19.2%
14.5	14.5	16.6	14.5	9.9	9.9	17.7	11.3
23.5	23.5	25.0	23.5	19.6	19.6	23.7	22.3
48.0	48.0	49.3	48.0	41.4	41.4	44.9	47.2
491	487	500	486	443	432	464	475
16.1	16.3	13.2	17.4	25.0	27.5	19.8	21.3
2.4	2.8	9.0	9.0	2.5	3.2	24.3	13.8
36.0	35.7	34.8	34.9	33.4	33.7	29.9	33.5
19.0	19.4	18.3	18.2	20.1	19.8	16.1	16.5
27.5	28.2	29.3	29.6	27.5	28.7	34.6	32.3
17.5	16.7	17.6	17.2	18.9	17.8	19.4	17.6

[c] A parent with the highest education has a bachelor's degree.
[d] At least one parent has an advanced degree.
[e] A high school in which at least 40 percent of students were eligible for a free or discounted lunch.

Table A8.3 Pre- and Post-Sensitivity Analysis with Different Thresholds: Characteristics of the Student Bodies of Elite U.S. Institutions, by Prototype, 1995–1996

	(1)	(2)	(3)	(4)	(5)
		Basic Simulations: 25% Threshold			
	Current	Economic	SES	Structural	Multi-dimensional
Test scores (mean)	1,190	1,210	1,200	1,200	1,180
High school GPA (mean)	5.6	5.6	5.6	5.7	5.6
AP courses taken (mean)	1.9	1.9	1.9	1.9	1.9
Black	7.0%	3.6%	3.4%	4.3%	5.9%
Hispanic	8.7	6.4	6.5	6.5	7.8
Asian	13.5	14.3	14.3	14.8	14.1
Other	1.0	1.0	1.0	1.0	1.0
White	69.9	74.7	74.8	73.4	71.2
% URM	15.7	10	9.9	10.9	13.7
% Immigrants	12.0	12.4	12.6	12.3	12.3
Black	5.1	2.9	2.9	2.9	2.9
Hispanic	14.1	11.8	12.5	9.8	11.8
Asian	54.5	58.8	58.7	60.8	57.8
Other	0.0	0.0	0.0	0.0	0.0
White	26.3	26.5	26.0	26.5	27.5
Parents, high school degree or less[a]	13.0	11.0	14.0	12.0	16.0
Parents, some college education[b]	8.0	7.0	10.0	8.0	8.0
Parents, bachelor's degree[c]	27.0	28.0	25.0	27.0	25.0
Parents, advanced degree[d]	53.0	54.0	51.0	53.0	51.0
Family income (mean)	$84,747	$82,532	$82,265	$85,204	$82,004
Expected Family Contribution (mean)	14,797	14,327	14,327	14,805	14,325
Quartile 1 (bottom)	8.9%	14.0%	14.0%	8.8%	14.0%
Quartile 2	16.2	14.5	14.5	16.4	14.5
Quartile 3	25.2	23.5	23.5	25.3	23.5
Quartile 4 (top)	49.7	48.0	48.0	49.5	48.0
% of poverty level	502	491	488	501	485
% Pell grantees	13.7	16.2	16.0	12.6	17.4
High poverty high school[e]	3.0	2.4	2.5	9.0	9.0
Region					
East	36.8	35.9	35.8	34.8	34.9
Midwest	18.7	19.2	19.9	18.5	18.2
South	28.0	27.3	27.5	29.4	29.5
West	16.6	17.6	16.8	17.3	17.3

Source: National Center for Education Statistics, Beginning Postsecondary Students Longitudinal Study (BPS), 1996–2001.
[a] Both parents have a high school diploma or less.
[b] A parent with the highest education has some college education.

(6)	(7)	(8)	(9)	(10)	(11)	(12)	(13)
Basic Simulations: 50% Threshold				Basic Simulations: 100% Threshold			
Economic	SES	Structural	Multi-dimensional	Economic	SES	Structural	Multi-dimensional
1,210	1,200	1,190	1,160	1,200	1,180	1,170	1,150
5.7	5.6	5.7	5.5	5.7	5.6	5.7	5.5
1.9	1.9	1.9	1.8	1.8	1.8	1.8	1.8
2.2%	2.1%	3.4%	5.4%	1.1%	1.1%	4.2%	4.6%
5.1	5.2	6.0	7.9	1.8	2.8	3.5	4.3
15.0	15.0	14.8	14.2	15.7	15.8	15.1	15
1.1	1.0	1	1.0	1.1	1.2	1.0	1.0
76.6	76.7	74.9	71.4	80.3	79.1	76.2	75.1
7.3	7.3	9.3	13.4	2.9	3.9	7.7	8.9
12.6	12.5	11.9	12.4	12.5	12.0	11.6	12.0
0.0	1.0	0.0	0.0	0.0	1.0	0.0	0.0
11.5	11.5	10.1	13.6	7.8	5.0	6.3	6.3
62.5	61.5	62.6	58.3	66.0	67.0	65.6	63.2
0.0	0.0	0.0	0.0	0.0	0.0	0.0	0.0
26.0	26.0	27.3	28.2	26.2	27.0	28.1	30.5
11.0	16.0	12.0	18.0	12.0	19.0	14.0	18.0
7.0	11.0	8.0	9.0	9.0	12.0	9.0	9.0
28.0	24.0	27.0	24.0	28.0	22.0	27.0	24.0
53.0	50.0	52.0	50.0	51.0	47.0	50.0	49.0
$80,761	$80,454	$84,368	$80,051	$77,051	$76,183	$81,302	$79,001
14,003	14,004	14,740	14,001	13,229	13,229	14,192	13,904
17.0%	17.0%	9.3%	17.0%	21.7%	21.7%	10.1%	17.7%
13.5	13.5	16.5	13.5	12.5	12.5	17.9	13.1
22.4	22.4	25.0	22.4	21.2	21.2	24.6	22.3
47.2	47.2	49.1	47.2	44.6	44.6	47.4	46.9
483	479	498	476	465	458	484	474
17.7	17.8	13.6	19.7	20.0	21.4	15.5	20.2
2.3	2.3	12.1	12.1	2.1	2.5	17.0	12.7
35.6	35.2	34.3	34.3	35.1	35.0	33.0	34.4
20.1	20.1	18.5	18.0	21.1	20.5	17.9	18.2
26.6	27.5	29.8	30.6	27.2	28.4	31.9	31.3
17.7	17.1	17.3	17.1	16.7	16.1	17.2	16.2

[c] A parent with the highest education has a bachelor's degree.
[d] At least one parent has an advanced degree.
[e] A high school in which at least 40 percent of students were eligible for a free or discounted lunch.

Table A8.4 The Likelihood of Attending College, by Institution Selectivity Level, Four-Year Institutions, Odds Ratios, 1995–1996

	Barron's Categories of Competitiveness			
	Most	Highly	Very	Competitive
Black/Hispanic	3.098***	2.225***	1.122	0.709***
	(0.992)	(0.395)	(0.120)	(0.0581)
Test scores	1.011***	1.008***	1.005***	1.002***
	(0.000888)	(0.000465)	(0.000273)	(0.000212)
High school GPA	0.951	1.062**	1.034**	1.025*
	(0.0451)	(0.0290)	(0.0169)	(0.0130)
AP courses taken in high school	1.456***	1.456***	1.399***	1.185***
	(0.137)	(0.105)	(0.0865)	(0.0687)
Honors courses taken in high school	1.195**	1.074*	1.059**	0.977
	(0.0890)	(0.0456)	(0.0297)	(0.0231)
GPA attained in AP courses	1.004***	1.003***	1.001*	1.001*
	(0.000865)	(0.000612)	(0.000535)	(0.000510)
Constant	3.36e-07***	4.93e-05***	0.00578***	0.294***
	(3.43e-07)	(2.43e-05)	(0.00149)	(0.0550)
N	1,979	2,293	3,217	4,497

Source: National Center for Education Statistics, Beginning Postsecondary Students Longitudinal Study (BPS), 1996–2001.
Note: Standard errors are in parentheses. The comparison category is less competitive and noncompetitive institutions.
***$p < 0.01$; **$p < 0.05$; *$p < 0.10$

Table A8.5 The Characteristics of Students at Elite U.S. Institutions, Below and Above Category Thresholds, by URM Status, 1995–1996

Variable	Whites and Asians	URM	Whites and Asians: Above	Whites and Asians: Below	URM: Above	URM: Below
Test scores (mean)	1,205	1,083	1,267	1,018	1,223	947
AP courses taken	2.0	1.5	2.3	1.0	2.1	0.9
Expected Family Contribution, Quartile 1 (bottom)	7.2%	18.1%	7.9%	5.2%	11.3%	24.7%
Parents' education less than BA degree	17.0	38.0	15.0	22.0	27.0	48.0
High poverty high school[a]	2.0	11.0	1.0	4.0	10.0	12.0

Source: National Center for Education Statistics, Beginning Postsecondary Students Longitudinal Study (BPS), 1996–2001.
Note: The threshold is the twenty-fifth percentile of test scores within the category (1,210 points at most selective schools and 1,070 at highly competitive schools).
[a] A high school in which at least 40 percent of students were eligible for a free or discounted lunch.

Table A9.1: OLS and Logit Regression Models Predicting Various Academic Outcomes for Students at the Israeli Universities Who Fell Just Above and Just Below the Affirmative Action Threshold of Eligibility, AA Regime

	AA Score: Narrow Range (Plus or Minus 10)		AA Score: Full Range	
	Unadjusted Gap 1	Adjusted Gap[a] 2	Unadjusted Gap 3	Adjusted Gap[a] 4
OLS regression (person-major): Freshman GPA[b]				
Above threshold	−0.383	−0.00955	−1.312***	−0.676*
Standardized academic score		0.134***		0.155***
Major fixed effects		Yes		Yes
Constant	77.45***	81.52***	77.71***	77.39***
Observations	1,900	1,855	4,521	4,389
R-squared	0.000	0.249	0.002	0.241
Logit regression (person): Graduated from university[c]				
Above threshold	0.0206	0.0353	−0.149	−0.0983
	(0.185)	(0.220)	(0.127)	(0.146)
Standardized academic score		0.00549		0.00751
		(0.00780)		(0.00489)
Major fixed effects		Yes		Yes
Constant	0.716***	1.146	0.851***	−0.0651
	(0.153)	(0.838)	(0.108)	(0.552)
Observations	609	574	1,425	1,383
OLS regression (person-major): Final GPA in each major graduated from[d]				
Above threshold	0.492	0.535	−0.675*	−0.334
	(0.560)	(0.613)	(0.374)	(0.401)
Standardized academic score		0.0748***		0.0580***
		(0.0187)		(0.0122)
Major fixed effects		yes		yes
Constant	82.98***	79.30***	83.83***	80.89***
	(0.461)	(3.214)	(0.313)	(2.701)
Observations	481	425	1,074	927
R-squared	0.002	0.181	0.003	0.152

Source: TAU, BGU, HUJI, and TECH administrative data, AA regime.
Note: Standard errors are in parentheses.
[a] Control for students' standardized academic score and their major's fixed effects.
[b] Students' first-year GPA in each major studied at TAU (2003–2007), BGU (2006–2007), HUJI (2001–2008), and TECH (2004–2007).
[c] HUJI (2001–2005).
[d] HUJI (2001–2005).
***$p < 0.01$; **$p < 0.05$; *$p < 0.10$

NOTES

CHAPTER 1: THE SEARCH FOR AN ALTERNATIVE AFFIRMATIVE ACTION POLICY IN U.S. HIGHER EDUCATION

1. Regents of the University of California v. Bakke 438 U.S. 265 (1978), 306.
2. In 1974 the "special program" criteria targeted applicants who asked to be considered as members of a "minority group," which the medical school apparently viewed as "Blacks," "Chicanos," "Asians," and "American Indians." In 1973 the program's criteria targeted applicants who asked to be considered as "economically and/or educationally disadvantaged." The record demonstrated that only disadvantaged minority applicants were in fact considered as part of the special program. Ibid., 265, 274 (Justice Lewis Powell, Opinion).
3. Kaufman (2006) and Stefoff (2006).
4. Stefoff (2006).
5. Bowen and Bok (1998).
6. Tobin (2009).
7. Ibid.
8. Bowen and Bok (1998).
9. Of course, blacks were not the only applicants with limited access to the Ivy League. For decades Harvard, for example, maintained a quota for Jews, fearing that too many Jewish students would alienate its core Anglo-Saxon constituency. Women were entirely excluded from most of these schools until the late 1960s and 1970s. Princeton admitted its first female undergraduate in 1969; Harvard went coed in 1977, as did Columbia University in 1983.
10. Bowen and Bok (1998), 4.
11. Karabel (2005), 379, 392.
12. Reported in Bowen and Bok (1998), based on Kendrick (1967).
13. Bagde, Epple, and Taylor (2011); Bertrand, Hanna, and Mullainathan (2010); and Robles and Krishna (2012).

14. Celai W. Dugger, "Campus That Apartheid Ruled Faces a Policy Rift," *New York Times,* November 22, 2010, A1.
15. Almeida-Filho (2012), Francis and Tannuri-Pianto (2012), Guimaraes (2010), and Peria and Bailey (2014); see also Jon Jeter, "Affirmative Action Debate Forces Brazil to Take Look in the Mirror," *Washington Post,* June 16, 2003, A1; and Edward E. Telles, "WideAngle: Discrimination and Affirmative Action in Brazil," PBS/WNET, 2009, available at: http://www-tc.pbs.org/wnet/wideangle/files/2009/04/discrimination-and-affirmative-action-in-brazil.pdf (accessed: August 4, 2011).
16. Agrawal (2006).
17. Dugger, "Campus That Apartheid Ruled Faces a Policy Rift."
18. Bakke 438 U.S. 265 (1978), 412 (Justice John Paul Stevens, Concurring in part and dissenting in part).
19. Ibid., 369 (Dissenting in the portion of the judgment directing Bakke's admission and concurring in the holding that race can be considered in admissions).
20. Ball (2000).
21. Bakke 438 U.S. 265 (1978), 320.
22. Ibid., 313 (quoting, in part, Keyishian v. Board of Regents of Univ. of State of N.Y. 385 U.S. 589 [1967], 603).
23. Kaufman (2006).
24. One of the legal questions in Bakke was deciding which standard of review applied, as the precedent on this question was unclear. Should the Court's strictest review be limited to assessing policies that were intended to exclude racial minorities, or should it be extended to policies that were implemented to include racial minorities (such as voluntary affirmative action)? The majority of the justices voted for the latter interpretation—that the strict scrutiny standard should be applied to assess the constitutionality of the medical school's affirmative action policy, thus requiring that the admissions policy further a compelling interest in a manner narrowly tailored to that interest. This framing represented an important shift in constitutional jurisprudence, and in fueling the ongoing challenges to affirmative action—by providing a justification for individuals to challenge race-conscious policies as discriminatory, particularly against whites—it shaped the broader public debate regarding affirmative action.
25. Dworkin (1985), 304.
26. Bakke 438 U.S. 265 (1978), 324.
27. Holzer and Neumark (2006), 476.
28. Bowen, Kurzweil, and Tobin (2005) and Espenshade and Radford (2009).
29. The Portuguese text of the original law is available at: http://www.planalto.gov.br/ccivil_03/_Ato2011-2014/2012/Lei/L12711.htm.
30. The law defines "low-income" as a family income less than or equal to one and a half times the minimum wage.

31. In the affirmative action context of this book, I use "ethnicity" interchangeably with the term "race."
32. Cohen and Haberfeld (1998), Haberfeld and Cohen (1998, 2007), Lewin-Epstein and Semyonov (1986, 1992), Semyonov and Tyree (1981), and Yaish (2001).
33. Graglia (1993), Sander and Taylor (2012), Sowell (2003), and Thernstrom and Thernstrom (1997).
34. The other two institutions, Bar-Ilan University and Haifa University, did not adopt such a program. Both of these schools are less selective than the other four universities.
35. The application process and admissions are major-institution-specific.

CHAPTER 2: AFFIRMATIVE ACTION IN AMERICAN HIGHER EDUCATION: A STORY ABOUT RACE

1. "Unpublished Memorandum [of 1978] of Justice Marshall on Regents of the University of California v. Bakke (438 U.S. 265)," folders 2–3, box 204, Thurgood Marshall Papers, Library of Congress, Washington D.C.
2. Du Bois (1903), 9. W.E.B. Du Bois (1868–1963), an African American sociologist, historian, and civil rights activist, was the first black man to achieve a doctorate from Harvard University.
3. Howard University, "Brief History of Howard University," available at: http://www2.howard.edu/about/history.
4. Public Papers of the Presidents of the United States: Lyndon B. Johnson, 1965 2(301): 635–50 (Washington: US Government Printing Office, 1966).
5. The data indicate the share of the population who completed four years of high school or more and those who completed four years of college or more, respectively (U.S. Census Bureau 2014).
6. Schill and Wachter (1995), 141–67.
7. DeSilver (2013).
8. In 1961 President Kennedy signed Executive Order 10925, establishing the Committee on Equal Employment Opportunity. The order includes the provision, among others, that government contractors "must take affirmative action to ensure applicants are employed . . . without regard to race, creed or national origin." This was the first attempt at legislating affirmative action and, indeed, is the source of the term. In 1965 President Johnson signed Executive Order 11246, which requires federal contractors to develop guidelines for how they plan to enforce antidiscrimination requirements and to proactively document their efforts to do so.
9. Bowen and Bok (1998).
10. Alon and Tienda (2007), Bowen and Bok (1998), and Karabel (2005).
11. Alon (2010).
12. These estimates are based on Bowen and Bok (1998), Bowen et al. (2005), Espenshade and Radford (2009), and Alon (2010). I have found, for example,

that among undergraduate students attending elite colleges and universities in the fall of 1989, black students enrolled in more selective schools than their white counterparts within every test score band (Alon 2010). Among black and white students who scored between 900 and 1,000 on their SATs, 41 percent of blacks enrolled at a highly selective school (category 2, in which the median SAT score ranged from 1,150 to 1,250), compared to only 20 percent of whites. Likewise, in the 1,100–1,200 band, 29 percent of blacks found their way to the most selective schools (category 1, median score above 1250), while only 9 percent of whites managed to do the same.

13. Clayton and Tangri (1989) and Kellough (2006).
14. Bowen and Bok (1998).
15. Ta-Nehisi Coates, "The Case for Reparations," *The Atlantic,* May 21, 2014.
16. Massey et al. (2007) find that about one-third of black freshmen at selective colleges in 1999 were first- or second-generation immigrants. The majority came from the Caribbean, with some also from Africa and Latin America. (Two feeding countries are Jamaica and Nigeria, both of which are former British colonies where English is spoken by the upper echelon of society.)
17. Bakke 438 U.S. 265 (1978), 312.
18. U.S. Census Bureau (2013, 2015).
19. Grutter v. Bollinger, 539 U.S. 306 (2003), 308.
20. Bowen and Bok (1998) and Alon and Tienda (2007).
21. Hinrichs (2012).
22. American Social Science Researchers, brief in support of respondents in Fisher v. University of Texas 570 U.S. (2013), Amici Curiae 11(345) (2012). Eric Grodsky and Michal Kurlaender (2010) show that the large negative impact of Proposition 209 on URM enrollment at the most prestigious UC campuses trickled down to affect other sectors of California's higher education system.
23. American Social Science Researchers, brief in support of respondents in Fisher v. University of Texas . . .; see also Garces (2013).
24. American Social Science Researchers, brief in support of respondents in Fisher v. University of Texas . . . ..
25. Bowen and Bok (1998) and Alon and Tienda (2005).
26. Bowen and Bok (1998), Jaynes and Williams (1989, 273), and U.S. Bureau of Labor Statistics (2014).
27. Brand and Halaby (2006).
28. Alon and Tienda (2005).
29. Brown and Hirschman (2006), Card and Krueger (2005), and Long (2004a).
30. Skrentny (1996) and Kellough (2006).
31. Chin (1998), Malamud (1997), Sowell (2004), and Wilson (1987).
32. Bowen and Bok (1998) report that 86 percent of black students at elite institutions in 1989 came from middle- to high-socioeconomic backgrounds. According to Espenshade and Radford (2009), about three-quarters of both black and

Hispanic applicants to elite schools in 1997 considered themselves middle-class or above.
33. Graglia (1993), Sowell (2003), and Thernstrom and Thernstrom (1997).
34. See Students for Fair Admissions, Inc. v. University of North Carolina, et al., case 1:2014cv00954, filed November 17, 2014, at the North Carolina Middle District Court, document 1, paragraphs 158, 158–73; and Students for Fair Admissions, Inc., v. President and Fellows of Harvard College et al., case 1:2014cv14176, filed November 17, 2014, at Massachusetts District Court, filing 1 (complaint), paragraphs 383–99. "The 'mismatch effect' of racial preferences far too frequently put the supposed beneficiaries of race-based admissions policies in a position where they cannot succeed academically in order to fulfill the university's social-engineering vision."
35. Gratz v. Bollinger 539 U.S. 244 (2003), 275.
36. Grutter v. Bollinger 539 U.S. 306 (2003), 325 ("today we endorse Justice Powell's view that student body diversity is a compelling state interest that can justify the use of race in university admissions"). The Court also elaborated on the educational benefits of diversity, which included promoting "cross-racial understanding," better learning environments, "better prepared students for an increasingly diverse workforce and society," and a path to leadership that would be visibly open to talented and qualified individuals of every race and ethnicity.
37. Ibid., 339.
38. The Court noted, "We expect that 25 years from now, the use of racial preferences will no longer be necessary to further the interest approved today." Ibid. at 343. Grutter also introduces the idea of a critical mass of underrepresented minority students. This was not a term used in Bakke, and it added a new dimension and vulnerability to the affirmative action debate. (How does one know when "critical mass" has been reached?)
39. In Schuette v. Coalition to Defend Affirmative Action 572 U.S. (2014), the Court upheld the constitutionality of this legislative ban. The debate is far from over. For example, in California there is ongoing pressure to overturn Proposition 209, which outlawed race-conscious admissions.
40. Hopwood v. State of Texas 78 F.3d 932, 5th Cir. (1996).
41. Fisher v. University of Texas, Supra, 133 S. Ct. 2411 (2013) at 2420.
42. Fisher v. University of Texas 758 F.3d 633 (2014) at 653.
43. "Affirmative Action at Risk in Supreme Court Case," *Inside Higher Ed*, June 30, 2015, available at: https://www.insidehighered.com/news/2015/06/30/supreme-court-will-once-again-consider-affirmative-action-college-admissions (accessed August 15, 2015).
44. Based on telephone interviews conducted from February 27 to March 16, 2014, of a national sample of 3,335 adults, eighteen years of age or older, living in all fifty U.S. states and the District of Columbia (Drake 2014). Among

whites, the share of supporters was 50 percent and among blacks and Hispanics it was over 80 percent. The discontent among Republicans is higher: only 43 percent think that racial preferences are a good thing.

CHAPTER 3: THE SHIFTING OF TECTONIC PLATES: SOCIAL, ECONOMIC, AND ACADEMIC TRENDS IN THE UNITED STATES AND THE IMPACT ON INEQUALITY IN HIGHER EDUCATION

1. Tilly (1998), 34.
2. Piketty and Saez (2003).
3. Alvaredo et al.
4. Lee and Mather (2008) and U.S. Bureau of Labor Statistics (2015).
5. Pew Research Center (2014).
6. Jason DeParle, "Harder for Americans to Rise from Lower Rungs," *New York Times,* January 4, 2012; Rana Foroohar, "What Ever Happened to Upward Mobility?" *Time,* November 14, 2011; Sawhill and Morton (2007).
7. Pew Economic Mobility Project (2011).
8. Corak (2006).
9. Pew Economic Mobility Project (2012).
10. Ibid.
11. Fischer and Hout (2006).
12. Buera and Kaboski (2012).
13. Baum, Kurose, and McPherson (2013).
14. Bailey and Dynarski (2011).
15. Brand and Halaby (2006).
16. Hoekstra (2009).
17. Dale and Krueger (2014).
18. U.S. Census Bureau (2015).
19. Planty et al. (2008).
20. Duffy and Goldberg (1998).
21. *Barron's* (1982, 1992, 2003).
22. Amherst College (Massachusetts), Barnard College (New York), Bates College (Maine), Boston College (Massachusetts), Bowdoin College (Maine), Brandeis University (Massachusetts), Brown University (Rhode Island), Bryn Mawr College (Pennsylvania), Bucknell University (Pennsylvania), California Institute of Technology (California), Carleton College (Minnesota), Carnegie Mellon University (Pennsylvania), Case Western Reserve University (Ohio), Claremont McKenna College (California), Colby College (Maine), Colgate University (New York), College of the Holy Cross (Massachusetts), College of William and Mary (Virginia), Columbia University in the City of New York (New York), Connecticut College (Connecticut), Cooper Union (New York),

Cornell University (New York), Dartmouth College (New Hampshire), Davidson College (North Carolina), Duke University (North Carolina), Emory University (Georgia), Franklin and Marshall College (Pennsylvania), George Washington University (District of Columbia), Georgetown University (District of Columbia), Hamilton College (New York), Harvard University (Massachusetts), Harvey Mudd College (California), Haverford College (Pennsylvania), John Hopkins University (Maryland), Kenyon College (Ohio), Lafayette College (Pennsylvania), Lehigh University (Pennsylvania), Macalester College (Minnesota), Massachusetts Institute of Technology (Massachusetts), Middlebury College (Vermont), New York University (New York), Northwestern University (Illinois), Oberlin College (Ohio), Occidental College (California), Pomona College (California), Princeton University (New Jersey), Reed College (Oregon), Rensselaer Polytechnic Institute (New York), Rice University (Texas), Rose-Hulman Institute of Technology (Indiana), Scripps College (California), Stanford University (California), Swarthmore College (Pennsylvania), The College of New Jersey (New Jersey), Tufts University (Massachusetts), Tulane University of Louisiana (Louisiana), United States Air Force Academy (Colorado), United States Military Academy (New York), United States Naval Academy (Maryland), University of California–Los Angeles (California), University of Chicago (Illinois), University of Miami (Florida), University of North Carolina–Chapel Hill (North Carolina), University of Notre Dame (Indiana), University of Pennsylvania (Pennsylvania), University of Richmond (Virginia), University of Rochester (New York), University of Southern California (California), University of Virginia–Main Campus (Virginia), Vanderbilt University (Tennessee), Vassar College (New York), Villanova University (Pennsylvania), Wake Forest University (North Carolina), Washington and Lee University (Virginia), Washington Theological Union (District of Columbia), Washington University in St. Louis (Missouri), Webb Institute (New York), Wellesley College (Massachusetts), Wesleyan University (Connecticut), Whitman College (Washington), Williams College (Massachusetts), and Yale University (Connecticut).

23. Alon (2009), and Alon and Tienda (2007).
24. National Association of College and University Business Officers and Common Fund Institute (2013).
25. Harvard's endowment in 2012 was the largest per institution but not per student. Princeton had more than $2 million of endowment funds per student.
26. "Financial resources" here refers to a school's average per-student spending on instruction, student services, academic support, research, and other educational programs and activities.
27. The empirical analyses follow a cohort of American students who started college in the fall of 1995–1996. Their academic experience is summarized in the

U.S. Department of Education's Beginning Postsecondary Students Longitudinal Study (BPS), which is linked to the National Postsecondary Student Aid Study (NPSAS).
28. The U.S. side of the investigation in this book is based on data from this cohort.
29. Mullen (2010).
30. Alon and Tienda (2007).
31. Lemann (1999).
32. Carnahan and Coletti (2003), Edwards and Sawtell (2013), and Lemann (1999).
33. Alon and Tienda (2007).
34. Ibid.
35. Alon (2009).
36. Briggs (2001, 2009) and Buchmann, Roscigno, and Condron (2006).
37. College Board (2009a), figure 9.
38. College Board (2009b), figure 12b; College Board (2012b), figure 14b.
39. Ehrenberg (2005).
40. College Board (2009b, 2012b) and Heller (2002). This increase is related to new, broad-scale state merit scholarship programs that provide a subsidy (usually free tuition) to first-year students based on academic performance (measured by high school GPA or test scores). The subsidy is then renewed annually based on college performance. The best-known state merit scholarship program is Georgia's HOPE (Helping Outstanding Pupils Educationally) program, which began in 1993. The popularity of the HOPE program helped spur the development of similar programs in other states. To date, fifteen states have implemented merit-based scholarship programs.
41. College Board (2012b, 2013).
42. Alon (2011a).
43. Alon (2009).
44. Claire V. Watkins, "The Ivy League Was Another Planet," *New York Times*, March 28, 2013, A25.

CHAPTER 4: BROAD DIVERSITY AT ELITE COLLEGES
1. Milem, Chang, and Antonio (2005).
2. The research demonstrates that having more opportunities for interaction with students from different backgrounds is associated with better learning experiences for all students (ibid.).
3. Alon (2010), Bowen and Bok (1998), Bowen et al. (2005), and Espenshade and Radford (2009).
4. Alon (2010).
5. Regents of the University of California v. Bakke 438 U.S. (1978), 315 (Justice Lewis Powell, Opinion).

6. Grutter v. Bollinger 539 U.S. (2003), 392–93 (Justice Anthony Kennedy, Opinion).
7. Stephanie J. Monroe, Assistant Secretary for Civil Rights, U.S. Department of Education, Office for Civil Rights, "The Use of Race in Postsecondary Student Admissions," letter to postsecondary institutions, August 28, 2008, available at: http://web.archive.org/web/20100307104353/http://ed.gov/about/offices/list/ocr/letters/raceadmissionpse.html (accessed October 2, 2014).
8. Rana Foroohar, "What Ever Happened to Upward Mobility?" *Time,* November 14, 2011.
9. President Lyndon B. Johnson, "To Fulfill These Rights," commencement address at Howard University, June 4, 1965.
10. "Brief of Harvard University, Brown University, The University of Chicago, Dartmouth College, Duke University, The University of Pennsylvania, Princeton University, and Yale University as Amici Curiae Supporting Respondents," submitted to the U.S. Supreme Court in Grutter v. Bollinger et al. and Gratz v. Bollinger et al.," 20, cited in Bowen et al. (2005), 175–76.
11. Clarke and Shore (2001) and Hawkins and Clinedist (2006).
12. Bowen and Bok (1998), 29.
13. Kane (1998), 26.
14. Bowen et al. (2005), 175–76.
15. UCLA Undergraduate Admission, "Freshmen Selection—Fall 2015," available at: http://www.admissions.ucla.edu/prospect/adm_fr/frsel.htm (accessed November 23, 2014).
16. The number of Pell Grant recipients grew at an average rate of 4 percent per year from 2001–2002 to 2006–2007 and 13 percent per year over the second half of the 2000s (College Board 2012b). In 2006–2007, the average Pell Grant award was $2,755. It rose to $3,972 by 2010–2011. The maximum for a single award rose from $4,496 in 2006 to $5,751 in 2010 (in current dollars).
17. In his report, Hout analyzes the freshman admissions process at UC Berkeley for the 2004–2005 academic year and finds that parents' education and income had no effect on admission chances. He concludes that "for the most part, their effects were indirect. Socioeconomic resources improved grades and test scores, which, in turn, improved reading scores and admission chances" (Hout 2005, 16). Mare examines the effect of applicant and high school characteristics on an applicant's holistic score in UCLA admissions in 2007 and 2008. He finds that the effects of family income and parents' education are very small, noting that, "because these effects are so small in 2008, the changes in estimated effects of family income and parents' education . . . are not, in my judgment, large enough to merit further analysis" (Mare 2012, 62).
18. Harvard College, Griffin Financial Aid Office, "Removing Economic Barriers to Harvard," available at: https://college.harvard.edu/financial-aid/how-aid-works/harvard-financial-aid-initiative (accessed July 23, 2014); see also Har-

vard College admission brochure, 2014–2015, available at: https://college.harvard.edu/sites/default/files/HarvardCollege2014-15.pdf (accessed December 28, 2014).

CHAPTER 5: WHAT IS CLASS-BASED AFFIRMATIVE ACTION?

1. Sander and Taylor (2012).
2. Kahlenberg (1996), 166.
3. U.S. Department of Justice and U.S. Department of Education (2011).
4. A class-based policy may generate more public support than race-conscious admissions because the chances for creaming are lower if the eligibility criteria are class-based.
5. Bowen et al. (2005), 255.
6. Skrentny (1996).
7. Carnevale and Rose (2004).
8. Clayton and Tangri (1989) and Kellough (2006).
9. Kellough (2006).
10. Bowen et al. (2005) and Espenshade and Radford (2009).
11. Ainsworth (2002); Brooks-Gunn et al. (1997); Crane (1991); Datcher (1982); Duncan (1994); Entwisle, Alexander, and Olson (1997); Gamoran (1987); Hallinan (2001); Massey and Denton (1993); McLeod and Edwards (1995); Parcel and Dufur (2001); Pebley and Sastry (2004); Sampson, Morenoff, and Earls (1999); Sampson, Raudenbush, and Earls (1997); South and Crowder (1999); and Wilson (1987, 1996).
12. Blau (1977) and Massey (2007).
13. U.S. Department of Justice and U.S. Department of Education (2011), 7.
14. Alon (2011b).
15. Steven Erlanger, "Top French Schools, Asked to Diversify, Fear for Standards," *New York Times,* June 30, 2010; and Heather Horn, "One French School's Secret for Making Affirmative Action Work," *The Atlantic,* April 9, 2012.
16. Horn, "One French School's Secret. . . ."
17. Fischer et al. (1996).
18. Wilson (1987).
19. Kahlenberg (2012).
20. Ibid., 15.
21. American Social Science Researchers, brief in support of respondents in Fisher v. University of Texas (2013), Amici Curiae 11(345) (2012).
22. Tienda and Niu (2006).
23. Koffman and Tienda (2008) and Tienda, Alon, and Niu (2010).
24. Poor schools include the quartile of high schools with the highest share of economically disadvantaged students (see Tienda et al. 2010).
25. Long, Saenz, and Tienda (2010).

CHAPTER 6: ISRAEL: CONTOURS OF INEQUALITY, HIGHER EDUCATION, AND CLASS-BASED AFFIRMATIVE ACTION AT THE TOP FOUR UNIVERSITIES

1. OECD, "OECD Income Distribution Database (IDD): Gini, Poverty, Income, Methods, and Income," available at: http://www.oecd.org/social/income-distribution-database.htm (accessed June 18, 2013).
2. Ben Naim and Belinsky (2012).
3. Israel Central Bureau of Statistics (ICBS) (2013a).
4. Cohen and Haberfeld (1998), Haberfeld and Cohen (1998, 2007), Lewin-Epstein and Semyonov (1986, 1992), Semyonov and Tyree (1981), and Yaish (2001).
5. Since statehood, smaller numbers of immigrants have also arrived from America; they are generally grouped with Jews of European origin.
6. Cohen, Haberfeld, and Kristal (2007) and Dahan et al. (2002).
7. ICBS (2010).
8. Lewin-Epstein and Semyonov (1986, 1993) and Semyonov and Tyree (1981).
9. Endeweld et al. (2012), ICBS (2011a), Myers-JDC-Brookdale Institute (2012), and Yashiv and Kasir (2009).
10. ICBS (2011b).
11. Shamir (2005).
12. ICBS (2013a).
13. Lewin-Epstein and Semyonov (1993) and Lustick (1980).
14. Friedlander et al. (2002), Haberfeld and Cohen (2007), and Okun and Friedlander (2005).
15. Haberfeld and Cohen (2007).
16. I compared the gaps among the younger cohorts of the college-educated population. My calculations are based on several Israeli Income Surveys for individuals who had attended an institution of higher education and were between the ages of twenty-seven and twenty-nine in 2005–2008.
17. During the same period, Mizrachi Jewish women of the same age cohort earned 94 percent of the monthly salary of their Ashkenazi peers.
18. ICBS (2010).
19. Ofakim had 24,000 residents in 2010.
20. ICBS (2006).
21. ICBS (1995).
22. ICBS (2012b).
23. Alon (2004), Spilerman and Habib (1976), and Yiftachel (2000).
24. For the sake of parsimony, and as a consequence of the different structure of the higher education system in Israel, I use the term "university" in this chapter to refer to the four flagship research institutions (TAU, HUJI, BGU, and TECH), with the main focus on bachelor's study, and the term "college" to refer to the

academic but non-research-oriented bachelor's degree–granting institutions. This usage is in contrast to previous chapters, in which I used the term "college" as a general term for an undergraduate education or for the part of any institution that offers it (as is common in the United States), regardless of whether the institution itself is classified as a college or university.

25. Suzzman et al. (2007).
26. U.S. Census Bureau (2012).
27. Between 1999 and 2008, 23 percent of students who attended the top four universities in Israel were enrolled in the social sciences, 21 percent in engineering, and 11 percent in the humanities and life sciences (see figure A6.1).
28. Clark (1983), Davies and Guppy (1997), Hagstrom (1971), and Rumberger and Thomas (1993).
29. The earnings information was obtained from the published reports of the Israel Central Bureau of Statistics, which are based on the tax authorities' administrative records for salaried workers, by major and institution. The pay data, based on the monthly salaries of bachelor's graduates during their first two years in the labor market, were collected for four cohorts of university graduates (2000 to 2003).
30. Suzzman et al. (2007).
31. ICBS (2009).
32. Alon (2015).
33. Ibid.
34. Alon (n.d.).
35. ICBS (2013b).
36. Author's calculations using the four universities' administrative data.
37. ICBS (2012b) and author's calculations using the four universities' administrative data.
38. The account of the program at the Faculty of Law at Tel Aviv University and its consequences is based on Mautner (2004).
39. In Hebrew: Ra'oi Le'Kidum, ראוי לקידום.
40. Based on the localities' socioeconomic index. All localities in the bottom three clusters are included. In all other localities, only poor neighborhoods are included.
41. Based on the high school ranking in the "Nurture Index" developed by the Israel Ministry of Education. The index is based on several characteristics of students (parents' educational attainment, income per household, and immigration status) and their school's geographic location, http://cms.education.gov.il/EducationCMS/Units/Scientist/CareIndex/madad+tipuach.htm (accessed: June 7, 2015).
42. Throughout the book, all names of individuals are pseudonyms.

CHAPTER 7: THE FEASIBILITY AND DIVERSITY DIVIDENDS OF AFFIRMATIVE ACTION IN ISRAEL

1. Council for Higher Education, Planning and Budgeting Committee, "Perennial Plan" (in Hebrew), available at: http://che.org.il/?page_id=23140 (accessed September 30, 2014).
2. The preferential policy began in 2001 at HUJI, 2003 at TAU, 2004 at TECH, and 2006 at BGU.
3. The records were obtained for periods ranging from ten to twelve consecutive years (circa 1997 to 2008).
4. The analyses are limited to individuals under age twenty-eight because admissions criteria are different for older applicants and also because the affirmative action plan has the same age cap. Also excluded are students who benefited from a relatively new program at TAU that does not require the submission of test scores for applicants from disadvantaged schools who ranked at the top of their class. Also omitted are individuals of Ethiopian origin who benefited from other types of preferential treatment, international students, and students enrolled in various programs that combine military service and academic studies. During the AA regime, these deletions totaled 2,878 admits.
5. Alon and Tienda (2007), Bowen and Bok (1998), Espenshade and Radford (2009), Kane (1998), and Long (2004b).
6. Bowen and Bok (1998) and Shulman and Bowen (2002).
7. The third group includes those who would have been eligible for the simulated race-based affirmative action (race-based admits).
8. The Technion administrative data had no information about the ethnic origin of Jewish applicants, so I excluded that university from the main simulations, but included it in the Arab-only simulations.
9. A complete set of results can be found in table A7.1 (for all majors) and table A7.2 (for the most-selective majors). Table A7.3 (for all majors) and table A7.4 (for the most-selective majors) report the results based on a simulation for Arabs only, including TECH.
10. Israel Central Bureau of Statistics (ICBS) (2011b).
11. Both are true stories, but the names have been changed.
12. Foreign-born admits also represent 15 percent of Jewish admits.
13. ICBS (2012a).
14. Alon (2015).
15. The economic edge of FSU immigrants may also result from this group's lower rate of transition into higher education and low graduation rate.
16. The spatial segregation of recent immigrants, who are mostly from the FSU, is less pronounced than that of both the Arab population and the Jewish immigrants of previous generations. Yet even though, as of 1995, new immigrants

have been overrepresented in socioeconomically strong localities, most of these immigrants do not reside in the affluent parts of these localities (ICBS 1995).
17. Ainsworth (2002), Brooks-Gunn et al. (1997), Crane (1991), Datcher (1982), Duncan (1994), Entwisle et al. (1997), Gamoran (1987), Hallinan (2001), Massey and Denton (1993), McLeod and Edwards (1995), Parcel and Dufur (2001), Pebley and Sastry (2004), Sampson et al. (1999), Sampson et al. (1997), South and Crowder (1999), and Wilson (1987, 1996).
18. The results for other categories in the socioeconomic index for localities are reported in the appendix.
19. ICBS (2006).
20. Alon (2004), Spilerman and Habib (1976), and Yiftachel (2000).
21. The data on these indicators were available only for TAU.
22. The parallel results for mother's status are reported in the appendix.
23. In addition, there is aid granted by private foundations.

CHAPTER 8: THE FEASIBILITY AND DIVERSITY DIVIDENDS OF AFFIRMATIVE ACTION POLICY IN THE UNITED STATES

1. The empirical analyses are based on the restricted-use Beginning Postsecondary Students Longitudinal Study (BPS), which is linked to the National Postsecondary Student Aid Study (NPSAS). I use the BPS cohort based on NPSAS: 96, with the first BPS follow-up in 1998 and the second in 2001.
2. *Barron's* gives each college a score that indicates its competitiveness and selectivity levels, as determined by the academic profile of the freshman class. The index ranges from 1 to 6, in decreasing order of selectivity (*Barron's* 1982, 1992, 2003).
3. Bowen and Bok (1998) and Alon and Tienda (2007).
4. Alon and Tienda (2007), Kane (1998), and Long (2004b).
5. I assess whether underrepresented minorities received an edge in admission in 1995–1996 relative to whites and Asians with similar academic achievements, and at what type of four-year institution. I fitted a model of logistic regression to the data to predict the chances of attending an institution from a certain category compared to the chances of attending less-competitive and noncompetitive institutions (categories 5 and 6). The model controls for the high school academic achievements that typically predict college admissions: test scores, high school GPA, number of AP courses, AP course GPA, and number of honors subjects (see table A8.4).
6. Bowen et al. (2005) and Espenshade and Radford (2009).
7. Hoxby and Avery (2012) and Kane (1998).
8. Another issue is that socioeconomic status is based on student self-reports.
9. Bowen et al. (2005) also report conducting separate simulations that use a mea-

sure for parental education levels. Espenshade and Radford (2009) use a response to a survey question: "Which one of the following categories best describes your family's social class during your senior year in high school?" Response categories include "lower," "working," "middle," "upper-middle," and "upper" class.

10. Ta-Nehisi Coates, "The Case for Reparations," *The Atlantic,* May 21, 2014; Todd Lewan and Dolores Barclay, "Torn from the Land: Black Americans' Farmland Taken Through Cheating, Intimidation, Even Murder," Associated Press, December 2, 2001.
11. Oliver and Shapiro (1995), 18.
12. Kahlenberg (2012), 18–19.
13. Federal Student Aid Information Center, "The Guide to Federal Student Aid: Funding Your Education," U.S. Department of Education Federal Student Aid Office, available at: https://studentaid.ed.gov/sites/default/files/funding-your-education.pdf (accessed January 20, 2015).
14. The information about the type of high school attended was available for the BPS:96 cohort but no, unfortunately, for more recent cohorts of the BPS data.
15. Hoxby and Avery (2012).
16. Bowen et al. (2005) and Espenshade and Radford (2009).
17. Bowen et al. (2009), 287.
18. The thresholds are 1,210 points for category 1 schools and 1,070 for category 2 schools. I focus on test scores because they are the academic criterion that selective institutions emphasize the most in admissions decisions (Alon and Tienda 2007). Moreover, using a composite measure of academic standing (based on test scores, high school GPA, and AP courses) yields very similar results. Thus, for parsimony and clarity, I decided to use test scores for setting the thresholds.
19. Profile 2014-5: Princeton University, available at: www.princeton.edu/pub/profile/PU-profile-2014-15.pdf, relevant data appears on page 6.
20. Kahlenberg (2012), 15.
21. Sander (1997).
22. Bowen et al. (2005) and Espenshade and Radford (2009).
23. Hoxby and Avery (2012) and Kane (1998).
24. For example, Bowen and his colleagues (2005) report that minority enrollments could fall from 13 to 7 percent. In Espenshade and Radford's (2009) simulations, the decline is from 16 to 13 percent.
25. That is, blacks are more likely than whites to be raised in families from the bottom of both the income and wealth ladders: in 2009, 65 percent of blacks were raised in families from the bottom quintile of the income distribution, and 57 percent in families from the bottom of the wealth distribution (Pew Economic Mobility Project 2012).

26. This was revealed by replicating the simulations (performing additional simulations) using different thresholds (see table A8.3 for full results).
27. Currently, under racial and ethnic affirmative action, the share of black students at these institutions is 7 percent. This figure would be cut in half if class-based policies based on socioeconomic standing were implemented. The number is slightly higher if class-based policies based on high school type were chosen instead (4.3 percent). Both class-based policy options—socioeconomic standing and high school poverty level—would reduce the share of Hispanics at elite schools by about one-quarter (from 8.7 percent under current race-conscious admissions to about 6.5 percent under the class-based models).
28. I simulated this scenario by capping the number of admits with multiple disadvantages so that their test scores, on average, did not fall below the average scores of the race-based admits. Under this cap, the level of racial and ethnic diversity at these schools dropped to less than 11 percent.
29. Most of the URM who gained entry as a result of this slight advantage had test scores that placed them at the margin of admissions under the race-neutral class-based regime.
30. Park, Denson, and Bowman (2013).
31. The economic standing of the class-based admits selected based on high school type is only slightly lower than that of the race-based admits (with EFCs of $6,960 and $7,790, respectively).
32. If the share of URM who received an edge in admission is greater than what is assumed by the simulations, then a shift from race to class in affirmative action has greater potential to augment the level of socioeconomic diversity at elite schools.
33. David Leonhardt, "Measuring Colleges' Success in Enrolling the Less Affluent," *New York Times,* September 9, 2014, A3.
34. Bowen et al. (2005).
35. Espenshade and Radford (2009).
36. Alon (2011a).
37. Leonhardt, "Measuring Colleges' Success in Enrolling the Less Affluent."
38. Harvard University, "Admissions Statistics: A Brief Profile of the Admitted Class of 2018," available at: https://college.harvard.edu/admissions/admissions-statistics (accessed September 22, 2014).
39. Hoxby and Avery (2012).

CHAPTER 9: THE ACADEMIC OUTCOMES AND MOBILITY DIVIDENDS OF AFFIRMATIVE ACTION POLICY IN ISRAEL

1. OECD, "OECD Income Distribution Database (IDD): Gini, Poverty, Income, Methods, and Income." Available at: http://www.oecd.org/social/income-distribution-database.htm (accessed June 18, 2013).

2. OECD (2014a).
3. Ibid.
4. To illustrate the economic consequences of this disparity, consider the following two groups of graduates from the Technion: graduates in civil engineering, whose selectivity index was 0.55, earned an average starting monthly salary of 8,200 NIS (about $2,300), while their peers in mechanical engineering, whose selectivity index was 0.61, earned more than 12,000 NIS (about $3,300). Data are for the years 2000 through 2003. Later in this section, I examine the effect of the program on economic payoffs more systematically.
5. Altonji, Blom, and Meghir (2012) and Melguizo and Wolniak (2012).
6. Admits to professional fields had at least one major classified as a professional field; applicants can be admitted to several majors.
7. Alon (2009).
8. See figure A6.1 for details about how his score was calculated.
9. The data included the average annual earnings of graduates and the number of months employed. To adjust for differences in labor supply, I divided the annual earnings by the number of months employed for graduates in each field of study.
10. To illustrate the meaning of a gap of 900 NIS, consider the following example: male graduates of economics departments earned a salary of 9,900 NIS per month upon labor market entry, while graduates in communications earned about 1,000 NIS less.
11. Forty-six percent of all ethnic minority applicants were admitted to the elite universities during the class-based regime. If a race-based regime had been implemented instead, this share would have risen to 50 percent.
12. The yield among the non-AA pool was 68 percent.
13. At the application stage to university, the discrepancies in field-of-study choices between prospective students just above and just below the affirmative action threshold are minor (Alon and Malamud 2014). This is to be expected given that applicants who applied for affirmative action did not know the formula used to construct disadvantage-based eligibility and were never told whether they met the threshold or not.
14. These results were confirmed in a more refined analysis that I conducted with Ofer Malamud of the University of Chicago in which we exploited a similar strategy, known as a regression discontinuity (RD) design (Alon and Malamud 2014).
15. Bowen and Bok (1998), for example, find that grades correlate strongly and positively with future levels of compensation even among students attending a group of elite schools. The premium associated with doing well academically is unaffected by the field of study, test scores, and background or employment characteristics.
16. Chia and Miller (2008), Jones and Jackson (1990), and Thomas (2000).

17. Graglia (1993), Sander and Taylor (2012), Sowell (2003), Thernstrom and Thernstrom (1997).
18. Alon and Tienda (2005).
19. Thernstrom and Thernstrom (1997), 406.
20. Crawford (2000), Lerner and Nagai (2001), Pell (2003), and Thernstrom and Thernstrom (1999).
21. Alon and Tienda (2005); Bowen, Chingos, and McPherson (2009); Cortes (2010); Hoekstra (2009); Massey and Mooney (2007); Melguizo (2008); and Rothstein and Yoon (2008).
22. Sander and Taylor (2012).
23. Sterling and Smith (2011), xii.
24. For the full results, see table A9.1. I fitted several OLS and logit regression models predicting various academic outcomes for students at the Israeli universities who fell just above and just below the affirmative action threshold of eligibility. The models controlled for students' standardized academic score and their major's fixed effects.
25. Alon and Malamud (2014).
26. Alon and Tienda (2005), Bowen et al. (2009), Cortes (2010), Hoekstra (2009), Massey and Mooney (2007), Melguizo (2008), and Rothstein and Yoon (2008).

CHAPTER 10: THE ACADEMIC OUTCOMES AND MOBILITY DIVIDENDS OF AFFIRMATIVE ACTION POLICY IN THE UNITED STATES

1. Fisher v. University of Texas 758 F. 3d 633 (2014), 18.
2. Haynes (2013).
3. Corak (2006).
4. OECD (2014b).
5. Pew Economic Mobility Project (2012).
6. OECD (2014b).
7. Rana Foroohar, "What Ever Happened to Upward Mobility?" *Time,* November 14, 2011.
8. Sander and Taylor (2012), Sowell (2003), and Thernstrom and Thernstrom (1997).
9. Fisher v. University of Texas 758 F. 3d 633 (2014), 18.
10. I did not include those eligible under the multidimensional prototype.
11. The underprivileged students attending category 1 institutions were left as is and were not reassigned in the simulations.
12. An endowment of $35,000 per student (in 1995 dollars) compared to less than $6,000 per student, on average.
13. Astin (1984), Davis (1991), Mallette and Cabrera (1991), Nettles (1991), Nora (1987), Pascarella and Terenzini (1980), Terenzini and Pascarella (1977), and Tinto (1993).

14. This survey is part of the data set used in the analyses in this book; see discussion in chapter 3.
15. Students had only minor differences between them based on their eligibility for class-based affirmative action, be it economic, socioeconomic, or high school–based.
16. The responses were scored on a scale of 1 to 3, then added and multiplied by 100.
17. Altonji, Blom, and Meghir (2012); Arcidiacono (2004); and Roksa and Levey (2010).
18. Goyette and Mullen (2006) and Mullen (2010).
19. A large share (about 40 percent) of college graduates with degrees in the social sciences, humanities, or STEM fields in 1993 began studying in a graduate or professional school within four years of graduation (Goyette and Mullen 2006).
20. Mullen (2010).
21. Bowen and Bok (1998).
22. Alon and Tienda (2005), Bowen et al. (2009), Cortes (2010), Hoekstra (2009), Massey and Mooney (2007), Melguizo (2008), and Rothstein and Yoon (2008); see also American Social Science Researchers, brief in support of respondents in Fisher v. University of Texas (2013), Amici Curiae 11(345) (2012).
23. American Social Science Researchers, brief in support of respondents in Fisher v. University of Texas (2013), Amici Curiae 11(345) (2012).
24. Haynes (2013).

CHAPTER 11: RACE AND CLASS IN AFFIRMATIVE ACTION POLICY

1. Tocqueville (1835).
2. Moreover, these ideals have been internally reinforced as these colleges and universities have become production centers of knowledge about the issues of diversity and inequality.
3. For example, such a policy was proposed by Kahlenberg (2012).
4. Sander (1997).
5. Ibid., 473.
6. Richard Sander, personal correspondence, May 31, 2010.
7. Sander (1997), 476.
8. Ibid.
9. Almeida-Filho (2012), Guimaraes (2010), and Peria and Bailey (2014). See also Jon Jeter, "Affirmative Action Debate Forces Brazil to Take Look in the Mirror," *Washington Post,* June 16, 2003, A1; and Edward E. Telles, "WideAngle: Discrimination and Affirmative Action in Brazil," PBS/WNET, 2009, available at:

http://www-tc.pbs.org/wnet/wideangle/files/2009/04/discrimination-and-affirmative-action-in-brazil.pdf (accessed August 4, 2011).
10. Peria and Bailey (2014), 16.
11. Alon and Tienda (2005), Bowen et al. (2009), Cortes (2010), Hoekstra (2009), Massey and Mooney (2007), Melguizo (2008), and Rothstein and Yoon (2008).
12. For example, Sander and Taylor (2012), as discussed in chapter 9, justify their advocacy for class-based preferences on the need to skirt the supposed mismatch problem associated with race-conscious admissions.
13. Milem et al. (2005) and Park et al. (2013).
14. Hoover (2013).
15. Jencks (1988), 533.
16. Brown and Patten (2014), table 37.
17. U.S. Bureau of Labor Statistics (2013).
18. Brown and Patten (2014), table 36.
19. Urban Institute. 2013. "Less than Equal: Racial Disparities in Wealth Accumulation." Available at: http://www.urban.org/sites/default/files/alfresco/publication-pdfs/412802-Less-Than-Equal-Racial-Disparities-in-Wealth-Accumulation.PDF (accessed September 8, 2014).
20. Forty percent of white twenty-five- to twenty-nine-year-olds attained a bachelor's degree or higher, while only 20 percent of blacks and 16 percent of Hispanics did (NCES 2014).
21. Among college students in 2011, 54 percent of whites were enrolled full-time at four-year institutions, while only 42 percent of Hispanic students and 50 percent of black students were. Hispanic and black students were overrepresented at two-year schools: 27 and 23 percent of Hispanic and black students, respectively, were enrolled in such institutions, which do not grant a bachelor's degree (Davis and Bauman 2013, table 2).
22. These are the author's calculations using the Education Longitudinal Study of 2004 (ELS:2004) data set. The data are for high school graduates from the 2004 cohort. The estimates are weighted.
23. Peria and Bailey (2014).
24. Park et al. (2013).
25. The State University of Rio de Janeiro and the State University of North Fluminense.
26. The two state laws passed in the years before the Law of Social Quotas was enacted instructed Rio de Janeiro's state universities to allocate half of their slots to students from public schools and 40 percent to self-declared blacks (*negros*) and browns (*pardos*) (Peria and Bailey 2014).
27. Peria and Bailey (2014, 9) argue that, "notably, the public school quota was much less often contested in these cases, suggesting that class was apparently viewed as less vulnerable to criticism than race."

28. "Time to Scrap Affirmative Action," *The Economist*, April 27, 2013, available at: http://www.economist.com/news/leaders/21576662-governments-should-be-colour-blind-time-scrap-affirmative-action (accessed August 29, 2014).
29. Bowen and Bok (1998); Espenshade, Chung, and Walling (2004); and Golden (2006).
30. Golden (2006).
31. Espenshade and Chung (2005).
32. Josh Freedman, "The Farce of Meritocracy: Why Legacy Admissions Might Actually Be a Good Thing," *Forbes,* November 14, 2013, available at: http://www.forbes.com/sites/joshfreedman/2013/11/14/the-farce-of-meritocracy-in-elite-higher-education-why-legacy-admissions-might-be-a-good-thing/ (accessed August 15, 2015); Ivan Maisel, "What It Takes," *Stanford Magazine* (November–December 2013), available at: http://alumni.stanford.edu/get/page/magazine/article/?article_id=66225 (accessed August 15, 2015).
33. Maisel, "What It Takes," available at: https://alumni.stanford.edu/get/page/magazine/article/?article_id=66225 (accessed August 15, 2015).
34. Annie Costner, actor Kevin Costner's daughter, attended Brown University, as did Jessica Capshaw, filmmaker Steven Spielberg's stepdaughter, as well as other children of celebrities. The list includes two Beatles' offspring, Francesca Gregorini, Ringo Starr's stepdaughter, and Dhani Harrison, son of George Harrison; Willa Mamet, daughter of playwright and scriptwriter David Mamet; Allegra Beck, daughter of Donatella Versace; Vanessa Vadim, daughter of actress Jane Fonda; Miles Guthrie, son of actors Susan Sarandon and Tim Robbins; Rhonda Ross, daughter of singer Diana Ross; and Matthew Reeve, son of the late *Superman* actor Christopher Reeve.
35. Golden (2006).
36. Taken together, blacks and Hispanics represent fewer than 4 percent of players in men's golf and 3 percent of players in men's lacrosse (ibid.).
37. According to Golden (2006), the University of Notre Dame, a Catholic research university in Indiana, admits 70 percent of faculty and staff children who apply and half of legacy applicants, but only 19 percent of all other applicants. The median SAT score of children of staff and faculty is 90 points below the median of legacies and 100 points below the median of all admitted students.
38. The full results are reported in table A8.2.
39. The share of students eligible for Pell Grants under socioeconomic affirmative action is 28 percent, but because this number was determined based on attendance at less-expensive schools, the real share of grant aid recipients would probably be much higher.
40. For example, most of the poor students who meet the academic standards of elite colleges are white, have college-educated parents, and did not attend a high-poverty high school.

REFERENCES

Agrawal, Purushottam. 2006. "All Things Being Equal: Multiple Index Related Affirmative Action (MIRAA)—A More Effective System for Equal Opportunity." *Communalism Combat* 12(116, June).

Ainsworth, James W. 2002. "Why Does It Take a Village? The Mediation of Neighborhood Effects on Educational Achievement." *Social Forces* 81(1): 117–52.

Almeida-Filho, Naomar. 2012. "Breaking a Vicious Cycle of Social Exclusion." *ReVista: Harvard Review of Latin America* (Fall). Available at: http://revista.drclas.harvard.edu/book/breaking-vicious-cycle-social-exclusion (accessed September 20, 2014).

Alon, Sigal. 2004. "The Gender Stratification of Employment Hardship: Queuing, Opportunity Structure, and Economic Cycles." *Research in Social Stratification and Mobility* 20: 115–44.

———. 2009. "The Evolution of Class Inequality in Higher Education: Competition, Exclusion, and Adaptation." *American Sociological Review* 74(5): 731–55.

———. 2010. "Racial Differences in Test Preparation Strategies." *Social Forces* 89(2): 463–74.

———. 2011a. "Who Benefits Most from Financial Aid? The Heterogeneous Effect of Need-Based Grants on Students' College Persistence." *Social Science Quarterly* 92(3): 807–29.

———. 2011b. "The Diversity Dividends of a Need-Blind and Color-Blind Affirmative Action Policy." *Social Science Research* 40(6): 1494–1505.

———. 2015. "Field of Study Inequality Throughout the College Pipeline and the Earnings Gap Between Ethnic and Immigrant Groups in Israel." *Social Science Research* 52: 465–78.

———. N.d. "The Pipeline–to–Labor Market Inequality: Field of Study of Arabs from Application to Israeli Flagship Universities to Graduation." Unpublished paper. Tel Aviv University, Jerusalem.

Alon, Sigal, and Ofer Malamud. 2014. "The Impact of Israel's Class-Based Affirmative Action Policy on Admission and Academic Outcomes." *Economics of Education Review* 40: 123–39.

Alon, Sigal, and Marta Tienda. 2005. "Assessing the 'Mismatch' Hypothesis: Differences in College Graduation Rates by Institutional Selectivity." *Sociology of Education* 78(4): 294–315.

———. 2007. "Diversity, Opportunity, and the Shifting Meritocracy in Higher Education." *American Sociological Review* 72(4): 487–511.

Altonji, Joseph G., Erica Blom, and Costas Meghir. 2012. "Heterogeneity in Human Capital Investments: High School Curriculum, College Major, and Careers." *Annual Review of Economics* 4: 185–223.

Alvaredo, Facundo, Anthony B. Atkinson, Thomas Piketty, and Emmanuel Saez. "Top 0.1 Percent Incomes, U.S., 1910–2013." *The World Incomes Database*. Available at: http://topincomes.g-mond.parisschoolofeconomics.eu (accessed June 18, 2015).

Arcidiacono, Peter. 2004. "Ability Sorting and the Returns to College Major." *Journal of Econometrics* 121(1–2): 343–75.

Astin, Alexander W. 1984. "Student Involvement: A Developmental Theory for Higher Education." *Journal of College Student Personnel* 25(4): 297–308.

Bagde, Surendrakumar, Dennis Epple, and Lowell J. Taylor. 2011. "Dismantling the Legacy of Caste: Affirmative Action in Indian Higher Education." Unpublished paper. India Ministry of Finance and Carnegie Mellon University (September). Available at: http://www.econ.wisc.edu/workshop/AA111011-1.pdf (accessed August 15, 2015).

Bailey, Martha J., and Susan M. Dynarski. 2011. "Gains and Gaps: Changing Inequality in U.S. College Entry and Completion." Working Paper 17633. Cambridge, Mass.: National Bureau of Economic Research.

Ball, Howard. 2000. *The Bakke Case: Race, Education, and Affirmative Action*. Lawrence: University Press of Kansas.

Barron's Educational Series. 1982. *Profiles of American Colleges*. Hauppauge, N.Y.: Barron's Educational Series Inc.

———. 1992. *Profiles of American Colleges*. Hauppauge, N.Y.: Barron's Educational Series Inc.

———. 2003. *Profiles of American Colleges*. Hauppauge, N.Y.: Barron's Educational Series Inc.

Baum, Sandy, Charles Kurose, and Michael S. McPherson. 2013. "An Overview of American Higher Education." *Postsecondary Education in the United States* 23(1): 17–39.

Ben Naim, Galit, and Alexey Belinsky. 2012. "Israel's Wage Divergence: An Analysis of Wage Mobility in the Last Decade." *Israeli Tax Quarterly* (Hebrew) 131: 7–40.

Bertrand, Marianne, Rema Hanna, and Sendhil Mullainathan. 2010. "Affirmative

Action in Education: Evidence from Engineering College Admissions." *India Journal of Public Economics* 94(1–2): 16–29.
Blau, Peter M. 1977. *Inequality and Heterogeneity: A Primitive Theory of Social Structure.* New York: Free Press.
Bowen, William G., and Derek Bok. 1998. *The Shape of the River: Long-Term Consequences of Considering Race in College and University Admissions.* Princeton, N.J.: Princeton University Press.
Bowen, William G., Matthew M. Chingos, and Michael S. McPherson. 2009. *Crossing the Finish Line: Completing College at America's Public Universities.* Princeton, N.J.: Princeton University Press.
Bowen, William G., Martin A. Kurzweil, and Eugene M. Tobin. 2005. *Equity and Excellence in American Higher Education.* Charlottesville: University of Virginia Press.
Brand, Jennie E., and Charles N. Halaby. 2006. "Regression and Matching Estimates of the Effects of Elite College Attendance on Educational and Career Achievement." *Social Science Research* 35(3): 749–70.
Briggs, Derek C. 2001. "The Effect of Admissions Test Preparation: Evidence from NELS: 88." *Chance* 14(1): 10–18.
———. 2009. "Preparation for College Admission Exams." Discussion Paper. Arlington, Va.: National Association for College Admission Counseling (NACAC). Available at: http://www.nacacnet.org/research/PublicationsResources/Marketplace/Documents/TestPrepDiscussionPaper.pdf (accessed September 21, 2014).
Brooks-Gunn, Jeanne, Greg J. Duncan, Tama Leventhal, and Lawrence J. Aber. 1997. "Lessons Learned and Future Directions for Research on the Neighborhoods in Which Children Live." *Neighborhood Poverty: Context and Consequences for Children* 1: 279–97.
Brown, Anna, and Eileen Patten. 2014. "Statistical Portrait of Hispanics in the United States" Pew Research Center: Hispanic Trends, April 29. Available at: http://www.pewhispanic.org/2014/04/29/statistical-portrait-of-hispanics-in-the-united-states-2012/ (accessed August 24, 2014).
Brown, Susan K., and Charles Hirschman. 2006. "The End of Affirmative Action in Washington State and Its Impact on the Transition from High School to College." *Sociology of Education* 79(2): 106–30.
Buchmann, Claudia, Vincent J. Roscigno, and Dennis J. Condron. 2006. "The Myth of Meritocracy? SAT Preparation, College Enrollment, Class, and Race in the United States." Paper presented to the annual meeting of the American Sociological Association. Montreal (August).
Buera, Francisco J., and Joseph P. Kaboski. 2012. "Scale and the Origins of Structural Change." *Journal of Economic Theory* 147(2): 684–712.
Card, David, and Alan Krueger. 2005. "Would the Elimination of Affirmative Action Affect Highly Qualified Minority Applicants? Evidence from California and Texas." *Industrial and Labor Relations Review* 58(3): 416–32.

Carnahan, Kristin, and Chiara Coletti. 2003. "SAT Verbal and Math Scores Up Significantly as a Record-Breaking Number of Students Take the Test: Average Math Score at Highest Level in More Than 35 Years." Report N0218. Washington, D.C.: College Board (August 26). Available at: http://www.collegeboard.com/prod_downloads/about/news_info/cbsenior/yr2003/2003-cbs.pdf (accessed August 11, 2014).

Carnevale, Anthony P., and Stephen J. Rose. 2004. "Socioeconomic Status, Race/Ethnicity, and Selective College Admissions." In *America's Untapped Resources" Low-Income Students in Higher Education,* edited by Richard D. Kahlenberg. New York: Century Foundation Press.

Chia, Grace, and Paul W. Miller. 2008. "Tertiary Performance, Field of Study, and Graduate Starting Salaries." *Australian Economic Review* 41(1): 15–31.

Chin, Gabriel J. 1998. "Bakke to the Wall: The Crisis of Bakkean Diversity." In *Affirmative Action and the Constitution,* edited by Gabriel Chin. Florence, KY: Taylor & Francis.

Clark, Burton R. 1983. *The Higher Education System: Academic Organization in Cross-National Perspective.* Berkeley: University of California Press.

Clarke, Marguerite, and Arnold Shore. 2001. *The Roles of Testing and Diversity in College Admissions.* Boston: National Board on Educational Testing and Public Policy, Lynch College.

Clayton, Susan D., and Sandra S. Tangri. 1989. "The Justice of Affirmative Action." In *Affirmative Action in Perspective,* edited by Fletcher A. Blanchard and Faye Crosby. New York: Springer-Verlag.

Cohen, Yinon, and Yitchak Haberfeld. 1998. "Second-Generation Jewish Immigrants in Israel: Have the Ethnic Gaps in Schooling and Earnings Declined?" *Ethnic and Racial Studies* 21(3): 507–28.

Cohen, Yinon, Yitchak Haberfeld, and Tali Kristal. 2007. "Ethnicity and Mixed Ethnicity: Educational Gaps Among Israeli-Born Jews." *Ethnic and Racial Studies* 30(5): 896–917.

College Board Advocacy and Policy Center. 2009a. *Trends in Higher Education: Trends in College Pricing.* New York: College Board.

———. 2009b. *Trends in Higher Education: Trends in Student Aid.* New York: College Board.

———. 2012a. *Trends in Higher Education: Trends in College Pricing.* New York: College Board.

———. 2012b. *Trends in Higher Education: Trends in Student Aid.* New York: College Board.

———. 2013. *Trends in Higher Education: Trends in Student Aid.* New York: College Board.

Corak, Miles. 2006. "Do Poor Children Become Poor Adults? Lessons from a Cross-Country Comparison of Generational Earnings Mobility." In *Research on Eco-*

nomic Inequality, vol. 13, *Dynamics of Inequality and Poverty,* edited by John Creedy and Guyonne Kalb. Bingley, U.K.: Emerald Group Publishing.

Cortes, Kalena E. 2010. "Do Bans on Affirmative Action Hurt Minority Students? Evidence from the Texas Top 10% Plan." *Economics of Education Review* 29(6): 1110–24.

Crane, Jonathan. 1991. "The Epidemic Theory of Ghettos and Neighborhood Effects on Dropping Out and Teenage Childbearing." *American Journal of Sociology* 96(5): 1226–59.

Crawford, Curtis. 2000. "Weighing the Benefits and Costs of Racial Preference in College Admissions." *Society* 37(4): 71–80.

Dahan, Momi, Natalia Mironichev, Eyal Dvir, and Shmuel Shye. 2002. "Have the Educational Gaps Narrowed?" *Economic Quarterly* (Hebrew) 49(1): 159–88.

Dale, Stacy, and Alan B. Krueger. 2014. "Estimating the Return to College Selectivity of the Career Using Administrative Earning Data." *Journal of Human Resources* 49(2): 323–58.

Datcher, Linda. 1982. "Effects of Community and Family Background on Achievement." *Review of Economics and Statistics* 64(1): 32–41.

Davies, Scott, and Neil Guppy. 1997. "Fields of Study, College Selectivity, and Student Inequalities in Higher Education." *Social Forces* 75(4): 1417–38.

Davis, Jessica, and Kurt Bauman. 2013. "School Enrollment in the United States 2011: Population Characteristics, Table 2: Enrollment in Undergraduate and Graduate College by Selected Characteristics: 2011." P20-571. Washington: U.S. Bureau of the Census (September). Available at: http://www.census.gov/prod/2013pubs/p20-571.pdf (accessed September 23, 2014).

Davis, Robert B. 1991. "Social Support Networks and Undergraduate Students' Academic Success–Related Outcomes: A Comparison of Black Students on Black and White Campuses," In *College in Black and White: African American Students in Predominantly White and in Historically Black Public Universities,* edited by Walter R. Allen, Edgar G. Epps, and Nesha Z. Haniff. Albany: State University of New York Press.

DeSilver, Drew. 2013. "Black Unemployment Rate Is Consistently Twice That of Whites." Pew Research Center, August 21. Available at: http://www.pewresearch.org/fact-tank/2013/08/21/through-good-times-and-bad-black-unemployment-is-consistently-double-that-of-whites/ (accessed September 12, 2014).

Drake, Bruce. 2014. "Public Strongly Backs Affirmative Action Programs on Campus." Pew Research Center, April 22. Available at: http://www.pewresearch.org/fact-tank/2014/04/22/public-strongly-backs-affirmative-action-programs-on-campus/ (accessed September 9, 2014).

Du Bois, W. E. B. 1903. *The Souls of Black Folk.* Chicago: A. C. McClurg & Co.

Duffy, Elizabeth A., and Idana Goldberg. 1998. *Crafting a Class: College Admissions and Financial Aid, 1955–1994.* Princeton, N.J.: Princeton University Press.

Duncan, Greg J. 1994. "Families and Neighbors as Sources of Disadvantage in the Schooling Decisions of White and Black Adolescents." *American Journal of Education* 103(1): 20–53.

Dworkin, Ronald. 1985. *A Matter of Principle*. New York: Oxford University Press.

Edwards, Kelcey, and Ellen Sawtell. 2013. "Landscape of Higher Education: Human Capital." Washington, D.C.: College Board (February 15). Available at: http://research.collegeboard.org/sites/default/files/publications/2013/3/presentation-2013-1-landscape-of-higher-education.pdf (accessed August 25, 2014).

Ehrenberg, Ronald G. 2005. "Reducing Inequality in Higher Education: Where Do We Go from Here?" Working Paper 79. Ithaca, N.Y.: Cornell University, Cornell Higher Education Research Institute (September). Available at: http://digitalcommons.ilr.cornell.edu/workingpapers/61/ (accessed August 13, 2014).

Endeweld, Miri, Netanela Barkali, Daniel Gottlieb, and Alexander Fruman. 2012. "Annual Report 2011: Poverty and Social Gaps." Jerusalem: National Insurance Institute, Research and Planning Administration. Available at: http://www.btl.gov.il/English%20Homepage/Publications/Poverty_Report/Documents/Poverty%20Report_2011.pdf (accessed September 20, 2014).

Entwisle, Doris R., Karl L. Alexander, and Linda S. Olson. 1997. *Children, Schools, and Inequality*. Boulder, Colo.: Westview Press.

Espenshade, Thomas J., and Chang Y. Chung. 2005. "The Opportunity Cost of Admission Preferences at Elite Universities." *Social Science Quarterly* 86(2, June): 293–305.

Espenshade, Thomas J., Chang Y. Chung, and Joan L. Walling. 2004. "Admission Preferences for Minority Students, Athletes, and Legacies at Elite Universities." *Social Science Quarterly* 85(5): 1422–46.

Espenshade, Thomas J., and Alexandria W. Radford. 2009. *No Longer Separate, Not Yet Equal: Race and Class in Elite College Admission and Campus Life*. Princeton, N.J.: Princeton University Press.

Fischer, Claude S., and Michael Hout. 2006. *Century of Difference: How America Changed in the Last One Hundred Years*. New York: Russell Sage Foundation.

Fischer, Claude S., Michael Hout, Martín S. Jankowski, Samuel R. Lucas, Ann Swidler, and Kim Voss. 1996. *Inequality by Design: Cracking the Bell Curve Myth*. Princeton, N.J.: Princeton University Press.

Francis, Andrew M., and Maria Tannuri-Pianto. 2012. "Using Brazil's Racial Continuum to Examine the Short-Term Effects of Affirmative Action in Higher Education." *Journal of Human Resources* 47(3): 754–84.

Friedlander, Dov, Barbra S. Okun, Zvi Eisenbach, and Lilach L. Elmakias. 2002. "Immigration, Social Change, and Assimilation: Educational Attainment Among Birth Cohorts of Jewish Ethnic Groups in Israel, 1925–29 to 1965–69." *Population Studies* 56(2): 135–50.

Gamoran, Adam. 1987. "The Stratification of High School Learning Opportunities." *Sociology of Education* 60(3): 135–55.

Garces, Liliana M. 2013. "Understanding the Impact of Affirmative Action Bans in Different Graduate Fields of Study." *American Educational Research Journal* 50(2): 251–84.

Golden, Daniel. 2006. *The Price of Admission: How America's Ruling Class Buys Its Way into Elite Colleges—and Who Gets Left Outside the Gates.* New York: Crown Publishers.

Goyette, Kimberly A., and Ann L. Mullen. 2006. "Who Studies the Arts and Sciences? Social Background and the Choice and Consequences of Undergraduate Field of Study." *Journal of Higher Education* 77(3): 497–538.

Graglia, Lino A. 1993. "Racial Preferences in Admission to Institutions of Higher Education." In *The Imperiled Academy,* edited by Howard Dickman. New Brunswick, N.J.: Transaction Publishers.

Grodsky, Eric, and Michal Kurlaender. 2010. "The Demography of Higher Education in the Wake of Affirmative Action," In *Equal Opportunity in Higher Education: The Past and Future of California's Proposition 209,* edited by Eric Grodsky and Michal Kurlaender. Cambridge, Mass.: Harvard Education Press.

Guimaraes, Antonio S. A. 2010. "Entrance into Prestigious Universities and the Performance of Discriminated Groups on the 'Vestibular': Black Students in the University of Sao Paulo, 2001–2007." In *Growing Gaps: Educational Inequality Around the World,* edited by Paul Attewell and Katherine S. Newman. New York: Oxford University Press.

Haberfeld, Yitchak, and Yinon Cohen. 1998. "Earnings of Native-Born Jewish and Arab Men in Israel, 1987–1993." In *Research in Social Stratification and Mobility,* vol. 16, edited by Kevin T. Leicht. London: JAI Press.

———. 2007. "Gender, Ethnic, and National Earnings Gaps in Israel: The Role of Rising Inequality." *Social Science Research* 36(2): 654–72.

Hagstrom, Warren O. 1971. "Inputs, Outputs, and the Prestige of University Science Departments." *Sociology of Education* 44(4): 375–97.

Hallinan, Maureen T. 2001. "Sociological Perspectives on Black-White Inequalities in American Schooling." *Sociology of Education* (extra issue): 50–70.

Hawkins, David A., and Melissa Clinedist. 2006. *State of College Admission 2006.* Alexandria, Va.: National Association for College Admission Counseling (NACAC). Available at: http://www.nacacnet.org/research/research-data/Documents/06StateofAdmission.pdf (accessed August 15, 2015).

Haynes, Berneta. 2013. "Views: Affirmative Action Helped Me." *Inside Higher Ed,* March 12. Available at: https://www.insidehighered.com/views/2013/03/12/affirmative-action-helped-me-and-benefits-society-essay (accessed September 20, 2014).

Heller, Donald E. 2002. "Is Merit-Based Student Aid Really Trumping Need-Based Aid? Another View." *Change* 34(4): 6–7.

Hinrichs, Peter. 2012. "The Effects of Affirmative Action Bans on College Enrollment, Educational Attainment, and the Demographic Composition of Universities." *Review of Economics and Statistics* 94(3): 712–22.

Hoekstra, Mark. 2009. "The Effect of Attending the Flagship State University on Earnings: A Discontinuity-Based Approach." *Review of Economics and Statistics* 91(4): 717–24.

Holzer, Harry J., and David Neumark. 2006. "Affirmative Action: What Do We Know?" *Journal of Policy Analysis and Management* 25(2): 463–90.

Hoover, Eric. 2013. "The Digital Campus 2013: Creating Software to Enhance Admissions Diversity." *Chronicle of Higher Education,* April 29. Available at: http://chronicle.com/article/Software-to-EnhanceDiversity/138789/?cid=at&utm_source=at&utm_medium=en (accessed July 23, 2014).

Hout, Michael. 2005. "Berkeley's Comprehensive Review Method for Making Freshman Admissions Decisions: An Assessment." Berkeley: University of California (May). Available at: http://academic-senate.berkeley.edu/sites/default/files/committees/aepe/hout_report_0.pdf (accessed August 15, 2015).

Hoxby, Caroline M., and Christopher Avery. 2012. "The Missing 'One-Offs': The Hidden Supply of High-Achieving, Low-Income Students." Working Paper 18586. Cambridge, Mass.: National Bureau of Economic Research.

Israel Central Bureau of Statistics (ICBS). 1995. "Table C1: Population in Jewish Localities, Mixed Localities, and Statistical Areas, by Continent of Origin, Period of Immigration, and Sex." In "Demographic Characteristics of the Population in Localities and Statistical Areas: Census of Population and Housing Publication." Jerusalem: Central Bureau of Statistics.

———. 2006. "Statistical Abstract of Israel 2006, No. 57: Census of Population and Housing Publication." Jerusalem: Central Bureau of Statistics.

———. 2009. "Statistical Abstract of Israel 2009, No. 60: Census of Population and Housing Publication." Jerusalem: Central Bureau of Statistics.

———. 2010. "Statistical Abstract of Israel 2010, No. 61: Census of Population and Housing Publication." Jerusalem: Central Bureau of Statistics.

———. 2011a. "Statistical Abstract of Israel 2011, No. 62: Census of Population and Housing Publication." Jerusalem: Central Bureau of Statistics.

———. 2011b. "Localities File" (in Hebrew). Available at: http://www.cbs.gov.il/ishuvim/ishuv2011/bycode.xls (accessed September 20, 2014).

———. 2012a. "Table 2.24: Jews, by Country of Origin and Age." Central Bureau of Statistics. Available at: http://www.cbs.gov.il/shnaton63/download/st02_24x.xls (accessed September 20, 2014).

———. 2012b. "Table 2.6: Population, by District, Sub-District and Religion." Central Bureau of Statistics. Available at: http://www.cbs.gov.il/shnaton63/download/st02_06x.xls (accessed September 20, 2014).

———. 2012c. "Characteristics of Studies and Integration into the Labour Market among First-Degree Recipients from Institutions of Higher Education in Israel, 1999–2008." Central Bureau of Statistics. Jerusalem, Israel. Publication No. 1471.

———. 2013a. "Statistical Abstract of Israel 2013, No. 64: Census of Population and Housing Publication." Jerusalem: Central Bureau of Statistics.

———. 2013b. "Characterization and Classification of Geographical Units by the Socio-Economic Level of the Population 2008." Publication No. 1530. Jerusalem: Central Bureau of Statistics (June 23). Available at: http://www.cbs.gov.il/webpub/pub/text_page_eng.html?publ=100&CYear=2008&CMonth=1 (accessed September 20, 2014).

———. 2014. "The Higher Education System in Israel." Central Bureau of Statistics. Available at: http://che.org.il/wp-content/uploads/2012/05/HIGHER-EDUCATION-BOOKLET.pdf (accessed September 15, 2015).

Jaynes, Gerald D., and Robin M. Williams Jr., eds. 1989. "A Common Destiny: Blacks and American Society." Washington, D.C.: National Academies Press.

Jencks, Christopher. 1988. "Whom Must We Treat Equally for Educational Opportunity to Be Equal?" *Ethics* 98(3): 518–33.

Jones, Ethel B., and John D. Jackson. 1990. "College Grades and Labor Market Rewards." *Journal of Human Resources* 25(2): 253–66.

Kahlenberg, Richard D. 1996. *The Remedy: Class, Race, and Affirmative Action.* New York: Basic Books.

———. 2012. *A Better Affirmative Action: State Universities That Created Alternatives to Racial Preferences.* New York: The Century Foundation Press. Available at: https://tcf.org/assets/downloads/tcf-abaa.pdf (accessed September 23, 2014).

Kane, Thomas J. 1998. "Misconceptions in the Debate over Affirmative Action in College Admissions." In *Chilling Admissions: The Affirmative Action Crisis and the Search for Alternatives,* ed. Gary Orefield and Edward Miller. Boston: Harvard Education Press.

Karabel, Jerome. 2005. *The Chosen: The Hidden History of Admission and Exclusion at Harvard, Yale, and Princeton.* Boston: Houghton Mifflin Harcourt.

Kaufman, Burton I. 2006. "Bakke, Allen." In *Presidential Profiles: The Carter Years.* New York: Facts on File.

Kellough, Edward J. 2006. *Understanding Affirmative Action: Politics, Discrimination, and the Search for Justice.* Washington, D.C.: Georgetown University Press.

Kendrick, S. A. 1967. "The Coming Segregation of Our Selective Colleges." *College Board Review* 66(Winter): 6–13.

Koffman, Dawn, and Marta Tienda. 2008. "Missing in Application: The Texas Top 10 Percent Law and Campus Socioeconomic Diversity." Texas Higher Education Opportunity Project Working Paper. Princeton, N.J.: Princeton University (March). Available at: http://theop.princeton.edu/reports/wp/ApplicantSocialClass.pdf (accessed December 22, 2010).

Lee, Marlene A., and Mark Mather. 2008. "U.S. Labor Force Trends." *Population Bulletin* (Population Reference Bureau) 63(2, June). Available at: http://www.prb.org/pdf08/63.2uslabor.pdf (accessed August 14, 2014).

Lemann, Nicholas. 1999. *The Big Test: The Secret History of the American Meritocracy.* New York: Farrar, Straus and Giroux.

Lerner, Robert, and Althea K. Nagai. 2001. *Racial and Ethnic Preferences and Consequences at the University of Maryland School of Medicine.* Washington, D.C.: Center for Equal Opportunity.

Lewin-Epstein, Noah, and Moshe Semyonov. 1986. "Ethnic Group Mobility in the Israeli Labor Market." *American Sociological Review* 51(3): 342–52.

———. 1992. "Local Labor Markets, Ethnic Segregation, and Income Inequality." *Social Forces* 70(4): 1101–19.

———. 1993. *The Arab Minority in Israel's Economy: Patterns of Ethnic Inequality.* Boulder, Colo.: Westview Press.

Long, Mark C. 2004a. "Race and College Admissions: An Alternative to Affirmative Action?" *Review of Economics and Statistics* 86(4): 1020–33.

———. 2004b. "College Applications and the Effect of Affirmative Action." *Journal of Econometrics* 121(1–2): 319–42.

Long, Mark C., Victor Saenz, and Marta Tienda. 2010. "Policy Transparency and College Enrollment: Did the Texas Top Ten Percent Law Broaden Access to the Public Flagships?" *Annals of the American Academy of Political and Social Science* 627(1): 82–105.

Lustick, Ian S. 1980. *Arabs in the Jewish State: A Study in the Control of a National Minority.* Austin: University of Texas Press.

Malamud, Deborah C. 1997. "Assessing Class-Based Affirmative Action." *Journal of Legal Education* 47(4): 452.

Mallette, Bruce I., and Alberto F. Cabrera. 1991. "Determinants of Withdrawal Behavior: An Exploratory Study." *Research in Higher Education* 32(2): 179–94.

Mare, Robert D. 2012. "Holistic Review in Freshman Admissions at the University of California–Los Angeles." Report prepared for UCLA Committee on Undergraduate Admissions and Relations with Schools. Available at: http://www.senate.ucla.edu/committees/cuars/documents/uclareportonholisticreviewinfreshmanadmissions.pdf (accessed August 15, 2015).

Massey, Douglas S. 2007. *Categorically Unequal: The American Stratification System.* New York: Russell Sage Foundation.

Massey, Douglas S., and Nancy A. Denton. 1993. *American Apartheid: Segregation and the Making of the Underclass.* Cambridge, Mass.: Harvard University Press.

Massey, Douglas S., and Margarita Mooney. 2007. "The Effects of America's Three Affirmative Action Programs on Academic Performance." *Social Problems* 54(1): 99–117.

Massey, Douglas S., Margarita Mooney, Kimberly C. Torres, and Camille Z. Charles. 2007. "Black Immigrants and Black Natives Attending Selective Colleges and Universities in the United States." *American Journal of Education* 113(2): 243–71.

Mautner, Menachem. 2004. "The Affirmative Action Program at the Faculty of Law of Tel Aviv University and Its Implications." In *Affirmative Action and Equal Representation in Israel* (in Hebrew), edited by Anat Maor. Tel Aviv: Tel Aviv University, Ramot.

McLeod, Jane D., and Kevan Edwards. 1995. "Contextual Determinants of Children's Responses to Poverty." *Social Forces* 73(4): 1487–1516.

Melguizo, Tatiana. 2008. "Quality Matters: Assessing the Impact of Attending More Selective Institutions on College Completion Rates of Minorities." *Research in Higher Education* 49(3): 214–36.

Melguizo, Tatiana, and Gregory C. Wolniak. 2012. "The Earnings Benefits of Majoring in STEM Fields Among High-Achieving Minority Students." *Research in Higher Education* 53(4): 383–405.

Milem, Jeffrey F., Mitchell J. Chang, and Anthony Lising Antonio. 2005. "Making Diversity Work on Campus: A Research-Based Perspective." Association of American Colleges and Universities. Available at: http://siher.stanford.edu/Antonio MilemChang_makingdiversitywork.pdf (accessed September 22, 2014).

Mullen, Ann L. 2010. *Degrees of Inequality: Culture, Class, and Gender in American Higher Education.* Baltimore: Johns Hopkins University Press.

Myers-JDC-Brookdale Institute. 2012. "The Arab Population in Israel: Facts and Figures 2012." Jerusalem: Myers-JDC-Brookdale Institute (March). Available at: http://brookdale.jdc.org.il/_Uploads/dbsAttachedFiles/Myers-JDC-Brookdale-Facts-and-Figures-on-Arab-Israelis-March-2012.pdf (accessed September 1, 2014).

National Association of College and University Business Officers and Common Fund Institute. 2013. "U.S. and Canadian Institutions Listed by Fiscal Year 2012 Endowment Market Value and Percentage Change in Endowment Market Value from FY 2011 to FY 2012." Available at: http://www.nacubo.org/Documents/research/2012NCSEPublicTablesEndowmentMarketValuesFinalJanuary232013.pdf (accessed August 10, 2014).

National Center for Education Statistics (NCES). 2014. *The Condition of Education: Educational Attainment.* Washington: U.S. Department of Education, Institute of Education Science. Available at: http://nces.ed.gov/programs/coe/indicator_caa.asp (accessed September 11, 2014).

———. "Beginning Postsecondary Students Longitudinal Study, 1996–2001." Washington: U.S. Department of Education, Institute of Education Science. Available at: https://nces.ed.gov/surveys/bps/.

———. "Education Longitudinal Study of 2004." Washington: U.S. Department of Education, Institute of Education Science. Available at: http://nces.ed.gov/surveys/els2002/.

———. "High School and Beyond." Washington: U.S. Department of Education, Institute of Education Science. Available at: http://nces.ed.gov/surveys/hsb/.

———. "Integrated Postsecondary Education Data System." Washington: U.S. Department of Education, Institute of Education Science. Available at: http://nces.ed.gov/ipeds/.

———. "National Education Longitudinal Study of 1988." Washington: U.S. Department of Education, Institute of Education Science. Available at: https://nces.ed.gov/surveys/nels88/.

———. "National Longitudinal Study of the High School Class of 1972." Washington: U.S. Department of Education, Institute of Education Science. Available at: http://nces.ed.gov/surveys/nls72/.

Nettles, Michael T. 1991. "Racial Similarities and Differences in the Predictors of College Student Achievement." In *College in Black and White: African American Students in Predominantly White and in Historically Black Public Universities,* edited by Walter R. Allen, Edgar G. Epps, and Nesha Z. Haniff. Albany: State University of New York Press.

Nora, A. 1987. "Determinants of Retention Among Chicano College Students: A Structural Model." *Research in Higher Education* 26(1): 31–59.

Okun, Barbara S., and Dov Friedlander. 2005. "Educational Stratification Among Arabs and Jews in Israel: Historical Disadvantage, Discrimination, and Opportunity." *Population Studies* 59(2): 163–80.

Oliver, Melvin L., and Thomas M. Shapiro. 1995. *Black Wealth/White Wealth: A New Perspective on Racial Inequality.* New York: Routledge.

Organization for Economic Cooperation and Development (OECD). 2014a. *Education at a Glance 2014: Israel.* Paris: OECD Publishing. Available at: http://www.oecd.org/edu/Israel-EAG2014-Country-Note.pdf (accessed September 20, 2014).

———. 2014b. *Education at a Glance 2014: United States.* Paris: OECD Publishing. Available at: http://www.oecd.org/edu/United%20States-EAG2014-Country-Note.pdf (accessed September 20, 2014).

arcel, Toby L., and Mikaela J. Dufur. 2001. "Capital at Home and at School: Effects on Student Achievement." *Social Forces* 79(3): 881–911.

Park, Julie J., Nida Denson, and Nicholas A. Bowman. 2013. "Does Socioeconomic Diversity Make a Difference? Examining the Effects of Racial and Socioeconomic Diversity on the Campus Climate for Diversity." *American Educational Research Journal* 50(3): 466–96.

Pascarella, Ernest T., and Patrick T. Terenzini. 1980. "Predicting Freshman Persistence and Voluntary Dropout Decisions from a Theoretical Model." *Journal of Higher Education* 51(1): 60–75.

Pebley, Anne R., and Narayan Sastry. 2004. "Neighborhoods, Poverty, and Children's Well-being: A Review." In *Social Inequality,* edited by Kathryn Neckerman. New York: Russell Sage Foundation.

Pell, Terence J. 2003. "Racial Preferences and Formal Equality." *Journal of Social Philosophy* 34(2): 309–25.

Peria, Michelle, and Stanley R. Bailey. 2014. "Remaking Racial Inclusion: Combining Race and Class in Brazil's New Affirmative Action." *Latin American and Caribbean Ethnic Studies* 9(2): 156–76.

Pew Economic Mobility Project. 2011. "Does America Promote Mobility as Well as

Other Nations?" Washington, D.C.: Pew Charitable Trusts (November). Available at: https://www.russellsage.org/sites/all/files/does-america-promote-economic-mobility.pdf (accessed August 15, 2015).

———. 2012. "Pursuing the American Dream: Economic Mobility Across Generations." Washington, D.C.: Pew Charitable Trusts (July). Available at: http://www.pewtrusts.org/~/media/legacy/uploadedfiles/pcs_assets/2012/PursuingAmericanDreampdf.pdf (accessed August 15, 2015).

Pew Research Center. 2014. "Middle Easterners See Religious and Ethnic Hatred as Top Global Threat." Pew Research Center: Global Attitudes & Trends, October 16. Available at: http://www.pewglobal.org/2014/10/16/middle-easterners-see-religious-and-ethnic-hatred-as-top-global-threat/ (accessed August 15, 2015).

Piketty, Thomas, and Emmanuel Saez. 2003. "Income Inequality in the United States, 1913– 1998." *Quarterly Journal of Economics* 118(1): 1–39.

Planty, Michael, et al. 2008. *The Condition of Education 2008*. NCES 2008-031. Washington: U.S. Department of Education, National Center for Education Statistics (NCES), Institute of Education Sciences (June). Available at: http://nces.ed.gov/pubs2008/2008031.pdf (accessed September 2, 2014).

Robles Frisancho, Verónica C., and Kala Krishna. 2012. "Affirmative Action in Higher Education in India: Targeting, Catch Up, and Mismatch." Working Paper 17727. Cambridge, Mass.: National Bureau of Economic Research (January).

Roksa, Josipa, and Tania Levey. 2010. "What Can You Do with That Degree? College Major and Occupational Status of College Graduates over Time." *Social Forces* 89(2): 389–415.

Rothstein, Jesse, and Albert Yoon. 2008. "Affirmative Action in Law School Admissions: What Do Racial Preferences Do?" *University of Chicago Law Review* 75(2): 649–714.

Rumberger, Russell W., and Scott L. Thomas. 1993. "The Economic Returns to College Major, Quality, and Performance: A Multilevel Analysis of Recent Graduates." *Economics of Education Review* 12(1): 1–19.

Sampson, Robert J., Jeffrey D. Morenoff, and Felton Earls. 1999. "Beyond Social Capital: Spatial Dynamics of Collective Efficacy for Children." *American Sociological Review* 64(5): 633–60.

Sampson, Robert J., Stephen W. Raudenbush, and Felton Earls. 1997. "Neighborhoods and Violent Crime: A Multilevel Study of Collective Efficacy." *Science* 277 (5328): 918–24.

Sander, Richard H. 1997. "Experimenting with Class-Based Affirmative Action." *Journal of Legal Education* 47(4): 472–503.

Sander, Richard H., and Stuart Taylor. 2012. *Mismatch: How Affirmative Action Hurts Students It's Intended to Help, and Why Universities Won't Admit It*. New York: Basic Books.

Sawhill, Isabel V., and John E. Morton. 2007. "Economic Mobility: Is the American Dream Alive and Well?" Washington, D.C.: Pew Charitable Trusts, Economic

Mobility Project. Available at: http://www.pewtrusts.org/~/media/legacy/uploaded files/wwwpewtrustsorg/reports/economic_mobility/EMPAmericanDreamReportpdf.pdf (accessed October 22, 2014).

Schill, Michael H., and Susan M. Wachter. 1995. "Housing Market Constraints and Spatial Stratification by Income and Race." *Housing Policy Debate* 6(1): 141–67.

Schmitt, Carl M. 2009. "Documentation for the Restricted-Use NCES-Barron's Admissions Competitiveness Index Data Files: 1972, 1982, 1992, 2004, and 2008 (NCES 2010-330)." Washington: U.S. Department of Education, Institute of Education Sciences, National Center for Education Statistics.

Semyonov, Moshe, and Andrea Tyree. 1981. "Community Segregation and the Costs of Ethnic Subordination." *Social Forces* 59(3): 649–66.

Shamir, Shimon. 2005. *The Arabs in Israel: Two Years After the Or Commission Report.* Tel Aviv: Konrad Adenauer Program for Jewish-Arab Cooperation.

Shulman, James L., and William G. Bowen. 2002. *The Game of Life: College Sports and Educational Values.* Princeton, N.J.: Princeton University Press.

Skrentny, John D. 1996. *The Ironies of Affirmative Action: Politics, Culture, and Justice in America.* Chicago: University of Chicago Press.

South, Scott J., and Kyle D. Crowder. 1999. "Neighborhood Effects on Family Formation: Concentrated Poverty and Beyond." *American Sociological Review* 64(1): 113–32.

Sowell, Thomas. 2003. "Damaging Admissions: Increasing Faculty Diversity." *Capitalism* (February 8). Available at: http://capitalismmagazine.com/2003/02/damaging-admissions-increasing-faculty-diversity/ (accessed August 12, 2014).

———. 2004. *Affirmative Action Around the World: An Empirical Study.* New Haven, Conn.: Yale University Press.

Spilerman, Seymour, and Jack Habib. 1976. "Development Towns in Israel: The Role of Community in Creating Ethnic Disparities in Labor Force Characteristics." *American Journal of Sociology* 81(4): 781–812.

Stefoff, Rebecca. 2006. *The Bakke Case: Challenging Affirmative Action.* New York: Marshall Cavendish Benchmark.

Sterling, Joyce, and Catherine E. Smith. 2011. "Forward: Social Class, Race, and Legal Education." *Denver University Law Review* (special issue on economic diversity and American legal education) 88(4): i–xiii.

Suzzman, Noam, Orly Furman, Tom Caplan, and Dmitri Romanov. 2007. "The Quality of Israeli Academic Institutions: What the Wages of Graduates Tell About It?" (in Hebrew). *Economics of Higher Education (EHE)* (Samuel Neaman Institute).

Terenzini, Patrick T., and Ernest T. Pascarella. 1977. "Voluntary Freshman Attrition and Patterns of Social and Academic Integration in a University: A Test of a Conceptual Model." *Research in Higher Education* 6(1): 25–43.

Thernstrom, Stephan, and Abigail Thernstrom. 1997. *America in Black and White: One Nation Indivisible.* New York: Simon & Schuster.

———. 1999. "Reflections on the Shape of the River Book Review." *UCLA Law Review* 46(5): 1583–1631.
Thomas, Scott L. 2000. "Deferred Costs and Economic Returns to College Major, Quality, and Performance." *Research in Higher Education* 41(3): 281–313.
Tienda, Marta, Sigal Alon, and Sunny X. Niu. 2010. "Affirmative Action and the Texas Top 10 Percent Admission Law: Balancing Equity and Access to Higher Education." *Sociétés Contemporaines* 79: 19–39.
Tienda, Marta, and Sunny X. Niu. 2006. "Capitalizing on Segregation, Pretending Neutrality: College Admissions and the Texas Top 10% Law." *American Law and Economics Review* 8(2): 312–46.
Tilly, Charles. 1998. *Durable Inequality.* Berkeley: University of California Press.
Tinto, Vincent. 1993. *Leaving College: Rethinking the Causes and Cures of Student Attrition.* 2nd ed. Chicago: Chicago University Press.
Tobin, Eugene. 2009. "The Modern Evolution of America's Flagship Universities" (Appendix A). In *Crossing the Finish Line: Completing College at America's Public Universities,* edited by William G. Bowen, Matthew M. Chingos, and Michael S. McPherson. Princeton, N.J.: Princeton University Press.
Tocqueville, Alexis de. 1835. *Democracy in America,* vol. 1. New York: Alfred A. Knopf.
U.S. Bureau of Labor Statistics. 2013. "Labor Force Statistics from the Current Population Survey: Employed Persons by Detailed Occupation, Sex, Race, and Hispanic or Latino Ethnicity." Available at: http://www.bls.gov/cps/cpsaat11.htm (accessed August 20, 2014).
———. 2014. "Labor Force Characteristics by Race and Ethnicity, 2013." Report 1050. Washington: U.S. Government Printing Office.
———. 2015. "Current Employment Statistics—CES (National)." Available at: http://www.bls.gov/ces/ (accessed August 6, 2014).
U.S. Census Bureau. 2012. "School Enrollment—CPS [Current Population Survey] October 2012: Detailed Tables." Washington: U.S. Census Bureau, Population Division. Available at: https://www.census.gov/hhes/school/data/cps/2012/tables.html (accessed August 20, 2014).
———. 2013. "Annual Estimates of the Resident Population by Sex, Race, and Hispanic Origin for the United States, States, and Countries: April 1, 2010, to July 1, 2012." Washington: U.S. Census Bureau, Population Division (June).
———. 2014. "The Condition of Education: Educational Attainment, Table A-2: Percent of People 25 Years and Over Who Have Completed High School or College by Race, Hispanic Origin, and Sex, 1940–2013." Available at: http://www.census.gov/hhes/socdemo/education/data/cps/historical/index.html (accessed January 20, 2015).
———. 2015. "Population Estimates: National Estimates by Age, Sex, Race: 1900–1979 (PE-11)." Available at: http://www.census.gov/popest/data/national/asrh/pre-1980/PE-11.html (accessed on January 21, 2015).

U.S. Department of Justice and U.S. Department of Education. 2011. "Guidance on the Voluntary Use of Race to Achieve Diversity in Postsecondary Education." Available at: http://www.justice.gov/crt/about/edu/documents/guidancepost.pdf (accessed September 2, 2014).

Wilson, William J. 1987. *The Truly Disadvantaged: The Inner City, the Underclass, and Public Policy.* Chicago: University of Chicago Press.

———. 1996. *When Work Disappears: The World of the New Urban Poor.* New York: Alfred Knopf.

Yaish, Meir. 2001. "Class Structure in a Deeply Divided Society: Class and Ethnic Inequality in Israel, 1974–1991." *British Journal of Sociology* 52(3): 409–37.

Yashiv, Eran, and Nitsa Kasir. 2009. "Arab Israelis: Patterns of Labor Force Participation." Working Paper. Jerusalem: Bank of Israel, Research Department, (November 11).

Yiftachel, Oren. 2000. "Social Control, Urban Planning, and Ethno-Class Relations: Mizrahi Jews in Israel's Development Towns." *International Journal of Urban and Regional Research* 24(2): 418–38.

INDEX

Boldface numbers refer to figures and tables.

AAE (Association for the Advancement of Education), 117, 130, 152
academic integration, 54–56, 219–21
academic outcomes, 206–11
academic selectivity, affirmative action policy effects, 136–38, 171–73, 256
ACT, 49–50
admissions practices: comprehensive review, 70–72, 96–97; data sources, 132; in Israel vs. U.S., 110–13, 123–24, 132; legacy admissions, 252–53; percent plans, 94–96; socioeconomic diversity impact, 67–74
admissions rates, 4–6, 51–53, 56–57, 194–96
advanced degrees, 34
affirmative action: broad diversity link, 73–76; comparative investigation, 16–18; data sources, 18; definition of, 6, 79; eligibility for, 86–89, 122, 235, 237–40; at elite colleges and universities, 4–6; goals for, 257–58; "mismatch effect," 36, 80–81, 206–11, 215, 226–29, 243–44; policy design considerations, 257–58; public opinion, 40; "race within class" model, 176–77, 187, 249–50, 256–57; social and economic context, 42–47; stigma associated with, 213, 229. *See also* class-based affirmative action; legal challenges; race-based affirmative action; race-neutral policies
African Americans. *See* blacks
Alvaredo, Facundo, **43**
American Dream, 43–44
American Sociological Review, 57
application process, for affirmative action programs, 122
Applications Quest, 245
Arabs, Israeli: affirmative action policy gains, 140–41; earnings, 104; employment disparities, 103; field of study stratification, 115–16; population, 15, 101; segregation, 102–3; socioeconomic status, 16; spatial inequality, 107
Arizona: affirmative action bans, 10
Ashkenazi Jews: academic fields of study, 115; assimilation in Israel, 102; definition of, 15; earnings, 104; educational attainment, 103; field of study, 115; immigration to Israel, 101; socioeconomic status, 16, 102

INDEX

Asian Americans: affirmative action lawsuits file by, 36; at competitive four-year colleges, **33**
Association for the Advancement of Education (AAE), 117, 130, 152
Atlantic, 30
Avery, Christopher, 167

Bailey, Stanley, 239–40, 294*n*27
Bakke decision, 3–4, 8–11, 30–31, 65, 66, 74
Barron's Profiles of American Colleges, 32, **33**, 49–51, 160
Bass, Robert, 252
Beginning Postsecondary Students Longitudinal Study (BPS), 17–18, **50**, 160–161, **164**, 166–167, **173, 175, 179, 184, 218, 220, 224, 255, 266–273**, 288*n*1
BGU (Ben-Gurion University), 18, 108, 117, 118, 131
Blackmun, Harry, 8, 9
blacks: college graduation rate, 28; at competitive four-year colleges, 32–34; disadvantage status, 247; earnings, 28; educational attainment, 248; at elite colleges and universities, 6; high school graduation rate, 28; household income, 248; mobility, 34–35, 44; socioeconomic status, 162–63; unemployment, 28, 248; wealth, 248
Black Wealth/White Wealth (Oliver and Shapiro), 162
BLS (Bureau of Labor Statistics), 28
Bok, Derek, 34–35, 279*n*32, 291*n*15
Bollinger; Gratz v., 36, 65, 67
Bollinger; Grutter v., 31, 36–37, 65, 66–67, 74
Bowen, William, 34–35, 67, 70, 83, 162, 180, 279*n*32, 289*n*9, 291*n*15
BPS (Beginning Postsecondary Students Longitudinal Study), 18, **50, 164**, 166, **173, 175, 179, 184, 218, 220, 224, 255, 266–273**, 288*n*1
Brazilian affirmative action programs: design of, 14–15, 91, 92, 249; eligibility, 239–40; enrollment, 7; lawsuits, 250; mandatory nature of, 236; quotas, 7
Brennan, William J., 8, 9
broad diversity: affirmative action model best for implementation of, 154–56; class-based affirmative action effects, 82–83, 154–56, 185–87, 253–57; definition of, 246–47; difficulties in targeting, 245–46; ideal of, 65–67; Israeli-U.S. policy comparison, 244–50; race-based affirmative action effects, 154–56; research considerations, 73–76; Supreme Court rulings, 66–67, 73–74, 244–45
Brown University, 4, 253
Bureau of Labor Statistics (BLS), 28
Burger, Warren, 9
Bush, George H.W., 6
Bush, George W., 6

California: affirmative action bans, 10, 32–34, 94–95; percent plans, 95
Canada: mobility in, 44
Caribbean immigrants, 278*n*16
celebrities, affirmative action for, 253
census data, **46**
The Century Foundation (TCF), 92–93, 162–63, 174
Chronicle of Higher Education, 245
Chung, Chang, 252
Civil Rights Act of 1964, 4, 9, 27, 28–29, 36
class: definition of, 12; importance in American society, 64
class-based affirmative action: academic integration effects, 219–21; academic outcomes, 206–11; academic selectivity effects, 136–38, 171–73; admission rate

impact, 194–96; Bakke decision and, 11; broad diversity generation, 82–83, 154–56, 185–87, 253–57; college destination effects, 216–18; comparison with race-based affirmative action, 16–18; cost vs. race-based policy, 180–83, 256; "creaming" effects, 156–58, 240–43; cross-country comparisons, 14–15; definition of, 11–12, 79; and degree attainment, 221–23, 227; demographic diversity impact, 138–43; diversity achievement, 12–13; eligibility, 237–40; and fields of study stratification, 196–206, 223–25; financial issues, 13; introduction, 79–80; Israeli policy features, 235–36; misconceptions of, 94–97; mobility dividends, 225–29, 243–44; prototypes of, 85–94; "race within class" model, 176–77, 187; racial-ethnic diversity impact, 173–77; rationales for, 80–85; simulation study, 163–64, 166; social integration effects, 219–21; socioeconomic diversity effects, 150–54, 177–83; spatial diversity impact, 143–50, 183–85; U.S. experiments with, 238–39. *See also* multidimensional affirmative action; socioeconomic affirmative action; structural affirmative action

Clinton, Bill, 6

Coalition to Defend Affirmative Action; Schuette v., 279*n*39

Coates, Ta-Nehisi, 30

college destination, affirmative action policy's impact on, 216–18

college graduation and graduates: earnings of, 45–46; economic premium for, 45–47; rates, 28, 213–14, 221–23, 226–27

colleges and universities: academic barriers to attending, 56–58, 73; admissions rates, 4–6, 51–53, 56–57, 194–96; changes in, 47–56; climate and student integration, 54–56; economic barriers to, 59–61; eco-nomic premium for degree, 45–47; enrollment data, 48–49; financial aid, 59–61; in Israel, 108–16; stratification in, 53–56; tuition, 59–60. *See also* admissions practices; elite colleges and universities; *specific colleges and universities*

Columbia University, 4, 5, 6, 275*n*9

comparative investigation of Israeli and American affirmative action policy, 233–58; broad diversity generation, 244–50; case for class-based program in U.S., 250–57; case for hybrid program in U.S., 257–58; data sources, 17, 18, 131–32, 160, 166–68; introduction, 16–18, 233–35; mobility dividends, 243–44; similarities and differences in policy, 235–43

comprehensive review, 70–72, 96–97

Cornell University, 4, 6, **53**

court cases. *See* legal challenges

Cox, Archibald, 4

"creaming" argument against race-conscious admissions, 36, 80, 88, 130, 156–58, 240–43

cross-country comparisons: class-based affirmative action programs, 14–15; income inequality, 100; race-based affirmative action programs, 7–8. *See also* comparative investigation of Israeli and American affirmative action policy; *specific countries*

Dale, Stacy, 47

Dartmouth College, 4

data sources: Israeli affirmative action policy, 18, 131–32; Israeli earnings, 200; U.S. affirmative action policy, 17, 160, 166–68

degree attainment, 28, 213–14, 221–23, 226–28

democracy, 43

demographic diversity, 138–43

Denmark: mobility in, 44

Denver University Law Review, 207

development towns, in Israel, 107, 116, 145, 148–50
discrimination, 28–30
diversity: benefits of, 64–65; class-based affirmative action impact, 12–13; demographic basis for, 138–43; economic basis for, 178, 182, 186, 256; at elite colleges and universities, 64–74; geographic basis for, 143–50, 183–85, 256; by immigration status, 141–43, 278n16; race-based affirmative action successes, 32–34; as race-conscious admissions policy rationale, 10–11, 30–31, 65–67; socioeconomic basis for, 67–74, 82–83, 150–54, 177–83, 256; spatial basis for, 143–50, 183–85, 256; at U.S. elite colleges, 173–76. *See also* broad diversity
Du Bois, W.E.B, 27
Dworkin, Ronald, 10

earnings. *See* wages and earnings
economic affirmative action, 88–89, 164–65, 171, 186
economic diversity, 178, 182, 186, 256. *See also* socioeconomic diversity
economic inequality, 42–43, 64, 98, 99–101
The Economist, 251
Education, U.S. Department of, 18, 49, 54–55, 67, 82, 219
education level: inequality in, 45; of Israeli Jewish vs. Arab citizens, 103–4; Israeli neighborhood differences, 106, 107; racial-ethnic differences, 248
egalitarianism, 35
eligibility, for affirmative action programs, 86–89, 122, 235, 237–40
elite colleges and universities: admissions rates, 4–6, 51–53, 56–57; admittance statistics, **266–71**; diversity at, 64–74; earnings premium for graduates of, 47; growth in number of, 49–51; in Israel, 111–13, 192–93; race-based affirmative action programs, 6–8, 29–31; SES differences in admissions to, 61–63; student characteristics, **273**
employment discrimination, 28
employment rates, 192
endowment, 53–54
equal opportunity, as affirmative action rationale, 31
Equal Protection Clause, 4
Equity and Excellence in American Higher Education (Bowen, Kurzweil, and Tobin), 67, 70, 83, 180
Espenshade, Thomas, 162, 252, 279n32, 289n9, 24
ethnic-conscious affirmative action, 131, 176–77, 187, 249–50, 256–57
ethnic inequality, in Israel, 101–5
ethnic origin, diversity based on, 138–41
Executive Orders: (10925), 277n8; (11246), 277n8
Expected Family Contribution (EFC), 164–65, 167

FAFSA (Free Application for Federal Student Aid), 164, 167
family income: affirmative action eligibility based on, 86–89; as proxy for class, 162; racial-ethnic differences, 248
fields of study, 111–16, 133–34, 196–206, 223–25, **259**
financial aid: and affirmative action, 97; cost of, 180–83, 256; decline in share of, 59–61; grant-based, 60–61; in Israel, 151–52; loan-based, 60–61; merit-based, 61; need-based, 72–73, 182–83
first-generation college students: comprehensive review process benefits, 70–71; at U.S. elite colleges, 178–80; at U.S. non-elite colleges, 165
Fischer, Claude, 45
Fisher v. University of Texas, 11, 37–40, 65, 79, 81, 215

Fitzsimmons, William, 253
Florida: affirmative action bans, 10, 32–34; percent plans, 95
Former Soviet Union (FSU), immigration to Israel from, 102, 104, 115, 141–43
Fourteenth Amendment, 4, 36
France: structural affirmative action programs, 91
Free Application for Federal Student Aid (FAFSA), 164, 167
Frist, Bill, 252

geographic diversity, 143–50, 183–85, 256
geographic periphery, in Israel, 103, 106–7, 146–47
Georgetown University, 6
Gilbert, Juan, 245
Gini index, 100
Golden, Daniel, 252–53
Gore, Albert, 252
grades, 208–9, 217
graduation likelihood, 211
grant-based financial aid, 60–61
Gratz v. Bollinger, 36, 65, 67
Great Recession, 42, 46
Grodsky, Eric, 278*n*22
group affiliation, affirmative action eligibility based on, 237–40
Grutter v. Bollinger, 31, 36–37, 65, 66–67, 69, 74

Harvard University: admission rates, 4, 52, **53**; affirmative action lawsuits, 36; endowment, 53–54, 281*n*25; female students, 275*n*9; financial aid policy, 71–72; geographic distribution of students, 183; homogeneity of student body, 6; Jewish student quotas, 275*n*9; legacy admissions, 252, 253; U.S. presidents graduated from, 5, 6
Haynes, Berneta, 213, 228–29
Hebrew University (HUJI), 18, 108, 116, 118, 131, 133, 209

high-achieving students: and academic selectivity, 173; and broad diversity generation, 186; class-based affirmative action outcomes, 88, 162, 229; college destinations, 217; data sources, 167; degree attainment, 221–22; field-of-study outcomes, 225; geographic distribution, 184, 185; race-conscious admissions impact, 31
higher education. *See* colleges and universities
high school graduation and graduates: earnings of, 45–46; rates, 28
high school type, affirmative action policy targeting, 14, 178, 180, 183–85, 187
Hill, Catharine Bond, 180, 183
Hispanics: affirmative action inclusion, 30; at competitive four-year colleges, 32–34; educational attainment, 248; household income, 248; poverty of, 248; social mobility, 34–35; socioeconomic status, 162; unemployment, 248; wealth, 248
Holocaust victims, compensation for, 30
Holy Cross, College of, 6
Hopwood v. Texas, 37–38, 94
household income. *See* family income
Hout, Michael, 45, 71
Howard University, Johnson's commencement address (1965), 27–28
Hoxby, Caroline, 167
HUJI (The Hebrew University), 18, 108, 116, 118, 131, 133, 209
hybrid affirmative action policy, case for, 257–58

ICBS (Israeli Central Bureau of Statistics), 105, **106, 110**
immigration status, diversity based on, 141–43, 278*n*16
income inequality, 42–43, 64, 99–101, 106
India: affirmative action policy, 7, 236
individualism, 35

industrial restructuring, 42–43, 45
Inside Higher Ed, 228–29
Institut d'Études Politiques de Paris (Sciences Po), 91
Integrated Postsecondary Education Data System (IPEDS), **72**
integration, of college students, 54–56
IPEDS (Integrated Postsecondary Education Data System), **72**
isomorphism, 237
Israel: admittance statistics for universities in, **259–65**; higher education in, 108–16; inequality in, 15–16, 98, 99–107; population of, 101
Israeli affirmative action policy: academic outcomes, 206–11; academic outcomes for students at universities who fell just above and below affirmative action threshold, **204, 205, 208, 274**; academic selectivity effects, 136–38; admission rates, 194–96; advantages vs. race-based programs, 124–25, 129–31; broad diversity generation, 154–56; "creaming" effects, 156–58; data sources, 131–32; demographic diversity impact, 138–43; design of, 92, 119–21, 125–26; eligibility, 235, 237–40; field of study entry, 196–206; goal of, 84; history of, 117–19; implementation stages, 122–24; introduction, 15–16, 98–99, 191–94; mobility outcomes, 211–12; research methodology, 133–36; socioeconomic diversity effects, 150–54; spatial diversity impact, 143–46; vs. U.S. policy, 16–18, 99, 235–43, 243–44; voluntary nature of, 236–37
Israeli Central Bureau of Statistics (ICBS), 105, **106, 110**
Ivy League, 4–6. *See also specific schools*

Jews: Harvard University quotas, 275n9; stratification in Israel, 15–16, 101–7, 115. *See also* Ashkenazi Jews; Israel; Mizrachi Jews
Johnson, Lyndon B.: Executive Order 11246, 277n8; Howard University commencement address (1965), 27–28
Justice, U.S. Department of, 82, 90

Kahlenberg, Richard D., 93
Kane, Thomas, 70
Karabel, Jerome, 6
Kennedy, Anthony, 66
Kennedy, John F.: Executive Order 10925, 277n8
"kitchen sink approach" to affirmative action, 92–93
Knesset, 118
Krueger, Alan, 47
Kurlaender, Michal, 278n22
Kurzweil, Martin, 67, 70, 83, 180

labor force participation, of Israeli Jewish vs. Arab citizens, 103
Latinos. *See* Hispanics
Law of Social Quotas (Brazil), 7, 8, 14, 91, 236, 239–40, 250
laws and legislation. *See specific legislative acts*
lawyers, 34
legacy admissions, 252–53
legal challenges: Bakke decision, 3–4, 8–11, 30–31, 65, 66, 74; Fisher decision, 11, 37–40, 65, 79, 81, 215; Fisher v. University of Texas, 11, 37–40, 65, 79, 81, 215; Gratz v. Bollinger, 36, 65, 67; Grutter v. Bollinger decision, 31, 36–37, 65, 66–67, 74; Hopwood v. Texas, 37–38, 94; Regents of the University of California v. Bakke, 3–4, 8–11, 30–31, 65, 74; Schuette v. Coalition to Defend Affirmative Action 572 U.S. (2014), 279n39; Students for Fair Admissions, Inc. v. President and Fellows of Harvard College et

al., 279*n*34; Students for Fair Admissions, Inc. v. University of North Carolina, et al., 279*n*34
life expectancy, of Israeli Jewish vs. Arab citizens, 102
loan-based financial aid, 60–61
low-income students: Brazilian affirmative action policy targeting, 14, 249; expensiveness of policies for, 180–83; high achiever status, 167; race as proxy for, 178; U.S. affirmative action policy targeting, 71–73

macrojustice, 29–30, 92, 124, 237
Malamud, Ofer, 209–11, 291*n*14
manufacturing, 42, 45
Mare, Robert, 71
Marshall, Thurgood, 8, 9, 27
Massey, Douglas S., 278*n*16
Mautner, Menachem, 117–18
merit-based financial aid, 61
meritocracy, 56–57
Michigan: affirmative action bans, 10, 32, 37, 94–95
microjustice, 88, 92, 124
Mismatch (Sander and Taylor), 80, 207, 211
"mismatch effect" of affirmative action, 36, 80–81, 206–11, 215, 226–29, 243–44
Mizrachi Jews: affirmative action policy gains, 140; definition of, 15; disadvantaged status, 130; earnings, 104; educational attainment, 103; field of study, 115; immigration to Israel, 101; socioeconomic status, 16, 102; spatial inequality, 107
mobility: of blacks, 34–35, 44; in Canada, 44; class-based affirmative action dividends, 225–29, 243–44; in Denmark, 44; Israeli trends, 100, 211–12; Israeli vs. U.S. affirmative action policy, 17, 243–44; and race-based affirmative action, 31, 243–44; in United Kingdom, 44; U.S. trends, 34–35, 43–44, 213, 225–29

Mullen, Ann, 55
multidimensional affirmative action: and academic selectivity, 173; broad diversity generation, 186; features of, **87,** 92–94, 166; geographic diversity effects, **184;** Israeli program design, 124

National Center for Education Statistics (NCES), **49, 50, 51**
National Postsecondary Student Aid Study (NPSAS), 18, 166, 288*n*1
natural experiments, 14, 15–16
NCES (National Center for Education Statistics), **49, 50, 51**
Nebraska: affirmative action bans, 10
need-based financial aid, 72–73, 182–83
neighborhood effects, 89–90
New Hampshire: affirmative action bans, 10
New York Times, 180
NPSAS (National Postsecondary Student Aid Study), 18, 166, 288*n*1

Obama, Barack, 6
O'Connor, Sandra Day, 37, 74
Ofakim, Israel, 105–7, 148–49
Office for Civil Rights (OCR), 66
Oklahoma: affirmative action bans, 10
Oliver, Melvin, 162
Organization for Economic Cooperation and Development (OECD), 99–100, 192, 213–14

parental education, affirmative action eligibility based on, 88–89, 178–80, **181**
Pell Grant, 5, 60, 182–83, 283*n*16
percent plans, 94–96
Peria, Michelle, 239–40, 294*n*27
Pew Charitable Trusts, 44
Pew Research Center, 40
physicians, 34
Piketty, Thomas, 42

poverty: affirmative action programs' potential for reduction of, 150–54, 177–83, 186, 256; and broad diversity definition, 154–55; Israeli affirmative action programs targeting, 144–46, 195–201, 243; of Israeli Jewish vs. Arab citizens, 102; rates, 248; underrepresentation of poor students at elite schools, 178

Powell, Lewis, 9, 10, 11, 30–31, 37, 65, 74

preferential treatment, 252–53. *See also* affirmative action

President and Fellows of Harvard College et al.; Students for Fair Admissions, Inc. v., 279n34

The Price of Admission: How America's Ruling Class Buys Its Way into Elite Colleges—and Who Gets Left Outside the Gates (Golden), 252–53

Princeton University: endowment, 281n25; female students, 275n9; homogeneity of student body, 6; Ivy League status, 4; preferential treatment practices, 252; racial-ethnic diversity, 173; U.S. presidents graduated from, 6

professionals: affirmative action programs, 3, 29; blacks, 34; Israeli graduates, 101, 111, 115, 130, 133, 192, 197–99, 202; Ivy League graduates, 5

public opinion, 40

quotas, 7–8, 10, 15

race, socioeconomic status as proxy for, 162–63, 174

race-based affirmative action: academic integration effects, 219–21; academic selectivity effects, 136–38, 137–38; broad diversity generation, 154–56, 187; comparison with class-based affirmative action, 16–18; controversy over, 35–40, 80–81, 206–7; cost vs. class-based policy, 180–83; "creaming" argument against, 36, 80, 88,
130, 156–58, 240–43; and degree attainment, 221–23, 227; demographic diversity impact, 141, 143; economic diversity effects, 178; eligibility, 237–40; fields of study, 201–2, 223–25; history of, 6–8, 27–31; mobility dividends, 31, 243–44; prototype of, 86; racial-ethnic diversity impact, 173–74; rationales for, 10, 30–31, 65–67; simulation study, 163; social integration effects, 219–21; socioeconomic diversity effects, 153–54, 178–80; spatial diversity impact, 145–46, 147, 150, **184**; successes achieved by, 32–35, 73–74, 161–62; U.S. policy features, 235; U.S. state bans, 10, 32, 37, 94–95

race-neutral policies: broad diversity generation, 12–13, 75, 154, 187, 245–46, 254–56; class as a Trojan horse for race, 81–82; class-based policy requirements, 256–57; diversity effects, 139–41, 176–77; Fisher decision, 11, 39, 79; in Israel, 15, 84, 98–99, 125, 129–30, 139, 193; shortcomings of, 248–49; in South Africa, 8; U.S. model, 247–50

"race within class" model of affirmative action, 176–77, 187, 249–50, 256–57

racial-ethnic diversity, 173–77. *See also* diversity

Radford, Alexandria, 162, 279n32, 289n9, 24

Regents of the University of California v. Bakke, 3–4, 8–11, 30–31, 65, 74

Rehnquist, William, 9

reparation, as affirmative action rationale, 30

Rice University, 5

Saez, Emmanuel, 42

Sander, Richard, 80, 207, 211, 238–39, 294n12

SAT, 49–50, 56–58

Schuette v. Coalition to Defend Affirmative Action, 279n39

Sciences Po (Institut d'Études Politiques de Paris), 91
segregation, 105
selective colleges and universities. *See* elite colleges and universities
service industry, 42
The Shape of the River (Bowen and Bok), 34–35
Shapiro, Thomas, 162
Shoham, Israel, 105–6
simulation studies, 134–36, 162–70, 201–2, 216–18, 254–57
Smith, Catherine, 207
social integration, 219–21
social mobility, 17, 31, 34–35, 43–44. *See also* mobility
socioeconomic affirmative action: academic selectivity effects, 171; broad diversity generation, 186; "creaming" problem, 241–42; economic diversity effects, 256; eligibility complexity, 237–40; features of, 86–89; geographic diversity effects, **184,** 185; racial-ethnic diversity impact, 174–76; simulation study, 165–66
socioeconomic diversity, 66–75, 82–83, 150–54, 177–83, 256
socioeconomic status: blacks, 162–63; Israeli Arabs, 16; Israeli Jews, 16, 102; measurement of, 239–40; as proxy for race, 162–63, 174; and standardized test performance, 57–58; of students at elite U.S. colleges, 67–75; of students at Israeli universities, 151
software, as application diversity generation tool, 245–46
South Africa: race-based affirmative action, 7–8
Southern Connecticut State University (SCSU), 55
spatial diversity, 143–50, 183–85, 256
spatial inequality, 105–7, 116
Spencer Foundation, 18

standardized tests, 49–50, 56–58
Stanford University, 5, 6, 252–53
state merit scholarships, 282*n*39
STEM fields, 142, 223–25
Sterling, Joyce, 207
Stevens, John Paul, 8, 9
Stewart, Potter, 9
stigma, 213, 229
structural affirmative action: academic selectivity effects, 171; features of, **87,** 89–91; geographic diversity effects, **184,** 185; Israeli policy, 124; racial-ethnic diversity effects, 176; simulation study, 166; socioeconomic diversity effects, 178–80
student grants, 60–61, 180, 182–83
student loans, 60–61
Students for Fair Admissions, Inc. v. President and Fellows of Harvard College et al., 279*n*34
Students for Fair Admissions, Inc. v. University of North Carolina, et al., 279*n*34
Supreme Court decisions: Fisher decision, 11, 37–40, 65, 79, 81, 215; Fisher v. University of Texas, 11, 37–40, 65, 79, 81, 215; Gratz v. Bollinger, 36, 65, 67; Grutter v. Bollinger decision, 31, 36–37, 65, 66–67, 74; Regents of the University of California v. Bakke, 3–4, 8–11, 30–31, 65, 66, 74

TAU (Tel Aviv University): affirmative action program features, 236–37; affirmative action program history, 117–18; data description, 18, 131; demographic diversity, 139–40; field-of-study stratification, 133; selectivity of, 108; socioeconomic diversity, 151
TAU, HUJI, BGU, and TECH administrative data, 18, **112, 114, 125,** 131–132, **138, 139, 142, 145, 147, 148, 149, 152, 153, 155, 195, 197, 202, 204, 205, 208,**
Taylor, Stuart, Jr., 80, 207, 211, 294*n*12

TCF (The Century Foundation), 92–93, 162–63, 174
TECH (The Technion), 18, 108, 117, 118, 131, 133
The Technion (TECH), 18, 108, 117, 118, 131, 133
Tel Aviv, Israel, 146
Tel Aviv University (TAU): affirmative action program features, 236–37; affirmative action program history, 117–18; data description, 18, 131; demographic diversity, 139–40; field-of-study stratification, 133; selectivity of, 108; socioeconomic diversity, 151
test preparation industry, 58
Texas: affirmative action bans, 10, 32–34, 94; percent plans, 95–96
Thomas, Clarence, 213, 215
threshold effects, 202–6, **274**
Tienda, Marta, 57, 228
Tilly, Charles, 41
Time magazine, 66
Title VI of Civil Rights Act of 1964, 9, 36
Tobin, Eugene, 67, 70, 83, 180
Tocqueville, Alexis de, 233
"Trojan horse" rationale for class-based affirmative action, 81–82, 84–85, 248–49
tuition, 59–60

UCLA (University of California–Los Angeles), 5, 71, 174, 238–39
underprivileged students, definition of, 86
unemployment, 28, 103, 248
United Kingdom: mobility in, 44
United States: admittance statistics for universities in, **266–71**; higher education system in vs. Israel, 108–11; income inequality in, 42–43, 100; likelihood of attending college in, **272**; mobility in, 34–35, 43–44, 213; student characteristics at elite institutions, **273**

United States affirmative action policy: academic and social integration effects, 219–21; Bakke decision, 3–4, 8–11, 30–31, 65, 66, 74; and college destination, 216–18; degree attainment effects, 221–23; design considerations, 257–58; eligibility, 235, 237–40; fields of study analysis, 223–25; introduction, 213–15; vs. Israeli policy, 16–18, 235–43, 243–44; mobility dividends, 225–29; voluntary nature of, 236–37
United States affirmative action policy, simulation of shift to class-based policy, 159–87; academic selectivity effects, 171–73; broad diversity generation, 185–87; case for, 250–57; college destination impact, 216–18; data sources, 160, 166–68; geographic diversity impact, 183–85; introduction, 159–61; racial-ethnic diversity impact, 173–77; research methodology, 160–70; socioeconomic diversity effects, 177–83
United States Census Bureau, **46**
United States Department of Education, 18, 49, 54–55, 66F, 82, 219
United States Department of Justice, 82, 90
United States Supreme Court. *See* Supreme Court decisions
University of Brasilia, 7
University of California–Berkeley, 5, 32, 71
University of California–Davis, 3–4, 8–11
University of California–Los Angeles (UCLA), 5, 71, 174, 238–39
University of Cape Town, 7, 8
University of Michigan, 5, 36–37
University of North Carolina, et al.; Students for Fair Admissions, Inc. v., 279n34
University of North Carolina–Chapel Hill, 36
University of Notre Dame, 295n37
University of Pennsylvania, 4, 52, **53**

University of Texas–Austin, 5, 37–40, 96
University of Texas; Fisher v., 11, 37–40, 65, 79, 81, 215
U.S. News & World Report, "Best Colleges" ranking system, 51, 54

Vassar College, 180, 183
vocational fields, 223–25
Voting Rights Act of 1965, 27

wages and earnings: blacks, 28; data sources, 200; of Israeli Arabs vs. Jews, 102, 104–5; of U.S. college vs. high school graduates, 45–47, 192
Washington: affirmative action bans, 10, 32–34, 94
Washington State University, 53–54

Watkins, Claire Vaye, 62
wealth, 162–63, 248
White, Byron, 8, 9
whites: college graduation rate, 28; at competitive four-year colleges, **33**; high school graduation rate, 28; household income, 248; poverty, 248; unemployment, 248; wealth, 248
Wilson, William Julius, 92
women, exclusion by Ivy League schools, 275*n*9

Yale University: academic integration, 55; admission rates, 4, 52, **53**; tuition at, 59; U.S. presidents graduated from, 5, 6

Zofnass, Paul, 252